Jesuit and Feminist Education

Jesuit and Feminist Education

INTERSECTIONS IN TEACHING AND LEARNING FOR THE TWENTY-FIRST CENTURY

Edited by Jocelyn M. Boryczka
and Elizabeth A. Petrino

FORDHAM UNIVERSITY PRESS
New York   2012

Fordham University Press has no responsibility for the persistence or accuracy of URLs for external or third-party Internet websites referred to in this publication and does not guarantee that any content on such websites is, or will remain, accurate or appropriate.

Fordham University Press also publishes its books in a variety of electronic formats. Some content that appears in print may not be available in electronic books.

Library of Congress Cataloging-in-Publication Data
Jesuit and feminist education : intersections in teaching and learning for the twenty-first century / edited by Jocelyn M. Boryczka and Elizabeth A. Petrino.—1st ed.
    p. cm.
  Includes bibliographical references and index.
  ISBN 978-0-8232-3331-1 (cloth : alk. paper)
  ISBN 978-0-8232-3332-8 (pbk. : alk. paper)
  ISBN 978-0-8232-3333-5 (epub)
    1. Jesuits—Education (Higher)—United States. 2. Feminism and education—United States. 3. Women in higher education—United States. 4. Critical pedagogy—United States. I. Boryczka, Jocelyn M. II. Petrino, Elizabeth A., [date]
LC493.J355 2012
378.0820973—dc22

                                    2011009369

Printed in the United States of America
14 13 12   5 4 3 2 1
First edition

Contents

Afterword
Charles L. Currie, S.J.

APPENDIX

Decree 14: Jesuits and the Situation of Women in Church and
Civil Society. Thirty-fourth General Congregation of the
Society of Jesus, 1995.

Foreword

JEFFREY P. VON ARX, S.J.

The history of the relationship between St. Ignatius and the early Jesuits and the women with whom they established relationships is a
nuanced and complex one, and a story that needs to be revisited in
the light of current historical scholarship and cultural understanding.
Certainly, women have played a critical role as benefactors in the development of the Society of Jesus, and the Ignatian way of proceeding
and the Spiritual Exercises themselves have likewise had a hand in the
spiritual formation of many women, particularly those in religious life.

Having said this, I find that what is unquestionable is that while
many women have exercised a profound influence on the Society, the
contingencies of our historical and cultural contexts have meant that
there has been a blind spot in the consciousness of the Society where
women are concerned. A willingness to allow women to be treated as
second class, or as limited and auxiliary to the work of the Society, has
prevailed based on the cultural customs and assumptions of the historical periods in which we have found ourselves.

But the wheels of history keep on turning and it is perhaps only now
in recent years, with a general rise in consciousness concerning this
issue, that the Society is in a place to openly reflect on the ways in
which it has turned its back on and participated in the systematic discrimination against women, not only within the Society itself, but
within our areas of mission. In Decree 14 of the Society's Thirty-fourth
General Congregation, the Society concedes that as Jesuits, "we have
been part of a civil and ecclesial tradition that has offended against
women," and that we have "often contributed to a form of clericalism
which has reinforced male domination with an ostensibly divine sanction."[1] The decree calls for a conversion of heart within the Society and

lays out steps the Jesuits must take in order to address these historical oversights.

Among the ways forward for the Society in this area that are outlined in the decree, perhaps the essential one is the one most baldly stated: "In the first place, we invite all Jesuits to listen carefully and courageously to the experience of women. Many women feel that men simply do not listen to them."[2]

The decree then goes on to list areas in which Jesuits should align themselves "in solidarity with women," which include the "support for liberation movements which oppose the exploitation of women and encourage their entry into political and social life," "respectful cooperation with our female colleagues in shared projects," and the "promotion of the education of women and, in particular, the elimination of all forms of illegitimate discrimination between boys and girls in the educational process."[3]

The decree states the commitment of the Society in "a more formal and explicit way to regard this solidarity with women as integral to our mission" and to work for a fuller reconciliation of men and women. The decree thus concludes, "We know that a reflective and sustained commitment to bring about this respectful reconciliation can flow only from our God of love and justice who reconciles all and promises a world in which 'there is neither Jew nor Greek, there is neither slave nor free, there is neither male nor female, for you are all one in Christ Jesus' (Gal 3:28)."[4]

Perhaps the richest arena where Jesuits are in a position to work toward this fuller reconciliation, and to explore how we will evolve as a Society to meet this commitment, is in our Jesuit universities. From October 27 to 29, 2006, Fairfield University hosted "Jesuit and Feminist Education: Transformative Discourses for Teaching and Learning" the first conference in the United States to look specifically at the points of intersection between the traditional Ignatian pedagogical tradition and emerging feminist pedagogies. Approximately 125 faculty, students, staff, and administrators from nineteen of the twenty-eight U.S. Jesuit colleges and universities attended. Many of the papers presented are included in this volume, which we hope will open up rich areas for discussion throughout the network of Jesuit institutions and more broadly in higher education.

As many of the contributors to this volume point out, there are some remarkable points of convergence between the almost five-hundred-year tradition of Ignatian pedagogy and the relatively recent and emergent feminist pedagogies. The most obvious of these, and certainly the central one, is a shared commitment to the pursuit of the truth in the interests of the service of justice. While most institutions of higher learning would agree that their mission is to form men and women for the benefit of society, I would argue that the Ignatian pedagogical tradition is unique in that, as Jesuit educators, we are specifically obligated to create learning environments actively engaged in the work of the liberation of the human spirit, and the transformation of social structures for the betterment of the society at large. That is our purpose and mission. Pedro Ribadeneira, one of the early Jesuits, would explain in a letter to King Philip II of Spain that the reason the Jesuits ran schools was because "the proper education of youth will mean the improvement for the whole world."[5] In essence, our mission has never wavered from this. Our universities must evaluate their effectiveness, but not based on the size of our endowments, the triumphs of our varsity athletes, or even the intellectual and scholarly achievement of our faculty. Instead, as universities and colleges, we need to evaluate what kind of impact we have on the community around us in terms of how we have contributed to the spiritual, intellectual, and imaginative liberation of those whom we are called to serve. As Ignacio Ellacuría, S.J., once put it, the question for all of us in Jesuit higher education is this: "How does a university transform the social reality of which it is so much a part?"[6]

So, in broad terms, both feminist and Ignatian pedagogy are interested in the search for truth that will serve the promotion of justice and the transformation of society. The aim of both is to try and identify what is unjust, broken, or unmet in the world around us and actively develop strategies to address these deficiencies. Feminist pedagogy has an explicit end: the transformation of existing social structures, the critique of established power relations, and the illumination of biases and prejudices that obscure the truth. Its purpose is the liberation of the learner, giving him or her the ability to see how what might appear to be unquestionable truths are in fact, in many cases, constructed to further the interests of a dominant political and cultural constituency.

Once this awareness has arisen, one expects students informed in this manner to have acquired greater latitude of action in their lives, and greater capacity to discern what is truthful and act accordingly. As Jesuits, we would hope that our student-centered methodologies and emphasis on critical thinking and the inherent dignity of every human person are in harmony with these aims.

What feminists and Jesuits also share at this juncture is a commitment to a fuller embrace of diversity within our institutions of higher education. Certainly, in recent years there has been a renewed commitment to a greater cultural, racial, religious, gender, and socioeconomic diversity at Fairfield University and on other Jesuit campuses. This commitment is critical to the vitality of our universities and colleges as they seek to educate men and women who are at ease in a multiplicity of cultural contexts and so able to be of service in our increasingly pluralistic and interconnected world. This renewed commitment and fuller appreciation of the importance of diversity within Jesuit education constitutes a radical renewal of the tradition of cross-cultural dialogue, which has been at the heart of our mission from the beginning, as it was for those missionary Jesuits of the early generations who traveled the globe and found God present in every culture with which they came into contact. As a result of their eye-opening encounters with the wider world, the network of Jesuit schools that began to spring up in the sixteenth century was almost immediately intercultural in practice and global in outlook. Jesuit pedagogy, at its best, has thus always been inclined to embrace a heart-to-heart dialogue with the "other" as a means to a deeper understanding of the complexities of the world, and as a means to a more profound apprehension of the nature of God as He is present in all people and places.

Feminist pedagogy shares this appreciation of the critical importance of a diversity of voices and perspectives as integral to an education that liberates the mind from unfounded assumptions and prejudices. As feminism has developed, through the process of actively illuminating the relationship between cultural assumptions and the power relations that those assumptions obscure, it has also had to look at its own assumptions and to question its own priorities. In short, feminist pedagogy has come to serve as the vanguard within our universities as the voice that calls for a greater diversity of backgrounds, genders, sexual orientations, races, and national and socioeconomic perspectives within our institutions. The gender issues that feminist pedagogy has addressed have broadened under that inquiry and become more complex as the work of feminist scholars has also illuminated how race, poverty, class, and other cultural factors are interwoven with gender into inequities of social power. In this respect, feminist pedagogy has proved to be a critical pedagogy open to self-critique. This, in my view, is also characteristic of a true Ignatian pedagogical approach, and feminist scholars within our universities play a vital role in ensuring that our institutions are self-reflective and self-questioning in this manner.

Jesuit and Ignatian pedagogy also share certain methodological features. Feminist pedagogy, like Ignatian pedagogy, takes as a point of departure that the work of learning is primarily a relational experience. In the Ignatian tradition, this begins with Ignatius's own education. Ignatius came to the understanding that he was being taught, guided, and liberated through a one-to-one relationship with God, who was leading him toward the truth. Education, for Ignatius was a process of vocational discovery guided through an active and relational engagement with the Divine person. This experience established the model for the Ignatian teaching methods that were to follow: emphases on one-to-one engagement with a teacher, raising questions, and personal reflection. So in this arena, feminist and Ignatian pedagogy share similar approaches to education as a transactional process of engagement. This is opposed to the idea that education is primarily a matter of imparting a fixed body of information to a student. This then is yet another area where Jesuit and feminist pedagogies are very much at ease with one another.

Also, feminist pedagogy, with its willingness to embrace our subjective and emotional experiences as valued mediums of self-awareness, is in harmony with the emphasis that Ignatian pedagogy places on the power of imagination, the role of empathy, and the validity of our instinctual responses in the work of reflection and discernment at the heart of the Spiritual Exercises.

There are many other rich areas where feminist pedagogy and Ignatian pedagogy share similar aims and methods, many of which are elegantly discussed in the following chapters. It should be noted too that there are likely to be significant areas where the paths of some feminists and some Jesuits are likely to diverge. The roles available to women within the Church provide rich areas for disagreement, as do issues concerning reproductive rights and obligations, and other questions pertaining to the family, sexuality, and the traditional roles of both men and women.

But it was the purpose of the conference at Fairfield and the hope of this book that we should begin the conversation with an appreciation for those areas where we share a common ground and mission. One thing that we do know for certain as we move forward, and as the number of men in the Society of Jesus continues to decline, is that the future of the Jesuit mission will become increasingly a collaborative one, a fact affirmed by Decree 6 of the Society's Thirty-fifth General Congregation. For centuries, we Jesuits have expected to take on the leadership roles in the pursuit of our goals to spread the liberating message of Jesus Christ and to work to preserve and enhance the dignity of the human person. Increasingly we will find that our emerging role is as collaborators, to support and encourage "those women and men of good will from all nations and cultures, with whom we labour in seeking a more just world."[7]

There are many works that we will be called to collaborate upon, but Decree 6 identifies an appropriately Ignatian work as one apt for collaborative engagement when it "intentionally *seeks God in all things*; when it practices Ignatian discernment; when it engages the world through a careful analysis of context, in dialogue with experience, evaluated through reflection, for the sake of action, and with openness, always, to evaluation."[8] As Jesuits moving into the future, we will find that our mission will be more fully revealed as we engage in thoughtful and respectful dialogue with those who labor alongside us in the service of our fellow men and women. Even where our paths may at times diverge, the respectful conversation and the collaborative spirit remain essential, because it is through these conversations that we will "come to know our own journey better and to follow it with new zeal and understanding."[9]

Acknowledgments

We would like to acknowledge the extensive network of colleagues who participated in bringing this book to fruition. The Fairfield University community provided the essential support for this project, which began at the Dover Retreat many years ago, continued at the "Jesuit and Feminist Education" conference in 2006, and now takes the form of this volume. In particular, we wish to thank Jim Bowler, S.J., Jeffrey von Arx, S.J., Mary Frances Malone, Tim Snyder, and Orin Grossman for helping to spearhead this project at Fairfield. Other colleagues at Fairfield University provided invaluable input on the formation of the conference and this volume. In particular, Paul Lakeland and Elizabeth Dreyer offered critical insights throughout the entire process, as did Wendy Kohli during the early formations of the conference. In addition, we wish to thank all the participants in the 2006 conference that generated the work for this volume and, of course, we wish to acknowledge the contributors to this volume. Other colleagues, including Bren Ortega Murphy and Rosemary Carbine, offered intellectual companionship and a sounding board during the conference that proved important to the final project, and the anonymous reviewers of the manuscript for Fordham University Press gave us valuable insights for revision. We would like to give special thanks to Ed Ross at Printing and Graphics Services at Fairfield University for his creative expertise in designing our cover image. Our research assistants, Shawne LoMauro and Diana Minnocci, also aided us in preparing the final manuscript. We could not have completed this project without the support of our families, especially our husbands, Tony and Thomas, and the advice of our friends and colleagues. This book is dedicated to all those feminist educators, men and women alike, who model holistic, compassionate education and embody the social change to which they are committed.

Jesuit and Feminist Education

Introduction

Educating for Transformation—Jesuit and Feminist Approaches in the Classroom and Beyond

JOCELYN M. BORYCZKA

AND ELIZABETH A. PETRINO

My hope emerges from those places of struggle where I witness individuals positively transforming their lives and the world around them. Educating is always a vocation rooted in hopefulness.

bell hooks, *Teaching Community: A Pedagogy of Hope*

We should be particularly sensitive to adopt a pedagogy that does not drive a further wedge between men and women who in certain circumstances are already under great pressure from other divisive cultural or socio-economic forces.

Decree 14, Thirty-fourth General Congregation

Three years ago, heading to a retreat on Jesuit pedagogy in higher education attended by faculty and administrators from Fairfield University, Boston College, and the College of the Holy Cross, we began a conversation that has resulted in far-reaching effects neither of us could have anticipated. As feminist, liberal, progressive, even activist scholars, we discussed how we felt about teaching at a Jesuit university, which eventually led us to ask: How could we, as feminists, find our way into a dialogue about Jesuit higher education? This question turned our attention toward intersections between Jesuit and feminist pedagogy, which are the focus of this volume.

The vibrant and intellectually rich dialogue that took place at the "Jesuit and Feminist Education: Transformative Discourses for Teaching and Learning" conference, which we co-organized at Fairfield University in October 2006, inspires this collection. One hundred twenty-five participants from nineteen of the twenty-eight Jesuit colleges and universities in the United States attended this conference—the first ever to examine the relationship between Jesuit and feminist education.

Contributors to this volume, most of whom participated in the conference, consider this relationship in their chapters by looking through a gendered lens to identify and underscore similarities between these two pedagogical approaches while critically engaging with their important differences. Taken together, the chapters in this volume open a much-needed discussion about how feminist and gender-focused approaches in the classroom can complement, rather than contradict, the methods that St. Ignatius of Loyola, founder of the Jesuit Order, taught over five hundred years ago. The intersection of Jesuit and feminist education explored here also holds much promise for addressing the demands of an increasingly global and multicultural world and, as such, for helping to map out the terrain of higher education for the twenty-first century.

This volume blends Ignatian pedagogical methods and a developing feminist methodology. The resulting intersectional approach locates individual and collective standpoints in relation to political, social, and economic structures, creating a space in which the dynamics of power and possibilities for liberation become visible. Kimberlé Crenshaw's pathbreaking work initially conceptualized this analytic framework as the intersection where two streets meet, expanding into an interconnected system of roads, avenues, boulevards, parkways, and interstate highways, which together constitute a map.[1] This intersectional approach is meant to disrupt the stable dualistic categories that maintain the impermeable boundaries which marginalize vulnerable classes of people. Applying this feminist framework to classrooms and campus communities facilitates our ability to chart relationships and the flow of power across boundaries that often separate teachers and students, administrators and faculty, living and learning, and campus and communities. Intersectionality, for this volume's purposes, provides an analytic tool for tracking the points of convergence and divergence between feminist and Jesuit education in order to facilitate an understanding of how educators at Jesuit universities and colleges and other religious and secular schools engage the multifaceted challenges and opportunities we face in the twenty-first century.

Furthermore, intersectionality locates points of convergence related to various identities, beliefs, ideologies, and epistemologies without assimilating differences that, in this volume, function to account for the divergent and even antagonistic Jesuit and feminist ways of understanding the world. Humanism, for example, orients both of these perspectives toward a focus on how embodied people living in communities relate to each other, encompassing their internal emotional, psychological, and spiritual lives and external realities. Feminism emphasizes difference in terms of variables such as gender, sex, sexuality, race, class, religion, age, and beliefs as inherent to achieving the humanistic goals of equality, social justice, and freedom for all. A Jesuit perspective, in comparison, assumes the existence of shared values as foundational to a common good that reflects a worldview shaped by sameness rather than difference.

Clearly, other points of divergence also exist. The Jesuit tradition is religious, whereas feminism, though inclusive of religious perspectives, is largely grounded in secularism. This difference, coupled with the fact that the Jesuit Order and tradition belong within the Catholic Church, generates a range of contentious issues in relation to feminism, including women's ordination, gay marriage, reproductive rights, and comprehensive sex education. Controversies on Jesuit and other Catholic campuses over condom distribution, performances of *The Vagina Monologues*, and forums on gay marriage represent important points of departure between feminist and Jesuit positions on issues related to gender, sex, and sexuality.

While such differences remain crucial to this volume, we bring to the foreground the intersections of feminism and Jesuit education in order to focus on how they can form, inform, and transform each other, our institutions, and the people in them. Shared commitments to educating the whole person by integrating reason and emotion, developing students into engaged citizens of the world, establishing meaningful connections between theory and practice by understanding and applying knowledge in context, and achieving social justice and ending oppression in its many forms become the focus of consideration. This involves the epistemological move integral to intersectionality—overcoming dualistic categories by attending to the permeability of constructed boundaries separating people, communities, and belief systems. In this way, this volume takes an approach that is intended to bring into dialogue the bodies of literature in Jesuit and feminist education as a way forward for twenty-first-century education. We hope that it will encourage teachers who inspire change in the world and are themselves inspired by their principles and moral values to view teaching as a transformative act.

Jesuit and Feminist Approaches to Teaching

This volume, in many ways, continues to carry out the charge delivered by Fr. Pedro Arrupe, S.J., in 1973 to reeducate for social justice and action by focusing on the formation of "men and women for others" as "the paramount objective of Jesuit education."[2] Arrupe's address "Men for Others," delivered to the Tenth International Congress of Jesuit Alumni of Europe, frames Jesuit education as a means of translating the abstract ideal of social justice into structural change with explicit attention to the people—including women—engaged in and affected by such change. In interesting ways, Fr. Arrupe's position resonates with the second-wave feminist slogan "The personal is political," which started gaining traction in the early 1970s. Nearly two decades later, Decree 14 of the Thirty-fourth General Congregation of the Society of Jesus specified in greater detail how Jesuit education could achieve the goal of forming men and women for others. Female faculty at Jesuit universities and colleges began reflecting on how women related to institutional settings and campus contexts built and shaped by an exclusively male hierarchical religious order. Lisa Sowle Cahill and Susan A. Ross, among others, gave voice to this issue initially by focusing on how to change the campus culture to make it more inclusive of women and their issues and, furthermore, as Ross argued, to make the question "What about women?" a standard for Jesuit educational institutions.[3] Rosemary A. DeJulio, among others, examined the role of women such as Mary Ward and Madeleine Sophie Barat in St. Ignatius's life and the development of the Jesuit tradition.[4] This work in Jesuit education and the tradition from which it comes attend to the changes necessary for women to be more fully included in campus culture, decision-making structures, and the translation of the ideals of social justice into reality.

This volume, while taking its lead from this body of work in Jesuit education, directs attention to how the Ignatian paradigm's five elements—context, experience, reflection, action, and evaluation—can inform approaches to teaching and learning. With the advantage of nearly thirty years of development, feminist pedagogy can now be related in meaningful ways to the Ignatian paradigm that anchors the broader Jesuit commitment to educating the whole person. The essays collected here represent the first of what we hope will become many direct explorations of teaching and learning that, in addition to taking Ross's "What about women?" question seriously, will examine how feminist and Jesuit pedagogy inform each other in ways that can extend beyond Jesuit campuses to transform educational practices for the twenty-first century. In doing so, this volume hopes to address a gap in the literature of Jesuit education regarding the specific contributions that "women's ways of knowing" the world and translating them into teaching practices make to this approach to teaching and learning.[5] Neither *The Jesuit "Ratio Studiorum": 400th Anniversary Perspectives* (2000) nor *A Jesuit Education Reader* (2008), for example, includes chapters that explore Jesuit educational practices from a woman's perspective. The increasing number of female faculty, students, administrators, and staff; the presence of women's studies programs on nearly every Jesuit campus; a focus on how laypeople carry on the Jesuit mission amid the order's declining numbers; and a commitment to diversity and social justice suggest that now is the time for examining how feminist or woman-oriented teaching and learning practices intersect with Jesuit education.

Helping students begin to realize their talents and God-given abilities in a value-driven education frames the Jesuit pedagogical tradition. The International Commission on the Apostolate of Jesuit Education has succinctly described its purpose: "The ultimate aim of Jesuit education is . . . that full growth of the person which leads to action—action, especially, that is suffused with the spirit and presence of Jesus Christ, the Son of God, the Man-for-Others. This goal of action, based on sound understanding and enlivened by contemplation, urges students to self-discipline and initiative, to integrity and accuracy. At the same time, it judges slip-shod or superficial ways of thinking unworthy of the individual and, more important, dangerous to the world he or she is called to serve."[6] The pedagogical ethic of developing persons who will be leaders in service is and has always been a defining characteristic of what we mean by a Jesuit, rather than a purely Catholic or religious, education.[7] Whereas Catholic service projects seek to aid the poor, Jesuit education encourages students to engage in service with others, including the poor, as a means to promote their moral growth and acknowledge the need for social justice. According to Fr. Kolvenbach, service programs should be a mainstay of Jesuit education in order to personalize the struggle against oppression for our students and acquaint them with the "gritty reality of the world," so they can respond critically to its demands.[8] Intellectual rigor and excellence also differentiate Jesuit from Catholic or secular education, given its establishment as the first teaching order within the Catholic Church amid sixteenth-century Renaissance humanism.[9] This context anchors Jesuit education, to this day, in a commitment to the humanities that views studying languages, poetry, history, rhetoric, and logic alongside mathematics, sciences, and the philosophy of nature as critical to teaching for expanding the intellect, sharpening critical analysis, developing good character, and learning to move others to action for causes consistent with advancing the common good. Today, the core curricula at Jesuit universities and colleges most clearly represent this humanist legacy, which continues to define a Jesuit education.

St. Ignatius of Loyola, in founding the Society of Jesus, sought to create a systematic approach to learning that would result in a learned ministry and educated lay class more apt to serve its people. He understood that the rapid growth of colleges would serve the Jesuits' life and missionary work but was not its totality. By 1548, eight years before his death, the Society had founded at least thirty colleges for the formation of Jesuit students and externs. At the rate of four or five colleges opening a year, these institutions vastly outnumbered the "professed houses," residences dedicated to housing members of their itinerant society.[10] The involvement of the Society in what Kolvenbach calls the "intellectual apostolate" emerged from a desire to enlighten others about Christian teaching through education. Rather than betray its initial promise to serve the poor, the turn toward education became an expression of the *magis*—"the result of the search for a greater apostolic service through an insertion into the world of culture."[11] The desire to engage in the pursuit of social justice, rather than provide an education from a purely academic standpoint, underscores the potential for Jesuit education to coexist with feminism and other activist movements in addressing a host of social issues, such as interdisciplinary education, internationalization, and the promotion of equality worldwide.

To that end, Jesuit education encourages the growth of the whole person through pedagogical methods embodied in the Ignatian paradigm and expressed in part in the *Ratio Studiorum*, a "code of liberal education which became normative for all schools."[12] Over the centuries, other methods were adapted to refine further a student's development as a fully human person and provide a model of justice in their daily lives—one central aspect derived from the Spiritual Exercises of Ignatius, originally penned as a guide to spiritual life rather than as a pedagogical text.

Nevertheless, the first ten lessons of the Exercises offer a dynamic model of teaching that evolved into the Ignatian paradigm: context, experience, reflection, action, and evaluation. First, the familiarity of the teacher with the student's actual life provides a context for building a shared and authentic relationship. According to the International Commission on the Apostolate of Jesuit Education, context includes a teacher's knowledge of "family, peers, social situation, the educational institution itself, politics, economics, cultural climate, the ecclesial situation, media, music, and other realities."[13] Second, through experience of the real world—the world outside the classroom, where theory and praxis meet—students begin to consider how their emotional responses (e.g., "I like this," "I'm threatened by this," "I'm bored") affect their intellectual understanding (e.g., "What is this?" "How does it work?"). Comprehending the larger dimensions of the world then involves relating experience to our personal situations. For this reason, the third critical aspect of intellectual and moral growth requires reflection. Memory, imagination, and feelings allow students to consider "the essential value of what is being studied, to discover its relationship with other aspects of knowledge and human activity, and to appreciate its implications in the ongoing search for truth and freedom."[14] Teachers must grant students the opportunity to come to terms, freely and without coercion, with their own role in and responsibility for local or global social issues without imposing their own points of view. Fourth, after reflecting deeply on the causes of social ills, students might be moved to act. As they become driven by a new understanding of how the personal and social worlds intersect and begin to apply a personal, human point of view to social problems, their wills are engaged. Fifth, routine evaluation, which includes tests and examinations to ensure academic mastery, extends to periodic reassessment of a student's personal and moral growth. By questioning, pointing out absences of vision in the student's original point of view, and broadening the student's perspective, the teacher gently encourages her or him to think more broadly, perhaps initiating once again the circuit of Ignatian teaching. Together, the five elements of this humanistic paradigm engage teachers and students with the world around them, and in the critical evaluation of personal values and roles within a world system and global economy, in such a way that they see themselves not as receivers but as producers of knowledge, not as takers but as actors for the larger good.

Feminist pedagogy, in contrast, lacks a centuries-old historical tradition, as this approach emanates from women's struggle for equality, freedom, and political inclusion during feminism's second wave in the 1960s and 1970s. Rooted in political struggle and social movement strategy, this pedagogical perspective is oriented toward opposition to dominant institutions, structures, and ways of knowing the world. A critical standpoint then binds the pluralistic impetus of feminist pedagogical practices and theories. The Church continues to represent an institutional focus of feminist critique in terms of its male-dominated hierarchical structure resistant to women's full inclusion and its positions on a range of social issues. And yet feminism has moved into the Church's educational contexts, as marked by the integration of women's writings, ideas, and theories into the curriculum despite such resistance as emerged in the controversy over the idea of an education based on "Great Books" in the 1980s. In addition, women's studies programs currently exist at twenty-seven of the twenty-eight Jesuit universities and colleges in the United States. A vibrant literature indicating the critical and multifaceted nature of feminist pedagogy now exists.[15] Much recent scholarship points toward the formation of an identifiable set of practices and theories constituting feminist pedagogy. Yet neither this literature nor that of Jesuit education examines how these two approaches to teaching and learning relate to each other—the purpose of this volume.

Similar to Jesuit education, feminist pedagogy lacks one clear definition or methodology, though certain approaches, methods, and perspectives distinguish it from other teaching and learning perspectives.

Feminism and pedagogy, as Crabtree, Sapp, and Licona highlight, remain highly contested concepts. They point toward a philosophy of teaching and learning grounded in analyzing classroom strategies and substantive course material from the position of how gender, sex, and sexuality intersect with other variables to shape how we understand the world as teachers and students.[16] At its core, feminist education assumes difference among people, in its most simple form between men and women, as inherent to working toward social justice, freedom, and equality. This position differentiates it from the humanistic foundation of Jesuit education, which takes sameness among people as the starting point for teaching and learning. While some feminists emphasize the sameness between men and women, and others focus on their differences, the recognition of variation based in gender, sex, and sexuality anchors feminism in a worldview that begins with accounting for difference as a way of addressing humanistic concerns such as justice for all.

Furthermore, feminism's orientation toward difference complicates what we mean by "women," "men," "black," "Latino/a," "Asian," "Christian," "Muslim," "Jewish," "poor," "middle class," "gay" and "lesbian," and "able bodied." Standpoint theory in feminist theory and pedagogy offers a framework for understanding the complex dimensions of people's identities, and their centrality to liberation, that result from their definition according to the standards of the dominant in society.[17] Giving voice to the silenced and visibility to the oppressed and marginalized groups that represent various standpoints is a primary goal of feminist pedagogy. Feminist educators Frances Maher and Mary Kay Thompson Tetreault translate feminist standpoint theory into classroom strategies by moving toward what they call positional pedagogies, which involve understanding our students' positions, including their identities and contexts, in the world.[18] Lee Anne Bell, Sharon Washington, Gerald Weinstein, and Barbara Love extend this approach to teachers by asserting that they must also interrogate their standpoints and how they shape the classroom community: "We struggle alongside our students with our own social identities, biases, fears, and prejudices. We too need to be willing to examine and deal honestly with our values, assumptions, and emotional reactions to oppression issues. The self-knowledge and self-awareness that we believe are desirable qualities in any teacher become crucial in social justice education."[19] Standpoints then play a vital role in feminist pedagogy by providing a powerful tool for specifying how the identities of teachers and students shape classroom dynamics and the educational contexts of our colleges and universities. Indeed, bringing feminist pedagogy into dialogue with the Jesuit approach can deepen how the latter attends to issues of gender, sex, and sexuality, as well as other variables that constitute a person's identity, and deepen our understanding of the subject and her or his subjectivity.

Against this topography of Jesuit humanism and feminist commitments to difference, three roads—the relational, subjective, and action oriented—come together to form a major intersection where these two seemingly divergent approaches to education meet. First, the relational refers to how both approaches locate the individual within a complex network of relationships between and among various groups of people. The connection between students and teachers in and outside the classroom orients both approaches toward locating teaching and learning within the broader structures of society. Second, the subjective relates to a person's emotions, spirituality, and experiences, which, when integrated into pedagogical practices and curriculum development, challenge objectivity as the dominant means of knowledge acquisition in higher education. Indeed, this commitment locates Jesuit education alongside feminism in terms of the culture wars that raged in the 1980s and 1990s. Opponents of critical pedagogies and particularly women's studies programs, such as Allan Bloom in *The Closing of the American Mind* (1987), argued that these approaches lacked empirical grounding, given their relativism and reliance on self-expression, which rendered them incompatible with the academic enterprise premised on reason. Third, action as a requirement of learning anchors both approaches, which emphasize taking direct political action in the world as necessary for redressing the inequalities, injustices, and oppression experienced by all vulnerable classes of people.[20] Where these three roads intersect indicates that Jesuit and feminist education present a powerful pedagogical means for rethinking individualism, apathy, and consumerism as the dominant ways, particularly in liberal democratic and capitalist societies, for people to engage the twenty-first-century world. Such transformative possibilities for higher education unfold through the following chapters.

Overview

The chapters in this volume make unique contributions to the literature in Jesuit and feminist pedagogy by addressing the theoretical and practical aspects of an education that is both Jesuit *and* feminist. This collection brings the work in Jesuit and feminist pedagogy into greater proximity by focusing on their relationship to each other, with an eye on how the two can transform teaching and learning in contemporary higher education.

Offering a broader context for understanding women's contributions to Jesuit education, the section "Mapping the 'Herstory' of Jesuit Education" investigates the rich tradition of female acolytes surrounding Ignatius and the wide spectrum of female influence that has long been neglected in more traditional histories of Jesuit education. Elizabeth A. Dreyer investigates in "'Do as I Do, Not as I Say': The Pedagogy of Action" the sixteenth-century European context, including the development of the printing press and vernacular literature, which led to improved literacy rates, giving rise to women's involvement in religious life. In her revisionist account, she traces the lives of many women, too numerous to mention here, who become central to her argument that lay females exerted political power and influence among the Jesuits, albeit within the limits imposed on them by their society and time. Basing her argument mainly on their letters to Ignatius and current historical investigations, Dreyer provides a new way of understanding the role women took in ministry within the early Church. In "Mary, the Hidden Catalyst: Reflections from an Ignatian Pilgrimage to Spain and Rome," Margo J. Heydt and Sarah J. Melcher share their fascination with Mary's formative influence on Ignatius, which arose during a pilgrimage on which they visited important spiritual sites in Spain and Rome. European images of Mary differ dramatically from her conventional iconic depiction, often portraying increased agency through eye contact or positioning with respect to the viewer or other figures in the work of art. They contend that viewing these lesser-known representations of Mary and uncovering her role as a "hidden catalyst" in Ignatius's spiritual life allow us to appreciate more fully the need for more gender-balanced discussions both in scholarship and in the classroom. Colleen McCluskey explores in "Early Jesuit Pedagogy and the Subordination of Women: Resources from the *Ratio Studiorum*" the extent to which the *Ratio Studiorum* (1599), a cornerstone of Ignatian pedagogy, contains methods for self-critique that might have allowed the early Jesuits to conceive of a more liberal attitude toward women. Although the typical course of study for university students, heavily weighted toward Aristotle and St. Thomas Aquinas, contained biased notions of gender, the authors of the *Ratio Studiorum*, McCluskey claims, also advocated exclusive "domains of responsibilities" that accorded females some independence and equality as wives. She concludes that Jesuit pedagogy allows for—even encourages—the active self-questioning that would permit a critical reading of philosophers and theologians. Hence, McCluskey reasons, "the *Ratio Studiorum* could have provided the early Jesuits with tools that might have enabled them to recognize and challenge the unjust subordination and oppression of women." Recovering a rich tradition of female influence in Jesuit education, these chapters have broad implications for our current classroom practices and open the way to a fuller understanding of the role gender played in early Jesuit life.

The next section, "Intersection I: Transformative Visions for Educating the Whole Person," engages with the first intersection where Jesuit and feminist education meet, opening up a dialogue that challenges us to reconceptualize the power dynamics within our classrooms and on our campuses to achieve a more liberatory and encompassing approach to education. In "'The Personal Is Political': At the Intersections of Feminist and Jesuit Education," we map out a general topography of points of convergence and divergence between these two pedagogies. We draw out their relationship by exploring how the five central elements of Ignatian education—context, experience, reflection, action, and evaluation—relate to a feminist pedagogy premised on the idea that "the personal is political." To describe how this connection can inform and transform educational practices, the chapter builds on the practical example of consciousness-raising and direct action projects employed in an Introduction to Feminist Thought course. Paul Lakeland similarly takes a broad view of both educational visions in "*Paideia* and the Political Process: The Unexplored Coincidence of Jesuit and

Feminist Pedagogical Visions." Lakeland argues for abandoning the term "pedagogy," which, he claims, fails to capture the Jesuit movement of seeking social justice by moving beyond the confines of the classroom, in favor of *paideia*—the total educational role of the entire institution as it prepares students to become citizens of the world. Furthermore, Lakeland asserts that Jesuit universities and colleges stand to benefit from a convergence of these two methods in a strategic alliance between the two in calling on our Jesuit institutions to pay closer attention to their social and religious responsibilities. Robbin D. Crabtree, Joseph A. DeFeo, and Melissa M. Quan contribute to our understanding of how these pedagogies operate in relation to each other in "Feminist Pedagogy, the Ignatian Paradigm, and Service-Learning: Distinctive Roots, Common Objectives, and Intriguing Challenges," which introduces the additional dimension of service-learning. This chapter looks at three "liberatory" pedagogies—feminist, Ignatian, and service-learning—to explore how their shared assumptions about teaching and learning can lead to the transformation of societies and individuals. Thoroughly reviewing the literature of each field and drawing from personal experience, the authors provide a framework for understanding the way that these pedagogies contribute to Jesuit education and undercut "hegemonic educational practices that tacitly accept or more forcefully reproduce an oppressively gendered, classed, racialized, and androcentric social order." Together the chapters in this section map out some primary throughways of Jesuit and feminist pedagogy in order to provide a basis for considering further some specific points of their convergence and divergence.

The following section, "Intersection II: The Power of Difference for Teaching Social Justice," then turns to the dynamics of difference. Identities, standpoints, and social locations related to race, class, gender, sexuality, ability, and religion that operate in various classroom contexts, these chapters show, illustrate how difference represents a powerful tool for teaching social justice, a goal shared by Jesuit and feminist approaches to education. In "The Intersection of Race, Class, and Gender in Jesuit and Feminist Education: Finding Transcendent Meaning in the Concrete," M. Shawn Copeland analyzes the terms "Jesuit" and "feminist" to explore their commonalities and interrogate what we mean by them. In this chapter, which was the keynote address at the

"Jesuit and Feminist Education" conference in 2006, Copeland considers the impact of social context on the structure of higher education and, more broadly, on the social arrangement of class privilege and racial coding within the United States. Copeland, an exponent of "political theology," the liberatory movement within the Catholic theological tradition that seeks to effect political transformation based on the application of religious principles, explores the ways that a Jesuit and feminist education might begin to redress the systemic inequalities of class, race, and gender. These class divisions and the process of racial formation, including the romanticization of race as "essence" and "the unconscious persistence of racism in the post–civil rights era," have obscured our understanding of the need for social change. Against this backdrop, Copeland argues, a critical pedagogy that attends to particular historical, cultural, and social contexts resists the tendency to make the experience of individuals abstract and generalized, instead fostering a "concrete" understanding of "transcendent" matters. By nurturing an "Eros of the mind, the passionate desire and drive to know," Jesuit and feminist approaches to teaching implicitly raise awareness of the structural inequalities that permeate society and encourage a more sensitive response to the need for change.

In "Teaching for Social Justice in the Engaged Classroom: The Intersection of Jesuit and Feminist Moral Philosophies," Karen L. Slattery, Ana C. Garner, Joyce M. Wolburg, and Lynn H. Turner explore how teachers within the Jesuit and feminist traditions share assumptions that underlie both Christian ethics and the feminist ethic of care. This chapter applies this ethical understanding to a service-learning project in which students worked for a Native American development organization. Subtle forms of resistance became evident in their engagement with a social group constructed as different. The authors outline how these two ethical perspectives helped teachers and students navigate these power dynamics of difference, leading them to argue for Jesuit and feminist pedagogies as an effective means of working toward ending oppression and achieving social justice. Theresa Weynand Tobin's "Transformative Education in a Broken World: Feminist and Jesuit Pedagogy on the Importance of Context" relates the concept of positionality from feminist theory and pedagogy to the Ignatian paradigm to show how its focus on the individual, at the expense of the structural, fails to acknowledge the unequal power relationships that disadvantage students from minority groups. Focusing on the positionality of gay and lesbian students in her classroom at a Jesuit college, Tobin explores how becoming attentive to our own positions with respect to our students allows us better to examine "how relationships of domination and subordination between members of oppressed and privileged groups in larger social and ecclesial contexts are re-created at the micro-level in the classroom." Drawing on a history course offered at Valparaiso University called Faith and Feminism in America, Mary J. Henold's "Consciousness-Raising as Discernment: Using Jesuit and Feminist Pedagogies in a Protestant Classroom" offers concrete examples of several teaching methods that reflect how feminist consciousness-raising among students intersects with the Jesuit practice of discernment. Henold specifically discusses strategies that nurture the consciousness-raising central to feminist and Jesuit learning among a religiously mixed, though predominantly Protestant, and fairly conservative group of students. The chapters in this section bring theory from feminism and Jesuit pedagogy into the practical context of the classroom and campus, extending beyond the Jesuit context to outline the power of difference in teaching social justice.

The chapters in the last section, "The Fault Lines of Gender, Sex, and Sexuality: Debates, Challenges, and Opportunities for the Future," consider the possibilities for change that arise when attitudes toward gender, sex, and sexuality intersect with Catholic and Jesuit teaching and tradition. David Gudelunas considers in "De Certeau and 'Making Do': The Case of Gay Men and Lesbians on a Jesuit Campus" the implications of applying the French Jesuit Michel de Certeau's theories about "everyday life" to the lives of gay men and lesbians on college campuses who are trying to create a hospitable space for learning and working. According to Gudelunas, de Certeau's notion that individuals employ tactics to counteract the hegemonic "strategies" permeating society and embodied in its institutions, such as the law, language, rituals, and discourse, empowers minority voices on Jesuit campuses. He offers the example of a student-driven report at Fairfield University that outlined recommendations for improving gay and lesbian life on campus and, adapting the language of de Certeau, argues that "poaching" from the mainstream culture affords gay men and lesbians an opportunity to thrive on Jesuit campuses. In "Textual Deviance: Eve Ensler's *The Vagina Monologues* and Catholic Campuses," Heather Hathaway, Gregory J. O'Meara, S.J., and Stephanie Quade discuss reasons for staging Eve Ensler's controversial play, *The Vagina Monologues,* which some colleges and universities have chosen not to present, largely as a result of the Cardinal Newman Society's negative reactions to it. Investigating the reasons the play has become a *cause célèbre*, arousing heated debate on Catholic campuses among feminists, students, and administrators, they refute the programmatic, theological, and aesthetic grounds that have been adduced to keep the play from being produced. They argue that an open-minded encounter with the issues the play raises can engage students in discussion about values—such as the dignity of human beings, violence against the oppressed, and solidarity with the poor and vulnerable—that are at the heart of Jesuit and feminist education. Susan M. Mountin examines the mixed messages that university campus ministry programs send to women concerning their role in the Church in "Tilling the Soil: Preparing Women for the Vocation of Ministry—A Challenge and Call." She argues that a major challenge for Jesuit schools in the twenty-first century will be nurturing and educating women for ministry. Drawing on the Manresa Project at Marquette University, she offers strategies for creating programs based on the Ignatian principles of introspection and discernment that "invite college students to think about both lay and ordained professional church ministry as a life goal." Finally, in "Women in Jesuit Higher Education: Ten Years Later," Susan A. Ross considers the situation of women at Jesuit universities and colleges, a topic she first addressed a decade ago in an article for *Conversations.* Despite significant improvements, she concludes that more work needs to be done, as the pressures of work and family life discourage both men and women from accepting administrative roles in women's and gender studies programs. These chapters reveal how discussing gender, sex, and sexuality with students gives teachers the opportunity to engage them at a critical moment in their struggles to form a personal identity. Such moments of student development become "teachable," the authors suggest, when related to broader social concerns that intersect with issues such as religion, academic freedom, and campus politics.

Charles L. Currie's afterword picks up where Jeffrey von Arx's fore-word left off by offering a Jesuit perspective on how to advance social justice in institutions of higher education by urging us to apply the lessons from Decree 14 (included as an appendix) to everyday practice in our classrooms and on our campuses. Educating for others by employing elements from Jesuit and feminist pedagogies, they suggest, offers powerful tools for teaching and learning in the twenty-first century.

Conclusion: Jesuit and Feminist Teaching and Learning for the Twenty-first Century

The chapters in this volume lead to two further questions: What is the transformative potential for exploring the intersections of Jesuit and feminist education? And how can we recognize and learn from the diversity in the world and become more aware of the political, social, and economic structures affecting us and our students in the twenty-first century? This volume, for example, challenges us to consider how spirituality and religious belief constitute a dimension of a person's identity and, thereby, a standpoint that holds implications for how educators at secular and non-secular universities and colleges engage with their students inside and outside of the classroom. Such a perspective derives from explorations of the intersection of Jesuit and feminist approaches in which entrenched positions regarding either the central-ity of religion or its absence become destabilized.

The positive value of caring for others in relationships and commu-nity building in Jesuit and feminist education provides a foundation for a more constructive dialogue about spirituality's role in teaching and learning. As feminist theorist, educator, and activist bell hooks explains, "To be guided by love is to live in community with all life. However, a culture of domination, like ours, does not strive to teach us how to live in community. As a consequence, learning to live in com-munity must be a core practice for all of us who desire spirituality in education."[21] Spirituality, broadly conceived, involves an expansive capacity to see contextual reality and to look beyond it—to accept dif-ference and be inclusive of all members, regardless of gender, race, or creed.

Hope for the future then emanates from such a capacity to reach across these divides with a larger purpose in mind. M. Shawn Copeland, in this vein, argues in this volume that an ongoing dialogue inclusive of Jesuit and feminist perspectives will enable students and teachers to reach their fullest potential. "Human persons," Copeland states, "learn best when engaged by and with experience, and human persons live best in collaborative efforts to realize one another's flourishing as human persons. . . . Jesuit and feminist pedagogy take seriously what it means to know with our lives and to live with our knowledge." We hope that the following chapters contribute to the development of classroom practices, campus initiatives, and administrative policies built on collaboration across fault lines of difference, including those created by religion, gender, sex, and sexuality, with the intention of human flourishing. This intersection may hold the potential for transforming higher education in ways that will help our students, faculty, staff, and administrators meet the dynamic demands and take full advantage of the opportunities of the twenty-first century.

Part I: Mapping the "Herstory" of Jesuit Education

1 "Do as I Do, Not as I Say"

The Pedagogy of Action

ELIZABETH A. DREYER

This volume is a welcome contribution to the many conversations about pedagogy. It places in dialogue two groups deeply engaged in active, creative, and liberating educational strategies from feminist and Ignatian perspectives. Important background for this conversation is an inquiry into the lives of the women who were part of the early Jesuit mission. Who were they? What did they do? What were their gifts, virtues, and failings? How did they present themselves? What kinds of relationships did they have and how did these associations affect those involved? What hopes did they have for their lives and the world?[1] Detailed studies of women in the early modern period document their diversity and creativity, revealing them to be agents in their own right, albeit within a wide range of social networks.

Interpreting the past is a challenging, complex task. We inevitably bring to this work lenses through which we view the world, lenses that are, of course, highly dependent on our personal history and upon the mind-sets, concerns, and biases of our time. In a book on Jesuit and feminist pedagogies, we are right to ask about the sources in order to shed light on the identity of the women around Ignatius, their relationships with the Jesuits, and especially how they taught by example as participants in the mission of the Society of Jesus.[2] A number of helpful recent studies have addressed medieval and early modern female-male relationships in Church and society.[3] They show that relationships between women and men are complex, vary over time, and are affected by class, age, and circumstances. Women operated within but also challenged social mores, expected behaviors, and power arrangements.[4]

My goal in this chapter is twofold. First, I lift up the active engagement of women in the ministries of the Society of Jesus, through which they became teachers by example—keeping in mind the social, ecclesial context of sixteenth-century Europe. Second, I contrast this portrait with the image of women found in Hugo Rahner's *Saint Ignatius Loyola: Letters to Women*. There are 139 extant letters exchanged between Ignatius and women—89 written by Ignatius, 50 written by women.[5] Other letters have, regrettably, been lost. Since my primary interest is lay ministry/philanthropy related to the establishment of Jesuit schools and ministries, I focus on the letters to and from Ignatius and female royalty, nobility, and select friends.[6]

Sixteenth-Century European Context

The roles of women in sixteenth-century Europe must be viewed in light of key sociocultural developments, which included both advance and decline.[7] Spanish and Portuguese exploration of the New World and travel to the Orient broadened horizons and possibilities, increased knowledge, and created enormous wealth. It was also a time of significant turbulence. Parts of Europe experienced economic depression, famine, plague, bloody sieges, and epidemics. Syphilis, more widespread as a result of increased mobility, urbanization, and the mainstreaming of prostitution, was named and explained as divine retribution for sin. The Protestant Reformation produced profound social upheaval, violence, and political conflict among cities, nation-states, and the papacy. Throughout Europe, in both Protestant and Catholic circles, a profound ambivalence toward women manifested itself in the ways women were treated and portrayed.[8] The tensions related to women included authority and humility, public/social and private/domestic roles, control and obedience, enclosed convents and public ministry, and fear of women's power versus need for their contributions.[9] For example, in public, Isabella of Spain presented herself as both a pious woman and a warrior queen. Let us examine some of these tensions in more detail.

Empowerment

The printing press and vernacular literature contributed to increased literacy of the laity—including women.[10] For example, women in the circle of the Italian poet Vittoria Colonna (1490–1547), a friend of Ignatius, were noted for their erudition (129). This meant that an increasing number of mostly elite women were able to read tracts and books, listen to sermons and discuss aspects of the spiritual life in an informed manner. They could imagine themselves as participants in an intentional spiritual life. Developing virtue, praying, and using their intellectual and material resources for the needy were seen as signs of divine grace.[11]

Medieval and early modern women had access to a variety of forms of religious life beyond enclosed convents. These opportunities for religious affiliation included many forms of intentional community life for laywomen that continued to grow during the Reformation period. Titles varied from country to country: *beguines, humiliate, beatas, mulieres sanctae, pinzochere.* Third orders, confraternities, congregations, and penitential societies allowed women to remain in the world and combine active lives with spiritual involvements.[12] Wealthy women went on pilgrimages and engaged in public ministry. Many of the women around Ignatius seized such creative opportunities—in spite of growing social and ecclesial efforts to restrict women's movement and activity. For example, the noble widow Donna Costanza Pallavicini Cortesi helped the Jesuit Silvestro Landini found a society of women in Modena dedicated to the poor and the sick, and to protecting girls in moral danger (203–4). In Ferrara, Jesuit work with endangered girls was taken over by a women's guild called the Congregation of Love (212). While new male saints far outnumbered female saints in the first half of the sixteenth century,[13] the number of Catholic and Protestant women professing their faith publicly grew; this included female prophets, charitable workers, Anabaptist martyrs, and Reformation women who began preaching in public.[14]

Growth in literacy and spirituality was put at the service of social and ecclesial renewal. Reform had been in the air for centuries but took on a new immediacy during the sixteenth century. Luther's challenge to the Roman Church elicited fresh energy and commitment to improving the moral tone of family, society, and Church. The desire of Protestants and Catholics to "best" each other in these efforts resulted in increased charity and social services for the poor, ill, and marginalized but also produced misplaced fervor that resulted in religious wars and witch hunts. In tandem with humanism's advocacy of improved social morality and the active life, the Council of Trent mandated moral reform and reinforced the practice of good works in an effort to reinscribe tradition against the Protestant *sola gratia*. Thus was born a newly sensitized social conscience in response to the urban poor that produced a range of philanthropic initiatives in which women played a significant part. Qualities of compassion and tenderness were lauded. It is in this context of reform that we must place the women around Ignatius.[15]

Constraint

These types of renewed opportunity and increased ministerial activity were counterbalanced by a downturn in the fortunes of women.[16] Jobs and salaries waned and manuals prescribing humble, self-effacing behavior for women appeared.[17] Suspicion about women's emotions and religious experience had arisen in the late fourteenth century and continued to grow.[18] The Inquisition and Indices of Prohibited Books (the Valdes Index was promulgated in 1559) severely limited access to spiritual manuals written in the vernacular language accessible to women without formal training in Latin.[19]

In the wake of the Catholic Reformation and the Council of Trent, the Church became more vigilant about oversight of vowed religious women. During the twenty-fifth (and last) session of the Council in 1563, it was ordered that "the enclosure of nuns be carefully restored, wheresoever it has been violated and that it be preserved, wheresoever it has not been violated."[20] Clerical supervision of nuns increased and greater enforcement of rules concerning cloister became the rule of the day—in spite of resistance by nuns who fought, ignored, or subverted unwelcome reforms.[21]

In general, the role of confessor was broadened to include spiritual direction, with an emphasis on sacraments and obedience to clerical authority—a response to Luther's challenge to clerical elitism and the attempt to control grace through the sacraments. The virtue of female charitable work and humble behavior was lauded over courage and prophesy. But those who practiced or taught interior prayer (*alumbrados, illuminati*) were suspect and often persecuted (123). Ignatius himself was interrogated and imprisoned by the Inquisition for teaching interior prayer (often to women) without proper credentials.

The trend was toward limiting women to the private sphere. These limitations varied significantly, depending on whether women were in the cloister, at court, or in urban centers and bourgeois households. Deepening concern about demonic activity among women opened the door to charges of possession and witchcraft and increased the importance of the role of confessors, who could vouch for (or deny) a woman's spiritual authenticity.[22] While trials leveled off in the early sixteenth century, we know of trials and executions in France (1553), Spain (1548), and Italy (1523). Witch hunts took on renewed fervor after 1560.[23] It is hard to imagine that Ignatius would not have been aware of the accusations and punishments of these mostly poor, unattached, and elderly women. In all cases, competition between the voice and the silence of women intensified.

The centralization of ecclesial power was mirrored by a strengthening of patriarchal power in emerging nation-states and within the nuclear family. The moral order of the family, enforced through increased male control over women, children, and servants, was seen as the foundation of a moral society.[24] State, Church, and family were interwoven in a complicated web of support, challenge, and intrigue. Popes and monarchs, clergy and nobles, monks and knights were enmeshed in a tangle of familial, political, economic, military, ecclesial, and spiritual concerns. This web is apparent in the letters between Ignatius and royal and noble women.

Members of royal and noble families had the power to support or thwart the ministerial activities of the Jesuits. This uneven distribution of power required Ignatius to modify the tone of his letters, depending on the situation. He was at times diplomatic, creative, firm—or obsequious, ingratiating, and compliant. A blunt "no" to an unwelcome request was not an option—kings and queens held one's future and even one's life in their hands (472–73). Without their cooperation, Ignatius would have been unable to pursue his dream. As we will see, Rahner's commentary on the letters reinforces the double standard regarding the exercise of power among women and men. The reader might conclude that kings who exercised power in less than ideal ways were "just being kings," while queens, princesses, and female regents were arrogant, capricious, or unreasonable. An alternative interpretation posits that these women had power, knew how to use it, and expected their wishes to be fulfilled (162–63).

Sexual Purity and Family Honor

A preoccupation—some would say an obsession—with sexual purity also marked this period. The male role included preserving family honor, which rested in large part on female sexual purity. Both single and married women had to be protected, their lives held up as models of integrity and virtue. Prostitution was tolerated and even supported by civil and ecclesial authority as a way to keep order by channeling male libido and preserving the honor of legitimately married women. After Trent, both Catholics and Protestants supported reform in the guise of new taxes and legal restrictions for houses of prostitution. One of Ignatius's first ministerial activities in Rome was the founding of St. Martha's, a house focused on the rescue of women from prostitution and their relocation as nuns, wives, or trade workers. Preoccupation with sexual purity and family honor also fueled gossip and malicious talk (121, 208, 222). Male-female relationships that fell outside the narrow confines of accepted behavior were especially subject to rumor. The Jesuits were not immune.

Letter Writing

In the increasingly far-flung global exploration of the sixteenth century, letters functioned to maintain social and kinship ties, facilitate business, and communicate discoveries and the flow of life in other parts of the world. They might convey messages, teach, influence politics, or explore inner emotions and spiritual experience. Building on epistolary traditions such as Jerome's letters to aristocratic women in the early Church (c. 340–420) and Catherine of Siena's large corpus of letters (1347–80; canonized in 1461), Italian women took advantage of what Albrecht Classen calls an "excellent breeding ground for female epistolary literature in the 16th century."[25] In their directness, letters provide insight into the existential aspects of life not visible in formal treatises. Letters could also serve as legal documents or theological works intended for oral reading, public distribution, or later collection and dissemination.[26] Often the personal or politically sensitive substance of a communication was omitted from the letter itself, entrusted to the memory of the messenger to be delivered orally to the recipient. Literate women were active letter writers.[27] Scholars note a growing distinction between medieval women who followed religious vocations and those who remained "in the world," but the letter remained a medium common to both.[28]

Like many in his culture, Ignatius saw letter writing as an important part of life (1). In a letter to Peter Faber, Ignatius wrote, "The written word remains and bears perpetual witness." A glance at an autograph of one of Ignatius's letters reveals the care with which he wrote. One of the earliest biographers of Ignatius, Ribadeneira, wrote: "He was so careful in the drafting of letters, especially to persons of high rank or when dealing with important questions, that he spent much time in revising what he had written. He read and re-read his letters, examined every word, crossed out and corrected wherever he thought necessary. Then he had the letter copied out several times. He regarded the time and labour that this involved as well spent" (6).

Letters to and from women were written between 1524, when Ignatius returned to Barcelona after his trip to the Holy Land, until his death in 1556 at the age of sixty-five. Rahner describes Ignatius's letters as "laconic"—terse, concise. The founder of the Society of Jesus kept spontaneity and affection in check, choosing his words carefully. As a public figure with a mission to accomplish, he guarded what he said through an often austere and aloof style.[29] Rahner writes: "With Ignatius there are no intimacies, no unguarded moments, even in the final sentence of a letter, or in the briefest note" (6). These qualities are due not only to Ignatius's native caution and political acumen but also to the formal, epistolary topoi of the time that are so foreign to the "laid-back" style of twenty-first-century American culture.

I am also struck by the contrast between the austere tone and economy of these letters and the detailed directions of the Exercises, which delve deeply into the emotions as a means to discipleship.[30] Letters helped Ignatius engage women in the mission of the Society, provide them support and pastoral care, and contribute to their spiritual growth. We can also surmise that he was instructed and affected in diverse ways by the relationships behind this correspondence. Throughout history, letters have served to construct communities of friendship and networks of ministry. They overcome physical absence by sharing information and establishing emotional bonds that nourish a sense of belonging and further the work of mission.[31]

Women's Ministry

It is safe to say that among Ignatius's earliest experiences of pastoral work, his encounters with women are prominent. He conversed with women about the things of God, directed women in the Spiritual Exercises, helped reform female convents, and engaged women of means in ministries to women in need. His lifelong desire to "save souls" led him to favor practical works of mercy over theory and abstraction (132). This stance allowed women involved with the Society to become collaborators in its mission.[32] Women's service included reform efforts, financial support, cultural education (weaving, music, art, homemaking), catechetical instruction, feeding the hungry, caring for the poor, healing the sick, and comforting the dying.[33] Even Teresa of Avila, a crusader for Carmelite enclosure, lamented that, as a cloistered woman, she was unable to preach and work in the world to save souls.[34] Social and ecclesial restrictions curtailed women's efforts to found religious organizations engaged in active ministry. In spite of Church pressure to revise their rules and modify their vision of public ministry, many religious women made notable contributions to female education in the early modern period.[35] Wealthy laywomen with more freedom of movement engaged in an even wider range of ministerial activities.

Catherine of Genoa (1447–1510) is one example of a lay female engaged in ministry. From an aristocratic family, she became a spiritual leader of a group of laypersons and clerics serving the poor and the sick, including plague victims.[36] A collection of her writings appeared in print in 1551, five years before the death of Ignatius. Another is Angela Merici (1474–1540), a single laywoman and member of the Franciscan Third Order who, like Ignatius, made a pilgrimage to the Holy Land and founded schools for the Christian education of young girls. In 1535 in Brecia, she gathered together a group of women, the nucleus for what would become the Ursulines. Other Italian women engaged in active ministry include Francesca de' Ponziani, Angelina of Montegiove, and Colomba of Rieti.[37] Later, after Ignatius's death, and in spite of the growing enforcement of strict cloister, Mary Ward

(1585–1645) and others such as Louise de Marillac (1591–1660) and Jeanne de Chantal (1572–1641) founded institutes that included active ministries of teaching, nursing, and service. Even though Mary Ward ended up in jail for heresy in 1631 for trying to start a female order of "Jesuitesses" modeled on the Society, her work heralded future orders of religious women engaged in public ministries.[38]

The impetus for the Jesuit emphasis on ministry stemmed from Ignatius's early encounter with God as beneficent Creator. He never tired of acknowledging the generous service offered by people in response to God's love. From the very first meditations of the Exercises, the exercitant is asked to appreciate creation—a principle that lies at the heart of Jesuit pedagogy. Awareness of the gifted nature of existence is a prerequisite for everything that follows. Ignatius never forgot the early help he received from Inés Pascual in Barcelona, who nursed him when he was ill and helped finance his studies. He wrote to the archdeacon Jaime Cazador that he "owed more gratitude to that city than to any other place" he had lived in (245). Ignatius wrote to Inés: "Thus for the love of our Lord let us make an effort in his service since we owe him so much, for we shall much sooner tire of receiving his gifts than he will in bestowing them" (178). Hugo Rahner rightly argues that, for Ignatius, ingratitude ranked as one of the most egregious sins (169–72).[39] Ignatius's conviction that God can be found in all things led to an acute sense that everything anyone did to minister to others was a form of participation in this divine giftedness.

The letters under consideration are replete with references to service. The linguistic structures related to service reflect the chivalric and courtly milieu Ignatius experienced at Arévalo, as well as the popular romance literature of the time—*Amadís de Gaula* is one example in which the courteous, gentle, devout knight's only desire is to perform heroic feats and obey the commands of his lady. After his conversion, Ignatius transferred such courtly sentiments to the Virgin Mary and to ministry more generally.[40] In a letter to Donna Costanza Pallavicini Cortesi, Ignatius wrote: "To your service in our Lord Jesus Christ I am greatly devoted" (209). Doña Aldonza González voiced her wish that Ignatius would "increase and prosper" in God's service so that God would be "served and praised" by her contribution of a house for a college in Saragossa (237).

When favors are rendered, recipients are indebted to the benefactor through obligation (136), incurring feelings of gratitude, and a duty to please (217). Vittoria Colonna, poet and friend of Michelangelo, wrote to Ignatius: "I think my deeds and my obeying in whatever you order me to do, sufficiently show you my goodwill" (131). In a letter to Francis Borgia's sister, Doña Luisa de Borja y Aragón, Ignatius says: "In the matter of the prayers that your Ladyship asks me to make and in all the rest that you command me for the glory of God our Lord, I shall obey with a right good will, as is, indeed, my duty" (125). In addition to the traditions of chivalry, Ignatius would have been aware of the scriptural and theological language of service (*diakonia*). All service to others was rooted ultimately in service to God.

Material Resources

A major ministry of women of means was financial.[41] Research on medieval women reveals the extent to which women's economic resources influenced religious ideas and practices—art, books, architecture, and ministry.[42] Shortly after his conversion, Ignatius depended on women in Barcelona such as Inés Pascual, Isabel Roser, Juana Ferrer, Michaela Canyelles, and Brianda Paguera to provide him with clothing, books, supplies, travel money, and nursing when he fell ill. Later, Ignatius needed to raise money to acquire property and buildings, staff schools, provide scholarships, and serve the poor.[43] A sampling of benefactresses includes Juana of Spain (60), Margaret of Austria (78, 84, 88), Elenora of Florence (107), Francis Borja's sister-in-law, Doña Juana (126), Donna Maria Frasoni del Gesso in Ferrara (188), Donna Costanza Pallavicini Cortesi in Modena (204), Donna Margherita Gigli (211–12), Aldonza González de Villasimplez (227), and Leonor Mascarenhas (418). They participated in the Jesuit mission by making financial contributions to houses for catechetical instruction, refuges for prostitutes, churches, schools, and scholarships for Jesuit students.[44] Donna Maria Frasoni arranged for a loan to help the Roman College at a time of crucial need (196), and many women regularly sent personal gifts (197).

Isabel de Vega, the daughter of Doña Leonor Osorio, helped establish the first Jesuit novitiate in Messina (459), established a school at Bivona

(467), and carried on her mother's tradition of sending Lenten gifts to Ignatius, including special foods and wax candles for liturgy (442, 446, 454, 470). In 1554 she provided a sumptuous Easter banquet for the entire Jesuit community at Palermo (469). Pedro de Ribadeneira, trusted friend of Ignatius and later a general of the Society, wrote to the father of Isabel de Vega after her death: "Our hearts sincerely sympathize with you in your sorrow, for we too have lost in the Duchess a peerless lady and patroness of the whole Society of Jesus" (478).

Influence

Women benefactresses also provided influence. As governess to the royal family, Leonor Mascarenhas used her position to encourage a favorable disposition at court toward the new Society of Jesus. Leonor de Vega Osorio, wife of Charles V's ambassador to Rome, was also an ardent advocate for Jesuit ministries. Doña Juana, Francis Borgia's sister-in-law, provided a friendly presence at the court of the Infanta María, regent of Spain, and Maximilian of Austria (127–28). Margaret of Austria supported Jesuit causes during the papacy of Pope Paul III, her influence deriving from her husband, Ottavio Farnese, who was the pope's grandson (76). A specific case involved Ignatius's request that Margaret intercede with the pope on behalf of a Dominican priest who had been in trouble with the Inquisition. Since this Dominican had done penance and spent time in prison, Ignatius thought he deserved to be released from his penalties. Ignatius called on Margaret to intervene by practicing a spiritual work of mercy—comforting "a soul much distressed and in tribulation" (80–81).

Personal Ministry

Many of these wealthy women also personally staffed houses for prostitutes and girls.[45] Leonor de Vega Osorio went out into the streets (as did Ignatius) to recruit fallen women for the House of St. Martha, bringing them back to her own palace until a place for them could be found (435). Later she founded similar houses in Messina and Trapani. In Bologna the women's Congregation of Love collected clothes, flour, and bread and visited the homes of the poor (213). Some women began to dress more simply, giving up rich dress and jewelry (212).[46] After donating money and her home to the Jesuits in Naples, Donna Lucrezia di Storento adopted the lifestyle of poverty as a Franciscan tertiary. In her case, roles were reversed when the Society had to provide funds for the indigent benefactress (224).

These women caught the spirit of Ignatian service on behalf of a God who showered the world with gifts and graces. They chose to become disciples, passing on to others what they had received, especially to those most in need. In spite of the Roman Church's rejection of Luther's theology of the priesthood of all the faithful, the women around Ignatius embraced their priesthood wholeheartedly, giving of their wealth, time, and talent for the succor and education of many.

Clashing Images of Women

Hugo Rahner's decision to gather the letters exchanged between Ignatius and women has produced a valuable resource for the study of early modern women and, in particular, the women around Ignatius. Rahner carefully situates the letters in their sociohistorical context, employing a wide range of sources. He notes that from the beginning, women gave Ignatius the most abundant help in his work to establish the Kingdom of God on Earth (4–5). However, the interpretive lens of the mid-twentieth century through which he views the women needs to be updated. In particular, we need to revisit the uncritical, hagiographic aspects of Rahner's portrait of Ignatius and his frequent negative stereotyped portraits of women (139, 149, 162).

For example, we read of Ignatius's relationship with Margaret of Austria: "One can hardly blame Ignatius if he occasionally with tact, restraint, and complete lack of self-interest made use of Madama's intervention with the Pope" (79). Other descriptions of Ignatius suggest that nothing could disturb his unruffled calm and patience (473).[47] Rahner presents Ignatius as the insider with superior and controlling knowledge: "In women, tears and anger often follow close upon one another: that Ignatius knew" (71). Ignatius becomes the rescuer amid political and matrimonial intrigue—a last sure resort when all else fails: "The whole world was talking of the Colonna marriage. Pope and Emperor were furious. It was time to call Ignatius" (139).

In contrast to the portrait of Ignatius, women are presented as melancholy (460), petty (99), a nuisance (469), and difficult correspondents (94). Female intelligence and strength are explained through gender reversal. Rahner describes Princess Juana of Spain as having manifested masculine intelligence and strength of will (54). Rahner cites Ludwig Pfandl's description of Margaret of Austria as "perhaps a shade" too harsh—she was "distinguished neither by intelligence nor feminine charm, and liked to play the part of a misunderstood, injured, ill-treated woman." But then Rahner adds: "Out of this unmanageable clay, Ignatius formed a great figure" (75). In another instance, Rahner writes that Jacqueline de Croy "could not follow [the] diplomatic verbiage. . . . [She] could not understand such things" (162). The content of a letter to Ignatius from Doña Leonor de Vega Osorio is described as "a truly feminine medley of important and trivial affairs. Everything, absolutely everything could be told to Father Ignatius" (442; see also 211). In other words, the reader leaves this analysis with an image of women as—among other things—infantile, difficult, unintelligent, and bent on pestering Ignatius with their petty demands, testing his patience, and jeopardizing his health (113, 452, 456, 469).

We know that cultural and ecclesial misogyny are not only perpetrated from outside but also interiorized by women.[48] For example, in the *Way of Perfection*, Ignatius's contemporary, Spanish mystic Teresa of Avila (1515–82), comments that she is more likely than learned men to know how to write of the "ordinary things" of women—fair enough. But she continues: "Since these learned men have other more important occupations and are strong, they don't pay so much attention to things that don't seem to amount to much in themselves. But everything can be harmful to those as weak as we women are."[49]

Happily, feminist scholars are revisiting this material, inquiring how such language might have functioned as a linguistic strategy to resist female disempowerment.[50] In light of the accomplishments of women such as Teresa—genuine holiness, service to the world, reform, and writing—it seems clear that while such expressions of lowliness signal cultural attitudes about gender roles, they may also have resulted in enhancing women's power rather than diminishing it. Such self-deprecating language is noticeably absent in the letters to Ignatius from aristocratic and royal women.[51]

When we view these women as individuals in their own right, we discover their ideas, creativity, virtue, and agency. For example, when we find out that, at the behest of the young Isabel de Vega, Ignatius trudged through Rome to find Clara, a wronged woman, we want to interpret the event in a more even-handed fashion than Rahner allows. He writes, "So the weary apostle [Ignatius] set out to look for her [Clara], limping through the streets of Rome and climbing stairs— merely to fulfill the wishes of young Isabel" (452). But there are certainly alternative interpretations of Ignatius's words in a letter to Isabel: "If it seems to Your Ladyship that I can serve you in anything to God's glory, it will be for you to command and me to obey in all things, for I consider it a very signal favour that Your Ladyship may be served at any rate by my whole-hearted desires, when in works I cannot do so, through my insignificance and little worth in our Lord" (454). Should we reduce this expression of gratitude for allowing him to participate in Isabel's ministerial efforts to a camouflage for irritation, literary "chivalrous courtesy," as Rahner suggests, or might there be elements of genuine humility and gratitude?[52]

Conclusion

The letters exchanged between Ignatius and women show that they were a significant presence in each other's lives. As difficult as it is to "cross over" and understand the world of sixteenth-century Europe, we can say that these relationships were, on all sides, a mix of friendship, loyalty, attachment, manipulation, need, pragmatism, and dedication. Women's public efforts to aid the Jesuits in a sustained, substantial ministry reveal a spirituality of action characterized by commitment, self-direction, and action. These women functioned as mediators of divine compassion, made possible in significant ways through their association with, and participation in, the spirituality and mission of the Society of Jesus.[53]

It has often been noted that Jesuit spirituality has an activist, this-worldly cast to it.[54] In spite of being barred from official leadership positions, these women succeeded in teaching by their actions and thus exerting influence on Church and society. Wealthy women were attracted to the Spiritual Exercises, which provided a foundation for such activism. The Exercises "offered alluring power and authority and freedom to move about the world . . . with confidence and with something to offer others."[55] The women modeled a way of living a public virtuous life that continues to move us and attract our attention. They embody the desire of other early modern Christian women to engage in active ministry in spite of social constraints and the Catholic and Protestant backlash against strong women spiritual leaders.

Hugo Rahner's portrait of Ignatius as always in control, "handling" naive women in the interest of what he perceived to be the greater glory of God, does not do justice to the evidence. Women of royal and noble rank held real personal, social, and pastoral power in ways comparable to their male peers.[56] Some of their letters reveal an unveiled struggle of wills in which individual women disagree with Ignatius's wishes, especially regarding the appointment of Jesuit personnel.[57] Both Ignatius and his female correspondents used persuasive, even demanding, tactics; employed rational arguments; and appealed to the will of God. In spite of deeply misogynist attitudes and practices, the privileged women around Ignatius exercised real power of voice, action, and holiness in ministry and in their interior spiritual lives. The playing field was definitely more complex and probably a bit more level than we have been led to think.[58]

All those involved—female and male—functioned at various times as patron, benefactor, or beneficiary. Ignatius came from wealth, gave it up, and then needed financial support from many, including women. These women sought to gain from and contribute to Ignatius's spiritual ideas and practices. Ignatius's emphasis on inner freedom must have been distinctively empowering for women, learning as they did to discern the truth or falsity of their religious experience. These women were in a good position to appreciate the values of the Ignatian way that ultimately led to apostolic roles that otherwise would have been denied them. Thus, women benefited from their Jesuit connections ministerially and spiritually as well as interpersonally. Ignatius and the Jesuits benefited through conversation, friendship, and donations of money, property, and influence necessary to create the Jesuit educational empire.

We have seen that in early modern Europe, social, political, and economic prosperity depended on a complex network of personal and professional bonds.[59] The Church was an integral part of these networks. Good patron-client relationships marked by trust and reciprocity were crucial to reform and ministry. But there was more than simple pragmatism at work. These letters also reveal faith, hope, love of God and neighbor, and generous hearts. Since Ignatius and the women to whom he wrote were born to privilege, the letters reveal little about relationships with workers, peasants, and others born to low estate. But women of the upper classes around Ignatius were empowered to teach by action; to live out the ideal of an active public ministry to those in need; and to contribute to, and benefit from, the spiritual genius of Ignatius and his early companions.

2 Mary, the Hidden Catalyst

Reflections from an Ignatian Pilgrimage to Spain and Rome

MARGO J. HEYDT AND SARAH J. MELCHER

In the summer of 2006, we undertook a ten-day Ignatian pilgrimage along with several Jesuit university colleagues. Our intention when we began our journey was to write from a feminist perspective about our experiences learning about the history of a religious order of men. We set out to discover how women fit into the history of the early Jesuits to which we would be exposed, thinking that the focus would arise from the holes in the story—the places where women should have been found but were missing. What we encountered on the pilgrimage, however, differed from what we expected in several ways. This chapter develops one of our discoveries: the influence of Mary, the mother of Jesus, on the transformation of Ignatius of Loyola from a Spanish soldier of nobility to the spiritual founder of the Jesuits. It is illustrated by photographs we took during our journey.

These reflections on our journey in this chapter, combined with our research, demonstrate the impact that such an exploratory trip can have on two Protestant feminist pilgrim professors. The trip led us to a new understanding of the role that women played in the life of Ignatius of Loyola and so to a better grasp of the individual himself and the order that he founded. Two standard texts had been suggested to all on the pilgrimage: *The First Jesuits,* by John W. O'Malley, S.J., and *Saint Ignatius of Loyola: Personal Writings,* translated by Joseph A. Munitiz and Philip Endean.[1] The historical information we learned from tour guides and artifacts throughout the pilgrimage revealed the role of Mary to be considerably more significant to Ignatius throughout his life and in the founding of the Society of Jesus than had been portrayed in the books we read. The visual representations of Mary and of the life of Ignatius that we saw on the pilgrimage left a great impression, making the recommended readings come alive. The extent of Mary's impact was confirmed by the research we began upon our return. In this chapter, through the lens of the pilgrimage, we invite the reader to journey along with us and see images of Mary, who so strongly influenced St. Ignatius.

The Pilgrimage and Imagery in Art

The pilgrimage retraced the steps of the early Jesuits, with stops at important Ignatian sites in Spain and Rome. It spanned the lifetime of Ignatius of Loyola, from his birth (1491) at the Loyola family castle to his death at age sixty-five (1556) in his simple apartment next to the Gesù, the church of the Society of Jesus in Rome. Along the pilgrimage path, we were delighted to find that representations of women were considerably more abundant in European religious settings than (in our experiences) in the United States. This was particularly true of the art we observed at the religious sites we visited in Spain. Not only were these representations more numerous, but most were also qualitatively different. We became fascinated by differences between the images of Mary we observed in Spain and Rome and those more commonly described images of Mary by those we queried from the United States during the pilgrimage and later.

Before you continue reading, we invite you to pause for a moment and close your eyes to see what image of Mary comes to mind. In informal questioning of others, we found that the image that comes to mind for many is that of a solemn, light-skinned bust with downcast eyes, surrounded by folds of flowing blue and white fabric. Some envision a simple gold halo floating above her head. If the image is full bodied, it is usually of a full-length version of that bust. Often she is seated and holding a barely visible infant well-wrapped in more blue and white fabric. There is no visible hair, no eye contact, and no hint of activity in the depiction of either Mary or the baby Jesus (see Figure 2-1).

The representations in Spain and Rome were quite diverse from this more conventional image. The eyes of the woman depicted in the sculpture or painting appeared to be looking at the viewer or at other figures in the artwork itself. The figure's hair was often visible. In addition, the representation was more likely to be full bodied or standing. Mary's arms or hands were often raised or engaged in some kind of

FIGURE 2-1. *Purisima Concepcion*, Basilica de santa maria del Mar—Barcelona, Spain

activity rather than folded or used only to hold the baby. The images of Mary that included Jesus showed him making eye contact and represented him at various stages of childhood instead of as a perpetually sleeping infant with closed eyes (see Figure 2-2).

A wide range of colors was present in Mary and Jesus's skin tones and the fabrics they wore. Crowns of many styles worn by both Mary and Jesus tended to be large and ornate. In some images, there was both a crown and a halo. Most significantly, these empowering representations tended to portray a woman as agent very much engaged with and affecting those around her. This was especially true of the statue of Mary in the Basilica of St. Mary Major in Rome, where Mary appears to be blessing her audience while holding a squirming Jesus as a toddler (see Figure 2-3).

The extent of Mary's influence on Ignatius of Loyola became increasingly evident to us throughout the pilgrimage. From the very first stop at the hospital where Ignatius was treated for his war wounds, we were intrigued to hear of his vision of Mary while he was hospitalized and to see the displays telling the story. At the Loyola family castle, a diorama (a collection of figurines arranged in twenty-six vignettes) illustrated the major events of Ignatius's life. Almost immediately, we were struck by how prominently Ignatius's devotional relationship to Mary was portrayed throughout the vignettes. Later, however, what stood out to us was the minimal emphasis given in most Jesuit history accounts to this relationship. The vignettes and the accompanying narrative demonstrated how images of the Madonna inspired Ignatius's initial conversion experience. Along his lengthy spiritual path, the continued appearance of such images was instrumental in confirming Ignatius's decisions. The diorama clearly showed that Ignatius became devoted to Mary, imploring her throughout his lifetime to help him be more like her son, Jesus.

To our knowledge, neither the diorama nor the accompanying text is a product of critical historical research. Since we found them at the Loyola family castle, they could represent authentic family history or be significantly embellished or both. They are, however, building blocks in a hagiography of Ignatius of Loyola. The diorama focused our interest on the influence of Mary on Ignatius and sparked our pursuit of further evidence of this, as well as our joint reflections, prompted us to begin

FIGURE 2-2. *Mary and Jesus*—Xavier Family Castle, Spain

FIGURE 2-3. *Basilica of Mary Major—Rome*

researching the relationships among Ignatius, the Jesuits, Mary, and other women. In this chapter, we share both our reflections and some of our research thus far.

Mary and Ignatius

Supporting the story told by the diorama at Loyola Castle, numerous sites along the pilgrimage path emphasized the spiritual connections that Ignatius experienced with Mary and how pivotal these were in his turning away from his previous lifestyle and in his founding of the Society of Jesus. We learned of a number of significant Marian visions, occurrences of spiritual inspiration sparked by a painting or statue of Mary, and other kinds of Marian connections in Ignatius's life:

> Ignatius's father and nurse taught him about Mary when Ignatius was a child, setting a foundation that made him receptive to Marian influence later.[2]
>
> He is profoundly affected by a painting of Mary hanging in the family castle.
>
> Ignatius's first vigil of conversion, during which he pledges to live his life as Jesus lived his, takes place before an image of Mary in Aránzazu.
>
> Ignatius seriously considers murdering a Muslim who questions Mary's virginity, in order to defend her honor.
>
> After a three-day vigil, Ignatius lays down his sword in front of the Black Madonna at Montserrat to take up the life of a religious.
>
> Ignatius feels the strong influence of Mary at Manresa while meditating and writing the Spiritual Exercises in the cave.
>
> Ignatius has a vision of Mary in the hospital of the Magdalena at Azpeitia.
>
> He takes vows with some companions in front of the Mary statue at St. Paul's Outside-the-Walls Basilica in Rome.
>
> A painting of Mary and Jesus hangs in a prominent location in his simple apartment in Rome.
>
> The first church ever held by the Jesuits, and the site of the future Gesù in Rome, is called Santa Maria della Strada, or Our Lady of the Way.

It is possible that the early circumstances of Iñigo de Loyola's life explain his openness to the influence of Mary, the mother of Jesus. According to Azpeitian witnesses at Ignatius's canonization process (1595), Ignatius was one of thirteen children of Beltran Yáñez de Loyola. His mother, Marina Sánchez de Licona, died soon after his birth. The boy was raised and taught religious devotion in the home of María de Garin, his nurse and the wife of a local blacksmith.[3] According to W. W. Meissner, "the combination of the loss of his mother and exile from the castle of Loyola must have had great psychic impact on the infant who was to become the great saint and founder of the Society of Jesus."[4] Meissner observes that the early loss of a parent can result "in attachment to idealized substitute figures or devotion to idealized causes."[5]

As James W. Reites explains it, Mary's more prominent role in Ignatius's life began with the wedding gift of a painting of Mary from Queen Isabella the Catholic to Ignatius's sister-in-law Magdalena, who had been a lady-in-waiting to the queen.[6] Young Ignatius contemplated this painting, which played a role in his conversion.[7] According to the diorama text, Ignatius first considered following a spiritual path after reading about the lives of saints in books that Magdalena brought him during his convalescence from his war wounds.[8] Despite Ignatius's request for some of the tales of chivalry that he loved, Magdalena brought him a *Life of Christ* and *The Golden Legend*.[9] He formed an idea of living out his life in the "land of Jesus," afflicting upon himself penances more severe than those endured by the saints. Ignatius felt that this plan was confirmed by a vision he had one night of the Madonna with the infant Jesus in her arms, a vision that filled him with immense joy: "Being awake one night, he saw clearly a likeness of Our Lady with the Holy Child Jesus, at the sight of which, for an appreciable time, he received a very extraordinary consolation."[10]

The Loyola Castle diorama text and Ignatius's *Reminiscences* relate how Ignatius's devotion to Mary continued. After leaving Loyola Castle to make his way to Jerusalem and the land of Jesus, Ignatius stopped first at Aránzazu, a Marian sanctuary in the village of Oñate. There Ignatius hoped to gain strength for his journey to Jerusalem through a vigil before a statue of Mary.[11] The diorama text describes this as Ignatius's premier vigil of conversion, during which he pledged to live his life like Jesus before an image of Mary. In a letter written much later (1554), after the sanctuary at Aránzazu was damaged by fire, Ignatius describes how much his experience in the chapel there had meant to him: "Indeed, the fire was a great pity and misfortune, especially for those of us who are acquainted with the devotion which flourished there and the great service rendered to God our Lord. Whatever measures are necessary for the restoration of the monastery should be undertaken with much devotion. I may say I have a particular and personal reason for desiring it. When God our Lord granted me the grace to make some change in my life, I remember having received some benefit for my soul while watching one night in that church."[12]

On the road to his next stop in Montserrat, Ignatius seriously disagreed with a Muslim who questioned the virginity of Mary. After the encounter, Ignatius apparently experienced an intense internal battle, feeling that he had not done his duty toward Mary.[13] In reconsidering the disagreement, Ignatius felt that he should have defended Mary's honor more devotedly and contemplated catching up with the man to kill him. In the end, however, he headed in another direction, one literally determined by the mule on which he was riding, and he left the Muslim alone.

According to the well-known and broadly circulated medieval (pre-1250) poem *Ordene de chevalerie*, a chivalrous man must make himself available to a woman in need, honor her, and perform whatever mighty deeds may be necessary.[14] Ramon Lull of Majorca, author of *Libre del ordre de cavayleria*, indicates that a knight had the obligation to "maintain and defend the holy Catholic faith, by which God the father sent his son into the world to take human flesh ain [sic] the glorious virgin our lady Saint Mary."[15] Ignatius's background prepared him for religious devotion, as the classic orders of chivalry recommended daily attendance at Mass. Lull closely follows the earlier *Ordene de chevalerie*, in declaring that the "office of a knight is to maintain and defend women, widows and orphans, men diseased; and those who are neither powerful nor strong."[16] Perhaps even more pertinent is the requirement outlined in Geoffroi de Charny's *Libre de chevalerie*: "Hence all good men-at-arms are rightly bound to protect and defend the honor of all ladies against all those who would threaten it by word or deed."[17] Ignatius's background as a noble prepared him to defend and honor Mary in the encounter with the Muslim and probably played a role in the later events that occurred on his journey.[18]

Both O'Malley and the diorama offer the better known story of Ignatius's conversion experiences at the Benedictine monastery of Montserrat, where he undertook a vigil before the famous Black Madonna statue in the basilica. The full-bodied statue is of a dark-skinned Mary and Jesus. Mary sits straight and tall, with Jesus as a little boy sitting in her lap. They are wearing heavy gold crowns and gold robes and sit regally on a massive throne, looking straight at the viewer. Both the tour guides and our research revealed several possible explanations for the darkness of the skin other than that this was the artist's intention. But as far as we have been able to determine, there is no consensus as to whether the skin color seen today is the original. The colors of their apparel are all golds, browns, and black. At another location in the same basilica was a ceramic tile relief of the Black Madonna that bears little resemblance to the statue in terms of colors (see Figure 2-4). This representation shows Mary and Jesus wearing crowns and about the same age as they appear in the statue, depicted in a similarly straightforward and regal pose. In this tile representation, however, both Mary and Jesus are portrayed in incredibly full and colorful attire. The Black Madonna statue that Ignatius honored as well as the ceramic tile representation in the same basilica emphasized the authority and power radiating from a queen mother through colors and her attire, facial expressions, and pose.

In spite of the fact that Ignatius's legs were not fully recovered from his battle wounds when he was in Montserrat, he was determined to perform a traditional chivalrous act toward the Black Madonna statue of Mary. As a noble in the age of chivalry, he was conscious of his obligation to maintain religious devotion and to honor women with all his might. Ignatius maintained his vigil of arms for Mary, standing for the entire night despite his war wounds. He then made the commitment to become a man of peace, laying his sword and dagger down in surrender before the Black Madonna.[19]

Continuing on his way to Jerusalem from Montserrat, Ignatius next journeyed to Manresa, where he wrote the Spiritual Exercises during lengthy meditations in a cave. The Spiritual Exercises became the foundation piece of the Society of Jesus. The cave of Ignatius's meditations was later enclosed by a marble wall and is now a small chapel replete with a wide variety of grand works of art. Although several pieces of art, including the one within the altar of the Manresa cave itself, show Ignatius looking up at Mary while he writes the Spiritual Exercises in the cave, to date we have not found supporting textual documentation of that vision of Mary.

Mary is, however, frequently cast as intercessor in the Spiritual Exercises. For instance, the Third Exercise suggests a series of colloquies,

FIGURE 2-4. *Black Madonna*, Benedictine monastery basilica—Montserrat

the first addressed to "Our Lady." The colloquy asks for her to intercede with Jesus Christ.

> This is to be made to Our Lady, so that she will obtain for me grace from her Son and Lord for three things, (i) that I may feel an interior knowledge of my sins and an abhorrence for them, (ii) that I may feel a sense of the disorder in my actions, so that abhorring it I may amend my life and put order into it, (iii) I ask for knowledge of the world so that out of abhorrence for it I may put away from myself worldly and aimless things. Then a Hail Mary.[20]

Similarly, in the meditation on the Two Standards, Ignatius recommends another colloquy that also asks for Mary to intercede with Jesus so that the reader may obtain physical and spiritual poverty, receive insults and reproaches, and have the ability to accept these without sin.[21] Mary is mentioned as well in the "First Day: First Contemplation on the Incarnation," where Ignatius exhorts his reader to reflect upon Gabriel's appearance to Mary in the annunciation story.[22]

The Loyola Castle diorama text closes by stressing again the role of Mary in Ignatius's life. Reflecting on what it means to be a Jesuit, the narrative suggests that Jesuits should emulate Ignatius, who prayed to Mary without ceasing to place him at the side of Jesus, her son. Investigating this devotion in the life of Ignatius, we discovered numerous instances of Ignatius entreating Mary to intercede with God or Jesus to enhance his relationship with the Deity. Particularly notable in this regard is *The Spiritual Diary*, in which Ignatius asks Mary to intercede on his behalf with God. Throughout *The Spiritual Diary* Ignatius perceives Mary as being very receptive to him. In his meditations, he sees her as highly willing and ready to intercede with God.[23] So central was Mary in this role of intercessor in the *Diary* that Ignatius recalls his meditation during the Mass of Our Lady in the Temple, saying, "I could not but feel or see her, as though she were part or rather portal of that great grace that I could feel in my spirit."[24]

In some of Ignatius's letters, his devotion to Mary is evident when he indicates his intention to pray to the Mother on behalf of the addressee.[25] On a number of occasions in his autobiography, Ignatius speaks of Marian visions or of his devotion to and communication with the Madonna. In the epilogue to the autobiography, Gonçalves da Câmara relates how Ignatius envisioned Mary or received confirmation from her throughout the forty days during which he meditated upon the *Constitutions*.[26]

Jesuit Women Who Wished to Follow Ignatius

The pilgrimage, the background readings for the pilgrimage, and the text accompanying the diorama at Loyola Castle, as well as the diorama itself, opened up to us an important aspect of Ignatius's spiritual life and sparked our interest in researching the Marian connection. Our research indicates that Mary was a very influential figure throughout Ignatius's spiritual journey. Our discoveries about this, along with the varied representations of Mary that we encountered, fueled an interest not just in Mary but in the role of women in general in the life of Ignatius and the early Jesuits. During the pilgrimage, we heard stories about Ignatius and women—from tour guides and other pilgrims. From the confluence of all this, we began to focus on some areas of special interest to us beyond Ignatius's devotion to Mary, including the secret ordination of one woman, Princess Juana of Austria, into the Society of Jesus very early in its history.[27] In addition, we discovered information about an early Jesuit-affiliated order composed of a handful of women who were engaged in the ministries to prostitutes under Ignatius himself. Unfortunately, as a result of some difficulties arising from interactions with the women who wanted to join the Jesuits, Ignatius approached the pope, who granted a decree in 1547 "freeing" the Jesuits from the spiritual direction of women; that decree has been in effect for almost five hundred years.[28]

Ignatius's devotion to Mary and her extraordinary influence upon his life were unknown to us—two Jesuit university faculty members and Protestant feminist researchers, one of us a biblical scholar, the other a clinician and social worker—prior to the pilgrimage. To the biblical scholar, this was a source of great "consolation," to use Ignatian terminology. To the clinician and social worker, the consistently empowering portrayals of Mary were of greater interest. As two feminist professors teaching at a Jesuit institution for nearly ten years, we pondered how it is that this aspect of Ignatius's spiritual development seems to have received much less attention than many other aspects of the founding of his order, such as his relationships with other early Jesuits. The secret agency of Mary as a hidden catalyst in the formation of the Society of Jesus through her influence on Ignatius was an exciting as well as puzzling discovery.

While it was personally gratifying to make the discoveries recounted here, as professors, we believe that the implications of these discoveries for Ignatian education serve as an example of how uncovering lesser-known "herstory" through the experiential learning of a pilgrimage sparked new insights into both "history" and "herstory." As feminists and educators have discovered through the decades, experiential learning can be a crucial means of delivering a holistic education in which the learner gains understanding in both cognitive and affective ways. Although the focus here is on the diverse, complex images of Mary in Spain and Rome and especially on the influence of Mary in the devotional life of St. Ignatius of Loyola, there are other important aspects of the influence of women in general on the early Jesuits.[29] The implications of this discovery for us are developing in unexpected ways that contribute to new understandings of how Jesuits and feminists can work together toward greater inclusion of women at every level, including in relating the "history" of the Society of Jesus.

Missing "Herstory" and Decree 14

Both our reflections and research emphasize the need for greater recognition of the historical role of women in the formation of the Society of Jesus. Some of our findings thus far regarding evidence of "herstory" in documented "history" follow. In his popular 1993 volume, *The First Jesuits*, O'Malley briefly mentions the vigil of Ignatius in front of the Black Madonna but includes nothing about the role of Mary in the conversion of Ignatius prior to that event. There is some description of Princess Juana of Austria as well as mention of the unsuccessful two-year venture when Ignatius "accepted a few 'devout women' to live in obedience to him."[30] In his more recent work published in 2007, *The Jesuits II: Cultures, Sciences, and the Arts, 1540–1773*, O'Malley includes a chapter by Elizabeth Rhodes titled "Join the Jesuits, See the World: Early Modern Women in Spain and the Society of Jesus." In the 1998 second edition of *Jesuit Saints and Martyrs: Short Biographies of the Saints, Blessed, Venerables, and Servants of God of the Society of Jesus,* Joseph N. Tylenda, S.J., does not mention Princess Juana of Austria or the other women who tried to become Jesuits. He does, however, briefly discuss the influence of Mary on both Ignatius and the Society in four sections of the book and states: "At all important junctures in the life of St. Ignatius, our Lady had an important role to play."[31]

In the hundred-plus-page glossy coffee table book *"Ours": Jesuit Portraits,* published in 2006, M. C. Durkin provides a fascinating illustrated review of the Jesuits who have contributed to Jesuit history through the centuries.[32] Chapter 1 highlights the beginnings of the Society, with a focus on Ignatius of Loyola, Peter Faber, and Francis Xavier. It includes a photo of the famous fresco of Mary and Jesus called *Madonna della Strada (Our Lady of the Way),* which was moved from the original church into the Jesuits' Church of the Gesù. Princess Juana of Austria is not included in the list of thirty-two significant Jesuits throughout the centuries. Even more recently than Durkin's volume, Amalee Meehan picks up the theme in her 2008 article "Partners in Ministry: The Role of Women in Jesuit Education." She examines the missing "herstory" in light of the cultural context of the times. Meehan concludes: "Jesuits, in their 'way of proceeding,' need to recognize that women are a rich and still largely untapped resource. Recalling the origins of the Society of Jesus, when Ignatius invited women to enter into the spirituality of the Exercises, will help us conserve the past while creating the future."[33]

Throughout the pilgrimage, the early stories we heard about women and the Society of Jesus offered historical lessons that can aid in the quest for greater solidarity among the Society, Jesuit institutions, and the many women like us who contribute to the Jesuit mission on a daily basis. We offer our reflection and research to stress the value of continuing to incorporate such experiential learning in the future in Jesuit institutional contexts, especially toward the end of making these contexts more inclusive. After nearly five hundred years of silence, the groundbreaking nature of Decree 14, "Jesuits and the Situation of Women in the Church and Civil Society," must be emphasized. Emanating from the Thirty-fourth General Congregation of the Society of Jesus in 1995, this amazing call for "solidarity" with women officially recognizes Jesuit complicity with the church and society in gender discrimination against women. Our research indicates, however, that when individual Jesuits take that brave step to truly align with women in solidarity, trouble tends to brew for them and the women themselves or the history of their roles is again omitted.

More specifically, Decree 14 calls for Jesuits "to listen carefully and courageously to the experience of women."[34] As Susan A. Ross points out, Decree 14 has indicated that solidarity with women is integral to the Jesuit mission. If that is so, states Ross, "Making such solidarity a reality will require a profound conversion, a conversion in which knowledge of women's lives and experiences is central."[35] In the context of Jesuit institutions, she also stresses how crucial it is for Jesuits and others to establish and nurture ongoing relationships with women: "Real listening is not possible apart from trusting relationships."[36] This is where experiential learning can become crucial to Jesuit education in the future by providing occasions and opportunities to "listen carefully and courageously to the experience of women" and establish healthy and lasting relationships with women.

This pilgrimage stands as a case in point. The pilgrimage introduced us not only to the significance of Mary in the life of Ignatius but also to other female figures who were influential among the early Jesuits and who may have had an impact on the very shape of the Society. If university administrations, faculty, staff, and students are given similar experiential learning opportunities to explore the influence of Mary as well as other women on the early Jesuits, they will be better able to analyze those historical interactions. Of course, it is in the reflection aspect of experiential learning where the greatest integration can take place. Participants are then more likely to draw out implications for today's relationships between Jesuits and women if they are thoroughly informed about the past. The influence of Mary on the early Jesuits was significant to their experience and thus it is significant for those involved in Jesuit education today.

Conclusion

In closing, we leave you with two final artistic images from our pilgrimage. For us, these images epitomize the role of Mary in the founding of the Society of Jesus. The first image, of which we do not have a photograph, is a grand painting within the Gesù in Rome, and one of the most powerful portrayals of Mary with several of the early Jesuits. The title of the painting is *Regina Societas Gesù*, or *The Queen of the Society of Jesus*. With Mary as the central figure, fondly gazing down upon many of the early Jesuits along with some of the followers of each, it recalls to us Ignatius's frequent references in *The Spiritual Diary* to Mary as being very receptive to him and, by inference, to his many followers as well. In our view, it resonates with the description of the diorama regarding what it means to be a Jesuit, suggesting that Jesuits should emulate Ignatius in his unceasing prayers to and relationship with Mary.

And finally, in the Loyola family castle was one of the most powerful Ignatius-Mary images of all: a life-sized statue of Ignatius cradling a doll-sized full-bodied Mary attired in flowing blue and white (see Figure 2-5). Although reducing Mary to the size of a doll may seem to minimize the significance of her role, the look of adoration on the face of Ignatius overrides that possibility, displaying his total absorption in the sense of "I will carry you with me everywhere." This is what he did.

Throughout the pilgrimage to Spain and Rome, experientially engaging with such diverse but lesser-known representations of Mary as agent and uncovering her significant role as a hidden catalyst to Ignatius's spiritual journey encouraged us to initiate research regarding the role of "herstory" in Jesuit "history." As well, the pilgrimage was spiritually empowering to us as women, as feminists, and as professors at a Jesuit institution of higher education. These unexpected outcomes move us to include a theological comment about the implications of experiential learning of this kind for Jesuit education. As Roger Haight, S.J., argues, the turn to the human subject and experience by the highly influential theologian Karl Rahner marked a "monumental achievement" in Catholic theology.[37] Haight derives a lesson from this: "The house of Christian meaning lies in the experience of the Christian subject."[38] Feminist theologians argue that Christian theology will not be balanced until the experiences taken into consideration are themselves gender balanced.

Experiential learning, such as the pilgrimage we were privileged to embrace, can help create that balance in individual theological reflection as well as institutional practice. Women will be more likely to

FIGURE 2-5. *Ignatius Cradling Mary*, Loyola Family Castle—Spain

occupy a position of equality with men when women's "herstory" is deemed as worthy of treatment and as integral to the narrative as men's "history." In addition to encouraging engagement in similar avenues of experiential learning, these reflections are shared in the hopes of stirring others to make similar discoveries, to dust off Decree 14, and to continue taking brave steps toward the kind of solidarity envisioned therein. We suggest that substantial and consistent support from Jesuit leaders and educational institutions is needed to restore the centrality of the role of Mary to its original prominence within the Society's historical documents. This in turn would begin to move the Society toward greater solidarity with women, in keeping with the stated intent of Decree 14. Along with the Jesuit emphasis on the whole person, the history of the Jesuits also needs to be made whole.

3 Early Jesuit Pedagogy and the Subordination of Women

Resources from the Ratio Studiorum

COLLEEN McCLUSKEY

Having built one of the most prestigious and influential systems of education in the world, the Jesuits have been and continue to be well positioned to influence social and public life. Although the *Ratio Studiorum*, the blueprint of studies published in 1599, is no longer the official guiding document for Jesuit educational institutions, still its influence in the curriculum remains, especially in the emphasis placed upon philosophy and theology in undergraduate programs and in the prominent position given to the history of philosophy and medieval philosophy in particular within the curricula of many philosophy graduate programs. My main question in this chapter concerns the extent to which Jesuit educational techniques and ideas, especially as developed in the *Ratio Studiorum*, could have enabled the Jesuits early in their history to recognize and confront the oppression of women. This would not have been easy, since those authors whose writings contribute to the backbone of the document are well known for their patriarchal views. The Jesuits were also products of the culture of their time. But from its inception, the Society of Jesus has demonstrated a willingness to challenge the system if justice requires such challenge. For example, early in their history, Jesuits accepted so-called New Christians (Jews who had converted to Christianity, often several generations prior) into their order at a time when other Catholic religious orders rejected them.[1] Had the Jesuits recognized the subordination of women to be the evil that it is, they could have used their educational institutions to defy the status quo in the early modern period and help bring about justice for women.

With the recent publication of a new translation of the *Ratio Studiorum* by Claude Pavur, S.J., and the recent (1999) five hundredth anniversary of its promulgation, there is renewed interest in this

foundational document. An examination of its possibilities in addressing injustice might help to provide Jesuit educational institutions with
new ways of visualizing strategies for change.

The *Ratio Studiorum*: Historical Background

By the time the *Ratio Studiorum* was published in 1599, the Jesuits
had been running educational institutions for fifty years. The first was
founded in 1548 at the request of community leaders in Messina, Sicily.
By the end of the sixteenth century, the Jesuits had charge of over two
hundred schools in Europe and Asia.[2] Although many of these schools
were what today we would call high schools, by this period in history,
the Jesuits had established some colleges as well. Their educational
institutions were so successful that the Jesuits felt pressured to open
and operate more institutions of learning. A formal plan of studies was
urgently required.

The document itself was developed over a number of years, and
several drafts circulated among Jesuits teaching at various schools.[3] It
was based at least in part on the so-called *modus Parisiensis*, which
reflected the basic structure of studies at the University of Paris, at
which Loyola and his original companions earned their graduate
degrees, and one of the premier European educational institutions.[4] On
the Paris model, the faculty had charge of the programs of studies, and
students, having been assigned to specific grade levels based on their
preparation and ability, progressed through a set regimen with regular
lectures, course exercises, and examinations, features that are familiar
to us today.[5] This was in contrast to the so-called Italian model, in
which the student body had a greater voice in the running of the institution and the development of its policies.[6]

The *Ratio Studiorum* starts with the most advanced level of education
and progresses to the least advanced level. It begins with the duties,
rules, and expectations of the higher administration within what we
would today call a college or university, moving through the ranks of
the faculty, and continuing to the duties of the administrators and
teachers in what we would call a secondary or high school. At each
level, it specifies both the structure of the offices and, for the teaching
positions, the content of what is to be taught, including specific texts

to be covered, as well as the nature of the classroom experience, and the structure of the exercises and examinations. One might conclude from this that the *Ratio Studiorum* specifies a rigid, highly regimented program of studies, and to a certain extent, this is true. But as I hope to demonstrate, there is a remarkable degree of flexibility within the Jesuit vision of education, as specified in the *Ratio*, and it is this flexibility, I shall argue, that could have provided the Jesuits with tools to challenge the subordination of women.

The *Ratio Studiorum*: Pedagogical Resources

There are two aspects of the *Ratio Studiorum* that support my optimism: first, the fact that its specifications extend beyond strictly academic matters to include a general concern for the spiritual and moral well-being of the students, and second, a particular degree of liberty granted to professors regarding the implementation of their courses. I will explore each of these aspects in turn.

Ignatius Loyola's original vision for the Jesuits included care and concern for the spiritual well-being of individual persons. Presumably this includes female persons as well, and there is evidence that Loyola established ties and enjoyed friendships with prominent women in various communities.[7] Although he used these contacts to raise funds to support the order, he also demonstrated a concern for their spiritual well-being and functioned as a spiritual adviser to them.[8] Furthermore, in 1554, Loyola permitted, in strict secrecy and under stringent conditions, the admission into the order of Juana of Austria, who at the time was regent of Spain.[9] The motivation for this was not entirely altruistic, for it did not spring from a desire to recognize the gifts and talents of women or to challenge the injustice of their subordination. Rather, the hope was that admitting a prominent member of the Spanish court, even in secret and as a permanent Jesuit scholastic, would provide the Jesuits with a measure of support and protection.[10] Juana's admission turned out to be a mixed blessing in Loyola's eyes; it did not persuade him to follow the example of the Franciscans and Dominicans and establish a female branch of the order. It was only under a great deal of pressure that he had allowed Juana to be admitted to the Jesuits at all; he had in fact previously issued a decree, with the approval of Pope

Paul III, maintaining the Jesuits as an all-male order.[11] Nevertheless, the Jesuits did serve as confessors and spiritual advisers to women, and they encouraged them to undertake the Spiritual Exercises. Furthermore, they established as one of their ministries outreach programs for the reform and care of prostitutes.[12] Thus, they did not regard their mission as one directed exclusively toward the well-being of males.

Nevertheless, their educational institutions, which increasingly occupied much of their time and resources, were virtually exclusively male until the twentieth century.[13] They were at least in theory egalitarian with respect to class. The schools charged no tuition, although students were responsible for their own material support. The *Ratio Studiorum* explicitly states that no student was to be turned away on the basis of poverty or social status.[14] Admission was strictly on the basis of achievement and ability (118 [261]). Their policy was not entirely praiseworthy insofar as incoming students had to have some degree of literacy prior to admission even to the lower studies, and the Jesuits seemed oblivious to the obstacles that lower social and economic status would have posed to the achievement of even a basic level of preparation. Furthermore, the Jesuits were not immune to class influence; the *Ratio Studiorum* states that the better seats in the classroom are to be assigned to the students of aristocratic origin (123 [279]). Nevertheless, they are to be commended for trying to break down at least some barriers to education and at least in principle focusing on the more relevant factor of native ability. Their willingness to challenge class privilege makes it at least plausible that they could have challenged gender privilege.

In keeping with the broader mission of care for souls, the *Ratio Studiorum* makes clear in a number of places that Jesuit educational institutions are to be concerned with more than their academic mandate; they are also to promote and help develop their students' spiritual lives and moral character (29–30 [73]; 48 [129], [131]; 63 [178]; 198–99 [466]). Professors are to encourage and nurture the learning of their students, rich and poor alike, and refrain from scorning those from less privileged classes (154–55 [374]). They must be not only exemplary scholars in their areas of expertise but also innovative teachers who care about their students' progress (8–9 [10]). Jesuit scholastics are to be developed not only with respect to their intellectual abilities but also to have a care and concern for the well-being of others (30–31 [75]; 189–90 [434–35]). They should have an interior modesty, a humbleness of heart (18 [33]; 191 [440]). Thus, the Jesuits were committed to developing in both Jesuit and non-Jesuit students virtuous individuals who excelled in their studies.

This concern for the complete person could have helped set the stage for challenging the subordination of women. First, their direct contact with women in the community in their capacity as spiritual advisers could have enabled them to recognize the intellectual gifts of individual women, which might have led them to question the prevailing notion of the supposed inferiority of female cognitive capacities. Second, their willingness to challenge at least parts of the established social order and their commitment to justice could have enabled them to recognize further oppression that needed to be addressed. Third, their recognition of a connection between academic studies and the development of virtue might have helped them to realize that women too would have benefited from their educational programs.

The second factor that could have enabled the Jesuits to develop a strategy for challenging the oppression of women has to do with the ways in which they visualized the educational experience, both with respect to the actual content of the particular courses and with respect to the pedagogical methods to be employed. I shall consider each in turn.

Early Jesuit institutions were structured in such a way that the first course of studies involved literature and rhetoric, especially ancient Greek and Roman authors. The next level was a study of philosophy, in particular Aristotle, and then finally theology, especially that of Thomas Aquinas. From a feminist perspective, the study of Aristotle and Aquinas is at best a double-edged sword. On the one hand, feminists have mined the philosophical systems of both thinkers (albeit critically) for resources in developing accounts of human nature and of ethics that are amenable to feminist goals.[15] On the other hand, as is well known, both Aristotle and Aquinas exhibit sexist and arguably even misogynist attitudes toward women.[16]

As far as the philosophy curriculum is concerned, most of the texts from Aristotle listed in the *Ratio Studiorum* are not explicitly problematic from a feminist perspective (see 99–106 [207–29]). The *Ratio Studiorum* specifies the study of Aristotelian philosophy as a three-year course. The first year is devoted to Aristotle's logical treatises, including *Categories*, *On Interpretation*, and parts of *Prior Analytics*. From there, the curriculum covers Aristotle's *Physics* and parts of *De anima*. In the second year, the students pick up *On the Heavens*, *On Generation*, and *Meteorologica*. The third year is devoted to the rest of *De anima* and *Metaphysics*.

It is not entirely clear which of Aristotle's two treatises on generation is to be covered, and from a feminist perspective, this might make a difference. *On Generation and Corruption* deals with the issues of coming to be and passing away in a very general manner, focusing on nonliving systems such as the heavens and the doctrine of the four elements. The other text, *Generation of Animals*, looks at the subject from the standpoint of living beings, including human beings. The latter text includes some of Aristotle's reasons for holding that women are inferior to men.[17] I suspect, however, that the text covered in early Jesuit institutions was the more general one, since its study follows the study of *Physics*, which is largely concerned with Aristotle's account of change, and generation and corruption are specific types of change. It is also situated between the study of astronomy and geology (roughly speaking) and so would seem more akin to them than would a study of biological entities. If this is so, then at least with respect to Aristotle's non-moral philosophy, the curriculum does not involve texts that are problematic from a feminist perspective.

The case is a bit more complicated regarding the study of moral philosophy, where the curriculum includes the ten books of Aristotle's *Nicomachean Ethics*. In book 8, we find an explicit example of Aristotle's patriarchal commitments in his treatment of friendship, including that between husband and wife. In his discussion there, Aristotle makes it clear that he regards the relationship between husband and wife to be one of inequality.[18] Furthermore, he makes the highly reprehensible remark that in relationships of inequality, the member who is granted a higher status (i.e., the husband in the case of marriage) is to be accorded more love than he himself provides and is to receive more of what is good.[19] Such a division of goods in Aristotle's view is in accordance with justice; the one who has a greater status deserves more. This is the one place within the philosophy curriculum that expressly reinforces the status quo. About all that can be said here is that these remarks on marriage occupy a very small part of book 8 out of an ethics curriculum that covers ten books. Therefore, I suspect that Aristotle's ideas on the marriage relationship were not noted to any great degree.

There is one further important issue regarding the study of Aristotle, and that is, of course, the contextual problem made clear in recent years by feminists, namely, that Aristotle takes himself to be addressing an aristocratic male audience, especially in his ethics.[20] However, unless one is familiar with those texts that prominently display Aristotle's androcentric attitudes, his parochialism is not at all obvious, since he appears to be presenting a moral theory based upon human nature and thereby presumably applicable to all human beings. The texts that explicitly reveal Aristotle's views on women and clarify his intended audience for the ethics (and most likely the rest of his philosophical theories) include the *Politics* and his biological treatises. These texts are not listed in the *Ratio Studiorum* and so presumably would not have been included in the curriculum. Having said this about the program of studies for philosophy, I shall now consider Aquinas's place in the program of studies for theology.

The material from Aquinas is drawn from his most famous work, *Summa theologiae*.[21] Among the texts and topics included in the theology curriculum, only the discussion of matrimony raises potentially troubling views. It is not entirely clear which of the particular questions on matrimony are to be discussed.[22] The *Ratio Studiorum* specifies certain issues to be omitted altogether, for example, whether virginity is a virtue, or to be covered under other topics elsewhere in the curriculum, for example, the nature of vows (94–95 [130]). Nevertheless, a significant amount of material on matrimony remains to be taught. While Aquinas's views on marriage are very complex and presuppose some highly problematic views on the nature of women, the actual questions on the sacrament of marriage for the most part do not raise those views explicitly. It is quite clear that Aquinas wrote the questions on marriage with the husband's perspective in mind. For example, he addresses the issue of whether it is lawful for a husband to kill his wife upon discovering her to be unfaithful but does not consider the opposite possibility.[23] He examines the issue of whether a husband who converts to Christianity should remain with a wife who does not convert but once again never discusses whether a newly converted wife should remain with her non-Christian husband.[24] He also looks at polygamy, bigamy, and divorce primarily from the husband's perspective and often fails to consider that of the wife.[25] But much of the material on marriage has to do with technical matters pertaining to marriage as a sacrament and so does not often raise direct worries about Aquinas's underlying sexist views of women. There are some exceptions. Aquinas mentions, almost in passing, that wives are to be subject to their husbands and that husbands/fathers are nobler than wives/mothers, but he never argues for this position here in the questions on marriage.[26] Thus, his views on the nature of women, argued for more explicitly elsewhere in texts not listed in the *Ratio Studiorum*, would not necessarily have been read or discussed in class.

Aquinas's reasons for supporting the traditional subjection of wives to husbands reflect his commitment to the Aristotelian idea that women are less capable of intellectual activities than men and therefore ought to be ruled by men.[27] On the other hand, Aquinas argues that wives have their own domains of responsibilities with which husbands are not to interfere.[28] Furthermore, marriage is an arrangement to which consent must be given freely by both parties, and it involves a state of friendship between husband and wife, which requires a certain degree of equality.[29] Thus, on Aquinas's view, wives have rights and privileges, the content of which would not satisfy current feminist conceptions, but which provide some wiggle room, so to speak, for developing a more congenial view on the status of women.

Unfortunately, Aquinas's notion of equality between husbands and wives is rather thin. Husbands and wives have equality with respect to what was known as the marriage debt, which is essentially the right of either spouse to sex on demand.[30] He also believes that having one's own sphere of influence within the marriage confers a kind of equality on the spouses, duties that, for Aquinas, divide along the traditional private-public distinction.[31] As I have argued elsewhere, neither of these notions endorses a truly robust notion of equality, and both are entirely compatible with the continued subordination and oppression of women.[32]

Thus, scattered aspects of those texts that would have been covered in Jesuit colleges would have tended to reinforce the status quo of women. Nevertheless, most of the truly problematic claims and arguments that Aquinas makes about the nature of women that ground his acceptance of the status quo are not to be found among the texts explicitly set out for study by Jesuit colleges. Thus, these views are left in the background. Although unexamined background assumptions make it difficult to recognize their roles in maintaining oppression, the fact that the most blatant expressions of Aquinas's sexist views were omitted from the curriculum might have provided at least some leeway for change. The absence of these statements diminishes their availability as authoritative ammunition in maintaining the status quo.[33] Furthermore, basic Jesuit pedagogy as specified by the *Ratio Studiorum* contains resources that could have been used to challenge these background assumptions. I shall now go on to consider this resource. Once again this is not an unmixed blessing.

As we have seen, the *Ratio Studiorum* exhibits a deep respect for Aquinas and his views. This respect influences what the *Ratio Studiorum* has to say about the placement of teachers. It stipulates that only those who are "well disposed" toward Aquinas's views ought to teach in the faculty of theology (10 [15]). Those who are inclined to disagree with Aquinas or who lack enthusiasm for his views ought not hold the theological chairs (10–11 [15]). Furthermore, the *Ratio Studiorum* tends to discourage novelty, stating that free thinkers ought to be dismissed from academic appointments (13 [22]). Rather, instructors are to teach the interpretations most common and universal among Catholic institutions (49–50 [134]). Professors of the most advanced disciplines are to subject their teaching materials to a review by the prefect of studies and to adhere to the customary subjects and pedagogical methods (49 [132]). These policies suggest rigorous oversight of those teaching Aquinas's texts, as well as the expectation that they will faithfully adhere not only to Aquinas's views but also to their conventional interpretations, which would surely enforce the status quo.

On the other hand, the early Jesuits recognized that there could be more than one respectable interpretation and that reasonable people could disagree. They also recognized that knowledge develops over time and that views once held as irrefutable could be established as false. Therefore, the *Ratio Studiorum* stipulates that instructors are to raise problems and objections to the views they are teaching (although not too many, and only the strongest ones) (50 [135]). No one is to teach anything that is false or outdated (50 [135]). This directive applies even to Aquinas; although instructors are to follow and defend his views, they are not to do so slavishly (62 [175]). They must in fact follow their own judgment with respect to his positions, and if anything is deemed indefensible, they are either to disagree respectfully with him (100–101 [212]) or to omit it altogether (68 [195]). This modus operandi encourages thoughtful consideration and evaluation of the accounts being taught and at least leaves open the possibility that individual instructors might come to recognize and address problems with the status quo.

This openness of thought applies to students as well. The *Ratio Studiorum* encourages them to present and defend their own reasoned positions even if those positions contradict the teacher's interpretations, although the expectation is that their views will be compatible with those of Aquinas (195 [454]). Thus, Jesuit pedagogy allows for the possibility that independent-minded students could encourage their professors to reconsider their own positions. Instructors are to be available after class to answer their students' questions and respond to their concerns (51 [139]). Hopefully, this too would stimulate expression of new ideas, even with respect to Aquinas. These commitments from the *Ratio Studiorum* reveal that while the early Jesuits were convinced of the value of Aquinas's philosophical system and of the veracity of his positions, they were not willing to assent to Aquinas's infallibility. Thus, while there is little in the content of Aquinas's views, aside from an insistence upon a kind of equality between husband and wife, that would have aided the early Jesuits in recognizing the oppression of women, there are no insurmountable barriers to their doing so, and their own pedagogical methods and commitment to justice serve as an encouragement to do so.

Opportunities Missed and Taken

I have been arguing that in setting up a system of education along particular pedagogical lines and curricular content, the *Ratio Studiorum* could have provided the early Jesuits with tools that might have enabled them to recognize and challenge the unjust subordination and oppression of women. First, the early Jesuits, including Loyola himself, recognized that education is pivotal in developing effective and virtuous social leaders.[34] Had the Jesuits recognized the oppression of women, they could have educated their students to advocate social and cultural changes that would have benefited women. Second, feminists have long noted a connection between increasing educational opportunities for women and dismantling the oppressive structures that maintain women's subordination. The hope is that educating women helps them develop the ability to comprehend their situation in life and increases their political and economic opportunities, supplying at least some of the tools needed in the fight against injustice.[35] The Jesuits could have come to see that adopting the education of women as one of their missions not only would benefit individual women but also would have helped to challenge the unjust status quo.

Although a number of potential avenues of challenge were available to the Jesuits in virtue of their philosophy of education, in the final analysis, it would have taken a leader of extraordinary insight to seize these opportunities and press for changes in the status and opportunities for women. This is because the *Ratio Studiorum* specifies a hierarchal administrative structure whose highest official, the general prefect of studies, essentially has absolute control over academics at the various levels of instruction (8 [8]). Thus, addressing the subjection of women by the early Jesuits through their educational ministry would have required a leader with a countercultural vision. Although many Jesuits developed countercultural innovations in their missionary work overseas and in their academic studies, most of them seem not to have done so with respect to gender. The question, of course, is why they did not.

Answering this question requires further inquiry into the status of women's education in the European Renaissance and early modern period as well as examination of prevailing cultural attitudes toward women, including their perceived abilities, social roles, and place in European society. I will be able to sketch these topics only very briefly here. Although reality did not always reflect the ideal, a woman's proper place was thought to be in the so-called private sphere of the home and not in the public realm. This ideal has its roots in traditional views of women's capacities as child bearers and associated ideas about their supposedly diminished rational abilities. These ideas have their roots in and are reinforced by authorities we have just examined, namely, Aristotle and Aquinas (among others).

Given this ideal, girls' education was most often directed toward what they needed to know in order to fulfill their duties in the private realm, especially as married women.[36] Prior to the Protestant Reformation in the sixteenth century, those women who did receive a more formal education tended to be educated either in their parents' homes with a private tutor or in secluded schools within cloistered convents. With the advent of the Protestant Reformation, public schools began to open both for girls and for boys as the ability to read began to be viewed as an important part of religious training.[37] These schools were developed first in Protestant areas and later in Catholic areas, but the number of schools available to girls was generally much lower than those for boys, especially in urban areas, and the curriculum and length of study for girls were much more circumscribed, emphasizing those skills girls would need for their married lives.[38]

Catholic women who did not wish to marry had another alternative open to them, insofar as they could enter the religious life, but attitudes toward women in religious orders track the same results; members lived sheltered lives within the walls of their convents, largely closed off from the outside world.[39] Thus, women in the early modern period in Europe were expected to take on one of two roles, both of which relegated them to the private sphere.[40]

This attitude, that women belong to the private sphere, that the public sphere is not an appropriate venue for them, is reflected in Jesuits' interactions with women. Their contact with women was itself private, either through the medium of correspondence or as their confessors and spiritual directors, venues that reflect a personal and private relationship.[41] Even when women assumed the role of patron, their contributions to Jesuit enterprises were often not publicized or prominently acknowledged.[42] Prevailing attitudes concerning the proper place of women in the social realm would have made it difficult for the early Jesuits to visualize a new order for women.

It did not, however, make it impossible. Nicolas Caussin (1583–1651) was a prominent French Jesuit who was asked by the abbess of Longchamp to write a biography of Isabelle, the sister of St. Louis (Louis IX), who founded this well-regarded religious house in 1260.[43] Isabelle lived with the religious community from 1263 until her death in 1269, but she never entered the order itself. She also resisted strong pressure from her family and the pope to enter into a marriage with the son of the Holy Roman Emperor. Caussin championed Isabelle as a devout and admirable woman who adopted for herself a third way of life, that of a single woman, challenging the sanctioned societal dichotomy of marriage and vowed religious life.[44]

Here we have an example of a Jesuit who was able to visualize and defend a different path for women. Nevertheless, Caussin's vision is fairly restricted and leaves intact the predominant structures that disadvantaged women. On the one hand, he argues that the choice of a single life should be available to all women, regardless of their economic or social status, and that such a choice is admirable. He also notes the many reasons why women might not wish to marry, such as a husband's drunkenness or ill treatment at his hands, as well as reasons why they might not wish to enter a religious order, such as a lack of religious vocation,[45] but he fails to acknowledge the fact that single women often lived in extreme poverty, given their limited opportunities for meaningful employment or living wages.[46] He also fails to address or condemn those practices that, by his own acknowledgement, lead women not to desire the married state. In other words, he leaves largely intact the oppressive structures that reinforced women's subordination and disadvantage.

But if many of the Jesuit rank and file and leadership failed in this regard, it is interesting to note that some of their female contemporaries did not. There were women who recognized the value of the Jesuit plan of studies and its applicability to the education of women. Two women in particular established schools for girls based upon the model presented in the *Ratio Studiorum*: Mary Ward, a sixteenth-century Englishwoman who founded the Institute of the Blessed Virgin Mary, and the founder of the Society of the Sacred Heart, Madeleine Sophie Barat, a nineteenth-century native of France.[47] Both institutions are still active today, although Ward's schools were ordered to be closed by the pope in 1631 and were driven underground for a time.[48] Both women were mentored and encouraged by individual Jesuits.[49] Once again, we see that some Jesuits supported efforts to address the oppression of women. This support, however, did not extend to the Jesuit hierarchy, who would have controlled general policy. Ward, for example, encountered strong resistance to her plans for female education from members of that hierarchy.[50] Furthermore, those Jesuits who did support Ward and other women in their endeavors did not seem to regard it as part of their own mission to organize and establish educational opportunities for women; they were content to let the women themselves take on the task. Thus, even those sympathetic to the concept of quality education for women did not consider it to be an integral part of the Jesuit mission. This may stem from the fact that Loyola explicitly specified his order to be exclusively male, but that did not prevent the Jesuits from serving women in other ministries.

The question, therefore, remains: Why did the Jesuits not lend stronger support to the education of women and other activities on the behalf of women in the early centuries of their existence? As we have seen, they were very much involved in the spiritual direction of women, and they ministered to prostitutes. This is speculation on my part, but I wonder if perhaps they felt no need to advocate for women because they saw no real difficulties with the status quo. Prostitutes were "fallen women" and so in need of ministry. Women as well as men needed spiritual direction. But if a woman's reason for avoiding marriage was fear of abuse, then, at least to Caussin (and I doubt that he was alone in this), the solution was not to change *male* behavior but rather to allow women to opt out of marriage. The education of women may have been seen as best left to women, who would, after all, be intimately familiar with what girls needed to know in order to assume their stations in life, stations that most likely appeared perfectly natural and therefore acceptable to those living under that system. Furthermore, as we have seen, the Jesuits believed that a central goal of their educational system was to produce virtuous and capable social leaders. The fact that public roles were not deemed appropriate for women in the early modern period would have reinforced the idea that Jesuits need not support an educational ministry for women.

In accepting these notions, the Jesuits simply followed the conventions of their time, conventions that were often accepted by women themselves, even those who were highly educated. Increased educational opportunities for women in the early modern period were justified as an enhancement to a woman's religious devotion and a means to improve her competence in performing her domestic tasks, not as a reason to change the status quo.[51] Mary Ward, whose plan of studies was patterned after the *Ratio Studiorum* and emphasized a rigorous academic curriculum, included religious studies and training in the domestic arts in her program of study.[52] Those rare women who achieved the classical humanist education generally reserved for male elites virtually all recognized the incompatibility between continuing to pursue their studies and assuming the domestic roles expected of them; instead of arguing that such a choice was unjust, constituting a double standard, and insisting that the system be changed, those who wished to continue their studies opted for the single life.[53] Those women who achieved the highest levels of learning often regarded themselves as the exception to the rule, having somehow "overcome their sex."[54] Thus, women themselves did not often recognize or deem it appropriate to challenge the sexist assumptions underlying their own subordinate status.[55] Perhaps then, Jesuit reluctance to take on this challenge can be understood.[56]

Present Attitudes

While the examination of history for its own sake is of interest to those of us who engage in it, a fundamental part of a commitment to feminism involves the application of lessons learned from history in order to improve the lot of women. This raises questions regarding the implications of my discussion for the Society of Jesus in the contemporary world. In my view, the spirit of the *Ratio Studiorum* lives on in the Jesuit Order. The dedication to the pursuit of truth expressed in this document and an acknowledgement of the difficulty of doing so is reflected in recent Jesuit writings on the state of women, including those found in the *Documents of the Thirty-fourth General Congregation of the Society of Jesus*.[57] Decree 14, in particular, articulates the Jesuits' awareness of past failures to recognize the subordination of women as well as a commitment to gender justice in the future. This in turn gives rise to the hope that the Jesuits and feminists are in fact allies in the fight against the oppression of women.

In Decree 14, the Jesuits particularly acknowledge the many forms that women's subordination has taken: "It has included discrimination against women in educational opportunities, the disproportionate burden they are called upon to bear in family life, paying them a lesser wage for the same work, limiting their access to positions of influence when admitted to public life, and, sadly but only too frequently, outright violence against women themselves" (172 [362]). The Jesuits admit their historic failure to recognize and address these unjust states of affairs as well as their own complicity in maintaining them (174 [369]). They raise specific arenas for change, beginning with the urgent need to listen authentically to women and take seriously what women have to say: "Unless we listen, any action we may take in this area, no matter how well intentioned, is likely to bypass the real concerns of women and to confirm male condescension and reinforce male dominance."[58] Among the specific items identified as means of addressing gender injustice, the Jesuits list two in particular that follow directly from their educational mission: "explicit teaching of the essential equality of women and men in Jesuit ministries, especially in schools, colleges and universities" and "promotion of the education of women and, in particular, the elimination of all forms of illegitimate discrimination between boys and girls in the educational process."[59]

Here, the Jesuits articulate two of the ways I identified from the *Ratio Studiorum* in which they could have addressed the subordination of women, namely, by teaching their students that the oppression of women is wrong, and by recognizing the value of educating women and admitting women into their educational systems.[60] Elsewhere in the documents, the Jesuits rededicate themselves to the goal of character formation through their educational institutions as a method of challenge to all forms of social injustice.[61] Although here they do not mention gender injustice specifically, I trust that they would certainly include it. The objective of developing a virtuous character in their students is an important legacy of the *Ratio Studiorum*, a worthy tool in the struggle against the evil of women's subordination.

Finally the Jesuits acknowledge that it would be presumptuous to assume that all the important issues and concerns surrounding the subordination of women have now been identified.[62] They articulate a commitment to vigilance on gender issues "through committed and persevering research, through exposure to different cultures and through reflection on experience."[63] They argue that ongoing intellectual inquiry is imperative if they are to maintain their dedication to social justice.[64] Once again, the emphasis on the need for further intellectual inquiry expresses the spirit of the *Ratio Studiorum* insofar as it recognizes the fallibility of human understanding and the need for further intellectual investigation and reflection.

Conclusion

There are a number of points that follow from all of this. First, while the Jesuit educational system as specified by the *Ratio Studiorum* contains nothing that explicitly challenges the subordination and oppression of women and is certainly compatible with maintaining the status quo of the time, still it contains very little that is overtly sexist. In fact, it does not even specify that only males are to matriculate as students, although that would have been presumed in the sixteenth century. Furthermore, the document promotes at least some degree of innovation and openness of mind to changing views. The framers of the *Ratio Studiorum* wanted to maintain high intellectual standards and a certain intellectual rigor and defense of what they saw as truth, but they were also humble enough to recognize that fallible human minds might not always recognize the truth when they see it. Thus, they wanted to promote a certain flexibility in their pursuit and transmission of knowledge. This flexibility would have served them well had they recognized sexism for the sin that it is.

The Jesuits also had a broad view of what an education was supposed to accomplish. To them, education consisted of more than simply book learning or vocational training. It included a concern for the character of the student and promoted the inculcation of virtue in an attempt to bring about a wiser society that promotes justice. Thus, what was wanting was a recognition of the injustices done to women, as well as an acknowledgement that women too would benefit from this kind of education.

Finally, while most Jesuits, especially the hierarchy, did not deem the education of women to be their immediate concern, still some individual Jesuits supported early efforts to educate women along the lines of the pedagogy and course of studies outlined in the *Ratio Studiorum*. While Jesuits did not have a direct hand in educating women until the twentieth century, they did in fact influence efforts to develop quality educational programs for women.[65] And in the documents from the Thirty-fourth Congregation, they publicly acknowledge the failures of the past and commit themselves to renewed efforts on behalf of women, an effort that in my view is very much in keeping with the spirit of the *Ratio Studiorum*.

Part II: Intersection I
Transformative Visions for Educating the Whole Person

4   "The Personal Is Political"

At the Intersections of Feminist and Jesuit Education

JOCELYN M. BORYCZKA

AND ELIZABETH A. PETRINO

> When we, as educators, allow our pedagogy to be radically changed by our recognition of a multicultural world, we can give students the education they desire and deserve. We can teach in ways that transform consciousness, creating a climate of free expression that is the essence of a truly liberatory liberal arts education.
>
> bell hooks, *Teaching to Transgress*

Jesuit education, from its inception, has retained its vitality and relevance through its interaction with other faiths and philosophical traditions. It is a tribute to the early teachers of the Society of Jesus, led by Ignatius Loyola, that they maintained a core set of principles and beliefs informed by their sense of spirit and rigorous search for truth while contributing to many of the leading intellectual achievements that developed in different cultural and historical contexts. As in the past, social and cultural diversity still give rise to a range of opportunities and challenges for Jesuit universities. At the twenty-first century's outset, "diversity" generally refers to race, class, and gender as well as religion, ethnicity, age, sexual identity, and ability or disability. These variables remain critical to understanding how the complex puzzle of identity is pieced together within the context of social, political, and economic institutions on local, state, national, and global levels. With these intersecting individual, structural, and contextual elements in mind, here we explore the essential role of diversity in the Jesuit mission for social justice through the lens of gender in order to see where principles and practices of Jesuit and feminist education may intersect.

Three initial questions drive this discussion: What role do women and their issues play in the identity of a Jesuit university? How can attentiveness to female experience in society and culture enliven the authentic dialogue and practical witness that have been hallmarks of Ignatian styles of teaching for over four hundred years? How can we put feminism in dialogue with Jesuit ways of understanding the world, both informing and transforming our understanding of our mission?

To engage with such questions, we could take many different approaches, such as examining the treatment of faculty, staff, and administrators in terms of the glass ceiling and equal pay, the development of a curriculum inclusive of women's contributions to all intellectual traditions, and attentiveness to problems such as sexual harassment and eating disorders. Though these are all important issues, we focus on methods of teaching to explore how feminist and Jesuit approaches promote education of the whole person as critical to achieving social justice. Admittedly, at first glance, Jesuit and feminist ways of looking at the world appear to be divergent and even antagonistic. A deeper analysis, however, suggests their profound similarities. Both approaches, for instance, are committed to integrating reason and emotion in educating the whole person, and both attempt to join theory and praxis in meaningful ways by viewing knowledge in the context of real-world decisions and choices. Furthermore, both Jesuit and feminist ways of understanding the world openly articulate their commitment to social justice and ending oppression in its various forms. Although mindful of divergences, we take the position here that Jesuit education's principles and practices are not antithetical to—in fact, may intersect with and support—aspects of contemporary feminist theory and practice. To develop this position, we explore how feminist pedagogy, captured in the slogan "The personal is political," converges with and diverges from five key aspects of Jesuit education—context, experience, reflection, action, and evaluation—in order to understand how they can inform and even transform one another.[1]

Examination of pedagogy from feminist and Jesuit perspectives arises from the real need to attend to issues of gender discrimination on all college campuses.[2] Despite the fact that women make up 57 percent of undergraduates, gender inequality particularly manifests in ways of knowing and teaching that contradict the impression of females dominating college campuses conveyed by such a statistic. Studies, for instance, have found that males receive more attention from their teachers in the classroom.[3] While males tend to demand more attention, particularly by asking questions and raising their hands during discussion, teachers (male and female alike) not only call on male students more frequently but also ask them follow-up questions and show greater involvement during teacher-student interactions. This learning context contributes to lower self-esteem and confidence among female students, who often remain silent in class and are more likely to abandon academic tasks than males. Additionally, female students respond more positively to student-centered cooperative learning than to lecture-style teaching, which still dominates college education.[4] Such gendered inequalities in our classrooms emanate from and reflect those found in the broader society. Speaking to this situation, Decree 14 of the Thirty-fourth General Congregation states, "The dominance of men in their relationship with women has found expression in many ways. . . . We still have with us the legacy of systematic discrimination against women. It is embedded within the economic, social, political, religious and even linguistic structures of our societies. It is often part of an even deeper cultural prejudice and stereotype."[5]

To link this political context to our colleges, universities, and, most important, the personal lives of the students who attend them, Decree 14 recommends two approaches particularly pertinent in this context: the "explicit teaching of the essential equality of women and men in Jesuit ministries, especially in schools, colleges and universities," and the "promotion of the education of women and, in particular, the elimination of all forms of illegitimate discrimination between boys and girls in the educational process."[6] Feminist views on the goals of equal education would concur with such Jesuit practices designed to promote gender equality on our campuses and beyond. Yet determining the means to achieve such ends often remains difficult. At this juncture, exploring the relationship between feminist and Jesuit pedagogy may offer insight as to a process capable of achieving this goal.

Unlike the Jesuits, feminists lack a centuries-old tradition and a systematic articulation of pedagogical principles, in part because feminism remains a relatively new intellectual perspective still in the early stages of theory building. Here feminist pedagogy is loosely conceived of in terms of "The personal is political," a slogan that served as a clarion call to second-wave feminists. As the radical black feminist Charlotte Bunch explained, "there is no private domain of a person's life that is not political and there is no political issue that is not ultimately personal. The old barriers have fallen."[7] Such a perspective captures the permeability of boundaries between the individual and the collective; the public and the private; and, in this case, the classroom, the campus, and the world. Second-wave feminists articulated the necessary interrelationship between consciousness-raising and direct action, which represents a point of departure for identifying where feminist and Jesuit education converge.

To draw this connection, we explore the five central elements of Ignatian education—context, experience, reflection, action, and evaluation—first articulated in the *Ratio Studiorum* of 1599. This founding Jesuit document defines teaching and learning as a collaborative process between teachers and students and encourages discovery and creative self-exploration as a lifelong commitment to learning and action, which relates to a feminist pedagogy premised on the idea that the personal is political. Before we move forward, we stress that our feminist approach and Ignatian pedagogy emphasize permeable boundaries that, in this context, translate into the constant interplay of the five central elements of Ignatian education, which should not be understood as separable entities.

To describe how this connection can inform and transform educational practices, we use the example of a direct action project employed in Dr. Boryczka's Introduction to Feminist Thought course. First, the Ignatian principle of *context* involves navigation of the terrain between the personal lives of teachers and students and the political world, which includes their socioeconomic status, religion, race, culture, and sexual orientation, all of which affect how teachers teach, students learn, and vice versa. Viewed in this light, the context for learning might include not only the micro-level of students, teachers, and the classroom, but the macro-level of socioeconomic, political, and cultural institutions. An Introduction to Feminist Thought course, though ostensibly focused on the more abstract issues of second-wave feminism's political history and theory building, immediately engages individual students with larger contextual issues, since the terms "feminism" and "feminist" evoke many biases cultivated by the many negative stereotypes perpetuated in the broader culture against this intellectual approach. To address this initial barrier to the course material, the Introduction to Feminist Thought class begins with activities and discussions designed to engage students with stereotypes about feminism, to deconstruct them, and then to construct a working definition of feminism for the class that reflects their collective experience and knowledge. Such a process identifies their personal responses to the public arena, where images and language shape our beliefs. In short, context becomes reality as students individually and collectively reflect on their lives within a complex community and they are introduced to the theory of social constructivism through their experience, drawing theory and practice together.

Beyond this initial point, students engage in a semester-long direct action project that involves working in groups to carry out an action designed to raise consciousness in their campus community about an issue pertinent to women. By creating a situation in which students reach beyond the classroom to connect with their university context, this project operationalizes the immediate reality of students' lives as it relates to their institutional environment within their broader socioeconomic, political, and cultural contexts. Students start the project by drawing on their experiences to identify issues important to women, such as breast cancer, heart disease, women in the military, domestic violence, sexual harassment, body image, or eating disorders. Since their understanding of such issues usually emanates from their construction in the broader society, students immediately confront the challenge of connecting these issues directly to the lives of women and men at their university. One group, for instance, focused on heart disease as the number one killer of American women, though it is not generally perceived as a danger for college-age women, by holding a nutrition and exercise class to educate their peers about prevention. Such an approach requires students to navigate the micro- and macro-levels of context, which enables them to see the permeable boundaries between one's personal life, one's immediate context, and the larger political world.

Second, the Ignatian model specifies *experience* as signaling the need to fuse an intellectual and emotional approach to learning—to maintain openness to human reality in its complexity, which will provide the basis for analysis and contemplation. The Ignatian concept of experience intersects with the feminist practice of consciousness-raising, which translates personal experience into meaningful collective action. American women throughout the late 1960s started small group "rap sessions," where they told stories of their daily hardships in the home and sometimes the workplace, finding that other women shared their experiences. This process awakened them to their systematic oppression as women in a male-dominated society.[8] From these rap sessions evolved a theory of consciousness-raising, which usually involves the steps of opening up, sharing, analyzing and abstracting from shared experiences, and engaging in direct action.[9] Summarizing the thinking behind this process, Pamela Allen states that "we believe that theory and analysis which are not rooted in concrete experience (practice) are useless, but we also maintain that for the concrete, everyday experiences to be understood, they must be subjected to the processes of analysis and abstraction."[10] Starting with personal experience uses practice as a point of departure for analysis and theorizing that abstracts from an individual's material reality, a hallmark of feminism consistent with Ignatian pedagogy.

Students translate experience in the Introduction to Feminist Thought course by meeting in small groups organized around a specific feminist issue and then participating in a modified consciousness-raising exercise following these four steps. This exercise, unlike the relatively unstructured opening up and sharing of feminist consciousness-raising groups, asks students to open up by expressing how they feel about group work and then sharing why they chose the particular issue on which the group is focusing. This first step usually opens communication, since students often have either strong positive or negative feelings about group work, and later in the semester, many report that despite their initial reluctance to express themselves, this exercise resulted in a solid bond among the group members. In the second step, students are asked to respond to questions such as, What personal interests or experiences drew you to this particular issue? Why is it important to you personally? What do you hope to learn from engaging with this issue? To help ensure a space for groups to discuss these questions confidentially, the professor needs to specify that anything shared in the group stays in the group. Students should not take notes on this part of the discussion and the professor should observe groups carefully by walking around the class without intervening in the conversations.

This consciousness-raising exercise's third step of analyzing and abstracting shifts from experience to Ignatian pedagogy's third element—*reflection,* which values critical analysis and generates a deeper understanding of how one's experience relates to the lives of others. The personal translates into the political as students recognize the patterns that arise as they share their experiences in relation to their group's issue. On the basis of collective discussion, students speculate about societal responses to their issue and its role in a broader context. This analysis serves as the touchstone for more extensive student research on the issue, which is now grounded in personal experience, from which they may analyze and abstract. Such an approach often generates a high level of student investment in and responsibility for the project.

The three Ignatian concepts of context, experience, and reflection indicate how this paradigm, similar to feminist teaching methods, emphasizes a student-centered approach to learning. Feminist pedagogy turns more explicit attention than the Ignatian paradigm to teachers, who must also reflect on their contexts and experiences as part of a dynamic interplay with students and their communities. As Lee Anne Bell et al. explain, teachers "struggle alongside our students with our own social identities, biases, fears, and prejudices. We too need to be willing to examine and deal honestly with our values, assumptions, and emotional reactions to oppression issues. The self-knowledge and self-awareness that we believe are desirable qualities in any teacher become crucial in social justice education."[11] While comprehending our students' lives remains imperative, teachers also need to participate in the difficult work of identifying their own contexts and experiences, both inside and outside the classroom, through reflection. Here, feminist and critical pedagogy inform and highlight the teacher's essential part in the Ignatian paradigm.

Students, having engaged with context, experience, and reflection through consciousness-raising, turn to direct *action*—the fourth aspect of Ignatian pedagogy—which structures the entire student project and, ultimately, the course. Direct action serves as a powerful tool for showing students through experience that they can address a specific political issue within the broader community, cultivating their agency and sense of empowerment. Jesuits and feminists in this regard desire nothing less than to liberate and transform the individual through self-reflection and, eventually, to move each person to act in pursuit of social justice. Under the professor's guidance, students design a project that speaks directly to their fellow students. Students have developed and carried out projects ranging from fund-raising for breast cancer research and holding self-defense classes to bringing an attorney to campus to speak on the issue of domestic violence and the law.

A student project that focused on the treatment of women in the arts illustrates how direct action can affect the students, their campus community, and the broader society. One group of three women started their consciousness-raising activity by discussing the challenges confronted by women in the comic book industry, a profession still dominated by men despite an ever-increasing readership among young women. Initially, the professor failed to see how such a concern would translate into a viable direct action project, yet the students' persistence convinced her to allow the project to move forward. The group consisted of an avid reader of comic books, a female graphic artist, and a history major interested in how female images such as that of Rosie the Riveter have promoted different political agendas throughout American history. Graphic art, in their experience, conveyed images of women that reflected their oppression in the broader society. Their direct action then involved recruiting faculty, staff, and students from the campus community to contribute to creating a graphic novel based on their responses to various feminist terms such as "patriarchy" and images such as Wonder Woman. As contributors developed their drawings, collages, and accompanying story lines, the students held two consciousness-raising sessions with them to allow them to share their experiences and reflect upon them. After pulling their contributors' work together, the students arranged for a gallery showing of the graphic novel in a student space on campus, an event they advertised in the student paper and through fliers. With over sixty people attended the showing, where students displayed the work and encouraged people to reflect on the exhibit by writing or drawing on a huge piece of butcher-block paper hung on the wall. The student organizers and contributors were also on hand to talk with attendees, creating a vibrant atmosphere of discussion in which consciousness was raised through multiple levels of interaction. Much to the professor's surprise, one student organizer contacted a host of news agencies about covering the event. A local station, Connecticut News 12, invited the students to be interviewed on their "Educational Notebook" segment, which aired numerous times around the Christmas holiday. This group's direct action project ultimately reached well beyond their immediate campus community to the broader society, raising consciousness among the public.

Evaluation, the fifth element of the Ignatian paradigm, involves the learner, under the gentle guidance of a teacher, in defining lifelong goals and considering his or her beliefs in light of further experience or social and cultural change. Through self-evaluation, the Jesuit model is committed to *cura personalis*, an ethic centered on developing the person rather than teaching a curriculum. Feminist pedagogy tends to underemphasize evaluation as a step following direct action that enhances personal growth and may further political action. Realizing this weakness in the feminist approach, the professor cultivated the critical element of evaluation in the direct action projects. Groups were required to include an evaluation mechanism such as a questionnaire for participants in their projects. Research papers on their projects also constituted an evaluation mechanism, allowing space for considered reflection about the implications of their project for them, their group, the class, and the campus community. In this space, students assessed the overall experience and the obstacles that they encountered as well as how they overcame them. Additionally, students reflected on these issues as a class throughout the semester and during the final class, when they collectively evaluated the experience by considering how and where the personal meets the political and the obstacles to and opportunities for creating change in the world. In the Introduction to Feminist Thought course, Ignatian pedagogy offered a structured approach to developing consciousness-raising as a tool for the class to carry out direct actions premised on context, experience, and reflection while contributing the critical element of thoughtful evaluation.

Looking at this direct action project in light of these two teaching methods returns us to the question: How can we put feminism in dialogue with Jesuit ways of understanding the world, both informing and transforming our understanding of mission? A few responses emanate from this discussion. Identifying gender as critical to diversity and as valuable in the search for social justice represents a critical contribution of the feminist perspective and one recognized as essential in Decree 14. More specifically, the Ignatian model of context, experience, reflection, action, and evaluation provides structure and meaning to the feminist approach, framed here in terms of the phrase "The personal is political." These approaches share a commitment to valuing personal experience and reflecting upon it to determine direct courses of action designed to have an impact on the broader structures of society that shape our context and act as barriers to social justice. In particular, feminism highlights the teacher's significance in a student-centered model, which is implied in Ignatian pedagogy, while Jesuit education makes explicit the need to engage in careful evaluation, an element that is more marginal in feminist approaches.

The integrated approach developed here reflects a broader potential for transforming the Jesuit university and our role as educators in two more ways. First, it broadens our understanding of culture to include those populations that have been traditionally marginalized. Second, this approach redefines social action to include a range of social ills of particular concern to women. The Jesuit statement on "Our Mission and Culture" clearly states that respecting "a range of ethnic and new subcultures which are often ignored" within a larger culture comes close to meeting the need to validate the rights of those persons who are marginal within society.[12] Not only have Jesuits committed themselves to resisting living as a foreign presence in the cultures they encounter globally, but we educators at Jesuit universities must seek to change the lives of people in our midst, including women, the poor, the underprivileged, and the marginalized. If the order commits itself to "accompany[ing] people, in different contexts, as they and their culture make difficult transitions,"[13] shouldn't this apply to our roles in nurturing the female student who may be weighing whether or not to pursue a career or befriending the gay student who may be coming out during his time at the university? Similarly, by seeing women as "equal partners in dialogue,"[14] we can build a context of mutual respect and understanding that may result in deeper awareness and a sustained critique. As "Our Mission and Culture" declares, "the structural injustice in the world [is] rooted in value systems promoted by a powerful modern culture,"[15] and this is reflected in gendered issues such as self-esteem, body image, eating disorders, child care, unequal pay, ableism, and sexual harassment, as well as racial and sexual discrimination. Given the commitment of Jesuit universities and colleges to pursuing social justice, we should seek to understand how women's oppression reflects larger structural inequalities operating in our culture, every day and at every level. Making the political personal may enable us to envision a joint future and to rectify those injustices that exist within our community as well as those in the culture at large.

5 · *Paideia* and the Political Process
The Unexplored Coincidence of Jesuit and Feminist Pedagogical Visions

PAUL LAKELAND

There are two aspects to every university. The first and most evident is that it deals with culture, with knowledge, the use of the intellect. The second, and not so evident, is that it must be concerned with the social reality—precisely because a university is inescapably a social force: it must transform and enlighten the society in which it lives. But how does it do that? How does a university transform the social reality of which it is so much a part?

Ignacio Ellacuría, S.J.

I entered the classroom with the conviction that it was crucial for me and every other student to be an active participant, not a passive consumer . . . education as the practice of freedom . . . education that connects the will to know with the will to become. Learning is a place where paradise can be created.

bell hooks, *Teaching to Transgress*

Pedagogies are not, at their best, disembodied theories to be applied prescriptively in any and every conceivable situation. The best of them are flexible methods with an internal sensitivity to the context out of which they initially emerged and the many and varied contexts in which they might profitably be applied. Flexibility is essential, given the number of variables at work in the educational process. Even within the classroom—which is by no means the only or perhaps even the most important component in education—instructor, student, institution, and social context are each a moving target, never still and always changing. Pedagogy, then, if it is not to be simply an abstract, confining method, must be couched in the most general and generous of terms. A successful pedagogy shapes a learning environment; it does not control its outcome.

Both feminist and Jesuit pedagogies are significant precisely because of their expansiveness, their sensitivity to context, and their dis-ease with any suggestion of confining or determining the range of acceptable outcomes. It would make a mockery of bell hooks's understanding of education as "the practice of freedom" to suggest it must result in particular outcomes.[1] The anonymous author of a women's studies syllabus who wrote that "we will look at all questions and issues from as many sides as we can think of. . . . Skepticism about oneself is essential to continued growth and a balanced perspective" was right on the money.[2] As, by the way, was Ignatius of Loyola, a sixteenth-century Basque nobleman and founder of the Society of Jesus, in his insistence that we "should not dispute stubbornly with anyone," but rather "give our reasons with the purpose of declaring the truth . . . and not that we should have the upper hand."[3] This statement was far more revolutionary in its time than we might imagine, as the twentieth-century Jesuit Walter Ong made so clear in an essay on the "masculinity" of classical academic style, when he wrote that "until the romantic age, academic education was all but exclusively focused on defending a position (thesis) or attacking the position of another person."[4]

As we examine the relationships between feminist and Jesuit pedagogy, there is a danger that we will think solely in terms of the productive conversation or interaction that could take place between the two pedagogies. In my opinion, this is too narrow an outlook and we run the risk of failing to take advantage of what both have to offer to one another and to the missing third term, the Jesuit college or university. In what follows, I propose to explore some similarities between the two pedagogies, to unpack some of their respective complexities by suggesting that we look at each as *paideia* rather than as pedagogy, and to suggest the educational and political value of a strategic alliance between the two in calling our Jesuit institutions to pay closer attention to their social and religious responsibilities.

The best starting point for considering relationships between Jesuit and feminist approaches to teaching is in an examination of their respective positions vis-à-vis the larger umbrella of "critical pedagogy." Critical pedagogy, inspired by the work of the Brazilian educator Paolo Freire, takes it as axiomatic that education involves a critique both of society and of the norms employed in the educational process. Of its nature it challenges both the sociopolitical and the educational status quo. In 1992 Henry Giroux wrote that critical pedagogy "signals how questions of audience, voice, power, and evaluation actively work to construct particular relations between teachers and students, institutions and society, and classrooms and communities." This form of pedagogy "illuminates the relationship among knowledge, authority, and power."[5]

While there are those who still seem to be under the impression that the significance of feminist pedagogy is directly connected to sitting in a circle in the classroom or studiously refraining from suggesting a student could ever be wrong, feminist theorists have always known that the story is more complex than this. Jennifer Gore, for example, helpfully distinguishes the approach of women's studies to the issue of feminist pedagogy from that of schools of education. She suggests that the former emphasizes how to teach and what to teach, while feminists in the field of education promote a radical critique of educational practice informed by feminist theory. Then there are the various ideological subdivisions of the feminist enterprise across a fairly wide political spectrum, each of which subtly modifies the expectations of a feminist critique of society. We could doubtless argue that this too is an oversimplification, and Gore would probably agree, but what I find especially instructive is that, in Gore's words, "the two strands seem to similarly address classrooms."[6] It is as if whatever transformation feminist pedagogy imagines in society has its privileged locus, at least its starting point, in the classroom, perhaps because the feminist classroom, unlike society at large, is one in which feminist principles can set the rules.

The convergence of differing feminist pedagogies over the significance of the classroom is instructive not least because the classroom is modeling a vision of human relationships that an educator neither should nor could believe to have a place only in the classroom. It also importantly implies that there is a substrate to feminist pedagogies that exceeds the ideological standpoint of this or that variety of feminism. In feminist and other critical pedagogies, we are mapping a world by our praxis. Even in traditional classrooms there is an implicit vision of social relations. It would be foolish to imagine that a classroom devoted solely to the passive absorption and retention of facts could serve anything other than an instrumental vision of society. Feminist pedagogy seeks to overcome such sheer social replication in practice in the classroom and, by implication, in the world beyond it.

What may not be so readily noticeable is that Jesuit pedagogy stands in remarkably similar relationships with the traditional classroom and with the world beyond it. While Jesuit pedagogy is usually summarized by reference to the holy triad of experience, reflection, and action, the nuances are better captured by Peter-Hans Kolvenbach, current superior general of the Jesuits, as "a process by which teachers accompany learners in the lifelong pursuit of competence, conscience and compassionate commitment." Indeed, Kolvenbach has pointed out that Ignatius of Loyola himself "appears to place teachers' personal example ahead of learning or rhetoric." Somewhat surprisingly, Kolvenbach found support for this view in Pope Paul VI's encyclical letter *Evangelii Nuntiandi*, where he wrote that "Today students do not listen seriously to teachers but to witnesses; and if they do listen to teachers, it is because they are witnesses."[7] Evidently, the holy triad operates in the context of the Jesuit notion of *cura personalis*, the care of the whole person. Feminist pedagogues and others are going to be the first to agree with Kolvenbach that the care of the whole person has social and political connotations, and so it is for Jesuit pedagogy. "What then does a university do, immersed in this reality? Transform it? Yes. Do everything possible so that liberty is victorious over oppression, justice over injustice, love over hate? Yes. Without this overall commitment, we would not be a university, and even less so would we be a Catholic university."[8]

While there is no question that feminist pedagogy has been in the forefront of critical approaches, the same is not always assumed about Jesuit pedagogy. Indeed, those who have consulted the *Ratio Studiorum*, the founding document of Jesuit education produced in 1599, may be excused for thinking that the system was rigid and hierarchical, though the words on the page probably do not do justice to the extraordinary practice that led Jesuit colleges and schools to become such an important feature of seventeenth- and eighteenth-century Europe. Any pedagogical approach that promoted rhetoric, dance, and drama on the scale that Jesuit schools did had to be more than it seemed in print. Moreover, a careful reading of the *Ratio* shows its genius to have been a blending of the medieval scholastic pedagogical traditions of repetition and disputation with a true Renaissance humanism. However, it is true that after the Society of Jesus was suppressed by papal edict in 1773 and restored in 1814, its approach to education, as to so many other things, was much more formalistic and pedestrian than it had been in the pre-suppression Society.

The close connections of Jesuit pedagogy to critical pedagogy emerge in documents produced by the order in recent years. After the Second Vatican Council (1962–65), the Society of Jesus, like so many other orders, was redirected to its roots in search of an essential charism that might have become occluded and—among other things—found a need to produce a new vision of education, almost a new *Ratio*. Two documents, "The Characteristics of Jesuit Education" (1986) and "Ignatian Pedagogy: A Practical Approach" (1993), articulate this renewed vision. The first of the two proposes twenty-eight principles that should guide Jesuit pedagogy. It incorporates statements such as "The task of the teacher is to help each student to become an independent learner."[9] It encourages the adult members of the learning community to form personal relationships with students so that these adults can "be open to change" and can "continue to learn." Teachers should challenge students to reflect on their personal experiences so that they can "develop a critical faculty that goes beyond the simple recognition of true and false, good and evil."[10] The 1993 document, which attempts to offer practical proposals for implementing the principles, makes the enlightening claim that "pedagogy is the way in which teachers accompany learners in their growth and development."[11] Through reflection, learning is moved "beyond the realm of an objective grasp of facts, principles, and skills to the level of personal meaning" in order to promote "action based on conviction."[12] Moreover, lest the specter of indoctrination appear in the minds of readers, the claim is that "what is needed is a framework of inquiry that encourages the process of wrestling with significant issues and complex values of life, and professors capable and willing to guide that inquiry."[13]

There are clearly a number of structural similarities between the two pedagogies. In the first place, both pedagogies are learner centered. Second, both step firmly away from the supposedly traditional model of instruction, of a teacher imparting knowledge to a group of students who begin from a blank state. Third, they define themselves more in terms of the activity of learning than they do by the content of what is taught. Fourth, they see the classroom as a space for consciousness-raising that will, if successful, spill over into life beyond the classroom and beyond the college years. Fifth, they envisage the ultimate purpose of education to be personal and social transformation rather than social replication.

The connotations of the word "pedagogy" do not help to convey the idea that education is a process that is so much larger than the dynamics of the classroom. I therefore want to suggest the abandonment of "pedagogy" in favor of the term *paideia*. James Fowler has defined *paideia* in the following way. It involves "all the intentional efforts of a community of shared meanings and practices to form and nurture the attitudes, dispositions, habits, and virtues—and in addition, the knowledge and skills—necessary to enable growing persons to become competent and reflective adult members of the community."[14] *Paideia* is the term that best signifies the total educational role of the entire institution as it prepares citizens of the world. More attuned to Socrates than to the sophists, *paideia* encourages us to think of education as a process of learning to be in the world constructively, a way to take an attitude to the world that demands action. Education happens, sometimes despite our intentions, in the particular mix of classroom instruction, role-modeling, experiential learning, and peer interaction that makes up the entire life of the student during the four undergraduate years. *Paideia*, rather than pedagogy, should be our focus, because it forces us to pay attention to far more than the narrow confines of the classroom. The values and practices of the entire institution teach in ways that classroom instruction alone does not. They should lead our students to an intentional awareness of the world for which we are preparing them, to take a constructive attitude to that world. Above all, I think, *paideia* looks to consistency between classroom instruction and the social and political face of the academic institution, and it stresses the role of education, both in the classroom and outside it, as modeling a social vision.

I suspect that most of us have little difficulty recognizing feminist pedagogy in the shift to *paideia* but may find the inclusion of Jesuit pedagogy to be a little more challenging. The problem here is that feminist pedagogy, especially where it is allied with women's studies departments in Jesuit schools, often feels that it stands in a critical if not always oppositional relationship to the culture of the institution. My point is twofold. First, we should not make the mistake of automatically associating Jesuit pedagogy with the prevailing institutional structure of the Jesuit institution. Second, Jesuit pedagogy, rightly conducted, stands in a precisely similar relationship to the institution qua institution, as do most feminist pedagogues. The two pedagogies are oriented toward a particular *paideia*. Both may find themselves out of step in strikingly similar ways with the *paideia* of at least some Jesuit institutions. Jesuit colleges and universities are not guaranteed to have seen or made the connection between the values of their pedagogy and the lived choices of the institution. Jesuit pedagogy can, I think, learn something from the strategies of feminist pedagogy, especially its classroom strategies. And feminist pedagogy can learn from the way in which Jesuit pedagogy stresses a discernment process that is not immediately interpretable in ideological terms.

We can make the point a little clearer by spending a few moments with the key meditation on the Two Standards from the Spiritual Exercises of St. Ignatius. In Ignatius's formulation, the exercitant is invited to view a great plain where the armies of Christ and Lucifer are arrayed, and to decide under which banner to stand and fight. Pretty obviously, Ignatius did not expect the exercitant to choose Lucifer! But the imaginative exercise is directed toward seeing how the world is a place of struggle between the good and evil spirit, or we might prefer to say the forces of good and evil. My own reworking of this language asks for a choice between energies that promote the truly human in a world that is our home, and those that are in effect anti-human. Ignatius encourages us to use our imaginations to see beneath the surface of things, to see that the world is a site of decision making, that we really cannot just absolve ourselves from the need to take sides. Will we side with the forces of good, with everything that supports human flourishing? Or will we side with the forces of evil, of all that is destined in the end to narrow and destroy the truth of human community and solidarity?

This meditation contains the two critical components of Ignatian education. The first is the careful and imaginative attention to the details of the world, in other words, the educational importance of understanding the world in which we live in the most sophisticated and critically aware manner of which we are capable. This is where we can confidently affirm that everything taught in the most theoretical and the most practical of our classrooms, from pure mathematics to literary theory to accounting practice, is integral to Jesuit education, because it all contributes to the enrichment of our awareness of how our world really works. And the second component is the call to make a decision that will be consistent with the foundational understanding of the human person and the human community. This is where *paideia* is most apparent, because the capacity to make a good decision is not simply acquired in the classroom but comes to pass as a result of the entire educational process: in the classroom, in the values absorbed from living within a community that practices what it preaches, and in the informal exchanges within a community with a common vision.

A Christian university must take into account the gospel preference for the poor. This does not mean that only the poor will study at the university; it does not mean that the university should abdicate its mission of academic excellence—excellence which is needed in order to solve complex social issues of our time. What it does mean is that the university should be present intellectually where it is needed: to provide science for those without science; to provide skills for those without skills; to be a voice for those without voices; to give intellectual support for those who do not possess the academic qualifications to make their rights legitimate.[15]

At this point, we might consider the relatively recent Jesuit recognition of the importance of work for justice and the commitment to its inclusion in classroom pedagogy and institutional *paideia*. In the 1986 document referred to earlier on "The Characteristics of Jesuit Education," it is made quite clear that "in a Jesuit school the focus in on education for justice," and that the goal of the endeavors is "a new type of person in a new kind of society."[16] The three distinct aspects of this education for justice are that justice issues are treated in the curriculum, that "the policies and programs of a Jesuit school give concrete witness to the faith that does justice," and that "there is no genuine conversion to justice unless there are works of justice."[17] An important characteristic of this commitment is the decision to make "a preferential option for the poor." Although Jesuit educations must sometimes struggle to make this concrete, the public commitment is there. Those who are less powerful, whose lives and priorities are on the margins of society, not at its heart, should be the special concern of these educational communities of justice. Although the terms are not used here, the call is for a pedagogy that blends seamlessly into *paideia*.

There is no doubt that at times in its history the Jesuit tradition has been guilty of sexism and the preservation of patriarchy, but in its espousal of a preferential option for the poor it may have something to offer to enrich feminist pedagogy. The movements of womanist and *mujerista* thought within feminism testify to women's own awareness that the feminist movement can sometimes fail to recognize the roles of race and class in the plight of women and can indeed, in some of its forms, be frankly bourgeois. In their Thirty-fourth General Congregation in 1995, the Jesuit Order produced a document recognizing their past failures in sexism and committing themselves to a more positive future (Decree 14). But woven even within this document is the important recognition that gender issues are complicated by the intersecting oppressions of war, race, poverty, and migration.

The final complexity to note is an institutional one. While there remain a number of women's colleges, there are not, as far as I know, any feminist universities. Neither are there universities that have explicitly committed themselves to feminist pedagogy and *paideia*. However, I want to suggest that the Jesuit universities, of which there are twenty-eight in the United States alone and many more around the world, not only may provide the most supportive home for feminist pedagogy but are in fact already committed to a *paideia* that is utterly consistent with the principles of feminist pedagogy. Let me say it boldly: The nearest thing we have in American higher education to feminist educational institutions is Jesuit colleges and universities. Of course, there is no perfect fit. Jesuit institutions have made great strides in appointing women to faculty and administration positions and ensuring fair and equitable compensation, but there is little doubt that a lot more could be done. But the essential principles of Jesuit *paideia* mandate classroom openness and an institutional integrity that is at one with the vision of feminist education.

Where serious differences may exist between Jesuit and feminist visions, and consequently where most friction may occur and most growth may be possible, is in the area of religious identity and ethical vision. Of course, there are lots of Catholic feminists, but feminism itself is not distinctively religious, and many of its most outspoken communicators are secular people who are not at all well disposed toward institutional religion. More neuralgic still, while feminism is pluralistic, the majority of feminist academics take a position on reproductive rights that is not comfortable with the public position of the Catholic Church, to which Catholic academic institutions must be in some sense faithful. Many individual Catholics and even many Jesuits may as private individuals share pro-choice positions on abortion or advocate the rights of gays and lesbians to marry. But while they will recognize the rights of conscience and freedom of speech, they cannot in the end espouse an institutional position different from that of the Catholic Church.

The ultimate test of the compatibility of Jesuit and feminist pedagogies, curiously enough, will be how they negotiate their differences on religious and ethical issues. Jesuit academic institutions are safe havens for feminist pedagogy because, in the first instance, Jesuit pedagogy is very similar to feminist approaches and, in the second, because providing space for the civil and humane process of mutual learning over contested issues is a sine qua non of Jesuit institutions. We should argue, said Ignatius, so that the truth should appear and not that we may seem to gain the upper hand. Difference of opinion on important issues, say Jesuit and feminist pedagogies together, is where we test our unity of outlook about how the educational process must proceed. What students conclude about this or that issue is less important than that they submit themselves to an academic discipline that leads them to know why they think what they think, and to make it their own. And this must be facilitated by an institution that shows in its concrete practices that it is committed to the struggle for justice, and that it takes principled stands on justice issues.

The vision of the Jesuit and, yes, the Catholic university, has to be one—as the old saying goes—in which the noun is "university" and the adjectives are "Jesuit" and "Catholic." While Jesuit and Catholic institutions may, because of their religious affiliation, be unable to promote particular ethical choices or lifestyles, they may not and should not be anything other than entirely open to an ongoing and mutually enriching dialogue on the trickiest of moral issues between and among the different interest groups within the faculty. The commitment to justice woven into the *paideia* of the institution, at once Jesuit and feminist, should see to that. When you put limits on what may be discussed or place boundaries around points of view you consider not open to discussion, when you say, "This or that is not on the table," then you are not behaving in the manner of a university. But, at the same time, when you declare debate and research to be value free and when you place everything that is truly human "off limits," you are also not behaving in the manner of a university, certainly not a Jesuit or a feminist university. Feminist/Jesuit *paideia* takes the more difficult path, when it is true to its deepest impulses, of honestly confronting the most challenging issues of justice in our world as concerns of priority, and finding ways to ensure that the institution as a whole, not just the classroom, testifies to those convictions. All institutions have a little bit of the demonic within them. I suppose a Christian would say that this is the institutional face of original sin, and both Christians and others might agree on the category of structural injustices. The agenda of feminist pedagogy is always rightly sensitive to the need to correct the failings of the institution, whether on matters of race, gender, class, sexual orientation, or whatever. It is one of the consciences of the university. In Jesuit institutions, its greatest ally in this task is Jesuit *paideia* itself.

One of my proudest moments as a teacher at Fairfield occurred over ten years ago. At the end of a lengthy campaign on the part of students and a few faculty members to obtain union recognition and decent working conditions for our custodial staff, with little or no progress made, the students occupied Bellarmine Hall—the principal administration building—in the time-honored fashion of the late sixties and early seventies. At one point in the day or so of occupation before the university administration finally capitulated to the justice of the case, students hung from one of Bellarmine's windows a banner displaying the message: "Practice the values you teach us to live by." It brought tears to my eyes and to not a few others, I think, to see concrete evidence that sometimes the teaching process works. A significant number of students remembered things that had been said to them in philosophy and religious studies and many other courses. But more important, they had seen the difference between the simple iteration of truths in a classroom context and the force of an institutional commitment to those same truths. They had reflected long and hard on the injustice of what they saw around them, they had discerned carefully and at length, and they had taken action. In my view, this was a textbook example of the Ignatian pedagogical method and, even if some in the university community were as mad as hell with those students, they were a shining example to us of all that we ought to hold dearest.

Please note that some in the university community *were* as mad as hell, including some at the vice-presidential level and above. There is no guarantee that the Jesuit institution is living up to the value of Jesuit *paideia*. Like all institutions, it has a tendency toward what Dorothee Soelle, the great Lutheran theologian, so quaintly and accurately referred to as necrophilia. All institutions—she was talking about the Church—tend toward a love of what is dead, like rules and regulations and structures. If they make such things priorities, and a critical relationship to the wider society is played down, then the fabric of the institution quite literally works against the Jesuit and feminist agenda of social transformation, and toward the stultifying promotion of social replication. All institutions need bureaucratic structures, but they are means to an end. In the typically dense phrase of Jürgen Habermas, all societies need to struggle against "the colonization of the lifeworld by the system."[18] That colonization, that necrophilia, is what feminist and Jesuit *paideia* exist to challenge. If their respective lessons are learned, then the institutions will model much more successfully the kind of society we hope our alumni and alumnae will work to realize. Let us end with a few more words from Ignacio Ellacuría.

But how is this done? The university must carry out this general commitment with the means uniquely at its disposal: we as an intellectual community must analyze causes; use imagination and creativity together to discover the remedies to our problems; communicate to our constituencies a consciousness that inspires the freedom of self-determination; educate professionals with a conscience, who will be the immediate instruments of such a transformation; and constantly hone an educational institution that is both academically excellent and ethically oriented.[19]

6 Feminist Pedagogy, the Ignatian Paradigm, and Service-Learning

Distinctive Roots, Common Objectives, and Intriguing Challenges

ROBBIN D. CRABTREE, JOSEPH A. DeFEO, AND MELISSA M. QUAN

Many alternative or "liberatory" pedagogies share common or related philosophical roots and have evolved through decades (and in some cases centuries) of debate about the role of education in society, the appropriate curriculum, the ideal nature of classroom interaction, effective relationships among teachers and students, and the desired outcomes of education in a multicultural democracy. Three such pedagogies are explored in three usually divergent literatures: feminist pedagogy, Ignatian pedagogy, and service-learning pedagogy. This chapter brings these literatures together in an exploration of the commonalities among the three pedagogical traditions, in which their historical and philosophical roots are discussed, some shared assumptions about teaching and learning are identified, and the objectives of each for the production of individual and social transformation are described.

In addition to describing these three pedagogical traditions, we explore some of the divergences among them, using each perspective as a critical lens and analytical tool with which to examine and challenge the others. We share specific teaching experiences that illustrate both the strengths and shortcomings of each approach-in-action in order to demonstrate how an inter-articulation of the three approaches to teaching—each with its own social history, philosophy, and set of practices—can inform institutions, teachers, and students as we work together to create meaningful pedagogies that are truly transformative.

Three Pedagogical Traditions

A relatively in-depth description of each pedagogical approach is crucial. Even a cursory review of the academic literatures on feminist,

Ignatian, and service-learning pedagogy demonstrates that ideas from one are rarely referenced in the others (though there is a very small number of papers on service-learning in Jesuit education or about service-learning in women's studies). Moreover, our experiences at academic conferences and in working with faculty across the disciplines reveals that few university professors (outside departments of education) are schooled in *any* pedagogy, let alone truly learned in one of these three.

The traditional meaning of pedagogy is "the art and science of helping children learn," while andragogy is "the art and science of helping adults learn."[1] Commonly understood to be components of pedagogy are (1) *curriculum*, the knowledge and content that are taught; (2) *instruction*, the preferred modes of teaching and prevalent interaction patterns in teaching and learning contexts; and (3) *evaluation practices*, the methods for, criteria used in, and values that guide the assessment of student performance. In addition, an exploration of pedagogy must consider the ideological and political dimensions of education, as schools are sites where social hierarchies are organized, replicated, and reified.[2] Feminist, Ignatian, and service-learning approaches all address each of these components in unique, though largely compatible, ways.

The Roots and Practice of Feminist Pedagogy

Both "feminist" and "pedagogy" are contested concepts in the academic literature, and all things feminist are largely misunderstood in popular discourse. Nevertheless, consensus has emerged over the last few decades among feminist educators that we must critically engage in dialogue and reflection not only about *what* we teach, but about *how* we teach, as well as how *who* we are within the social and educational orders necessarily affects what and how we teach. Feminist pedagogy is a set of assumptions about knowledge and knowing, approaches to content across the disciplines, teaching objectives and strategies, classroom practices, and instructional relationships that are grounded in feminist theory as well as critical pedagogy.[3] In general, feminist pedagogy can be seen as a movement against hegemonic educational practices that tacitly accept or more forcefully reproduce an oppressively gendered, classed, racialized, and androcentric social order. It is an ideology of teaching inasmuch as it is a framework for developing particular strategies and methods of teaching in the service of particular objectives for student learning and social change.

Feminist pedagogy is a product of and a response to the feminist organizing and movement that have occurred since the 1970s.[4] As such, feminist pedagogy explicitly acknowledges and foregrounds the undeniable history and force of sexism and heterosexism in society.[5] Based in the principles of feminism and the material history of feminist organizing and consciousness-raising, feminist teaching is predicated on ideas about empowering individuals, especially females, within a larger project of social change, though there is not consensus on the political strategies for achieving this change or on the vision of what the world might look like after a feminist revolution. Nevertheless, individual consciousness-raising, collective political action, and social transformation are explicit goals of feminist pedagogy. Consciousness-raising and political action also are instructional methods or learning activities in feminist teaching.[6]

Like the consciousness-raising groups of the 1970s, feminist pedagogy emphasizes the epistemological validity of personal experience. Through a critique of the ways traditional scientific and academic inquiry have ignored or negated the lived experiences of women, feminist pedagogy acknowledges personal, communal, and subjective ways of knowing as valid forms of inquiry and knowledge production. Feminist pedagogy questions the ways traditional knowledge production and received knowledge serve particular (patriarchal) interests and configurations of power through the systematic exclusion or oppression of particular classes of people. It also emphasizes accountability for the use of knowledge.[7]

These alternative views of epistemology influence the kinds of interactions and student participation we might expect to see in a feminist classroom as well. Thus, feminist educators promote the linking of personal experience with course material, exploration and sharing of personal insights, and personal accountability in classroom dynamics. These practices illustrate feminist ideas about voice and authority; students are encouraged to find and use their voices and to share authority with the teacher in the exploration and production of knowledge. Feminist educators' critical analysis of authority structures and rhetorics relates not only to the analysis of the status of women in society at large but also to understanding the (often problematic) authority of female faculty in the academy and (female, in particular, but all) students in the classroom.[8]

Closely related to the concept of authority is the problem of power in the classroom.[9] Feminist pedagogy is marked by the promotion of less hierarchical relationships among teachers and students and reflexivity about power relations, not only in society, but in the classroom as well. The vision of egalitarian and empowering communities of learners who share a sense of mutual and social responsibility ideally manifests in participatory classroom structures and dynamics, collaborative evaluation, and respect for individuals and differences.[10] Power relations within the feminist classroom must be part of this analysis, since "one way to resist the dominance of the professor and to subvert gender polarities [is] to make our authority in the classroom self-reflexive by making our pedagogy a part of the class, a subject of investigation and critique along with the subject matter of the course."[11] Within contemporary feminist pedagogy, then, there is an explicit attempt to name and reflexively shift the dynamics of power and powerlessness that exist in the classroom, whether in the complex relationships among students (and groups of students) or between students and teachers. The essence of feminism—in the production of theory, as a social movement, and in teaching—is the awareness of "power as a dynamic in the world—that it is central to who we are and what we teach."[12] As part of this process, it is also important to understand the experiences of and constraints on differently situated teachers in the complex web of institutional power structures.[13]

Perhaps one of the most frequently cited hallmarks of feminist teaching is the "ethic of care";[14] some have even used the word "love."[15] Feminist teachers demonstrate sincere concern for their students as people and as learners and communicate this care by treating students as individuals, helping students make connections between their studies and their personal lives, and guiding students through the process of personal growth that accompanies their intellectual development. This process involves special care for women students, inside and outside the classroom, and a commitment to advancing and improving the educational experiences, professional opportunities, and daily lives of women.

Feminist pedagogy links classroom-based teaching with opportunities for application in communities through the use of strategies such as service-learning, feminist action research, social action projects, and other methods of engaged and community-based learning. This tenet of feminist pedagogy recognizes the links between the personal (including the individual's educational experience) and the political, and the importance of working to understand and change the collective social reality. The phrase "The personal is political" not only validates the political nature of women's individual experiences and voices but acts as a reminder that theory and intellectual inquiry have a responsibility to society.[16] In many ways, the other characteristics of feminist pedagogy are expected to strengthen students' sense of self and empower them as social actors and change agents.

In terms of learning objectives and outcomes, feminist pedagogy seeks to enhance students' conceptual learning (not only in women's studies but in all disciplines) as well as to promote consciousness-raising, personal growth, and social responsibility. It offers teachers and students alike the intellectual skills to expose ideology and to participate in the contestation and realignment of gender politics in society. Feminism (particularly postmodern and poststructural feminisms) provides teachers and students with a language of critique to analyze differences among social groups and how they are constructed within and outside the academic setting, as well as to interrogate their own roles in various forms of domination, subordination, hierarchy, and exploitation.[17] Feminist classrooms create environments where students and teachers examine relationships of power in culture, reject false dichotomies of either/or and essentialist binaries (such as masculine/feminine, homosexual/heterosexual), and cultivate the ability to problematize commonsense viewpoints, discover similarities within difference, and learn to understand phenomena through multiple lenses.[18]

Critical analysis of the educational environments within which teaching takes place is also important within feminist pedagogical theorizing, including recognizing the ways schools and classrooms have been hostile environments for girls and women, and monitoring the evolving status of women at all levels of education.[19] As well, feminist teachers engage actively in the exploration of how *who* we are within these environments necessarily affects *what* and *how* we teach. This approach includes an explicit commitment to address the intersections and inter-articulations of gender, race, ethnicity, class, and sexuality not only in the content of the academic disciplines but in the dynamics of the specific classroom as well.[20] The influence of postmodernism and poststructuralism on feminist theory and pedagogy has been considerable.[21] Analysis of the ways power, knowledge, and identity are constituted in discursive practices and everyday interactions has influenced the structures of women's studies curricula, constitutes a growing proportion of feminist course content, and increasingly frames our understanding of classroom dynamics, the broader educational context, and the larger social milieu in which students learn, work, serve, and live.

It should not be superfluous to add that feminist pedagogy is not simply about learning theory and applying it in a classroom, but it is also, more importantly, a way of living life professionally and personally.[22] As Pagano has pointed out, "to act is to theorize."[23] Our actions inside and outside the classroom, especially the ways we conceptualize and enact our relationships with students, are all statements about and evidence of the theories we use as educators. As Ropers-Huilman notes, "it is imperative that we, as feminist educators, consciously model what we value and how we think values should take shape in educational environments."[24] Thus, feminist pedagogy is both the reflection of feminist principles and the practice of feminism in the classroom, mentoring relationships with students, and work life in the academy. This holistic way of thinking about pedagogy beyond the classroom walls and grounded in relationships has much in common with the Ignatian pedagogical paradigm.

The Ignatian Pedagogical Paradigm: Vision and Methodology

The Ignatian pedagogical paradigm flows from a 450-plus-year-old spiritual tradition begun by Ignatius of Loyola (1491–1556). Although it was not originally considered one of the main missions or ministries of the young Society, Ignatius and the first Jesuits eventually recognized that their involvement in education could be one more way to recognize "in all things . . . the presence of God" and to be of "loving service" to those in need.[25] The early Jesuits engaged in the ministry of education in the same way they engaged in any Jesuit ministry—by using their spiritual foundation and distinctly Jesuit "way of proceeding."[26] Influenced as he was by the tradition of ancient Greek and Latin thinkers, Ignatius's vision quite naturally included a desire to transform or "help souls."[27] These elements are within the Spiritual Exercises of St. Ignatius, a retreat program developed by Ignatius. According to Jesuit historians, the Jesuits' "ministries and how they went about them were quintessential to the Jesuits' self-definition."[28] Most of the Jesuits' self-definition, past and present, comes from their experience of their founder's Spiritual Exercises. In this sense, Ignatian pedagogy is merely this quintessential Jesuit spiritual foundation and way of proceeding applied to the ministry of education.

Ignatian pedagogy is a dynamic formation process in which the teacher seeks to "accompany learners in their growth and development."[29] Ignatian pedagogy raises the bar of academic excellence by promoting a vision of the human being that includes, in addition to the intellectual dimension, "human, social, spiritual, and moral dimensions."[30] The Ignatian pedagogical paradigm adheres to the way the spiritual director of Ignatius's Spiritual Exercises facilitates the process and guides the retreatant toward a direct encounter with God. Figure 6-1 illustrates the similarities between relationships among participants in the Spiritual Exercises and those in an educational setting.

Guiding students toward or accompanying students in direct encounters with truth requires a realignment of traditional teacher-student power structures within the classroom environment. Like feminist and service-learning pedagogies, Ignatian pedagogy requires the student to encounter truth directly so he or she may personally appropriate it and make it part of his or her sense of self. Yet Ignatian pedagogy is distinct: Not only is a direct encounter with truth sought but it can also include a direct encounter with the Divine through loving and serving others, transforming the soul, or fostering an interior freedom.[31]

Within the context of education, the goal of Ignatian pedagogy is the development of the whole person. It involves caring for every student often referred to as *cura personalis*, and the formation of "men and

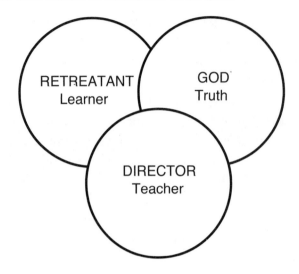

FIGURE 6-1

women for others."[32] As well, in Jesuit educational philosophy and Ignatian pedagogical practice "the promotion of justice is an absolute requirement."[33] Ignatian pedagogy involves fostering growth in human development, which is realized through one's developed attitude and action of serving those in need. As such, Ignatian pedagogy is not simply a method for learning. Rather, it is a formational and transformational process, a way of proceeding toward the full development of the human being. The International Commission on the Apostolate of Jesuit Education writes, "If truly successful, Jesuit education results ultimately in a radical transformation not only of the way in which people habitually *think* and act, but of the very way in which they live in the world, men and women of competence, conscience and compassion, seeking the *greater good* in terms of what can be done out of a faith commitment with justice to enhance the quality of peoples' [*sic*] lives, particularly among the poor, oppressed and neglected."[34]

Operationalizing the broad vision and goals of Ignatian pedagogy is an active learning methodology that involves the dynamic interplay of five key areas: context, experience, reflection, action, and evaluation. At the heart of this methodology is an ongoing cyclical process of experience, reflection, and action, during which the teacher values and relates the student's individual context and lived experiences to the subject matter. The student continually reflects on his or her lived experiences (including experience with various academic subjects and perspectives) in relation to the larger context, which creates new understandings and perspectives. Structured and guided reflection promotes deeper understanding of the subject matter and also fosters a personal appropriation of the material being considered. These reflections can lead the student to take some action consistent with the new understanding and broadened perspective. Finally, evaluation not only of how well students have learned the material but also of the change or growth in their own human development, such as their newly increased sense of awareness of and biases and attitudes toward the subject material, rounds out the educational and formational process. The elements of experience, reflection, action, and evaluation with guiding questions for educators to consider are elaborated here. An example of context is provided later in this chapter.[35]

Experience for Ignatius meant "to taste something internally."[36] Beyond the intellectual grasp of learning, experience involves the use of the imagination and feelings along with the intellect. Human experience can be either direct (personal) or vicarious (experienced though a textbook, newspaper, story, movie, etc.). Similar to feminist and service-learning pedagogies, Ignatian pedagogy values and engages affective ways of knowing. Two questions that guide educators to engage the element of experience are: How do I engage my students' affective senses to promote learning? What experiences can I facilitate that can help my students care about or connect to my subject material?

In Ignatian pedagogy, *reflection* involves a personal appropriation of the subject, connecting one's existence and values to the subject in some way. Starratt offers two questions to promote reflection: "What does this subject mean to me? What does this subject mean for me personally?"[37] These questions

> force students to relate what they are involved with in class to their sense of the larger world and of their own lives, their sense of themselves. Those questions force them to consider relationships and connections among ideas and experiences. They often force students to reflect on personal values and social value systems. They occasionally force them to be critical of themselves and of their community.

> Those questions habituate them to seeing that knowledge should lead to understanding, to forming interpretive perspectives on various aspects of life, to the posing of new questions, to appreciating things and people in their own right, to forming opinions, grounding beliefs, expressing the poetry, the harmony, the pathos, the music embedded in reality.[38]

Through reflection, intellectual concepts become personally appropriated and contextually meaningful. They help deepen understanding of oneself and one's relationship to the world. In spiritual language, this is often referred to as a process of discernment, or an individual and communal process of reflection in order to relate one's "lives, talents, and resources to God's priorities."[39]

Action refers to "internal human growth based upon experience that has been reflected upon as well as to its manifestation externally."[40] Action is the response, a natural extension of the self, now more fully understood, directed toward the opportunities this new understanding reveals. It involves two steps: (1) interiorized choices, such as a shift in attitude, awareness, bias, or perspective, and (2) choices externally manifested, as in a physical action "consistent with this new conviction."[41] The action resulting from immersion in the Ignatian paradigm is expected to be one that serves those in need, that promotes the common good, and that enables students to become men and women for others.[42] To consider action, educators might ask: How do I encourage and provide opportunities for my students to make concrete choices or take some action consistent with their newly acquired perspective?

Evaluation includes "the periodic evaluation of each individual student's growth in attitudes, priorities, and actions consistent with being a person for others."[43] For the practitioner of Ignatian pedagogy, evaluative measures should not only assess the student learning of course material but also, as a manifestation of *cura personalis*, assist the student in growth and development. Helping students evaluate their own sense of awareness of, sensitivity and open-mindedness to, and biases toward the subject being studied throughout a semester as well as through the complete program of study is a distinct and intentional goal of Ignatian pedagogy. Two questions to consider are: How have my students' attitudes toward, awareness of, or sensitivity to the subject area shifted, changed, or grown? How might I learn how my students have grown intellectually, humanly, socially, spiritually, and morally?

The components of Ignatian pedagogy that shape the educational process foster a continual desire to know one's own personal life and truth, as well as the world. While the five-part methodology alone can inform effective teaching and learning techniques valuable for higher education, the richness and depth of Ignatian pedagogy only manifest when the vision and goals of the Jesuits remain intentionally connected to its pedagogical application. The broad educational vision and specific teaching methodologies, which include engagement with the self and the community and incorporate reflection on key issues of social justice, find common ground with feminist pedagogy as well as with service-learning.

Service-Learning: Educational Philosophy and Pedagogical Practice

Service-learning is a pedagogy based on the beliefs that "acting and thinking cannot be severed, knowledge is always embedded in context, and understanding is in the connections."[44] It is rooted in the experiential learning philosophies of John Dewey and David Kolb and, like feminist pedagogy, is informed by the critical pedagogy of Paulo Freire.[45] In service-learning, experience is defined as the interaction between the learner and the environment, and learning is a transformational process that results from reflection on experience—or what Freire calls "praxis."[46] Thus, similar to Ignatian pedagogy, service-learning involves a cycle of knowledge (of self and context), experience (through community-based learning), reflection (individually and in groups, also ideally with the community), and action (through life choices and civic engagement, for example).

Service-learning was formally named and recognized in the 1960s, a time when U.S. society was going through dramatic changes and issues of national service and social justice were receiving a great amount of attention in higher education. President John F. Kennedy launched the Peace Corps, the civil rights movement was at an apex, and students challenged their colleges and universities on social justice issues such as war, inequality, and the growing corporate influence on the academy. In addressing these issues, higher educational institutions were driven to reexamine their civic purpose.[47] Community activists and educators began to think about making connections between social and educational movements: They "found themselves drawn to the idea that action in communities and structured learning could be combined to provide stronger service and leadership in communities and deeper, more relevant education for students."[48]

Much work has been done to provide a formal definition for academic service-learning; one of the most accepted and often cited comes from the *Journal of Higher Education*, where it is defined as "a credit-bearing educational experience in which students participate in an organized service activity that meets identified community needs and reflects on the service activity in such a way as to gain further understanding of course content, a broader appreciation of the discipline, and an enhanced sense of civic responsibility."[49] Howard refers to service-learning as a "counternormative" pedagogy.[50] It promotes social responsibility and the common good rather than individualism, emphasizes both academic learning and community-based experiential learning, and challenges the student-teacher relationship to become more collaborative—the students share responsibility for the learning and the teachers are learners too. The goal of service-learning is not to deposit large quantities of information into the minds of students but instead to teach them to think critically about their current beliefs and ideas, always searching for alternative answers and explanations.

These definitions emphasize the main components of service-learning: (1) academic learning, (2) related and meaningful community service (the experience), (3) reflection, and (4) civic learning. These components are also foundational to both feminist pedagogy and Ignatian pedagogy, although one may place more emphasis on particular components or may interpret the components somewhat differently.

Studies show that service-learning leads to many positive outcomes with regard to student development, including enhanced academic learning, improved higher-order moral reasoning, advanced critical thinking and problem-solving skills, empowerment, self-knowledge, enhanced interpersonal skills, and increased desire and motivation to achieve advanced degrees.[51] However, as John Dewey noted, experience does not necessarily lead to learning; simply combining the various components of service-learning—academic learning, service, reflection, and civic engagement—will not necessarily lead to the desired outcomes.[52] In service-learning, academic learning is integral to good service, which is integral to purposeful civic engagement, and so the cycle functions. Reflection is the "bridge" that links experience and learning.[53] Through reflection, students make connections between the course subject matter and experience, and it is through these connections that learning and personal formation or transformation take place.

The most important function of service-learning is to enhance student academic learning. Thus, the service component should be treated as an integral component of the course, like a primary textbook as opposed to an additional activity.[54] Students should not be given extra credit for their service participation, as this would indicate that the service component is extraneous to the educational experience rather than integral to the course objectives.[55] As in other courses, students should be evaluated on their demonstrated ability to meet the course objectives, understand the subject matter, apply knowledge, and make connections between the subject matter and their service experiences.[56]

In the traditional classroom, learning is usually teacher centered, giving the teacher the primary responsibility of transmitting information to the students, who, in most cases, are relatively passive learners. The values of service-learning (as well as the politics of feminist pedagogy and the structure of Ignatian pedagogy) challenge the traditional student-teacher relationship. In practicing service-learning, teachers must feel comfortable relinquishing some control of their classrooms.[57] Dewey argued that to empower students for life in a democracy, schools themselves must operate under the values and principles of democracy.[58] Therefore, students must have more of a participatory role in their own learning. Service-learning offers students a more active role as teachers serve as facilitators of student learning rather than as transmitters of information. Similarly, knowledge is not only received from books or teachers but discovered and produced in and with communities.

Relevant (to the course) and meaningful (to the community) service distinguishes service-learning from other experiential educational approaches. Howard defines service as "contributions in and to the community that improve the quality of life for an individual, group, neighborhood, or for the entire community," including activities such as "public work, community development, social capital, community action."[59] The mission of service organizations, as well as the type of work that students engage in, should be relevant to the course objectives. In addition, the number of hours that students spend doing service should be adequate to enable them to achieve the learning objectives.[60] For instance, working on a two-hour neighborhood cleanup will do little to teach students about community revitalization and development. However, working with a community development organization consistently over the course of a semester, assisting with community outreach, attending community meetings to determine priority issues, and exploring and evaluating various approaches to community development can lead to meaningful student learning and meaningful service to the community partner and broader community.

Studies show that student learning is enhanced when the service experience challenges the students' beliefs and assumptions.[61] Such opportunities provide students with the chance to work with people in the community and to hear their stories and learn about their struggles. "The experiential and interpersonal components of service-learning activities can achieve the first crucial step toward diminishing the sense of 'otherness' that often separates students—particularly privileged students—from those in need."[62] Ideally, a reciprocal relationship is established between the service agency and university.[63] This ensures that both the community and the student will benefit from the experience. This will require teachers and students to work *with* the community to identify and formulate a relevant and meaningful service experience. Members of the university must recognize and value their community partners as co-educators, equal partners in the learning experiences, not merely placement sites for students.

The goal of purposeful civic learning as a part of service-learning is often overlooked.[64] According to many researchers, the service-learning of individuals and groups who operate without a clear understanding of purposeful civic learning represents a "charity model," which compromises the transformational purpose of service-learning and fails to promote responsible citizenship.[65] Howard defines civic learning as "knowledge, skills, and values that make an *explicitly direct and purposeful contribution* to the preparation of students for active civic participation."[66] Kahne and Westheimer argue that civic responsibility is often confused with giving and altruism, or charity, and that charity supports the replication of unjust structures because it does not promote their reconstruction.[67] For instance, while working at a soup kitchen, a student may become aware of poverty issues at the same time that he or she meets the immediate needs of hungry and homeless persons; however, serving food at a soup kitchen does little to change the unjust societal structures and policies that produce and perpetuate hunger and homelessness.

Consistent with the goals of feminist pedagogy, the purpose of service-learning as a transformative pedagogy is to teach students about their civic responsibility to challenge unjust structures and participate in effecting change. Kahne and Westheimer write, "Citizenship in a democratic community requires more than kindness; it requires engagement in complex social and institutional endeavors. . . . Citizenship requires that individuals work to create, evaluate, criticize, and change public institutions and programs."[68]

Much of the learning in service-learning results from the meaningful connections made between ideas and actions, the course subject and the service experience, and the individual and the community. These associations are facilitated by reflection. This is a critical component of what Freire refers to as praxis; it is "the reflection and action which truly transforms reality, [which] is the source of knowledge and creation."[69] Hatcher and Bringle define reflection as "the intentional consideration of an experience in light of particular learning objectives."[70]

The question often arises whether or not faculty should participate in service with the students. Some experts believe that student learning and enthusiasm may be enhanced if faculty members participate with them.[71] Because of their emphasis on fostering meaningful interpersonal relationships within the classroom community, this, in particular, is one area where feminist pedagogy and Ignatian pedagogy can inform service-learning. Faculty accompaniment of students in the service component of a course can only enhance and strengthen those important relationships.

Pedagogy-in-Action: Reflection on and Dialogue among Perspectives

While feminist, Ignatian, and service-learning pedagogies have shared similar historical influences on their development, there has been a surprising lack of dialogue between them.[72] In this section, we bring the three pedagogies into dialogue as we share teaching experiences in which one or more of the three pedagogies informed our approach to course content, classroom interaction dynamics, evaluation of student learning and course objectives, and critical analysis of the educational context. We explore what worked and what did not, using the three pedagogical approaches to consider avenues for improvement. In this way, we explore not only ways that these three approaches to teaching and learning are compatible but how considering them together can enhance our understanding of each individual approach. Each approach provides a critical lens through which to view the others, so that we as educational professionals might deepen our critical reflection on, as well as enhance the effectiveness of, the pedagogies that we use.

Robbin's Family Communication Class

When I teach family communication, I teach it from a feminist perspective and I use many aspects of feminist pedagogy. The course foregrounds exploration of how the historical and contemporary family as a social unit is a site for women's oppression and self-actualization, a site where women's personal and professional lives are both constrained and enabled. We examine family interaction patterns and the ways gender identities are constructed and performed within them. In addition to traditional exams, students write reflective papers connecting course concepts to their new and expanding understandings of their own family dynamics, experiences, and aspirations. The final project is the construction of a family shrine or altar; students are asked to use aesthetic media and symbolism to create the shrine and communicate the knowledge they've gained in the course.

Since coming to teach at a Jesuit university, I have been informed by Ignatian pedagogy in teaching this class. Context has always been a central component of this course, consistent with both feminist and Ignatian pedagogy. The historical course material, along with the readings on myriad family experiences (e.g., blended families and stepfamilies, various ethnic and religious family rituals, the phenomenon of interracial and international adoption, families headed by gay and lesbian parents) leads to deep explorations of students' own family experiences in relation to course content and concepts, as well as in relation to the broader social and historical context. The impact of the Catholic Church and other religious structures on their families is a welcome site of analysis and critique.

The Ignatian principle of reflection plays a key role in the family communication course. At Fairfield University, through my growing understanding of Ignatian pedagogy, I now feel more empowered as an educator to ask students to explore deeply their own lives and contexts related to course content. Discussion of students' family experiences is welcome, and these experiences are incorporated into paper assignments. Given the course material, students cannot help but be moved toward deeply personal, and often painful, realizations about their families' structures, interaction dynamics, and role relationships. We develop clear rules about confidentiality and respect, and students decide how much (or how little) self-disclosure they are comfortable with. My one-on-one-conversations with students reflect a broadened teacher role, as reflecting on course content requires me to be more of a mentor and support person, perhaps a role closer to that of director in the practice of the Spiritual Exercises. Of course, I refer students to the appropriate campus services if they are needed, but the dynamics of the course lead to closer relationships with the students than those I have with students in other courses. These processes and relationships deepen my experience as an educator, and this experience has informed and enhanced my interactions with students in other courses and settings.

Course assignments and in-class activities in the family communication course blend conceptual learning with reflection. Evaluation in the course considers students' abilities to communicate knowledge and critical thinking as well as thoughtful and reflective engagement with course material and the ways that they have made it meaningful in the context of their own conceptions of family and unfolding family lives. Drawing on Ignatian principles of evaluation (and, coincidentally, in keeping with an increasing emphasis on the assessment of student learning outcomes connected to the mission of Jesuit education), it may be helpful to consider employing intentional evaluative measures that focus more on the growth and development of each student beyond mastery of course concepts.

It is the feminist and Ignatian emphasis on action that has most eluded me, and sometimes troubled me, in relation to this class. To be clear, student knowledge acquisition and reflection do lead them to decisive action, whether internalized through changed attitudes about gender or family dynamics or externalized through altered behaviors toward a new stepparent or a decision to seek different kinds of romantic partners. Of course, I remind them before they go home for Thanksgiving or Easter break that they have not become family therapists armed with the means to "fix" their families. Nevertheless, their new understandings inevitably lead them to reexamine their perceptions of and feelings about themselves and their families, which often leads to behavior changes and uncharacteristic intervention in old family dynamics and patterns. I am thrilled to know that the family communication course helps students raise their expectations for developing quality relationships that are more empowering and fulfilling. But how are these actions related to social justice? What of the *common* good and positive actions beyond their personal lives?

I believe that a service-learning component could make a significant contribution in inspiring students to reflect and act upon social injustices facing families in our surrounding community and around the world. While the course curriculum includes readings that help students engage with issues facing families who are poor, oppressed, displaced, and otherwise marginalized, a service-learning experience might bring them into the context of these families. Service-learning experiences with, for example, immigrant families, domestic violence shelters, family literacy programs, teen parent services, or incarcerated women might move their actions beyond improving their own lives toward advocating for better policies and services for all kinds of families. Such experiences would also certainly strengthen the feminist content of the course, as the encounter with social injustice is also almost always a confrontation with gender injustice.

Joe's Mentoring Communities Program in the Ignatian Residential College

The Ignatian Residential College Mentoring Communities Program is part of an intentional living-and-learning community of two hundred sophomores organized around the question of vocation at Fairfield University. Through this program, groups of seven or eight students and a faculty or staff mentor are formed into a mentoring community. Each month all participants are asked to reflect on designated key questions in light of their lived experiences, participate in monthly mentor activities, engage with suggested readings, and respond to journal prompts. The goal is to develop an intimate and intentional community of peers in a trusting environment where each person seeks to learn about him- or herself and one another throughout this year-long experience. The experiences that I describe here arose when I served as director of the Ignatian Residential College through which I facilitated the mentoring communities program.

In one of the monthly activities, students are asked to have both a close friend and a family member write them a letter answering the question "Who do you say I am?" In this letter, writers are to offer their insights into the person's strengths, gifts, and challenges. At the same time, students write letters to themselves, attempting to answer the same question—"Who am I?" This has been a powerful experience for many students, as the level of insight provided by family members and friends is often surprising. Students find the letters quite accurate and characterized by profound honesty, vulnerability, and depth. The experience frequently overwhelms students, because they have rarely, if ever, received letters of this type from loved ones. As a personal development exercise, this activity is successful in helping students recognize elements of their own context: their many gifts and talents, the challenges that they face, and ways they are perceived by those closest to them.

In Ignatian pedagogy, educators must "adapt to the condition of the one who is to engage" and meet students where they are in order to guide them through the course material.[73] In this sense, the educator must be able to situate the material to be learned in relation to the subject matter of the course and semester, as well as in relation to the student's major department, its cross-curricular relationships, and the realities of the world in some way (i.e., the student's context). Ignatian educators may ask: How do I prepare to teach this material most effectively to these particular students at this particular time and place, given their particular needs, interests, skills, and reality? The letter-writing activity functions in important ways for the teacher and mentor as well as for the student.

To further increase learning from the letter-writing exercise, drawing on aspects of feminist and service-learning pedagogies can broaden the Ignatian exploration of individual context. Specifically, these pedagogies emphasize a greater critical and analytical exploration of one's identity within a social context. Feminist pedagogy squarely challenges students to consider who they are and their context in terms of race, gender, power, and politics, which has the potential to lead to serious recognition of one's relative power and privilege (particularly important with our university population). Similarly, service-learning experiences facilitate connections between students' identities and contexts in relation to the individuals, communities, and justice issues encountered in the service site or work. Reflective experiences associated with service-learning also help students develop the habit of personally connecting their lives to the subject matter, a process of appropriating knowledge through reflection. As this habit of reflection develops in students, they may then become more inclined to participate in the work of service, civic engagement, and social justice, and to develop the conscience and commitment associated with Jesuit education. These same perspectives could be brought to other exercises in the Ignatian Residential College.

The letter-writing activity often awakens students to a deeper sense of connectedness and fosters greater intimacy with friends and family. One of the presuppositions of Ignatius's Spiritual Exercises is the idea that God unconditionally loves each person and invites each person into intimate relationship with Him. This intimacy allows students the freedom to choose to respond (or not) to this love. This free choice may then translate into various types of actions.

The ideal of Ignatian pedagogy is to awaken in students the desire to serve others, take action, and work for social justice. It must be recognized, however, that students should be free to choose whatever action they wish to engage in. The actions then taken, if any, may be of two kinds: an interiorized choice, such as a change in one's attitude, increased compassion, or awareness of one's biases or limitations, or a choice that is manifested externally, such as a physical action that is consistent, through reflection, with one's new understanding and conviction. Both types of choices represent the student's response, which may or may not involve direct work for social justice yet does contribute to bettering one's authentic self and relationships and, in that sense, one's world.

The connectedness and intimacy that the letter-writing activity provides is an opportunity to develop students' self-understanding and relationships with those whom they care about deeply. After this exercise, students often reveal that they never realized some things about themselves or how much they really valued the perspective of their friends and family. Some share how this exercise was a significant breakthrough in their relationships, deepening the level of intimacy. Others reveal a stronger sense of self and self-confidence, leading some to become more involved and engaged with those in their community. Recognizing that the student has the free choice to respond (or not) to the new and heart-centered information that the letter-writing activity provides may generate a desire to respond or take action in some way, authentically benefiting themselves or others.

Another way Ignatian, feminist, and service-learning pedagogies can support the learning objectives that each approach articulates relates to reflection. The deep reflection of Ignatian pedagogy can assist the work of both feminist pedagogy and service-learning; that is, the formation of the individual student (through exercises such as the letter-writing activity) prepares him or her to consider being of service and working for justice in the future. As a student's habit of reflection develops, matures, and becomes a part of his or her way of learning, courses and experiences using feminist and service-learning pedagogies can further build upon this reflective skill and direct it toward issues of inequality and injustice. We might consider, then, how these pedagogies can form a sort of scaffolding for student learning within a four-year experience. While learning and development do not always occur in a linear progression or in the same sequence for all students, it seems fair to say that each of these pedagogies supports students' individual human development, personal and collective liberation from oppression, and the cultivation of civic engagement for social justice.

Melissa's Work in Service-Learning

Each of the three transformative pedagogies discussed in this chapter challenges the learner to consider issues of power and privilege and his or her own personal responsibility within oppressive and unjust structures and systems. In my experience working with students in cocurricular and curricular service-learning, I have found that reflection is one of the most challenging components in which to engage students in a meaningful way. As mentioned earlier, reflection is an integral component of any service-learning experience, as this is where the learning and personal growth and development take place. It is also through reflection that we challenge beliefs and assumptions; engage in difficult dialogue about inequality, race, class, and privilege; and empower students to move from the charity model of understanding service to one oriented toward change and justice. Students are often understandably resistant to engaging in this type of reflection, and I have often found it difficult to empower them to move from charitable intentions toward a productive restlessness and passion for justice.

When asked to share reflections on their service experience, students often report that it makes them feel good to help others or to make others happy. During a recent reflection exercise, I asked students to identify a goal that they have in regard to how they engage with their service experience or in terms of how they want to grow from their experience. Several students focused on how they wanted the service experience or the organization itself to change so that they could enjoy it more, rather than how they themselves could grow and develop new understandings or perspectives, or how they themselves could become agents of change. If we as educators fail to empower students to gain a deeper understanding of the root causes of injustices that they witness through their service and to move from an understanding of service as a feel-good activity toward recognition of their responsibility to be agents of change, then we run the risk of perpetuating stereotypes and a sense of "otherness" between students and service populations as well as paternalistic relationships. This is always a risk in service-learning pedagogy but often one well worth taking.

Feminist pedagogy can inform how educators address these important challenges because it provides a framework, language, and set of

practices for helping students move from "me" to "we" or, more importantly, toward an understanding of solidarity. Feminist pedagogy also
provides a framework for exploring issues of diversity, power, and privilege and, in particular, for examining the self in relation to power and
privilege. Utilizing the language, history, and practices of feminist pedagogy may help service-learning practitioners engage students in these
necessary explorations in such a way that they do not feel threatened
or become defensive but feel empowered to develop new understandings and become agents of change.

Additionally, both feminist pedagogy and Ignatian pedagogy build
from the personal, lived experiences of students as the context for these
types of conversations, whereas service-learning engages students in
new and often foreign experiences in the community. Initially using
students' lived experiences to engage in difficult conversations about
race, gender, class, privilege, injustice, and so forth, could help to prepare them for the new experiences that they will have in the community, thus laying the foundation for exploring these issues in relation to
their new experiences. With this foundation, they are more likely to
enter the new experience with a more mature and intellectually astute
perspective and to have the resources necessary to move from a focus
on the self to a focus on solidarity.

Conclusion

At a recent Campus Compact retreat, longtime service-learning practitioner and consultant Nadinne Cruz referred to service learning as a
practice rather than a *program*.[74] This responds to the fact that many
would-be service-learning practitioners focus merely on adding a service component to an existing course and fail to fully reconsider the
nature and purposes of knowledge production in light of the philosophies underlying service-learning pedagogy, or to becoming a critically
reflective teacher. Facilitating effective reflection in service-learning
pedagogy requires the professor to have unusual flexibility, as well as
improvisational skills and the willingness to engage authentically and
personally with the insights and relationships in the classroom and
community. Feminist pedagogy may be more a philosophy than a
method; there is no finite set of characteristics or components and

feminist teachers use all sorts of teaching methods. But feminist pedagogy, like service-learning, is also a *practice*, a way of being and inquiring that necessitates a reconsideration of knowledge, teaching, and
learning. Feminist pedagogy "require[s] us to turn answers into questions; [so] that it is not the answers we find but the questions we pose
that place knowledge . . . in the service of social transformation."[75]
Similarly, the Ignatian paradigm is a reflective *practice* for teaching and
learning. Even with its five key areas and established model based on
the Spiritual Exercises, it is not simply an educational philosophy or set
of teaching methods. In Jesuit parlance, it is *a way of proceeding.*

In this chapter we have illustrated what may be for some a surprising
compatibility between feminist and Ignatian pedagogy. Given the many
points of convergence between feminist and Jesuit approaches to education, teaching, and learning, it is no wonder so many feminist scholars
have found professional homes and communities at Jesuit colleges and
universities, even as we continue to struggle for equal representation,
treatment, and authority in those institutions. It is also no surprise that
Jesuit colleges and universities have been innovators in community-
based education and places where some form of service-learning has
been practiced for decades. Neither is it surprising, then, that we educators in the feminist, Ignatian, and service-learning traditions have
found allies in each other as we strive to create not only rigorous academic experiences for our students but personally and socially transformational ones as well. But there is more work to be done.

Unlike feminist and Ignatian pedagogical approaches, the outcomes
of service-learning have been subject to much empirical research.[76] In
fact, the growing academic literature and number of empirical studies
on service-learning have led to recent claims that service-learning has
moved beyond being an educational movement and is becoming,
instead, an academic field in its own right. Ignatian and feminist educators would do well to study their teaching methods and learning outcomes empirically. With its deepest roots in humanist (rather than
social science) inquiry, the feminist pedagogical literature is characterized by incisive critical analysis and inspirational argument, but almost
no empirical substantiation.[77] Similarly, the Ignatian paradigm flows
from a faith tradition; thus it is not surprising that it has not been
subjected to systematic empirical investigation. Nevertheless, in today's

higher educational environment, the assessment efforts used in service-learning could powerfully inform our understanding of feminist and Ignatian pedagogies.

This chapter represents our collective experience as educators, as well as our conversations across disciplines and pedagogical tendencies. What we have learned through the process of weaving together our ideas and experiences is that a consideration of diverse philosophies, theories, and methods of teaching and learning is a critical component of faculty and staff development, and crucial to the advancement of mission and identity for colleagues at Jesuit colleges and universities. As we struggle to become more multicultural and socially responsible institutions, an inter-articulation of the three pedagogical approaches may provide an important avenue for developing truly transformative discourses of teaching and learning, as well as transformative experiences for all of us in higher education today.

Part III: Intersection II
The Power of Difference for Teaching Social Justice

7   The Intersection of Race, Class,
    and Gender in Jesuit
    and Feminist Education

Finding Transcendent Meaning in the Concrete

M. SHAWN COPELAND

In May of 2006, the board of trustees and the administration
of Boston College announced their decision to invite then–U.S. secre-
tary of state Condoleezza Rice to address the graduating class and to
receive an honorary doctorate of laws. This decision provoked dissen-
sion within the university community. Kenneth Himes, chair of the
Department of Theology, and David Hollenbach of the Society of Jesus
wrote a measured letter objecting not to the address but to the conferral
of the degree. Across the university's colleges and schools, groups of
faculty and students protested—signing the letter; distributing leaflets;
organizing rallies, panel discussions, and debates. At the same time,
other faculty and students demonstrated support for the decision. Edi-
torials, op-ed pieces, and letters—pro and con—crowded the pages of
our three student-run newspapers. One faculty member repudiated the
Himes-Hollenbach letter in Boston's archdiocesan newspaper, the *Pilot*,
and the city paper of record, the *Boston Globe*, reported on something
other than Boston College's football prospects.

In the midst of this bristling activity, one bright May afternoon,
two of my students, a young woman and a young man, came by
appointment to my office. Our conversation proved to be a truly pre-
cious and memorable moment in teaching. These undergraduates
came to my office not, as I initially and shamefully suspected, to
inquire about the final examination; rather, they came to have a conversation with their teacher, a co-learner. They wanted to talk about
ideas and about books that they had read—not assigned course reading but books that they had read on their own. And so, for roughly
forty minutes, the three of us enjoyed a real conversation that ranged
from our anger and disgust at the war in Iraq to the memoir of General Roméo Dallaire, who had been posted to Rwanda as commander

of UN forces during the genocide; from Michael Walzer's book, *Politics and Passion,* to the contingency and challenge of creating a just society; from the brutal prison system in the United States to the failure of U.S. public education. As the students prepared to leave, one of them asked me, "How do you not get co-opted when you grow up?" I confess that I was stunned and, not for the first time that semester, my integrity as a person, as a teacher, was on the line. In reply, I said something like this: "You critically discern what is right, and you struggle to do it—no matter what it costs." This conversation with my students stays with me and influences what I have to say about Jesuit and feminist pedagogy.

My remarks are organized in three parts. I begin with the obvious— some clarification and limitation of terms—and point out some commonalities between Jesuit and feminist pedagogy. I ask, "Does Jesuit include Ignatius or what comes long after?" and "What do I mean when I use the word 'feminist'?" Because I want to address the social arrangements through which we create and incarnate the United States, in the second part, I consider some of the neuralgic features of the social context of our pedagogical efforts. I am a Roman Catholic, a teacher, a theologian. I focus my theological work—my questions, research, reading, thinking, teaching, writing—through the lens of political theology. Hence, in the third part, I reflect briefly on how we as teachers, women and men who employ critical pedagogical strategies, may influence human relations and social interactions that lead to the creation of a good and just society that strives to incarnate transcendent meaning in the concrete.

Jesuit and Feminist Pedagogy: Some Definitions and Commonalities

The terms "Jesuit" and "feminist" are freighted with internal contradictions and conflicting meanings. Jesuits and feminists refer to, define, even absolutize different and sometimes incompatible features when they name or single out just what is Jesuit, just what is feminist. These terms, "Jesuit" and "feminist," shift into standpoints or perspectives only upon critical interrogation.

The history of Jesuit education forms an intricate, nonlinear, and dynamic narrative stream about men who are companions, friends in Christ—about their ideas and ministry, their risks and hopes—that stretches over more than 450 years. I want to point out three shifts that bear on what Jesuits insist today signals the continuity and innovative character of their educational endeavor.

The establishment, administration, and staffing of secondary schools or colleges and universities was not Ignatius of Loyola's intention when he gathered his first companions. Jesuit theologian Michael Buckley writes that this company of friends was "to be wandering missionaries and preachers, ministers of the Word of God who promoted its interior realization through such ministries as confession, spiritual direction, the Spiritual Exercises, and the Eucharist, and its social embodiment in the works of charity and of reconciliation."[1] Ignatius and his companions set up residences, or colleges, attached to major universities in Europe for Jesuit students for the priesthood. Eventually, lectures designed to supplement the academic courses at the universities were held in the colleges. Within a few years non-Jesuit and secular male students began to attend the college lectures with Jesuit scholastics.[2] From their beginnings, then, Jesuits have had a taste for what a key document of Jesuit higher education describes as "creative companionship with their colleagues."[3]

Jesuit historian John O'Malley uncovers a shift in the universities of the fifteenth and sixteenth centuries that distinguishes them from their earlier counterparts—namely, an emphasis on *veritas* rather than *pietas*. The new university centered its curriculum no longer "on the development of the student or the betterment of society but on the solving of intellectual problems."[4] O'Malley argues that when Jesuits took up the task of formal education in the mid-sixteenth century, they did so in Italy, where the *studia humanitatis* had been in existence for more than one hundred years. Jesuit education came to bloom in an intellectual and cultural environment that affirmed and nurtured the "almost limitless potential for the individual and for society" and grasped the "correlation between the *pietas* [of the early humanists] and the kind of personal conversion and transformation that were the traditional goals of Christian ministry" in which Jesuits were engaged.[5] Such regard and care for the person and the person's potential still mark Jesuit education.[6]

Ignatius and his first companions wanted very much to "help people in the manner of Jesus and the early disciples . . . to be available to people where they were and as they were, to constantly devise new ways of making the Gospel meaningful to people."[7] And, as Timothy Hanchin observes, Jesuit education draws inspiration from Ignatius's penchant for and insistence on conversation. Conversation requires hospitality, openness, testing, revision, and discovery.[8] Genuine conversation may lead as well to the disruption of conventional opinion, to encounter with an "other" who may change us radically. Genuine conversation lays the ground for solidarity and justice.[9]

The emergence, waves, meanings, and varied instantiations of feminism are by now well known and need not be repeated here. In brief, feminism refers to a global phenomenon that assumes many forms, two of which bear upon this discussion: feminism as a social movement that seeks the liberation of women from all forms of sexism and feminism as a cross-disciplinary academic method of analysis.[10]

Taking into account the proto-feminism of the late nineteenth and early twentieth centuries, most scholars delineate three waves of feminism. But it is important to remember that these waves are not decisively linear; they overlap and interact with one another. The first wave surfaced in the latter half of the nineteenth century, following on other movements for human, social, and political liberation. White upper- and middle-class women of education and privilege directed and dominated this wave, which gave rise to at least four distinct types or expressions of feminism: liberal feminism, with its emphasis on women's full equality with men in all facets of social, political, and economic life, along with a demand that women have the right to make decisions about the sexual and reproductive disposition of their bodies; cultural feminism, with its accent on the "moral superiority of women over men" and the primacy of such values as compassion, regard for nature, nurturance, and peacemaking; radical feminism, with its insistence on female-male separatism, on the insidious character of patriarchy, and on the removal of patriarchy and men from every aspect of women's lives; and socialist feminism, with its critique of the white male domination of capitalist societies and advocacy of the eradication of class divisions and women's economic and social dependence upon men.[11]

Second-wave feminism stems from the global and differentiated critiques formulated by women of color—First Nations or indigenous women, Asian women, Latin American women, Latinas and *mujeristas* in the United States, working-class women of European descent, and black women of African descent on the Continent and throughout the diaspora. Second-wave feminism rejected the first wave's limitation of the meaning of women's experience to that of privileged white women and attempted to reimagine "the whole of humanity in relation to the whole of reality."[12] Third-wave feminism is associated with the young women who came of age in the mid-1990s and who set themselves to address the shortcomings of the first and second waves.[13]

As a black woman doing intellectual work in a society that continues to treat the very existence and presence of black people—indeed, people of color, poor people of all races, and most women—as deficient, I find that the term "feminist" imposes on my social location substantively. My use of the term "feminist" is shaded in black. A black feminist or womanist standpoint projects a social vision rooted in critical reflection on black women's experience of gender-based discrimination and oppression within both the black community and the larger dominant cultural and social matrix.[14] Black feminist pedagogy forms an oppositional discourse sensitized by joy in human sexuality and differences of human sexual orientation, by social analysis and class consciousness, by cross-generational openness and dialogue. Black feminist pedagogy resists unmindful surrender to the prevailing assumptions and ideas, habits and actions, cultural meanings and social conditions that hinder women and men of all races from living more human and humane lives.

Of course, there are important differences, but Jesuit and feminist pedagogy hold in common at least the following basic assumptions. First, the subject of education is the student, the woman, and the man as each is and might become. Jesuit and feminist pedagogy honor and value personhood in the concrete and are oriented by the goal of liberating men and women for others. Second, nurturing the Eros of the mind, the passionate desire and drive to know, forms the foundation of every pedagogical endeavor. To know critically is to resist the "flight from understanding,"[15] that is, the fearful escape into forms of abstraction that overlook or disregard concrete human experience as a source for theorizing. Third, critical pedagogy addresses particular historical, cultural, and social contexts. Such pedagogy entails differentiating and problematizing historical understanding; requires rigorous interrogation of the unquestioned assumptions, habits, symbols, and media representations that subtly and blatantly shape a cultural matrix; and demands serious investigation of social structures, "bureaucratic hierarchies, and market mechanisms" that limit the potential of some and expand that of others.[16] Fourth, critical pedagogy respects and attends to experience—biological, personal, psychological, practical, aesthetic, dramatic, religious, and intellectual.[17] Fifth, the liberation of "men and women for others" pedagogically means, above all, that we model the meaning of solidarity for our students—how to meet, to listen to, to converse with, and to grow in friendship with the children, women, and men whom our society has made invisible; that we help our students to grasp the essential humanity that levels and unites us all; and that we equip our students to sniff out and repudiate desiccated liberal do-gooding. Sixth, critical pedagogy embraces advocacy and struggle for social change on institutional or structural levels; education is personal and communal, cultural and political. Jesuit and feminist pedagogy not only argue but also demonstrate that individualism and detachment, dogmatism and exclusivity, arrogance and bias serve neither authentic human knowing nor authentic human action. Seventh, human persons learn best when engaged by and with experience, and human persons live best in collaborative efforts to realize one another's flourishing as human persons. In other words, Jesuit and feminist pedagogy call not only for what Lorraine Code named "epistemic responsibility" but also for ethical responsibility.[18] Jesuit and feminist pedagogy take seriously what it means to know with our lives and to live with our knowledge.

The Social Context of Our Pedagogical Praxis

The success or failure of Jesuit and feminist pedagogy lies in the ability to meet the cultural crises of our time. Culture can be understood as a set of meanings and values that inform a way of life. Those meanings and values are expressed concretely through the social order—the kinds of institutions and structures that we construct and maintain, the people with whom and the ways in which we cooperate and collaborate.

Critical analysis and reflection on the social order forms a crucial starting point from which to identify the crises we face and from which to develop, evaluate, and enact our pedagogical praxis.

The so-called New American Century is proving to be as deceitful, vicious, smug, and cruel as those that have preceded it. All around the world children, women, and men are consigned to the margins of society in disease, hunger, homelessness, war, and ignorance. "Every day," writes Jean Ziegler, the United Nations' Special Rapporteur on the Right to Food, "more than 17,000 children under the age of 5 die from hunger-related diseases. More than 5 million children [were] killed by hunger-related diseases by the end of [2005]."[19] The United Nations' most recent *Human Development Report* states simply: "At the start of the twenty-first century we live in a divided world. The size of the divide poses a fundamental challenge to the global human community."[20] The global transfer of power and resources from the natural world to human control, from local communities to transnational and neocolonial elites, from local to transnational power centers, reduces life expectancy, increases infant and child mortality, compromises health care, leads to a disregard for education and illiteracy, and distorts income distribution. "The world's richest 500 individuals have a combined income greater than that of the poorest 416 million. Beyond these extremes, the 2.5 billion people living on less than $2 a day—40% of the world's population—account for 5% of global income. The richest 10%, almost all of whom live in high-income countries, account for 54%."[21]

To borrow a phrase from Zygmunt Bauman, this global system results in "a new socio-cultural hierarchy, a world-wide scale" that correlates with race and gender: "the darker your skin is, the less you earn; the shorter your life span, the poorer your health and nutrition, the less education you can get."[22] The darker your skin is, the more likely you are to be imprisoned, a refugee, a forced migrant. The darker your skin is, the more likely you are to become infected with HIV/AIDS. If you are a woman, the darker your skin is, the more likely you are to bury your infant.

In the United States, the working poor, trapped in a quagmire of low wages, are pitted against economically desperate undocumented workers, whom we loathe, but on whom we resentfully depend for the manual labor we despise. Arab Americans, Asians, veiled observant Muslim women, olive-complexioned Puerto Rican men, Sikhs, Mexican American citizens, well-dressed Caribbean Canadians crossing the border—all trigger our suspicions. For most of the nation, the survivors of Hurricane Katrina have faded from not only our view but also from our consciousness as they continue to struggle with recalcitrant insurance companies and intermittent municipal services. Each campaign season seems to bring us political advertising dedicated to teasing out racial fear. From the shooting of young girls in an Amish schoolhouse to the murder of a college student in rural Vermont, violence against women and girls has become chronic. Violence in major cities is on the rise and, through it all, the middle-class suffocates, the rich get richer, and the poor get prison.[23] Of the many social breakdowns that press on our pedagogical praxis, I want to single out the unconscious persistence of racism in the post–civil rights era, even though white people in the United States insist vigorously that they are not racist.[24]

Sociologists Michael Omi and Howard Winant use the term "racial formation" to denote the complex historically situated process by which human bodies and social structures are represented and arranged and by which society is organized and ruled. From this perspective, "race is a matter of both social structure and cultural representation."[25] Racial formation process accounts for a cluster of problems regarding race, the dilemmas of racial identity, and the relation of race to other forms of difference, including gender and nationality. This perspective also discredits the romanticization of race as essence and its misrepresentation as illusion. Racial formation process maintains that race is *not* a deviation within a given social structure but a constant feature embedded within it.

The explanatory power of racial formation process functions to account for both macro- and micro-levels,[26] but I focus here on the micro-level, or everyday level, because it is on this level that unconscious racism arises so often. Attending to racial formation process on this level uncovers how the most mundane as well as the most important tasks can be grasped as racial projects—voting, banking, health care, registering for school, inquiring about church membership. We have been taught to *see* race, and we do, and we see it most vividly when we insist that we are color blind. Race is one of the first things that we notice about people (along with their sex) when we meet them. Furthermore, the ability to read race accurately, to categorize people (black or white, red or brown, Mexican or Indian, Chinese or Vietnamese), has become crucial for social behavior and comfort. The inability to identify accurately a person's race spells crisis, and even as we question such interpretation, we continue to analyze and interpret our experience in racial terms. Moreover, as Omi and Winant observe, "We expect differences in skin color, or other racially coded characteristics, to explain social differences."[27] This affects not only our relations to various social institutions, cultural activities, religious rites, and rituals but our relationships with other human persons as well as the constitution of our own identities. The very stereotypes we profess to abhor and repudiate break in on our encounters with physicians, professors, musicians, law enforcement officers, and elected officials of races different from our own. However, critical interrogation of racial formation process can uncover social conditioning for what it is—a set of learned behaviors and practices. At the same time, that critical interrogation can identify and support strategies to overcome the debilitating legacy of racism.

Although race is not an ideology, racism certainly is. Because racial formation process accords critical attention to both social structures and social signification, it can account for racism as ideology. Racism is the product of biased thinking, an ideology that willfully justifies, advances, and maintains the systemic domination of a certain race or certain races by another race. Racism goes beyond prejudice (feeling or opinion formed without concrete experience or knowledge) or even bigotry (doctrinaire intolerance) by joining these feelings or attitudes to the putative exercise of legitimate power in a society; in this way, racism never relies solely on the choices or actions of a few individuals but is institutionalized.

We racialized subjects sustain and transmit racism as an ideology through our uncritical acceptance of standards, symbols, habits, assumptions, reactions, and practices rooted in racial differentiation and racially assigned privilege. Racism penetrates the development and transmission of culture, including education and access to it; literary and artistic expression; forms of communication, representation, and leisure; participation in and contributions to the common good, including opportunities to work, to engage in meaningful political and economic activity; the promotion of human flourishing, including intellectual, psychological, sexual, and spiritual growth; and the embrace of religion, including membership and leadership, catechesis and spirituality, ritual, doctrine, and theology. Thus racism permeates every sphere of social relations.[28]

As an ideology, racism envelops the "normal" and "ordinary" social setup and spawns a negatively charged context in which flesh-and-blood human beings live out their daily lives and struggle to constitute themselves as persons. Racism is no mere problem to be solved, but a construal of the whole of reality, a distorted way of being in the world. Racism is not something out-there for us to solve; rather it is in our consciousness, shapes our discourse and practices.

Educating the Imagination, Disciplining the Heart

As educators, the persistence of racism must be understood as a most important challenge to our pedagogy. In our classrooms we daily pit human intelligence against bias—against the arrogant choice to persist in ignorance, stereotype, and irresponsibility, against the distortions and fear-driven inhibitions of our imaginations and hearts.[29]

What tasks and strategies can we develop to open ourselves and our students, our imaginations and theirs? What disciplines for our hearts and theirs might we propose so that we may participate in healing and creating in history? Let me suggest three—though surely there are more that we might devise.

First, Jesuit and feminist pedagogy must do more than reproduce subjects of the cultural matrix, for we are living out of a virtual, vulgar, and voyeuristic culture. We are deeply wounded in our living and our knowing. For all its creative tactics of destabilization, revision, and complexification, postmodernism fails to assist people of color in the struggle against invisibility, political indifference, or public surveillance and regulation. Postmodernism fosters the cannibalization of black popular culture and consumes its creators and producers.

Second, Jesuit and feminist pedagogy must address the persistence of racism in our society and in our schools. Attention to critical race theory in our pedagogy offers one approach in the effort to dismantle and interrupt prized notions of fairness, meritocracy, color blindness, and impartiality. Furthermore, we can model for our students how to discern the ways in which racism, sexism, class exploitation, and homophobia are structured through power relations, disguised, transmitted, and replicated in our major social (i.e., political, economic, technological), cultural, and religious institutions.

The negotiation of difference has become an important feature in critical pedagogy. Differences are real: After all, men are not women, women are not men, but men and women are human beings. "There is the 'difference,'" social theorist Stuart Hall observes, "which makes a radical and unbridgeable separation: and there is a 'difference' which may be positional [and] conditional."[30] However, as Anthony Paul Farley argues, "an ideology of difference [may also] function as denial in our culture by masking, on the ground of nature, the [actual] relationship between whites and [others]."[31] Critical race theory seeks to analyze actual racial relationships, grasping race not just as a matter of difference but also as a matter of power.

Third, Jesuit and feminist pedagogy must foster serious analysis of white privilege. We all know what it is like to try to have a conversation about race. Many of us have heard the rejoinders "I just do not see color or race" or "It does not matter to me if you are blue or green." Such statements serve to maintain the notion that all persons are treated equally without regard to color or race, the notion that it is time to move beyond race. Ironically, such statements disclose the uncomfortable awareness of race and racism that lies at the core of such adamant insistence. Such comments function to support white racial privilege and de-emphasize race; such comments permit raw as well as subtle forms of racism to pass unnoticed. Thus racism as power, as structuring hierarchy, is erased and reduced to the actions of a few unsavory bigots whom some people of color are forced to endure.

This erasure and reduction are possible, Stephanie Wildman observes, only because of a "sleight-of-mind" that allows for opportunistic shifts of racial location or position. Wildman writes: "We are each individuals, assured of individual rights. But sometimes we are group members, acting relationally. Understanding privilege requires conceptualizing individuals as part of groups. . . . Considering only the personal, individual holder of the knapsack of privilege results in missing a significant part of how privilege operates."[32] To advert only to the individual holder of privilege erases the systemic or structural way in which white racial privilege functions. Analysis of white privilege exposes just how white children, women, and men benefit individually and collectively from the so-called normalization of those advantages, and how racial privilege allows whites to evade personal or individual responsibility for biased (racist) acts and practices and to treat these as mere random occurrences.

Conclusion

Of course, there is much more to say about these issues, but underlying what I have said is an exercise in political theology. Theological reflection can go a long way toward complementing individual and communal responses to situations of dis-grace—pointing out some of the ways in which structures and systems are disordered and deformed. At the same time, political theology always ought to cast a light on the ultimate and transcendent solution to the realization of the common human good. That solution can only be located in the darkly luminous mystery of the cross of Jesus of Nazareth. For if the prophetic praxis of Jesus reveals the transcendent passion of an eschatological imagination in the midst of a concrete human setup, the cross shows us its radical risk.

I shared with you what I said to my students, but not all that I thought. For with the honorary degree and Dr. Rice's role in articulating the rationale for the war in Iraq in mind and with my heart heavy for the university I love so very deeply, for my alma mater, what I thought at the time was this: The answer to the question "How not to be co-opted when you grow up? How to resist the seductions of power, prestige, and privilege? How to keep one's integrity, one's honor, bright?" ought to be a Jesuit education—indeed, a Jesuit and feminist education.

Sitting with those two young people, what I felt was the embarrassing, sharp, and painful irony of the situation in which we found ourselves: We *were* sitting in a Jesuit university. As I have mulled over this conversation and my reaction to it, I have come to appreciate again that a Jesuit university, in fact, is the place in which such questions must be raised.

For some Boston College faculty and students, the events surrounding the May 2006 commencement amounted to "much ado about nothing"; for others, it was an upsetting display of bad manners; still for others, the situation was confusing. But for some, whether or not they dissented from the decision to confer an honorary degree on Dr. Rice, this was an occasion for critical self-examination. Certainly, these events were not peculiar to Boston College. Yet arguably the decisions to contest or concur with the decision of other vital members of our university community reinforced the significance of critical Jesuit and feminist pedagogy. Indeed, we were pushing Boston College to be better than its best self—pushing ourselves to be better than our best selves.

I close with this passage from Martha Nussbaum's *Cultivating Humanity*. Given the condition of the context in which we carry out our pedagogical praxis, I think it captures something of what we all hope to do in the classroom.

> It is up to us, as educators, to show our students the beauty and interest of a life that is open to the whole world, to show them that there is after all more joy in the kind of citizenship that questions than in the kind that simply applauds, more fascination in the study of human beings in all their variety and complexity than in the zealous pursuit of superficial stereotypes, more genuine love and friendship in the life of questioning and self-government than in submission to authority. We had better show them this, or the future of democracy in this nation and in the world is bleak.[33]

8 Teaching for Social Justice in the Engaged Classroom

The Intersection of Jesuit and Feminist Moral Philosophies

KAREN L. SLATTERY, ANA C. GARNER,
JOYCE M. WOLBURG, AND LYNN H. TURNER

Jesuit and feminist educators, despite what ideological differences exist between them, embrace the moral necessity of teaching for social justice.[1] Teaching for social justice involves creating a pedagogy focused on improving the lives of those disenfranchised by the larger culture.[2] This common goal reflects similar core values and assumptions arrived at from two different ethical perspectives: Christian ethics and an ethic of care.[3] While Jesuits and feminists share this common ground, they teach in a culture in which the moral concept of justice dominates. The concept of justice assumes independence, equality, and reason, while Christian ethics and an ethic of care assume interdependence, reason, emotion, care, and love. The tension that arises from these conflicting assumptions has underscored the care-justice debate in feminist literature and has enormous implications for the teaching of social justice in Jesuit institutions. Yet this debate and its implications have not been examined from a pedagogical perspective.

Thus this chapter seeks to fill this void by weaving together the threads related to social justice, Christian ethics, and the ethic of care. In the process, we establish a framework within which to interrogate feminist and Jesuit pedagogical practices related to teaching for social justice. This framework allows us to determine how social justice–related concepts, including emotion, power, and self-reflexivity, might more effectively be taught in university classrooms.

Specifically, we do the following in this chapter: First, we offer a definition of social justice. Second, we explore the similarities in foundational assumptions that animate both care-based and Christian moral theories and contrast those with the assumptions that underpin justice-based moral theories. We draw on the commonalities between Christian-and care-based assumptions to frame our critique of pedagogical practices germane to teaching for social justice and its related concepts. Third, we present and offer a critique of an example of teaching for social justice that took place in an undergraduate communication course offered by a university instructor who describes herself as a feminist. The critique allows us to explore how the intersections of Jesuit and feminist moral thinking inform teaching for social justice and, in turn, how practices of teaching for social justice inform the shared theories and concepts of feminism and Jesuit education.

In our application, we pay particular attention to the concepts of emotion, power, and self-reflexivity. Emotion is important to consider because both Christian- and care-based moral perspectives, in direct contrast to Kantian and Rawlsian justice-based ethics, acknowledge that emotions play a critical role in moral reasoning. According to ethics of care philosopher Held, emotion provides "at least a partial basis for morality itself, and for moral understanding."[4] Both Christianity and care are concerned with conditions of vulnerability and inequality, which give rise to issues of power.[5] Emotion grounds empathy, which in turn allows us to see and understand vulnerability and inequality, that is, those conditions that give rise to issues of power.

Power is an important concept because feminist and Jesuit quests for social justice recognize that disenfranchised people possess much less power than other groups. Feminist and Christian traditions compel feminist teachers at Jesuit institutions to help students recognize and understand their social, economic, and political interrelationships to others and to motivate students to engage in action that addresses unequal relationships and other factors that systematically promote inequality within a culture. Instructors interested in teaching for social justice must find ways for students to recognize the relationship between intellect and emotion in moral decision making.

Finally, self-reflexivity is formative and necessary for effective action. Empathy is needed to understand the emotional connection to vulnerability, which then leads to the recognition of power inequities and, when coupled with self-reflexivity, enables social action and change. This chapter examines specifically how we translate Christian ethics and an ethic of care into pedagogical practices.

Social Justice

The term "social justice," scholars generally agree, is difficult to define precisely because definitions are relative to one's political, economic, and social perspectives; what some may perceive as just, others may perceive as unjust.[6] Rawls's work on distributive justice is viewed as a major contribution to contemporary Western thinking on the issue. He notes that justice is required when people with competing interests "press their rights on one another."[7] He anchors justice to the individual rather than to the overall well-being of the greatest number of members of society, as utilitarian philosophers did, and advocates equality of basic liberties and rights to the resources necessary for survival. Rawls argues that primary social goods, including income and wealth, should be equally distributed unless an unequal distribution is to everyone's advantage. Injustices arise when unequal distribution of primary social goods advantages some people and disadvantages others. Amid the vast literature responding to Rawls's conception of distributive justice, feminist scholars, in particular, have argued that the possession of material goods is not synonymous with well-being and have expanded the concept of primary goods to include the right to care.[8]

Frey, Pearce, Pollock, Artz, and Murphy moved us closer to understanding how to teach for social justice when they urged a shift away from the focus on a precise definition of the concept and toward the development of a "social justice sensibility."[9] They stipulated that social justice is the "engagement with and advocacy for those in our society who are economically, socially, politically and/or culturally underresourced."[10] A social justice sensibility, these scholars suggest, is "a sufficient guide for action" in most of the unjust circumstances that require people to react.[11] This sensibility is informed by four commitments. To develop the sensibility, one must first be willing to foreground ethical concerns when thinking about community. Second, one must commit to examining and resolving structural problems that cause or perpetuate injustice. Third, one must adopt an activist orientation toward resolving the social injustice. Finally, one must move beyond oneself and be open to identifying with the other. Frey and his colleagues caution against confusing social justice with kindness, charity, or hospitality. They also note that this sensibility is not impartial; emotion plays a role in recognizing and acting on perceived social injustices.

Embedded within this concept of social justice sensibility are themes common to both Christian ethics and an ethic of care, which, as noted, differ from justice-based ethics in significant ways. Before describing the tension between justice- and care-based ethics, we offer overviews of care- and Christian perspectives and point to the intersections between the two. Then we explore how feminists and Jesuits can work together to reduce this tension on a practical level.[12]

Christian and Care-Based Theories of Morality

Christian ethics is the study of morality that draws on Judeo-Christian tradition to frame moral matters. Within this theoretical tradition, Harkness identifies frames of reference within which the term "Christian ethics is used," which includes the ethical teachings of Jesus, the Bible, the New Testament, and the ethics of the Christian church.[13]

These frames share a similar grounding in the concept of Christian love that is selfless and spiritual. The Roman Catholic religion describes Christian love as more than just affect. The Holy See describes it as "the service that the Church carries out in order to attend constantly to man's sufferings and his needs, including physical needs."[14] Furthermore, these frames assume the interrelatedness of God and all human beings. Jesus underscored the value of relationships when he told the Pharisee that the greatest commandment is to "Love the Lord your God with all your heart and with all your soul and with all your mind." The second greatest commandment is to "Love your neighbor as yourself."[15]

Situated within Christian ethics, and of particular interest here, is Catholic social teaching, a set of social and moral principles developed in the Catholic Church's writings since the late 1800s that address its positions on economic, political, and cultural issues. These principles relate to the individual and how they relate to one another. The dignity of personhood, rights and responsibilities to others, participation in and promotion of the common good, economic justice, stewardship of God's creation, peace, and global solidarity are assumed by these principles.

Governments, according to Catholic social teaching, play a role in promoting the principles. These writings are rooted in scripture, as well as the Catholic Church's philosophy and theology.[16]

Jesuit pedagogy reflects the principles of Catholic social teaching. The Society of Jesus formally adopted the pursuit of social justice as part of its educational mission in 1975 at its Thirty-second General Congregation when it decreed that the Society's mission was "'the service of faith, of which the promotion of justice is an absolute requirement.'"[17] The mission has evolved since then to recognize that injustices are rooted in cultural attitudes and economic structures, and that social justice emerges when cultures transform through the "'liberating power of the Gospel.'"[18]

Christian ethics has been associated with the Christian church in its various forms. Likewise, the ethic of care, which has been associated with women's morality, is reflected in a range of perspectives. Here we will briefly address the contributions of three: the feminine, maternal, and feminist perspectives. The feminine perspective offers the ethic of care as a corrective for Western moral philosophers' disregard or trivialization of female characteristics or traits that inform moral thinking. Gilligan points out that mainstream moral philosophers have privileged male voice, which speaks in terms of abstractions, justice, rights, and rules.[19] She argues that women use a language stressing relationships, responsibilities, and contexts, identified by Tong as a language of care.[20]

The maternal approach to the problem of morality relates to this feminine perspective. Maternalists advance a model based on relationships as they appear in the private sphere (e.g., between a mother and her child) to frame moral thinking. This model is a corrective for the contractual model at the heart of most traditional Western moral theories. The contractual model draws from relationships as they occur in the public sphere (traditionally dominated by males), where relationships are assumed to be independent, anonymous, and equal. However, maternalists point out that, as a practical matter, most relationships occur within specific contexts and between people of unequal power, knowledge, and access to resources.[21] Humans, they argue, are contextualized and interdependent rather than independent in both private and public spheres.[22]

The feminist perspective, while sharing many values with the feminine and the maternal, emphasizes the political. Care, from this perspective, as Tronto, among others, argues, is revisioned as a concept that, along with justice, should inform decision making in the public sphere. This reflects feminism's commitment to eliminating those institutions, structures, and attitudes that subordinate women and others who are oppressed.[23] Feminist thinking, while inclusive of many different perspectives, including Marxism, multiculturalism, globalism, and ecofeminism, aims to advance social justice.

While feminine, maternal, and feminist perspectives differ in some ways, each has evolved in response to criticism of mainstream philosophies that systematically ignore the relevance of women's ways of thinking and knowing. Together, they advocate an ethical system that acknowledges the experiences of all men and women, including the poor and the oppressed, and one that addresses the importance of interdependence among human beings rather than independence. They argue against ideas that the most fully developed self is separated from, or independent of, others and that reality is most truthfully captured by knowledge that is rational, universal, and abstract.[24] For the purpose of convenience, we will refer to these approaches as "care-based" in the rest of this chapter.

This broad overview of care-based and Christian moral thinking sets the stage for us to examine the ways in which these two approaches to moral thought intersect. Understanding the intersections offers insight into how Jesuit and feminist instructors might work together to enhance teaching for social justice in higher education.

Intersections

Christian-based and care-based moral theories intersect on at least four important points: the concept of human interdependence, the emphasis on humans as relational beings, the acknowledgement of an interplay between emotion and reason in moral thinking, and the link between justice and care.

The first important similarity between care-based and Christian moral theories is the assumption of human interdependence, although each grounds the claim differently.

Care-based theories are grounded in a pragmatic naturalism perspective and assume human interdependence as given. Accordingly, the human subject is understood as living in relationships with others in community to survive. Infants, for example, begin life dependent on others to meet their basic human needs.[25] As Tronto states, "All humans have needs that others must help them meet."[26] The Christian tradition, in comparison, draws on spirituality, as opposed to material needs, to frame human interdependence. Yet similar to the care perspective, Christian spirituality assumes a caring God reflected in all of us as "persons in community who can enrich or impoverish the lives of those around us by our actions."[27]

Deeply connected to this assumption of interdependence is the second important similarity—a shared emphasis on relations to others. Catholic social teaching underscores relations between oneself and others when calling on all people to "consider one's every neighbor without exception as another self, taking into account first of all life and the means necessary to living it with dignity, so as not to imitate the rich man who had no concern for the poor man Lazarus."[28] Care theorists point out that our humanity is "mutual," and as humans, we are "already and potentially in relation."[29] Therefore, care must be "the most basic moral value."[30]

In addition to emphasizing interdependence and relationships, both Christian and care-based moral perspectives view the interplay between emotion and reason, rather than rationality alone, as necessary for the development of the complete person. Christianity emphasizes the interconnectedness of reason and emotion, and the primacy of Christian love. Freedom and rationality are necessary if we are to decide what kinds of persons we wish to become.[31] The Catholic Church posits that the will and intellect must be engaged if Christian love is to mature.[32]

Rationality is a necessary part of the process of caring for the other according to the ethic of care. Noddings argues that the "well-spring of human behavior is grounded in human affective response."[33] Caring does not diminish rationality and may in fact, Noddings contends, enhance care through instrumental thinking. At the very least, she says, rationality ought to be engaged when one cares for the other.

While emotion is viewed as a necessary component of morality, it is important to note that Christian- and care-based ethicists differ in their views of the exact nature of emotion at the core of moral development. Christian theologians argue that the emotion is Christian love, that is, the love of God reflected in all human beings. Care theorists such as Noddings alternatively argue that the basic human affect is joy, an emotion rooted in the concept of relatedness.[34] We note that an exploration of the distinction regarding the exact nature of the emotion or emotions that underpin moral development is important; however, it is beyond this chapter's scope.

Finally, the relationship between the concepts of care and justice commands the attention of Christian and feminist scholars. Theologians link justice to Christian love, arguing that the ideal of justice grows out of faith that is social and communal.[35] Joseph Daoust, S.J., points out that the scripture loosely situates the idea of justice with "love, compassion, and the fullness of peace."[36] In his encyclical letter *Deus Caritas Est*, Pope Benedict XVI writes that "love—*caritas*—will always prove necessary" even in the most just of states.[37] He further describes the Church's duty to the ideal of justice, saying that while the state has the responsibility of structuring a just society, the Church has an obligation to "contribute to the purification of reason and to reawakening of those moral forces without which just structures are neither established nor prove effective in the long run."[38]

At the same time, care theorists continue to examine the relationship between justice and care. Some argue that care and justice are separate ethics, while others reason that care must logically precede justice, for without care there would be no reason for justice.[39] Held argues that care, as the most basic moral value, offers the "the wider moral framework into which justice should be fitted."[40] Feminist scholars extend their analyses into many arenas of society, including culture, the professions, and politics.[41]

Intersections between Christian ethics and the ethic of care inform our understanding of how to teach for social justice, a topic that we take up next. Before doing so, we must point out that these shared values and assumptions contrast starkly with those underpinning traditional Western moral philosophies, often categorized as justice-based moral theories. Justice-based theories, including Kant's duty ethics and utilitarianism, assume that humans are independent of one another, moral reason is only rational, and emotion rarely, if ever, should factor into the moral equation. Relationships qua relationships, likewise, are not called into play when one is making moral decisions. Justice-based theories assume the impartial application of abstract moral principles to humans, who are, in theory, equal and autonomous. In contrast to this liberal paradigm of justice, however, we contend that the intersections between Christian and care-based ethics, particularly as they relate to interdependence and emotion, offer a powerful perspective from which to think about teaching for social justice.

The Practice of Teaching for Social Justice

It is not surprising, given the shared assumptions between Christian- and care-based moral theories outlined here, that Jesuit and feminist pedagogies also share important commonalities related to teaching for social justice. Both call attention to the roles of context, lived experience, the integration of emotion and reason, and action in the student-centered learning process. Intersections between the moral and pedagogical perspectives of Jesuit and feminist educators, therefore, offer a common place from which to examine pedagogical practices related to teaching for social justice sensibilities in Jesuit higher education and elsewhere. Here we apply the framework developed in the previous section to one of our experiences of teaching for social justice in a communication course.

We use as an example a class project in a multicultural/international advertising and public relations class offered at a Jesuit university. Students majoring in advertising or public relations who completed basic introductory courses are eligible to take the course, and the multicultural component typically includes a service-learning project, in which students gain real-world experience with a local client from an organization. The relationship between students and service-learning partners simulates that of an advertising/PR professional and client, with the students creating a product of value to the client.

The course instructor and the director of a Native American economic development organization collaborated on a project with an assignment aimed at overcoming barriers to successful fund-raising. The organization set a goal of increasing its funding from grants and contributions from individual sponsors and philanthropic organizations. The organization's leaders, however, recognized that many potential donors lack an understanding of their mission and harbor misperceptions of Native people, many of which are based on inaccurate stereotypes. Failure to address these misperceptions and a lack of understanding would jeopardize the fund-raising efforts.

The Native American project was designed to encourage learning on two levels. On an intellectual level, the assignment charged students with helping the organization and its Native American administrators with their promotional activities. Students could accomplish this by identifying misperceptions that could tarnish the organization's image in the community and by providing strategic solutions, given that reputation management is a common need of organizations. On an emotional level, the assignment challenged students to care. Presumably, this could occur if students gained a better understanding of Native American people, were touched by the oppression that this group experiences, and felt a connection with Native American people. This blending of goals aimed to help each student develop as a "whole person, head and heart, intellect and feelings," which follows the Ignatian worldview.[42]

To meet the Native American organization's goal of more effective fund-raising, each of the twenty students in the class read a first-person account by Native writers and then interviewed five non–Native American people about their perceptions of Native Americans. None of the one hundred interviewees identified themselves as Native Americans. Four of the students in the class were African American, three were Asian American, and one was Hispanic; the rest were Caucasian. Most students reported that prior to this assignment, they had had little to no contact with Native people, and that their understanding was informed by media images, stereotypes, and reports about conflicts over the Native American mascots of athletic teams.

Recognizing Emotional Dimensions of Learning

While classroom activities such as the Native American project provide intellectual stimulation and opportunities for rational thought, it is critical to acknowledge the role of emotion in the process and to recognize its relationship to cognition. As Guerrero, Andersen, and Trost note, "clearly emotional experience and expression is part of a fabric of thoughts, feelings, and behaviors that blend together to characterize the tapestry of interpersonal interaction."[43] The interaction in classrooms is no less grounded in the blend of emotion and reason.

We as educators, however, must recognize that universities traditionally value intellectual accomplishment more highly than emotional expression. When faculty members set goals that involve not only the head but also the heart, they often go beyond the stated learning outcomes that they are trained to assess—even in Jesuit universities and colleges. Thus, attempting to teach emotional intelligence in the classroom is a complex and difficult endeavor that students, some instructors, and the university may resist unless the campus culture explicitly supports it.

While this assignment provided participants an unanticipated opportunity to examine the relationship between emotion and cognition, the presence of intense emotion should have been expected. Rockquemore and Schaffer note that students progress through three stages of development during this type of learning experience: shock, normalization, and engagement.[44] These stages certainly bring emotion to the forefront in the classroom. In this case, the initial shock occurred when Native American people suddenly went from being *invisible* to *visible*. Despite the presence of a Native American–owned casino near campus, students vastly underestimated the number of Native people in the area. They were equally surprised at their lack of awareness of two Native American schools located within a two-mile radius of their campus and a Native American senior citizens' group that met at a church across from the university dental school. One student commented that it is as though Native Americans and non–Native Americans live in parallel universes with no intersections.

In this particular exercise, some classroom attempts to grapple with the emotion raised by the assignment brought about fruitful discussions, and others did not. Students eventually got past the initial shock and normalized their understanding of Native American people, but not all students reached the engagement stage, going beyond identifying social problems to developing a new understanding. Moments when students spontaneously raised questions usually generated more

insightful interactions than planned discussions, and critiques of negative perceptions were more powerful when delivered by students than
by the professor.

Dealing with issues that arouse intense emotion compels us to set
aside time in the classroom for discussion. It is often difficult, however,
to anticipate how open to discussion the students will be, how the
relationship between the teacher and students will evolve, and how
much insight will emerge. Discussions on sensitive topics are often
beyond the comfort level of many faculty and students, who may
remain silent out of fear of saying the wrong thing. Faculty members
must recognize that an open atmosphere where students can speak
without judgment is essential so that prejudicial attitudes can be critically evaluated. Professors also must recognize that they need to prepare for surprises and be flexible, striking a balance between emotion
and cognition.

Feminists and Jesuits recognize emotion and intellect as involved in
experience, which leads to action and, hopefully, social change. Understanding problems relating to emotion and reason is critical because
"reason working in our emotional life forces us to take our feelings as
an awareness of things outside us, as a consciousness of meaning and
value of things other than ourselves."[45]

Power Relations and Minority Audiences

Challenges related to power dynamics are clearly tied to the emotional
dimensions of learning in an engaged classroom. The issue of power
emerges from the assumption of interdependence, a hallmark of both
Catholic social teaching and the ethic of care. Relationships vary in
levels of equality. It follows that developing a social justice sensibility
requires one to explore issues associated with the imbalance of power.
In this particular exercise, the issue of power emerged in unexpected
places as students worked their way through the process.

First, the assignment inadvertently viewed the students and faculty
member as benevolent helpers, and the Native Americans from the
local community as those in need of help. Service-learning classes in
communication often partner with the clients of nonprofit organizations for class projects at the university. When partners are members

of minority groups, however, the potential for reinforcing feelings of superiority among the students and for perpetuating the unequal power relationships that accompany white privilege intensifies.[46] Students and faculty members often believe that helping a group such as Native Americans leads to a positive outcome because it engages students and teachers in altruistic behavior. However, this model—which can, arguably, be ego driven—risks reinforcing unequal power relationships, and encourages belief in a one-directional learning experience in which only the Native Americans, not the students and teachers, are helped and educated.

Interrogating the dynamics of helping (especially as it differs from partnering) is one means of advancing the discussion on power relationships. A class discussion that challenges students to think about who is actually being helped may actually create new ways of thinking. For instance, Jesuits argue that learning experiences such as the one examined here are two-way experiences. As members of the "middle-class tribe," most students live in a world where they are too distanced from the life-and-death struggle that is the daily fare of the poor.[47] They see the poor as marginalized when, in fact, the marginalized are really at the center of things. As Dean Brackley, S.J., maintains, the middle and upper classes actually need the victims of oppression—the poor, abused women and children, racial and sexual minorities, and prisoners—more than the latter need the former, because they reveal both "the horror of evil in the world and the possibility for a more human way of living together."[48]

Second, this assignment may have unintentionally reified unequal power relationships between students and their client. When students submitted their collected interview data, it was clear that some very negative perceptions existed among the one hundred members of the larger community who had been interviewed, none of whom reported themselves to be Native American. Two perceptions stood out: the belief that Native Americans have become wealthy from running casinos and the contrasting view that Native American people are unemployed alcoholics living in poverty. Some participants interviewed were sympathetic in regard to the oppression that Native Americans experience. Others, however, expressed resentment that Native Americans receive too many "handouts" from the U.S. government, are powerless to take control of their lives, and have taken political correctness to an extreme with their sensitivity to university mascots that derive from Native American traditions (e.g., the Warriors, Fighting Illini).

Course readings and interviews, though intended to connect students to a minority group in a positive way, may have had the negative effect of reinforcing harmful stereotypes or, worse, creating them where none previously existed. Judging from the commentary on their interviews, some students clearly bought into their interviewees' inaccurate views, perhaps because the interviews offered a more accessible perspective and, therefore, one more real to students than the Native American first-person accounts they read for class.

Students were required to present their interview findings to the client, a task that might have required greater sensitivity than the students possessed. It was unclear how the findings themselves would be received—whether the harsh perceptions of the community would come as a surprise or whether they would confirm what the Native Americans already knew from experience. Clearly, the delivery of this information would require sensitivity. Otherwise, students might appear egotistical, arrogant, and prejudiced.

These power issues must be addressed because both the Jesuit and feminist traditions call upon us as faculty, when teaching for social justice, to confront issues; thus passing up important teaching moments is not an option for the Jesuit feminist classroom.[49] Jesuit universities and colleges are charged with providing students with significant intellectual training and morally preparing them "to change the world when they leave the university."[50] To be morally prepared requires, according to Brackley, an understanding of the world's suffering, its causes, and possible solutions. It also means caring about others.

Although an understanding of the world's suffering and its causes helps people to be morally prepared, faculty and students may need additional tools in order to confront power issues such as those discussed here openly. A class discussion about how students balanced interviewees' perspectives against their own as well as the first-person Native American accounts served as a first step in confronting power issues. However, the issues arose so unexpectedly that more work was needed to unpack all the nuances of the experience. In particular, discussions of how students felt changed as a result of the process were required.

One possible solution may lie in the concept of attentiveness, which requires the recognition of one's own need for care and the care-related needs of another.[51] An exploration of care of the self may put students in the position of having their own needs met by those who are receivers of care, resulting in a two-way exchange. If the concept of attentiveness and self-care were applied as a starting point, it would place the care-giver and care-receiver in the same space at the same time. This could lead to a shift in the balance of power and require systematic attention to emotions and self-reflexivity. In this case, the instructor unwittingly approached the class exercise from Rawls's liberal distributive justice paradigm, which focuses on rationality as opposed to emotion. Changing the beginning pedagogical stance to a care-based ethic, which includes attention to self-care, might have been a way of avoiding some of these difficulties.

Addressing these issues can be particularly difficult for faculty with no training in teaching people to care. They can set an example of caring and offer students the opportunity to be touched by the people with whom they interact. Yet some students will predictably regard the assignment as merely an intellectual exercise. For them, the Native American assignment was no different from other exercises about managing a client's reputation. Such assignments offer great opportunities for students to learn to engage with and care about the Other and ultimately learn to share power. There are no guarantees, however, that meaningful learning will occur.

Self-Reflexivity in Engaged Learning

Self-reflexivity, or evaluation, is an important part of the transformation process. This step leads to "a deeper understanding of how one's experience relates to the lives of others."[52] This part of the process enhances the integrity and wholeness of a person and the person's connections with others, which, in turn, can lead to social justice.[53]

Self-reflexivity is a significant goal; however, as with the challenge of teaching students to care, exerting control over how, when, and to what extent it occurs is not easy. Teaching students to engage in self-reflexivity requires that faculty members give up some control in the classroom and engage in difficult discussions. However, it also depends upon students' willingness to be introspective and honest with themselves. Confronting one's own prejudices and correcting stereotypical attitudes toward others can be painful.

One class session during the Native American project spontaneously generated some discussion about the level of responsiveness on the client's part, which directly led to a degree of self-reflexivity among some class members. During this class period, a student expressed criticism of the client's time commitment to the project and the amount of time he took to answer the students' questions. After a brief discussion, the faculty member defended the client by making note of the client's extensive involvement in meetings in the planning stages of the project, suggesting that the client's commitment to the project extended beyond what students were able to see. Though it was unintentional, this exchange probably sent the message to the class that the student's criticism of the client was incorrect. More important, the student's comment may have related to the larger and more complex issue of gratitude. When work is driven by altruism, the "helpers" usually expect some degree of gratitude from those who are "helped." The student's comment may have been an expression of frustration that the client had not shown proper gratitude. Going beyond the surface complaint and examining what was really happening could have led to a more fruitful discussion regarding students' expectations of gratitude, as well as a moment of reflection about different expectations for clients who are minority members.

Because the exchange was unplanned and occurred on a day when other course material needed to be covered, the discussion was cut short. Students, as a result, lacked enough time to explore the criticism, and the instructor realized too late that she had lost a valuable teaching moment. Such discussions provoke anxiety because faculty members do not have the power to prevent students from making disparaging comments. The instructor's real concern at the time was that the criticism of the client's action would be taken as one of the individual and, in turn, Native Americans in general. The reaction in such situations might be to try to maintain order and respect for the client, particularly if the client is the member of another race. However, the temptation to close the discussion and move on to a safer topic silences a voice that should be heard, precisely because it reflects a genuine although uncomfortable position. When these thoughts are spoken out loud, the student's voice conveys a concrete idea with which the instructor can deal. Left unspoken, the idea remains but is inaccessible and therefore potentially more damaging.

The responsibility to foster self-reflexivity in the engaged classroom rests on the instructor's shoulders, and first attempts at working through these pedagogical issues are predictably imperfect. Despite the lack of in-depth class discussions on issues such as the client's perceived commitment, some students engaged in self-reflection on their own, as evidenced by comments in their course evaluations. Furthermore, some students continued working with the organization through independent studies the following semester, and one pursued a summer job with the organization. Those who embraced what the Native American people could teach them benefited from the two-directional learning process, and engaging in self-reflexivity further enabled their personal transformation.

This class project and others like it, from the Jesuit perspective, encourage students to let the reality of others into their lives so that they can, in part, feel it and critically think about others in ways that help achieve social justice.[54] Similarly, a feminist approach to pedagogy focuses on the whole person and strives to enhance students' connections with others. As Shrewsbury states, feminist pedagogy "requires continuous questioning and making assumptions explicit, but it does so in a dialogue aimed not at disproving another person's perspective, nor destroying the validity of another's perspective, but as a mutual exploration of explications of diverse experiences."[55]

The demands of feminist and Jesuit perspectives can be difficult for faculty and students. Fear of rejection and retaliation for personal views about gender, race, ethnicity, social class, and sexual orientation can run quite high. These fears are especially apparent in classroom situations where the racial and gender composition of the students is mixed. At predominately white universities and colleges, where students of color are definite minorities in a classroom, these fears can promote student silence and faculty reluctance to confront difficult issues that need to be addressed. Issues of power, discrimination, representation, prejudice, and privilege come to the forefront and often challenge students' sense of identity and position within their communities. These issues likewise challenge a faculty member's own comfort level in deal-ing with these sensitive matters in an empathetic and caring, yet peda-gogically responsible, manner.

Within feminist and Jesuit pedagogical approaches, discussion of the topics of race, gender, and class requires that courses function as semi-nars that actively encourage discussion, reflection, and the exchange of views. Working with minority groups can be an especially effective way to encourage students to begin talking, sharing, and reflecting upon their position within the larger culture vis-à-vis those different from themselves. Illustrating that everyone has a stake in the outcome helps move discussions from personal stances to the larger issues in question.

Conclusions

Jesuit and feminist educators are charged with teaching for social jus-tice in Jesuit institutions of higher learning. These institutions are situ-ated in a larger culture in which justice-based theories of ethics that presuppose independence and equality dominate. These presupposi-tions create tension for Jesuit and feminist teachers, since their philo-sophical underpinnings assume human interdependence. This tension manifests itself in pedagogical practices. The common ground between Jesuit and feminist approaches offers a place to begin exploring ways to ameliorate such tensions and enhance teaching for social justice.

Our exploration of these intersections of Christian- and care-based ethics offers a solid position from which we offered a critique of an example of teaching for social justice by a feminist in a Jesuit classroom. We discovered that, in the teaching process, issues of emotion, power, and self-reflexivity were inescapable. For instance, a project designed to make students aware of social stereotypes and power relations with Native Americans may have inadvertently reinforced stereotypes and reified inequitable power relations for some students. We also noted the difficulties of addressing emotion, particularly when Native Americans became visible to students for the first time. Finally, we identified the difficulties in helping students learn to be self-reflective. Sometimes self-reflection occurred without specific action, and other times it fal-tered, despite the instructor's best intentions to foster the process. Fur-thermore, although we examined emotion, power, and self-reflexivity as discrete elements, we recognize their interconnectedness as they relate theoretically and practically to social justice. We suggested how theory can inform practice, so we now turn our attention to how practice can inform theory.

In the process of reflecting on this experience, it became apparent that faculty members can only go so far in solving problems related to emotion, power, and self-reflexivity in the classroom, given that each problem reflects issues too large for a single teacher to address. These issues must be engaged at the institutional level if helping students effectively develop social justice sensibilities is to become a reality. With this in mind, we propose institutional self-reflexivity and action in the following three areas: furthering the knowledge and understanding of emotion, the development of pedagogies appropriate to disseminating that knowledge, and the understanding of how justice and care relate.

First, we advocate scholarship and intellectual inquiry within the academy directed toward uncovering the knowledge of emotion. MacMurray points out that moral behavior depends on the "absolute value of human beings as free human spirits," not as male or female, child or adult, black or white, or young or old.[56] Part of the human spirit, he argues, has an emotional core, so being human requires a clear understanding of our intellectual *and* emotional selves.[57] Intellectual or rational approaches to the problems of social justice are not enough. Relational thinking as it applies to our emotional beings must be developed in order to bring about social justice grounded in care and spiritual love.

A true understanding of emotional knowledge should be on the university's research agenda, much the way that science has been for the last several centuries. Further, the subject of emotion should not be housed in women's studies departments or taught in an occasional philosophy course by a part-time instructor or in the psychology department, where it is treated as a variable that must be defined, categorized, isolated, and tested. Emotional knowledge as it relates to our physical and spiritual beings ought to permeate the entire university curriculum, particularly since we are told that the "central core of our experience is seeking to accept one another and to be accepted for what we are, so that we may be ourselves and express ourselves for one another."[58] That process requires a genuine emotional understanding of the significance of subjects outside ourselves. Such understanding and knowledge lead to genuine communion with others, which in turn evolves into friendship, cooperative living, society, and community. Within this sort of communion, social justice may flourish.

Second, if emotion, as some argue, is central to moral thinking, then developing pedagogies that foster meaningful engagements with emotion within the learning environment becomes imperative. In the short term, instructors must continue to rely on intuition and a willingness to take risks. The long term, however, requires a genuine commitment to fostering social justice sensibilities based on a knowledge of how to teach intellectual *and* emotional skills and knowledge.

Third, we insist on the pressing need to examine the relationship between justice and care. The theory of justice spelled out by Rawls, which accounts for much of our society's thinking about justice, does not account for care or emotion as do Christian- and care-based ethics. Rawls locates the starting point for justice within the individual on the assumption that individuals are autonomous and independent—not in relation to one another.[59] Rawls's theory of justice does not account for Christian love or care and its relationship to human well-being. We have identified bodies of thought that link care and justice, but the work in this area is incomplete. Certainly, scholars from Okin and Tronto to Kittay and Sevenhuijsen as well as Jacobson and Sawatsky and Daoust have explored the implications of the Christian- and care-based ethics from philosophical and theoretical perspectives. This debate, however, is not fully developed.

We encourage the academy to examine this argument further. We encourage Jesuit institutions of higher learning to put that problem before its faculty and students and ask for their best thinking. Theoretical and pedagogical questions such as "When might the individualism and rationality of the justice paradigm offer a counterbalance to the challenges of a caring paradigm?" and "How does justice inform caring practices in the classroom?" deserve to be asked and answered. We believe that the importance of the linkage between care and justice and its implications for understanding and teaching for social justice cannot be underestimated.

As a final note, we argue that Jesuit universities and colleges must continually engage in self-reflexivity about linking the theory of social justice with practice within their own institutions. If the institutions in which students are trained model injustice in any of their own behaviors, then one must ask whether it is reasonable to expect young men and women to move into the larger world and seek justice for all. Jesuit institutions must ensure that faculty genuinely understand Jesuit moral and teaching philosophies. Likewise, those who work within these institutions of higher learning must be willing to hear the voices of others, including feminist instructors. For it is only with a shared understanding of one another that we will realize our best efforts to provide opportunities for the transformation of students into men and women in service for others.

9 Transformative Education
in a Broken World

*Feminist and Jesuit Pedagogy
on the Importance of Context*

THERESA WEYNAND TOBIN

In a recent ethics class, my students and I were discussing the Civil Rights Act, in particular Title VII, on equal employment opportunity. This portion of the Civil Rights Act makes it illegal to discriminate in employment practices on the basis of race, color, religion, national origin, or sex. The class was considering whether or not sexual orientation ought to be added to the list. In some places it remains legal to fire someone simply because of his or her sexual orientation. We were considering whether or not this is fair and consistent with a principled commitment to the moral equality of all human beings. The discussion was proceeding fairly well, with some differences of opinion being expressed in a respectful manner, until one young man raised his hand and made the following comment: "We should not protect homosexual persons from discrimination because homosexuals are pedophiles, and we don't think we should protect them, right?" There were some audible gasps of shock among other students at this young man's comment, but the most dramatic response came from a openly gay young woman who spent the rest of the class in tears—angry, offended, and deeply hurt by this remark.

What Went Wrong?

As the instructor, I was really upset by this experience, in large part because a student got hurt in my classroom. I was seriously concerned about the pain that this young woman had endured and the breach of trust that had occurred in our classroom community. One of the central goals of philosophy is to teach students critical thinking skills, and so many people with whom I consulted about the experience commented that perhaps it was a "teachable moment," an opportunity to critically interrogate this line of reasoning as a class. While I am sympathetic to this view, this experience raised difficult questions for me about how to balance the goal of critical thinking about socially relevant topics with a genuine respect for each of our students, especially when the topics we discuss may touch the personal lives, indeed the very identities, of our students.

At the outset of the course, I had explained to my students that we would periodically be discussing socially relevant and contentious topics in this class. We had worked extremely hard to build a safe classroom environment where all students would feel comfortable sharing their views. I had stressed that listening to opposing viewpoints is an essential part of the process of growing in moral wisdom. I had also stressed repeatedly that we live out *cura personalis* in the classroom by treating each other with dignity and respect, especially when expressing opposing viewpoints. Up to this point, classroom discourse had been going quite well. What went wrong?

Recent work in feminist pedagogy helped me diagnose the problem as a failure to attend to a particular aspect of the learning context that feminists call positionality.[1] Part of what went wrong in my class was a failure to consider the ways in which the context of the teaching and learning environment, in particular the heteronormative and heterosexist features of that context, was influencing not only individual students' perceptions, beliefs, and intuitions but also relationships of relative power and privilege among students. The social structures that continue to marginalize gay men and lesbians were replicated at the micro-level in my classroom, locating the straight male in a relative position of power and authority in relation to the gay female. By considering only the ways in which social context influences my students *as individuals*, I was failing to account for the unequal social relations both within and outside the classroom that continue to disadvantage those students who are members of marginalized groups and to inhibit the goal of transformative education, a goal toward which both feminist and Jesuit pedagogy aim. While feminist and Jesuit pedagogy both emphasize the importance of context, feminists pay special attention to the ways in which context affects relationships among students. In this chapter, I explore the ways in which a feminist emphasis on positionality can enrich Jesuit pedagogy and facilitate the goal of transformative education.

Jesuit Pedagogy on the Importance of Context

One expression of the Jesuit commitment to transformative education is the graduation of "men and women of competence, conscience and compassion, seeking . . . to enhance the quality of people's lives, particularly among God's poor, oppressed and neglected."[2] While I remain deeply committed to this ideal, my recent classroom experience prompted difficult questions about how to achieve the goal of transformative education in a non-ideal setting, namely, a classroom context that is itself shaped by the kinds of injustices we aim to combat. One of the Ignatian paradigm's central concepts for education is attention to the context within which teaching and learning take place. Like all aspects of Ignatian pedagogy, the emphasis on context derives from the Spiritual Exercises. Ignatius believed that spiritual direction would not be fruitful if the director did not first get to know, as well as possible, the retreatant's predisposition to prayer and to God. He emphasized that a person's life experience, the real-world context within which the individual is situated and that influences his or her beliefs, perceptions, values, and relationships, should determine the shape and content of the spiritual exercises that are used.[3] Similarly, Jesuit education, which aims to be transformative, requires that teachers become as familiar as possible with the life experiences of their students, that we "meet them where they are," and that we be attentive to the real-world context within which teaching and learning take place. Attention to context means accounting for the influence of "family, peers, social situations, the educational institution itself, cultural climate, the ecclesial situation, media, music and other realities," all of which have an impact on students, for better or worse.[4]

Ignatian pedagogy stresses at least four levels of context that we must consider: the larger social context, current ecclesial context, institutional context of our particular university or college, and context of our individual classrooms. These levels of context are distinct but intimately related and in any particular instance they may be either mutually reinforcing or in tension with one another. First, attention to context requires that we understand as well as possible the socioeconomic, political, and cultural aspects of the larger social context. What's going on in contemporary American life, in politics and pop culture?

What are the nationwide disparities between rich and poor, and from which socioeconomic classes do our students come? Do they come from relative privilege or poverty, and how might these factors affect any particular student's learning experience? A student's socioeconomic background may, for example, influence her expectations about academic success, or a particular political environment may make freedom of expression about certain topics difficult for some students.[5]

Additionally we must account for the institutional environment of our particular university or college as both Jesuit and Catholic. We need to be familiar with the complex networks of norms and expectations within the university setting, the culture of teaching and learning that our particular Jesuit institution promotes. Is it an environment that promotes trust and respect for others despite differences of opinion? Moreover, what is the ecclesial situation at the present time and how might this influence the learning ethos of our particular institution as Catholic and as likely serving a large number of Catholic students? Finally, attention to context requires awareness of the ways in which each of these levels of context shapes the beliefs, values, concepts, and perceptions that students bring to the start of the learning process in our individual classrooms.

One aspect of context that helps make sense of what happened in my classroom is the heteronormativity and heterosexism influential at every level: the larger social context of American culture, current ecclesial context of the Catholic Church, institutional setting of my particular university, and individual classroom in which this incident occurred. The term "heteronormative," refers to the idea that sexual and marital relations are normal only when they involve two persons, one of each sex; and that heterosexuality is the only normal sexual orientation. "Heterosexism" here refers to various forms of bias, prejudice, and discrimination against persons who are not exclusively heterosexual. Much like racism and sexism, heterosexism can be more or less overt, and it can manifest either at the level of individuals in interpersonal relations or at the level of institutions in either formal rules and policies or informal social norms and expectations.[6] While an individual can behave in a heterosexist manner (in much the same way that an individual can behave in a racist manner), heterosexism does not necessarily reflect one individual's malicious intent to harm

another person. Rather, it often refers to systemic and structural prejudice that generates and maintains oppression in a myriad of ways, ranging from job discrimination to harassment, political disempowerment,
and brutal and life-threatening hate crimes.

Heteronormativity and heterosexism are logically distinct concepts.
That is, heteronormativity does not logically entail heterosexism. However, in reality they are often closely linked: In a context governed
by heteronormativity, people tend to produce and replicate political,
economic, and moral structures that are heterosexist. One reason for
this is that what is considered normal functions not just as a term
describing how most people allegedly are but also as a prescriptive term
setting a moral and cultural standard and leading people to treat those
who deviate from this standard as deviants (and so as inferior, less than,
threatening, morally corrupt), rather than just different. Despite an
increase in the more visible presence of gays and lesbians and relationships in American pop culture, for example, in TV shows such as *Will
and Grace* or movies such as *Brokeback Mountain*, heteronormativity
and heterosexism continue to shape the larger social context of American life. One can see this in political disputes over gay marriage, in
general public disapproval of and disgust at public figures who "turn
out" to be gay, in pronouncements by prominent religious leaders con-
demning gays and lesbians as moral abominations, in resistance by
many people to even consider protecting gays and lesbians from various
forms of discrimination, such as job discrimination, and in the preponderance of hate crimes perpetrated against gays and lesbians.

Moreover, with respect to the current ecclesial situation, though
some Church leaders condemn heterosexism, heteronormativity is the
very foundation of Catholic moral teaching about sexual identity and
norms about what constitutes morally permissible sexual relationships.[7]
And though the Church hierarchy does not draw an explicit connection
between homosexuality and pedophilia, they have sometimes implied a
connection in their response to the scandal of sexual abuse in the
Church by banning gay men from entering the seminary.[8]

In such a context, it is no surprise that some of my students hold
the view that homosexuality is a perversion and that gays and lesbians
are sexual deviants who cannot be trusted and who, like pedophiles, do

not deserve the same civil protections that the rest of us enjoy. However, Jesuit emphasis on the importance of context prompted deeper reflection on my part about how deeply entrenched heteronormativity is, and about just how much our students unreflectively absorb and perpetuate the heterosexism they see in the media and in the words and deeds of political figures, religious leaders, their parents, and their peers. Moreover, given that sexual orientation is not necessarily a "visible" identity, attention to context requires a heightened awareness of the possibility that diversity in the classroom may include diversity in sexual orientation and that discussions of topics that touch on this issue may evoke strong feelings and touch very deeply and personally the lives of some of our students.

This does not mean that we ought to avoid these topics. Graduating men and women who are ready, willing, and able to work toward a more just world requires tackling in the classroom the most blatant forms of injustice present in the world. What attention to context requires is that we create a classroom environment that is conscious of the contextual factors that shape people's identities and beliefs, and that we tread carefully and perhaps delicately in conversations that are so important but also may be so personal for some students.

While I wholeheartedly endorse the Ignatian emphasis on context as the starting point for transformative teaching and learning, I believe the Ignatian model remains somewhat limited in its ability to capture accurately what happened in my classroom and to generate adequate pedagogical responses to these sorts of incidents. As I understand it, attention to context is essentially about attention to identity. The call to know who our students are and where they are coming from is a call to know, as well as possible, the particular identities of our students as they are shaped by the various levels of context, and to allow these identities to inform as much as possible what we teach and how we teach it. Yet there are different ways of understanding the nature of identity. The Ignatian approach stresses how context at both the micro- and macro-levels may affect the beliefs, attitudes, perceptions, and intuition of each student considered *as an individual*. While this approach is worthwhile, its failure to highlight the way that context shapes relationships among students, and to address how relational aspects of identity limit its effectiveness. I now examine how feminist pedagogy can enrich Jesuit approaches to education and facilitate the goal of transformative education.

Feminist Pedagogy on Positionality

Feminist and Jesuit pedagogy overlap in many ways. Both view education as a transformative enterprise aimed at graduating men and women who are intellectually, emotionally, and morally prepared to work toward establishing a more just world. Both approaches also stress that transforming the world must start with personal transformation, and that personal transformation cannot happen without attention to context. As bell hooks comments about her teaching, "Whether a class is large or small, I try to talk with all students individually or in small groups so that I have a sense of their needs. How can we transform consciousness if we do not have some sense of where the students are intellectually, psychically?"[9] Nonetheless, despite the significant overlap, feminist and Jesuit approaches diverge in how they understand the nature of identity.

Ignatian pedagogy clearly recognizes that social context is relevant to an individual's identity formation. This is precisely why we need to understand the various contexts our students inhabit. However, the Jesuit model tends to presuppose a conception of the student that makes his or her identity a function of a particular set of characteristics that attach to the student as an individual. On this model, the classroom is viewed as a collection of equally situated individuals, each of whom may have a unique set of beliefs and values shaped by the social and cultural contexts he or she inhabits. The Ignatian emphasis on identity directs us to approach our students on an individual basis. When I attend to context, I attend to the ways in which various levels of context shape and affect my students qua individuals.

In contrast, feminists understand identity not as a fixed set of characteristics that an individual has but as relational and shifting, depending on context. The feminist conception of relational identity has its roots in feminist ethics, beginning most notably with Carol Gilligan's groundbreaking work on moral development, *In a Different Voice*, which gave rise to what is known as the ethics of care. The ethics of care emerged initially as a feminist response to a long history of claims in Western philosophy and psychology that women's moral capacities are inferior to men's capacities and that women are somehow less capable than men of moral maturity and development. Gilligan purports to demonstrate that women are not morally deficient, but rather that they often view moral problems from a different perspective, or in a "different voice," which she called a care perspective.[10] The justice perspective associated with the dominant moral paradigms of modern Western philosophy and society emphasizes independent, self-sufficient, discrete individuals who resolve moral dilemmas by applying abstract universal moral rules or principles. Gilligan found that the women she interviewed tended instead to emphasize the moral salience of relationships, to highlight the moral significance of dependence and interdependence, and to promote the moral value of care.[11]

While the ethics of care focuses on interpersonal relationships, more recent feminist work shows the significance of relational aspects of selfhood and identity for political and structural contexts.[12] For example, Iris Marion Young draws on Stephen Epstein's understanding of identity as "a socialized sense of individuality. . . . Identity is constituted relationally, through involvement with—and incorporation of—significant others and integration into communities."[13] According to Young, some of the most salient aspects of an individual's identity result from his or her membership in certain social groups and from interactions among social groups. Young distinguishes social groups from aggregates and associations. Grouping people on the basis of their zip code might be an aggregate. Examples of associations include neighborhood or parent organizations and religious groups. Social groups differ from aggregates in that they are more than just a mere collection or grouping of people based on some arbitrary shared feature or trait.[14] Social groups then differ from associations in that they are not formally organized institutions that people independently and freely choose to join. As Young notes, social groups differ from these in that "one *finds* oneself as a member of a group, whose existence and relations one experiences as always already having been. For a person's identity is defined in relation to how others identify him or her, and they do so in terms of specific attributes, stereotypes, and norms associated with them, in reference to which a person's identity will be formed."[15] In Young's analysis, social identity is a function of social relations. Identity is not simply a matter of how context influences the beliefs, values, and capacities an individual *has*; it is also a result of how others perceive and treat the person and how he or she perceives him- or herself in relation to others. These variable perceptions are mitigated in large part by social group membership and relations.

Most important, for our purposes, feminists emphasize relational aspects of identity as absolutely essential for understanding the nature of oppression. Characterizing the nature of identity as relational rather than individualistic allows us to see how oppression and privilege are also relational. Laurie Finke, a professor of women's studies and gender studies at Kenyon College, draws on Julia Kristeva's work to explain this idea to her students. Finke notes, "What we need is a description that is not based on categories but, as Kristeva says, on positionality, on relations. No group is in and of itself oppressed or marginal. It is only in relation to something else. So . . . for instance, we can say that women are marginal compared to men. But Black women are marginal compared to white, middle class women. What is perceived as marginal at any given time depends on the position one occupies."[16] On this view, identity, and whether or not one is oppressed or privileged in particular contexts as a result of her identity, is a matter of not merely the beliefs and attitudes an individual *has* but also her social position relative to others.

Starting from a relational rather than individualistic understanding of identity, feminists emphasize a feature of the teaching and learning context called positionality, which involves locating the self in relation to others within social structures that re-create and mediate those relationships. This approach allows us to see that students' identities are extremely complex and shift depending on context. Attention to positionality requires us to locate our students in relation to one another within a particular set of social structures that govern a particular context. The larger social and ecclesial contexts within which our universities are embedded and which are shaped by heteronormativity, and often also by heterosexism, position the heterosexual male in a space of relative power and privilege in relation to the gay female, especially in regard to epistemic authority and power to be perceived as a credible interlocutor. So the larger context does not just affect the particular beliefs, perceptions, and values that individual students bring to the start of the learning process; it has an impact on the relationships among students in the classroom.

Understanding the positional features of context requires teachers to examine how relationships of domination and subordination between members of oppressed and privileged groups in larger social and ecclesial contexts are re-created at the micro-level in the classroom, and how these relationships affect the acquisition of knowledge, including what views will be taken seriously, who has the authority to speak and be heard, and who has power to cause real moral harm. Accounting for positional features of context involves locating particular perspectives, views, or experiences that students might share in larger historical, cultural, religious, and economic contexts, to understand not only why an individual student may hold a particular view but also how unequal social relationships governing contexts outside the classroom automatically place some students at the center and others at the margins of the classroom.

What feminists draw our attention to is that the nature of oppression is relational and that oppression is manifest in and maintained by broken relationships. If I only focus on how context influences the realities and identities of my students as individuals (i.e., how it affects the beliefs, perceptions, and values each individual student brings to the start of the learning process) but fail to attend to the way context shapes relationships, I am in danger of fostering a classroom atmosphere where the broken relationships that underscore oppressive structures in larger social contexts are replicated and reinforced in the context of my classroom.

To use Young's language, the Jesuit paradigm implies a view of the classroom as an aggregate, or perhaps an association—a space made up of equally situated individuals with different starting points who come together in a classroom setting for sixteen weeks to explore a particular subject together. On the basis of this view, attention to context prompts me to get to know as well as possible each student's starting points. Moreover, from the perspective of viewing the classroom as an association, my response to this incident ought to have been to use this experience as a teachable moment. When a questionable view is put forth in the classroom, we should draw out the reasons for holding the view and, as a class, scrutinize the view, exposing whatever flaws in reasoning may be sustaining it. I do think this is a useful strategy in many circumstances, and I also think it is important to attend to individual aspects of our students' identities. But a student got hurt in my classroom. Viewing the classroom as an association of equally situated individuals obscures how social relations of power can be reinforced in our classrooms and cause real harm.

Feminist work on positionality encourages us to see that the social relations of oppression and privilege that inform larger contexts do not disappear when our students enter the classroom. Attention to positionality directs us to view the classroom as comprising social groups, the members of which may be situated in positions of unequal social power. The incident in my classroom was not just about an individual holding and expressing an offensive view; rather, it was a manifestation of the daily realities that many gay men and lesbians experience, which reinforces their marginalization in relation to heterosexual persons and culture. This classroom enactment of oppression reinforced the heterosexism that shaped the context in the first place. Even though I believe I was able to facilitate this young man's reflection on what he had said and why it was harmful, and to see that there is no good evidence to support the view that gay men and women are pedophiles, I left untouched the relational/positional aspects of the context. Yet it is precisely the relational/positional aspects of the context that help explain, at least in part, the harm this young woman suffered. The young man was not a malicious individual intending to offend, and in the end, he did come to understand why a gay man or lesbian might be offended by his remarks. Yet he had no conception of his positionality in a relative position of privilege and power vis-à-vis this young woman in this context. Interestingly, however, the young woman who was so hurt by this experience understood her positionality quite well. She articulated her constant struggle to be genuinely listened to and heard in the face of stereotypes and prejudices that, from the outset, give her less credibility in public discourse, including classroom settings.

Thinking about positionality also prompted me to ponder my own identity and the social relations that mitigate interactions between me and my students. Both the feminist and Jesuit pedagogy literature tend to be so student focused that they can render the presence of the teacher invisible. Yet teachers must also negotiate their identities in the classroom vis-à-vis their students in order to effectively engage students. This feature of the classroom context became crystal clear for me during this incident. My first response to this incident was to freeze; I was initially immobilized by not knowing how to respond, and I recall feelings of anger and fear. I believe part of my initial reaction had to do with certain positional aspects of my own identity as a young woman in a position (i.e., philosophy professor) still stereotypically associated with men, and as a Catholic and a feminist who often struggles to negotiate these two identities, which are not always obviously compatible. Interestingly, in the end, I believe my identity as a young Catholic and feminist woman played an important role in my ability to relate to both the young man who made the offensive comments and the young woman who was deeply hurt by them. Even though I did not manage at the time to address adequately the relational/positional aspects of the classroom, upon reflection I came to see that my positional identity did enable me to understand the power relations at work in this context and provide access to relationships of trust that allowed me to engage effectively with both of these students after the fact.

Positionality is an essential component of any approach to education that attempts to transform society by transforming the individual, because it focuses our attention on relationships. The brokenness of our world is, in large part, a function of broken relationships. As we diversify our universities and classrooms, we increasingly invite these broken relationships into the classroom. This is a good thing, but it means that we need to think about how to develop and implement pedagogies that do not inadvertently reinforce those broken relationships. Feminist emphasis on positionality invites us to pay explicit attention to these broken relationships at the micro-level and to devise pedagogies that facilitate students' awareness of their own positional locations.

The classroom setting offers a unique opportunity for students to see where they sit in the larger contexts that generate and perpetuate oppression and injustice in the world and to examine not only how their positionality influences their individual beliefs and perceptions but also how they interact with and treat other people, especially people situated on the margins of any particular context. One function of privilege is to make privilege invisible; making relationships of privilege and power visible and coming to know where one is positioned in those relationships are an essential part of transformative education. I believe attention to positionality is an absolutely crucial component of transformative education because transforming the world requires seeing the ways in which we are part of that which we aim to transform; it more intimately links the personal and the political.

Practical Strategies for and Obstacles to Positional Pedagogies

I am a philosopher who teaches courses primarily in ethics and feminism, and I am just beginning to think about how to develop and implement positional pedagogies in my classes. One crucial point is that implementing positional pedagogies means going well beyond diversifying the curriculum. Teresa McKenna argues persuasively that diversifying our universities must not be limited to merely incorporating a variety of diverse alternative texts into the curriculum.[17] As she puts it, "to change the lists is not sufficient. If the subjectivities of teacher and student are not questioned, exposed, integrated into the process of the classroom, then the 'reading' or even 'rereading' of texts will not make a qualitative difference."[18] In other words, transformative education requires more than simply exposing our students to a new and different angle or perspective on Western culture; it requires that we work toward transforming the broken relationships that sustain injustice and inhibit human flourishing.[19] Transforming relationships requires engaging with the positional identities of our students and ourselves in any particular classroom context.

Indeed, one crucial part of implementing positional pedagogies involves faculty (not just students) locating their own positional identities in the classroom context. Faculty need to be more self-reflective not only about what teaching methods we aim to employ and which texts we aim to discuss but also about who we are. We need to reflect on our own identities and how these identities position us in the classroom vis-à-vis our students in order to explore what we share with our students, our own vulnerability in the classroom, and our own struggles with bias, prejudice, and oppression.

So how can we do this? What I have discovered thus far is that positional pedagogies are radical and that other features of the teaching and learning context present significant barriers or obstacles to implementing them. One way of accounting for positionality in the classroom is through experiential learning. For example, a colleague who teaches graduate-level courses in psychology has a project where students go on public outings holding hands with a member of the same sex. They are asked to pay attention to what the experience feels like, the reactions of others, and so forth. This kind of exercise is certainly an example of a positional pedagogy because it begins to allow students to be explicit about their social identity, the identity of others, and their relationships to those who are members of different social groups. Yet this exercise is radical, requiring a certain level of maturity and openness on the part of students, as well as institutional support that I'm not convinced is readily available for undergraduate courses. This kind of exercise also requires time to process the experience as a class and expertise on the part of the teacher in facilitating fruitful discussions about the exercise.

bell hooks suggests the perhaps less radical strategy of creating space for and assigning real epistemic value to personal confession in the classroom, where all voices are heard and where people share their own experiences publicly. This may be more practicable in most of our classrooms, but in order for this to be effective, students must be willing and able to share their own experiences and, importantly, they must be able *to genuinely hear what others share*. The goal of positional pedagogies is to draw explicit attention to relationships of power and privilege, and this is risky business. It can be extremely painful for students to have this kind of consciousness-raising experience, and many students are likely to resist the kinds of exercises that might enable them to move toward this goal. Marquette has a wonderful service-learning program, and I am beginning to think about how service-learning might facilitate positional pedagogies.

Yet there are institutional barriers and other features of the teaching and learning context that make it difficult to implement positional pedagogies, including traditional grading systems, the role of student evaluations in tenure decisions, and concerns about being perceived as unfairly biased. For example, a grading system that assigns grades to individuals based on their ability to successfully communicate whatever information they are supposed to know does not easily support the kind of knowledge promoted by positional pedagogies. The traditional grading system cannot easily accommodate learning situations in which students are "learning as a group or learning from each other and not only from the teacher" or are learning about their positionality vis-à-vis others.[20]

Another obstacle is the role of student evaluations in tenure decisions. Positional pedagogies can be painful and uncomfortable as opposed to entertaining or engaging in the way that a really well-put-together lecture might be. bell hooks notes: "I began to see that work to shift paradigms, to change consciousness, cannot necessarily be experienced immediately as fun or positive or safe."[21] Often students do not fully understand or appreciate what they've learned until long after the fact, but the initial student scores and comments matter in tenure evaluations, making untenured faculty vulnerable and less free to explore alternative pedagogies.

According to hooks, one helpful strategy when one is implementing a radical pedagogy is to be explicit from the start about the terms of engagement, "to identify what we mean when we say that a course will be taught from a feminist perspective," making the class conscious of what it is they are doing. Can and should we implement positional pedagogies in all our classes, or should they be reserved for courses in certain specialized disciplines or on certain topics for students mature enough to engage in and benefit from them? I have more questions than I do answers. I have come to believe that attention to positionality is an absolutely crucial aspect of transformative education, but knowing how to develop and implement this kind of pedagogy is difficult. This chapter is offered as an attempt to explore precisely how and why an emphasis on positional pedagogy can facilitate the Jesuit mission of transformative education and to prompt further discussion about practical strategies for doing so.

10 Consciousness-Raising as Discernment

Using Jesuit and Feminist Pedagogies in a Protestant Classroom

MARY J. HENOLD

In the fall of 2004 I was a young history professor enjoying my second year of a postdoctoral fellowship at Valparaiso University, a Lutheran college in Indiana. I was given the opportunity to teach an honors course in my research area, a class I titled Faith and Feminism in America. Two weeks into the course I knew I had a problem. Naively, perhaps, I had crafted a straightforward history course, but after just a few class meetings, it was clear the subject matter would have an unintended impact on the course's structure and purpose. A religiously diverse group of female students' exposure to feminist ideas caused them to react to the material in unexpected ways that required a response. Having started out teaching an American history class, I was disconcerted to suddenly find myself in the middle of a full-blown feminist consciousness-raising group.

While this development was full of possibility, it also posed a serious pedagogical challenge. My students were not just struggling with the concept of liberation. Some also faced a spiritual crisis when they allowed their emerging feminist beliefs to influence their faith and religious practice, which the subject matter was continually encouraging them to do. Feminism, as it is often presented, implies (or expects) a sundering of ties to one's church if it remains patriarchal. Indeed, many of the students assumed at first that becoming a feminist meant denying their faith. However, I could already see that my students, so responsive to feminist inquiry, did not necessarily want to end their relationships to their faith traditions. Besides, I hoped to encourage an expansive view of feminism that validated feminist women of faith.

My goal, then, was to offer my students a different model, one that would encourage them to determine for themselves what form their feminism would take, and how it would shape their faith and religious practice. But how was I going to approach this problem pedagogically, making sure that students' spiritual needs were met as they explored their responses to feminism? I am a historian, not a chaplain. As I repeatedly handed tissues to weeping students, I could only think, "I have no training for this!" The sensitive nature of this situation was only compounded by the fact that all but one of the students came from a Protestant background, while I was a cradle Catholic.

My solution was to turn to my own faith, in particular my background in Jesuit spirituality and education, and bring those experiences to bear on the pedagogical question, despite the Protestant context in which I found myself. I developed an approach to my students and the subject matter that intertwined feminist and Jesuit pedagogies in subtle ways and therefore were more easily incorporated into my non-Catholic classroom. Ultimately, I came to believe that the best way to guide my students through their confusion was to turn to one of the foundations of Jesuit spirituality and present the adoption of feminist consciousness as a process of discernment.

The Course

Let me begin with some details about the course. The class comprised ten honors students, all female. All were white, midwestern, and middle class; four were ELCA Lutheran, three were Missouri Synod Lutheran, and the remaining three were an evangelical, a member of the United Church of Christ, and a Catholic. They ranged from fervent believers to religious seekers just beginning to explore their options. The students all knew each other, and there were two pairs of friends in the room, but they represented three different classes and for the most part did not interact much outside class.

Only two of the ten self-identified as feminists at the start of the course, although all admitted to being strong, intelligent women who were willing to stand up for themselves. Of the two self-identified feminists, one was in a particularly difficult position. She was raised Presbyterian by a strong feminist mother who held a master's of divinity, but this student began to practice in an evangelical church starting in high school (much to her parents' chagrin). By the time she was a senior in college, she had compartmentalized her life. She had a gender studies minor, and she was outspoken on many feminist issues, but rarely about sexism in her faith tradition. She had been taught to believe that evangelicals could not be feminists, and so to some degree she was leading a double life.

I designed the course to incorporate several feminist pedagogical approaches, one of which was reflected in their first assignment. In retrospect, the task probably contributed significantly to the path that the course took. I asked each student to interview another student in the class about her relationship to feminism and then write a paper in which the interviewer would tell that woman's story. Each student, then, would interview one woman and be interviewed by a second woman. Right off the bat, we established that every woman's experience was valid and valuable and worthy of being both listened to and reported. The assignment also suggested that each of us would begin our scholarly exploration rooted in our own experience. As a bonus, I got a quick sense of where everyone was, and students started to form close bonds immediately.

I designed the course as a reading seminar, and from the start I encouraged the students to study the texts analytically, but I also invited them to relate the texts to their own experiences as women and as women of faith. I modeled this by sharing my own reflections in discussions. Our readings began with a primer in feminist theory, which raised a few eyebrows. Their reactions were typical as they began to shed their media-created views of what a feminist is. The diversity of feminists struck them immediately. They could not relate to some of the more radical positions, but many were surprised to find that moderate feminist positions resonated with them. From there, we moved into a series of secondary and primary texts on the nineteenth century.

One day a group of them came to class obviously excited. One text had so captured their imagination that they had stayed up late discussing it and even went so far as to photocopy it and slip it under the doors of the women who lived in their dorm. I was flabbergasted, as I had taught the piece many times and had become inured to it. That Elizabeth Cady Stanton's *Declaration of Sentiments* should cause the first glimmer of feminist consciousness in so many of them astounded and delighted me. Moreover, their response to the reading led them to share their own stories of discrimination in their churches for the first time. The Missouri Synod women were particularly vocal on this score.

One had been selected to write a sermon for her youth group but was then told that she would have to let a young man read it for her. Another explained that women in her church could not teach Sunday school to boys beyond the age of twelve, as the children might gain the false impression that women have authority over men in spiritual matters. A third told of how the girls in her church were harangued by the pastor for wearing clothing that provoked the boys to sin. I encouraged them to share their stories and scrutinize their particular traditions for sexism and misogyny.

So I knew something was happening, but I was unprepared for the next meeting. They were asked to read an excerpt from *The Woman's Bible*, a collection of women's interpretations of scripture edited by Elizabeth Cady Stanton in the 1890s. Two of the students came in prepared for battle. Like other women in the class, they struggled to reconcile what they were learning with staunch beliefs in biblical inerrancy, a concept foreign to my own background. My evangelical student and my most conservative Missouri Synod student balked at the idea that one could refer to God as a female. They began to argue with the rest of the group, who seemed intrigued by the idea. The discussion reached a crescendo when my evangelical feminist started waving her hands in front of her body defensively as if to ward off some infectious disease, declaring that she would *not* believe that this was okay. Then the two of them promptly burst into tears.

What became obvious was that these women had started to question and were now confused, frightened, and defensive. The others in the class were less defensive, but they too were confused, as I was asking them to reevaluate some of their most deeply held beliefs and traditions, not to mention go against their families' wishes. But here the foundations we laid in the first days of class paid off. When the two students burst into tears, the rest of the class jumped in, some challenging them gently, others comforting them and offering support. Although I interjected once in awhile, the students themselves talked the women through it, sharing their own feelings on the subject.

I left class shaken, finally understanding that what I had unknowingly created was a consciousness-raising group, albeit one founded and rooted in an academic context. In the sixties and seventies, consciousness-raising groups were created by radical feminists looking for a new way to spread the word about feminism and organize at the grassroots level. Consciousness-raising quickly became a tool of feminist groups across a broad spectrum of the women's liberation movement. I have even found evidence of consciousness-raising groups among Catholic sisters in the early seventies. These groups encouraged participants to share their experiences as women with each other, not as therapy, but as a means of raising awareness. Their goals were to help lead women to take action against sexism in their homes and communities, and to see that they were not alone and that their personal experiences of sexism were rooted in a larger cultural phenomenon.

The seminar format encouraged students to share their own experiences and respond to those of their peers. In those conversations they began to see patterns of oppression in the world and discuss women's responses to them. The process was aided, of course, by the fact that this was a history course designed to reveal those patterns and responses. I just did not expect all the students to engage with the material at the personal level required to transform their small academic community in such a profound way.

Faith and Feminist Consciousness

As I contemplated a course of action, I turned to my own research for guidance. I am a historian with specialties in recent America, women's/ gender history, and the history of American Catholicism. At the time of this course, I was writing a history of the American Catholic feminist movement in the sixties and seventies.[1] It was no coincidence, perhaps, that one of the central investigations in that research concerned the process by which religious women come to embrace a feminist identification.

Feminists (and historians of feminism) tend to describe the adoption of feminism in language that suggests a conversion experience. For example, when explaining how they became feminists, many women describe a sudden moment of revelation, sometimes referred to as "the click." One feminist historian describes the click as "that awe-inspiring moment of vision and of commonality, when a woman was instantly and irrevocably transformed from naïve to knowing, from innocent to experienced, from apolitical to feminist."[2] Feminist scholars Rachel

Blau DuPlessis and Ann Snitow suggest that these revelation stories have taken on the features of myth and have become a means of providing "shared meaning and experience" for feminists.[3] I would argue, too, that the myth of "the click" reinforces the feminist movement's efforts to distance itself from institutional religion by providing feminists with a secular conversion experience on par with religious revelation. I do not intend to discount these experiences; too many personal narratives describe this phenomenon for them to be easily dismissed. However, it begs the question, What came after the click?

By describing the adoption of feminist consciousness in this fashion, historians imply that feminism is somehow whole and self-evident, and that upon conversion to it, newborn feminists simply turn their faces forward, ready to leave behind everything that does not fit their new consciousness. For religious women—and, indeed, any woman with conflicting loyalties—such an approach is problematic. One cannot safely assume that new feminists would immediately allow feminism to trump loyalty to faith or religious institution. Indeed, the Catholic feminists I study prove that while the decision to become a feminist may have been sudden, the process of fitting those new beliefs into a religious framework took time, was often extraordinarily painful, and did not necessarily end with a decision to cut ties with their churches. My research on this group led me to conclude that the adoption of a feminist identification is better understood as a complex process involving innumerable negotiated choices that needed to reconcile a feminist outlook with preexisting worldviews and loyalties. Deciding to be a feminist is not enough. Feminists must also decide *how* they will be feminists. In short, to adopt a feminist identification is to face choices.

Consciousness-Raising as Discernment

It occurred to me, then, that the process of becoming a feminist, particularly for women of faith, could fruitfully be viewed as a process of discernment. Discernment, of course, lies at the center of Ignatian spirituality. In my understanding, it is an invitation to use prayer and contemplation to examine the paths that our lives take, so that we might figure out what is bringing us closer to God and leading us away from God. Ideally discernment becomes habitual through such exercises as the daily examination of conscience, although it can also serve as a means of working through a particular dilemma or crisis.[4] For new feminist women of faith, discernment could provide an opportunity to ask questions of both the new belief system and the old. What aspects of her new relationship with feminism bring her consolation or desolation? How will this new way of looking at the world lead her to a better understanding of God's will for her? How does it change perceptions of justice and the need to take action for justice? How will relationships with loved ones change, and how can she approach these changes, which are likely to be fraught with tension? Viewing the process of becoming feminist in this light has the advantage of giving students space and time to work out conflicts that have already arisen, while encouraging them to see faith and feminism as mutually supportive instead of inherently combative.

The question remained, however, of how to introduce this idea of Ignatian discernment to a room full of Protestants. What they did not need, I decided, was a primer in Jesuit spirituality; what with trying to teach my history content, explain feminism, and moderate increasingly emotional discussions, I felt that my classroom had become confusing enough. I chose instead to provide them with some tools for discernment, but in a rather subtle fashion. I did not describe what I was doing as explicitly Jesuit or rooted in the Catholic tradition. I believe these Protestant students might have experienced such concepts as alien and therefore inapplicable to their situations. They might have dismissed them as they had my explanations of the rosary or patron saints: weird and strangely fascinating, but having nothing to do with them. I should add that nothing in their Protestant backgrounds seemed incompatible with the idea of discernment. They believed that they could establish a personal relationship with God through prayer, and all of them were accustomed to seeking God through the contemplation of scripture. My task, then, was to find ways of encouraging discernment without turning to explicit Ignatian spiritual exercises. In the end, I was able to teach a subtle form of Jesuit pedagogy through the following five approaches.

Acknowledge the Whole Person

The first approach was to acknowledge that within the small world of my classroom I was undertaking to educate the whole of my students, not just their intellects. This focus on the whole person is, of course, one of the hallmarks of Jesuit education, one that I had given lip service to for some time but had never been pressed to live out to such a degree. This first approach, then, had to begin with me. I had to be willing to treat them as whole people, recognizing that not just their academic needs but also their spiritual needs required my close attention and could be a subject for my teaching. I had to let my course become something besides a history class in order to meet their needs. Feminist pedagogy works in a similar fashion. An explicitly feminist classroom acknowledges multiple dimensions of students by openly encouraging them to apply academic learning to their personal lives and relationships to the world. Acknowledging the spiritual side of these students merely added another dimension to our relationships in the room and our commitments to each other.

Teach the Need for Discernment

First, I very deliberately explained to them that the process they were undergoing required discernment, which was not at all obvious. After all, the majority entered the course with the belief that a choice to be a feminist was an automatic choice to leave one's church. I also did not want to leave them with the impression that the revelation of feminist consciousness itself makes all things clear or that it should. Such an impression might suggest that if they had decided to be feminists and were still confused, they had somehow done something wrong.

But inviting them into discernment was not enough. I also had to make it clear that these new feminists had genuine options, and that the choices they faced were not obvious. Thankfully, I had already structured the course readings to include the works of feminists who had made a variety of choices concerning their faith traditions. I also added a panel discussion toward the end of the semester for which I brought in four women from the Lutheran tradition who worked on campus. All four identified themselves as religious feminists, and they represented a variety of approaches to being a feminist woman of faith, ranging from one woman's choice to establish an official lifetime affiliation with her church to the decision of another to cut ties with the faith tradition of her youth. Each told her own story of consciousness and discernment and shared her ultimate decision about feminism and faith in her own life.

I tried to present discernment as a means not just of simply deciding what to do, however, but of understanding what their fundamental desires were, and what kind of life God was calling them to lead. I found that this focus affected my students in unexpected ways, indicating that they had taken it very much to heart. Three students chose to break up with their boyfriends that semester, telling me independently of each other that what they had learned about themselves called their relationships into question. A fourth student became increasingly determined to accept her own identity and made the choice to come out as a lesbian to her classmates. Two other students shared their new understanding with their very conservative parents, who insisted their daughters stop listening to me. These students had to choose the best way to relate to the parents they loved and respected as they chose to defy them.

Encouraging Reflection

It was not enough to teach my students that they had options; I also needed to help them approach those options in a prayerful way. Following the Ignatian tradition, I deliberately emphasized the value of reflection. I chose not to introduce them to a particular spiritual exercise. Instead my goal was something more basic: just getting them to recognize the value of being quiet! Young women who spend much of their waking hours talking on their cell phones, text messaging, and leaving comments on Facebook pages place most of their energy and faith in communication, and practically none in careful consideration and personal, thoughtful reflection. I hoped that a gentle reminder to stop and be silent would teach them where I thought they were most likely to find the peace they sought.

This took concrete form at the beginning of every class meeting, when I invited the students to close their eyes and take a few moments for silent reflection. We came to call this our "thirty seconds." Thirty seconds of silence does not seem like much, but it can have a strong impact on this particular generation of students. If nothing else, it gets them focused on the tasks at hand. The thirty-second experiment had such an impact that I now use it in all my classes. It is not usually until after the semester is over that students come and tell me how important those few seconds came to be for them, since they experienced it nowhere else. In the Faith and Feminism course, I used the thirty seconds to teach students that only through prayerful reflection could they create the space they needed to discern the call of the Spirit in their lives and to detect the sense of consolation and desolation. Only by taking the time for reflection and listening could they wisely choose the path they needed to take.

The End of Discernment Is Action

Furthermore, I tried to teach them that discernment should result in action that is ultimately oriented toward an expansive love that seeks justice for God's people in the world. Here feminism and Ignatian spirituality are so clearly compatible. For both, transformation that begins with the individual ideally will turn into concrete action in communities to bring justice. I often called attention to the political actions taken by the religious feminists we read, and I highlighted the risks and sacrifices that they required.

Over the course of the semester several students reported actions they had been moved to take to challenge sexism in their congregations, young adult groups, and families. One of these actions had a measurable impact. About half the women in my class became involved in preparations for *The Vagina Monologues* the following semester. I had the pleasure of witnessing my students hatch a plan to take their production to Wabash College, an all-male college in Indiana. Together with a men's group at Wabash, they stimulated a lively discussion about domestic violence (and had to defend their actions vigorously in both schools' newspapers). This was the first time the play had been presented at an all-male college, and the play's author, Eve Ensler, was present to mark the occasion.

Grounded Discernment

I taught my students that any choices they made needed to be grounded in who they are. According to Ignatian scholar Pierre Wolff, one of the four criteria of discernment is being "incarnate," as he phrases it, "to be the one who I am, and no one else . . . to be reconciled and in harmony with myself."[5] Feminist narratives of consciousness can imply that rejection of one's past is a prerequisite for embracing the new worldview. If a feminist is slow to abandon aspects of her past that retain connections to oppressive institutions, she can be viewed as lacking commitment or feminist maturity. Obviously, this is of particular concern for feminist women of faith. It is true that many of these women may eventually reject their faith tradition in whole or in part, and I made it clear that such a choice was valid. But I also suggested that the students should reflect on how they had been shaped by these traditions. The traditions of wisdom, authority, revelation, and celebration that they grew up with may be revealed as oppressive, but they also contributed immeasurably to each woman's identity. "To be reconciled and in harmony with myself" in this context means making peace with that part of oneself that was shaped by tradition, whether oppressive or not. This is particularly true if that is the tradition through which the woman understands and communicates with God.

Effectiveness

So how effective was this approach that I put together largely on the fly? Thankfully, it appears to have been successful. For me, proof of its effectiveness was apparent in the group's final task. I gave the class a not-for-credit opportunity to design and celebrate a feminist liturgy outside class. I expected their liturgy to showcase what they had learned about feminist approaches to liturgy and faith practice, and it certainly did. They gathered in a circle, choosing not to have a celebrant but to share leadership of the service among themselves. They used female pronouns for God, beginning the opening prayer with the words "Mother Creator." "Sing praise to the Lord," they chanted. "To Her alone sing your praise." They gave all the participants a chance to light a candle in thanksgiving for the women who inspired them. Yet this liturgy was grounded in both their new understanding of feminism and their traditions. Not by chance did they call their service a "Liturgy of Unity." Their efforts to balance commitments to faith and feminism were evident throughout.

I anticipated that they would design a private service for the class alone, but they chose instead to invite the entire campus community to their liturgy, in the end drawing thirty other students, faculty, and staff, male and female, from a variety of traditions. Reflecting their Protestant backgrounds, the centerpiece of the liturgy was four individual testimonies on scripture passages chosen by the speakers. They all reflected in some way on how feminism changed their perspectives and spurred them to action, and each revealed how she turned to her faith, particularly to her relationship to Christ, to find the strength to take this feminism into the world. They ended with two prayers, a decidedly feminist benediction that began, "May God bless you and keep you in Her loving arms," and a closing prayer from the Lutheran Book of Worship: "Grant, O God, that your holy and life-giving Spirit may move every human heart, that the barriers which divide us may crumble, suspicions disappear, and hatreds cease, and that, with our divisions healed, we might live in justice and peace."

Faith and Feminism in America was an extraordinary class, perhaps a once-in-a-lifetime class; I have not been teaching long enough to know. But I can say for certain that the mingling of Jesuit and feminist approaches and principles bore fruit. All ten women left the course as self-identified feminists. All the students also considered themselves to be women of faith at the same time. An informal survey of the group two years later showed that they continued to view themselves as religious feminists. In fact, two are now in graduate school, studying feminist theology and preparing themselves for ordination. But to me, the more telling fact is that none of the ten was yet sure what her relationship to her church would be when she left the course. Not having been pressured to embrace or abandon, they chose to give themselves time to discern what form their feminism would take.

—☾ Faith and Feminism in America ☾—

Course Description

In this seminar we will explore the tumultuous relationship between religious faith and feminist activism in the United States. Although many, both proponents and opponents of feminism, would argue that no such relationship exists, feminist women of faith dating back to the mid-nineteenth century would argue otherwise. Through the writings of feminists and historians, we will learn how feminist women of faith from a variety of faith traditions justified their positions, agitated to end sexism in their churches, and struggled (often unsuccessfully) to reconcile feminist conviction with religious faith and practice. I've designed the course so that readings and discussion topics will be pertinent to your lives today and your own questions about the intersection of faith and feminism. You do not have to be a feminist to take this course. Moreover, the goal of this course is not to turn you into a feminist. All positions on feminism will be respected here. If all goes well, our discussions should emerge from a combination of the texts and your own experiences.

Goals

> To help you think about the intersection of faith and feminism in depth
>
> To learn how your foremothers addressed these questions
>
> To deepen your understanding of the spirituality of American women
>
> To help you formulate the arguments you will put forward in the world on this issue, whether as activists or not
>
> To help you discern your own position on the intersection of faith and feminism

Assignments

There will be three papers and daily writing assignments. For the first paper you will interview another student about her relationship to feminism, particularly in the context of her spirituality and religious practice. Your paper will be a narrative about your colleague's experiences (you will also introduce the student to the class by sharing some of your findings). Every student will interview another student and be interviewed by a second student. The second paper will be an analysis of C. S. Lewis's *Till We Have Faces*. Your third paper will be a synthesis, an invitation to revisit the course readings and put forward an argument about the intersection of faith and feminism in America and how it has changed over time. You will also have the option, as a class, to create and celebrate a feminist liturgy (not for credit).

Course Schedule
Part I: The Nineteenth and Early Twentieth Centuries

Week 1: Introductions: Josephine Donovan, *Feminist Theory*, chaps. 1 and 2

Week 2: Integrating the Story: Elizabeth Cady Stanton, "The Declaration of Sentiments"; Nancy Isenberg, "Firstborn Feminism," from *Sex and Citizenship in Antebellum America*; Ann Braude, *Radical Spirits*, intro, chaps. 1 and 2

Week 3: Faith and Feminism in the Nineteenth Century: Braude, *Radical Spirits*, chaps. 3 and 4; *The Woman's Bible* (excerpts). First paper due

Week 4: Radical Visions and Traditionalist Response: Kathi Kern, *Mrs. Stanton's Bible*, chap. 5; "Some Catholic Views on Women's Suffrage"; Charlotte Perkins Gilman, *His Religion and Hers*

Week 5: Faith, Feminism, and Race: Evelyn Brooks Higginbotham, "Unlikely Sisterhood" and "Feminist Theology, 1880–1900"; Kern, *Mrs. Stanton's Bible*, chap. 3

Part II: Interlude

Week 6: Practicing Feminist Analysis: C. S. Lewis, *Till We Have Faces*

Part III: The Second Wave

Week 7: Early Works in Second-Wave Feminist Theology: Valerie Saiving, "The Human Situation: A Feminine View"; Rosemary Radford Ruether, "Motherearth and the Megamachine"; Mary Daly, "After the Death of God the Father"; Donovan, *Feminist Theory*, chap. 6

Week 8: Women's Ordination: Gracia Fay Ellwood, "Should Men Be Ordained?"; selections from the 1975 Women's Ordination Conference; readings on the 1974 Episcopal Women's Ordination

Week 9: Feminist Liturgy: Nelle Morton, "The Dilemma of Celebration"; Mary Henold, "Making Feminism Holy." Second paper due

Week 10: New Forms of Feminist Spirituality: Rita Gross, "Female God Language in a Jewish Context"; Naomi Janowitz and Maggie Wenig, "Sabbath Prayers for Women"; Judith Plaskow, "Bringing a Daughter into the Covenant"; Aviva Cantor, "A Jewish Woman's Haggadah"; Starhawk, "Witchcraft and Women's Culture"; Carol P. Christ, "Why Women Need the Goddess"

Week 11: Feminism, Religion, and the Body: Rosemary Radford Ruether, "What a Catholic Mother Thinks about Birth Control"; *Humanae Vitae*; Karen Osman, "Sex, Babies, and Other Good Stuff"; Margaret Ellen Traxler, "Choosing Life: For Rich Mothers Only," "Religious Coalition for Abortion Rights: The Right to Choose"

Week 12: Feminism in Conservative Protestant Denominations: Julie Ingersoll, *Evangelical Christian Women: War Stories in the Gender Battles*

Week 13: Ingersoll, *Evangelical Christian Women* (continued)

Week 14: Staying and Leaving: Feminist Women of Faith Panel

Week 15: Optional feminist liturgy. Final paper due

Part IV: The Fault Lines of Gender, Sex, and Sexuality

Debates, Challenges, and Opportunities for the Future

11   De Certeau and "Making Do"

*The Case of Gay Men and Lesbians
on a Jesuit Campus*

DAVID GUDELUNAS

I remember being an undergraduate at a fine Jesuit institution when a priest walked into a lesbian, gay, bisexual, and transgender student meeting and offered to serve as a much-needed advisor. Many faculty members, awaiting tenure, swamped with teaching and research responsibilities, or simply uninterested, had previously turned us down, and the amicable Father was perhaps the one person on campus we hadn't asked. This definitely wasn't my parish priest from back home, and I remember distinctly, and perhaps understandably, being confused about how a man of the cloth could do what so many lay members of the campus community were unwilling to do—even in San Francisco, even in the 1990s. Being nineteen and somewhat brash, I of course asked him. He said simply, "Sometimes we just have to make do," joking in a dry way that he may not have been the advisor I had in mind but was about the best I was going to get. More than that, it was a fatalistic way of thinking about the very question that so many members of a Jesuit campus community—whether feminist, queer, Jewish, or of whatever marginalized position you could think of—face on a regular basis. We are often asked to "make do."

This chapter is about operationalizing this idea of making do. In particular, I want to reflect on the writings of French Jesuit scholar Michel de Certeau, an extremely influential cultural anthropologist of the twentieth century, whose dense and fascinating writings shed light on what more modern scholars might simply label "coping strategies." Central in de Certeau's work is his discussion of "strategies" and "tactics," whereby he links strategies with institutions and structures of power, while tactics are utilized by individuals to create space for themselves in environments defined by strategies. This chapter explores the relevance of this theoretical framework of "everyday life" to understanding the contemporary position of feminists as well as gay men and lesbians who are creating space for their own communities within the structure of a Jesuit university. In particular, this chapter explores how one group of students at a Jesuit university created a policy report as a tactical measure to document and make recommendations on how to best make life for gay men and lesbians on a Jesuit campus more welcoming.

Truth be told, this chapter is really a bit self-serving. I teach de Certeau in my classes here at Fairfield, and his work has been foundational in my own research, which delves into popular culture and media theory. I am also always searching for ways to make dense and at times obtuse theoretical trajectories relevant to students. Admittedly, I never realized that de Certeau was himself a Jesuit, though considering his geographically and intellectually diverse biography, his Jesuit credentials shouldn't have come as a surprise. Michel de Certeau was born in France in 1925 and his education was an eclectic mix of degrees in subjects including classics and philosophy from universities including Lyon and Paris. He entered the seminary in Lyon, and the Jesuit Order in 1950, and was ordained in 1956, initially hoping to join his brothers doing missionary work in China. The academy, however, maintained more of de Certeau's attention, and by 1960 he earned his doctorate in theology from the Sorbonne based on an influential thesis that examined the mystical writings of Jean-Joseph Surin. He was a founder of the journal *Christus* and also a founding member of an intellectual community in France that spearheaded that country's ruminations of psychoanalysis and particularly the works of Freud and Lacan. While an amazingly productive researcher, de Certeau was also a teacher and held posts throughout his long academic career at Geneva, Paris, and UC San Diego.[1] Curiously, he avoided Unites States Jesuit institutions, and he died in 1986. Presumably, there was no relationship between the two.

Michel de Certeau's influence in American academic circles happened late in his career, and most of his intellectual fame in fact accumulated just after his death. His works, which my undergraduates remind me semester after semester are obtuse at best, were not published widely in English until the 1980s. In the United States he was embraced most readily by cultural anthropologists and scholars engaged in the study of media, culture, and popular communication. Given de

Certeau's own interests, his position of privilege within United States cultural studies was far from inevitable, though today he is considered one of its canonical scholars.

Michel de Certeau's influence in the study of media and culture can be traced back to his seminal work *The Practice of Everyday Life*. Here de Certeau argues that because of its repetitive and tacit quality, everyday life is distinctive from daily existence. He spends a majority of the work thinking through the ways that we unconsciously navigate texts ranging from literary works to city streets. The theoretical trajectories of the book itself are quite ambitious, drawing on everyone from Kant and Wittgenstein to Foucault and Bourdieu. Like a true Jesuit, de Certeau was never afraid of some intellectual posturing. Interestingly, long before interdisciplinarity became a mantra in the academy, de Certeau moved between methods, disciplines, and historical periods with great aplomb.[2]

Translated into English at the same time scholars were attempting to justify their study of "everyday" media like television, fashion, and magazines, de Certeau's work coincided with the explosion of popular culture studies in the U.S. academy and "everyday life" became essentially synonymous with "popular culture." His discussion of tactics as a form of resistance was used to fuel research and theoretical inquiries into the way in which audiences are able to subvert the dominant meanings of mediated texts to both justify their enjoyment and empower themselves against the dominant strategies of homogenized and ultimately aesthetically unsatisfying corporate media.

For example, U.S. scholar Henry Jenkins draws on de Certeau's work to show how audiences of the television and film franchise *Star Trek* are able to form a legitimate community around alternative meanings they "poach" from the actual media texts.[3] Likewise, John Fiske has built a career on expanding de Certeau's ideas to demonstrate how media audiences use tactics of subversion to bring their own meanings to one-size-fits-all media texts that don't actually speak to their existence.[4] Central in all this work, and directly derived from de Certeau's writings, is the idea that no text, experience, or idea is ever without multiple meanings. Moreover, though some experiential meanings are preferred by their creators, negotiated, resistive, and downright subversive meanings are what propel us through life. Michel de Certeau's assertions that a society is never shaped by the products thrust onto it helped move U.S. cultural studies away from thinking about producers and texts and toward pondering the way in which audiences (or consumers) make use of those texts.

While de Certeau's thinking has been extrapolated to cover this terrain of popular culture, his actual writings are, in fact, less interested in our popular diversions than scholars like Jenkins and Fiske lead us to believe. Of course, even though this version of de Certeau being interested in how everyday folks subvert the status quo in everyday life is also the story I sell to my students when trying to explain his work, it is a bit of a pedagogical stretch. Michel de Certeau is really interested in something much grander than poaching alternative meanings from popular culture artifacts. He is interested in how humans survive, connect, and thrive not by rules and products that exist in a culture but rather by the creative recombining of those rules and by poaching on the territory of others.

I argue that applying de Certeau's theoretical framework to the question of feminists and queers on a Catholic campus, though not an obvious extrapolation, is in fact much more true to the spirit of his original work. It should come as no surprise that the position of gays and lesbians on a Jesuit campus is a tenuous situation. More often than not, my own revelation that I work at a Catholic institution is met with some mighty waxed and mighty arched eyebrows. As many of the other contributors to this volume can attest, the position for feminists is similar to that of queers. Sexuality in all forms is something that does not always have a logical space to fit into in the overall structure of the Jesuit institution. The question that people mean to ask, however, when a self-identified feminist or gay progressive acknowledges working toward the mission of a heterosexist and essentially patriarchal institution is "Are you insane?" The question, however, becomes less obvious if one considers not the institution or the dominant script or rituals of that institution but rather the ordinary people who animate that script. That is, the question de Certeau encourages us to ask is not how the university institution operates but rather how the feminist, queer, or other marginalized individual within the institution is able to "make do" and, indeed, thrive. In the discourse of my own discipline, we need to move from a model of communication generated by the sender to a model driven by the receiver. Michel de Certeau tells us: "The presence and circulation of a representation (taught by preachers, educators, and populizers as key to socioeconomic advancement) tells us nothing about what it is for users. We must first analyze its manipulation by users who are not its makers. Only then can we gauge the difference or similarity between the production of the image and the secondary production hidden in the process of its utilization."[5]

While I hesitate to apply the word "manipulators" to describe feminists or queers, the non-pejorative denotation of the word seems oddly appropriate. I don't doubt that more than a few of my own colleagues view discourse on feminism and Jesuit ideals as the ultimate co-option—or calculated manipulation—of a rich, male-dominated legacy. Likewise, since Betty Friedan first famously labeled lesbians the "lavender menace" within the feminist movement back in 1969, gay rights and feminist concerns have been equally strange bedfellows as feminists and Jesuits. Even at a time when the Jesuit academy has diversified to include many influential women in leadership roles, non-Catholics at all levels, and some of the most culturally diverse campuses in the United States, this question of marginality by a majority population (that is to say, non-Jesuits) becomes all the more intriguing. Michel de Certeau recognizes this contradiction of the marginalized majority, explaining, "Marginality is today no longer limited to minority groups, but is rather massive and pervasive. . . . Marginality is becoming universal. A marginal group has now become a silent majority."[6]

Indeed, de Certeau, reflecting a distinct contribution of the Jesuit intellectual tradition, is interested in the tactics of the majority without a voice. His central thesis posits a distinction between the "strategies" of institutions and the "tactics" of what he calls "non-producers." A strategy in his framework is any entity entrusted with power and authority. Michel de Certeau tells us, "I call a strategy the calculation (or manipulation) of power relationships that becomes possible as soon as a subject with will and power . . . can be isolated."[7] Strategies become dominant, in part, because they take form physically in the site of operations and through a variety of products (laws, language, rituals, discourse, and so forth). Notably, thanks to tradition and scope, strategies are unwavering. Strategies are, furthermore, hegemonic in nature and maintain their hegemony by constantly reproducing.

The tactical model, in contrast, describes weak and fragmented groups with no established central base of operations. Michel de Certeau describes a tactic as "a calculated action, determined by the absence of a proper locus. No delimitation of an exteriority, then, provides it with the condition necessary for autonomy. The space of a tactic is the space of the other. Thus it must play on and with a terrain imposed on it and organized by the law of a foreign power."[8] Tactical operations come about because of necessity (typically survival), and these tactical forces are able, according to de Certeau, to mobilize quickly. Unlike guerilla warfare, which de Certeau notes is not a tactic, tactical maneuvers never attempt to sabotage or take over an institution but rather seek to fulfill needs behind an appearance of conformity or, in other words, to simply make life more "habitable." Tactical operations, according to de Certeau, range from changing a recipe while cooking to changing a myth while retelling it. The key here is not the final product itself, but the method by which change was effected.

Michel de Certeau's example of "Walking in the City" helps concretize these concepts. In this chapter, de Certeau describes his experience standing on what was the 110th floor of the World Trade Center in lower Manhattan. For de Certeau, the city is a concept, and "to be lifted to the summit of the World Trade Center is to be lifted out of the city's grasp," and most importantly, "it transforms the bewitching world by which one was 'possessed' into a text that lies before one's eyes."[9] For de Certeau, this text is written by the maneuvering of governments, urban planners, and other sources of authority who generate products like maps, urban grid designs, and laws that allow so many people to live so close together in relative comfort. So much comfort, in fact, that one can't fully appreciate (or grasp) the concept of the city until he or she is "an Icarus flying above." If the city as a concept is a type of strategy, then the pedestrian at street level, 110 stories down, operates in a more tactical way. Michel de Certeau considers "walking rhetorics" and "pedestrian speech acts" that involves the appropriation of geography not unlike more traditional speech acts that involve the appropriation of language. Notably, these actions on the part of pedestrians are not completely determined by the strategies of the city. These tactical operations on the part of pedestrians are important because they demonstrate how weak, disorganized, and powerless pedestrians can, quite literally, fight city hall. Michel de Certeau's assertion is that "everyday life invents itself by poaching in countless ways on the property of others."[10] My cutting through the Duane Reade drug store that stretches nearly half a city block on my way home from my subway stop on a cold winter evening helps illustrate this point. The map of Manhattan doesn't show a street that cuts through this retail space, city planners intend for me to stay on the sidewalk, police officers and other forms of authority would rather I didn't make a street out of the cosmetics aisle, yet night after night I defy the very strategies that organize Manhattan.

Notably, my trip through Duane Reade, like most tactics of the weak and cold, is not mapped in the same way that authorities map the Manhattan grid. Key here is the idea that social science alone is unable to uncover the often creative "ways of using." Michel de Certeau says, "Only the effects (the quantity and locus of the consumed products) of these waves that flow in everywhere remain perceptible. They circulate without being seen, discernible only through the objects that they move about and erode. The practices of consumption are the ghosts of the society that carries their name. Like the 'spirits' of the former times, they constitute the multiform and occult postulate of productive activity."[11]

While de Certeau argues that the inability to map these tactics is part of the subversive power of tactical maneuvers, the coming together of feminists, gay men and lesbians, and other representatives of the silent majority on Jesuit campuses is an important attempt to map our own space within the strategies of the institution. I think the tactics of feminists and gays and lesbians on Jesuit campuses are wonderful examples of how the official institutional structure has often little to do with the way in which we can use, recombine, and essentially poach on the territory that was never organized, spatially or intellectually, for our purposes.

This may sound more insidious than it actually is. I don't want to suggest here that the Jesuits, the administration, or other forms of institutional power are consciously attempting to thwart the "non-producers." Strategies, by definition, are not individual forces but rather collective accumulations of authority. Just as the modern urban city is not the product of any one person, era, or idea (or even several), the modern academy and its contingent strategies are not the product of any one entity either.

What de Certeau's work on everyday life provides for us is an alternative way of conceptualizing not how feminists or queers would sabotage or co-opt the mission, identity, or tradition of an institution but rather the ways in which we can thrive while maintaining a distinct sense of ourselves. His point is that this is the way life works . . . my point is that one's position as a gay faculty member or a feminist or a Jew or whatever position one identifies with is not any more problematic or inherently challenging than walking down Madison Avenue. I make it to my home nightly, in fact, relatively easily. Similarly, my response to those who ask how I can support the mission of a Catholic institution is "Easily."

The analogy of a "strong" Jesuit strategic institutional position and tactics of a "weak," disorganized feminist or queer perspective within these institutional frameworks does not translate perfectly outside de Certeau's original context, but anyone who has identified as gay, lesbian, or feminist (or some combination thereof) certainly would agree that there are definitive constraints faced daily on our campuses. Both consciously and unconsciously, we subvert daily these constraints, and de Certeau's astute observation that this is historically how we make sense of our collective world in a variety of contexts is well worth heeding. In other words, we are wise to concern ourselves less with strategies and more with tactics.

In my case, I am loathe to get into conversation about where the Church stands on issues concerning sexuality and more inclined to think through how a wonderful mission of service to others, a worldview that privileges social justice, and a care for the whole person and concern for the most marginalized members of our society can be, to borrow de Certeau's language, poached to form my own sense of stability and belonging. When I teach courses on media and cultural studies, I spend a good amount of time discussing things—ranging from sexuality to feminism—that in my own personal framework are far from antithetical to the experience at a Jesuit institution of higher learning. Instead, I situate these discussions as central to the educational mission of a Jesuit university. In fact, one is hard pressed to think of another "brand" of educational approach that has such a hospitable mission to feminist and queer concerns. Similarly, I argue for a perspective that aims to find the similarities and connections between seemingly disparate missions—feminism and organized religion, homosexuality and Catholicism, and so forth—as opposed to dwelling on their points of divergence.

"Making do" does not mean simply compromising; "making do" actually implies something far more empowering. By making do, we are in fact making change. Michel de Certeau cleverly relies on reappropriated military terminology in much of his writing. The effect is, on the surface, one of the marginalized fighting for meaning, as well as defusing the language of war to apply to something far more productive—the empowerment of individuals and groups. While, as noted earlier, I use de Certeau in my classes, the real pedagogical value of his work became more apparent to me after a group of students approached me about making change on my own campus.

As part of a competitively awarded grant designed to promote diversity initiatives at Fairfield University, a group of students approached me about how best to address the topic of homosexuality on our campus. Initially these students, all bright and committed to justice, were unsure how to even ask the question. To borrow from de Certeau, they were unclear on how they could mobilize their "art of the weak." Eventually the student-led research team devised a project that later became known as "The Collegiate Closet." The project was divided into two main components: research and recommendations.

The first part, research, was a classic tactical maneuver that borrowed from strategies in order to create resistance. That is, these students used the tools of the academy—historical analysis, large-scale survey work, qualitative field work, and other social scientific tools—in order to make their own meaning. Just as de Certeau discusses how renters of apartments use decorations and other touches of personalization to transform "another person's property into a space borrowed for a moment by a transient," these students were appropriating the language of the academy to create their own meaning.[12]

The report itself produced interesting data that were instructive in gauging the climate for sexual minorities on a particular campus at a particular moment in time. It was really the second phase of the project, namely, the recommendations, where the students were able to think about how they could link theory, solid social science data, and historical perspective to practice. From a pedagogical perspective it was this tangible connection between theory and practice that was truly rewarding. Not only did the students present their data in the form of a policy report but they went on to make specific recommendations to multiple divisions on campus. From student services to academics, the students made bold and informed policy suggestions that were aimed to appropriate the strategies of their university and make life more habitable.

When students apply for diversity grants to track instances of homophobia on a Catholic campus or when faculty members reflect on how feminist and Ignatian concerns can intersect in enriching ways to enliven the classroom, we're essentially participating in what de Certeau labels strategies of resistance and subversion. In my own experience, de Certeau's dense and often fascinating writings work in practice as well as they work in theory. Ultimately, these pedagogical exercises that involve thinking about how we can work within the structure of the academic institution in order to create a more dynamic university community don't work apart from the Ignatian mission, but rather with it. We are, in other words, making do by making a tradition our own in order to make the world a more habitable one.

While this chapter has reflected on how gay men and women poach meaning from the dominant strategy of the university, it is worth thinking about how others in the minority similarly develop unmappable tactics in service of making do. When feminists or members of the gay and lesbian community do poach meaning from the Jesuit university mission, it is paramount to note that they aren't actually removing or in way disrespecting this tradition. It isn't stealing and it isn't co-option. Instead, it is something far more dynamic. What we are doing is enlivening it, making it relevant, and putting it to service in a way that makes the practice of everyday life not simply tolerable but in fact joyous.

12 Textual Deviance

Eve Ensler's The Vagina Monologues *and Catholic Campuses*

HEATHER HATHAWAY, GREGORY J. O'MEARA, S.J., AND STEPHANIE QUADE

The year 2008 marked the tenth anniversary of the V-Day Campaign, an effort to promote the production of Eve Ensler's play *The Vagina Monologues* in a variety of venues to raise awareness of and funds for groups opposing violence against women. While this annual event has clearly moved into the United States and international mainstreams (over 2,700 college performances were held in the United States as part of the 2006 V-Day Campaign, and numerous nations, including Hungary, Russia, and the United Kingdom, have launched their own V-Day organizations), participation in this movement has been the source of significant debate at Catholic colleges and universities. The frank sexual nature of the play, and, in particular, one of the monologues dealing with a lesbian encounter involving a teenage girl and an older woman, has raised concerns about whether the play conflicts so dramatically with Catholic teaching so as to render it inappropriate for Catholic campuses. Attention to the issue from the Cardinal Newman Society (CNS), an organization formed to strengthen Catholic values on Catholic campuses, moved this debate into the national spotlight. The resulting notoriety has brought significant attention to campus decision making regarding sponsorship of *The Vagina Monologues* and, more broadly, to campus processes and policies for program approval. This chapter examines the controversy surrounding *The Vagina Monologues* from three angles: the programmatic, theological, and curricular.

First, Stephanie Quade, dean of students, considers how the issue has been addressed by student development administrators in Catholic colleges as they weigh competing demands from students, alumni, and organizations external to the university. Second, Fr. Gregory O'Meara, S.J., associate professor of law, evaluates the assertion that the play conflicts with the teaching of the Catholic Church by applying the post–Vatican II theological method of Bernard Lonergan to such claims.

Third, Heather Hathaway, associate professor of English, analyzes the strengths and weaknesses of the play from aesthetic, cultural, and political perspectives to show that *The Vagina Monologues* actually provides a valuable vehicle through which to educate students about the fundamental ideals of Catholic, and particularly Jesuit, education. As a whole, this three-part chapter seeks to move beyond the political rhetoric that has dominated the discussion to show that by demanding from students a critical engagement with this text, Catholic institutions can initiate discussions about the very values—respect for the dignity of each person; call to community; service to those in need, particularly the poor, vulnerable, and suffering; and solidarity—that are the basis of Catholic/ Jesuit feminist pedagogy.

The Context
Stephanie Quade

In order to understand the central conflict surrounding the production of *The Vagina Monologues* on Catholic campuses, it is important to first clarify the distinction between programs covered by the principle of academic freedom and those that exist in the extracurricular realm. Academic freedom is defined by the American Association of University Professors as "the essential characteristic of an institution of higher education. It encompasses the right of faculty to full freedom in research and in the publication of results, freedom in the classroom in discussing their subject, and the right of faculty to be free from institutional censorship or discipline when they speak or write as citizens."[1] Under the realm of academic freedom, a wide variety of materials may be taught, discussed, and presented on campus, regardless of their relationship to the teachings of the Catholic Church. Extracurricular activities, however, are governed by seemingly more subjective policies administered by the student affairs arm of the campus, and it is here that the Catholic campus finds itself vulnerable to accusations of having abandoned the Catholic mission of the institution.

At Marquette University, it is the responsibility of the Office of Student Development to distinguish between programs and events that are considered to be predominantly educational in nature (and thereby governed by the principles of academic freedom) and programs considered extracurricular. The policy governing out-of-class programs, as defined in the Marquette University *Student Handbook*, states that

> Student organization requests for the distribution of literature, the sponsorship of visiting speakers and public performers and the screening of films will be considered in light of the educational purposes and the Catholic identity of Marquette University. Specific attention, therefore, will be paid to the context and purpose of the proposed material. The university has final discretion in decisions regarding the distribution of literature, the sponsorship of visiting speakers and public performances, and the screening of films. In keeping with the intellectual imperative of the university and the instructive value of dialogue, educational or artistic merit and a balanced perspective will be the normative bases for decisions.

According to this policy, student organizations are encouraged to contribute to the "role of the university as a forum for intellectual discussion, debate, investigation and/or artistic expression." Through comparable policies and procedures, student affairs administrators at Catholic schools try to ensure that there is a venue on campus in which important topics may be discussed, and that there is a home for artistic expression. Policies such as these are designed to allow for the free exchange of ideas within the context of a Catholic school. As will be noted, the challenge to these policies comes from the wide variety of persons (both on and off campus) trying to define what, exactly, "Catholic" means.

Typically, on Catholic campuses, these policies are most notably referred to when programs such as those addressing abortion, birth control, and sexual orientation are being considered. They may be referred to regarding which candidates are allowed to speak on campus during an election year, which student organizations will be granted official university recognition, and which movies will be shown. On many campuses, there is a great deal of discretion given to the young student affairs staff members charged with making these decisions, and most often, the program is approved with a disclaimer or a required post-performance discussion. Most approvals are not scrutinized or sent "up the ladder" for consultation. And yet there is one program that immediately challenges even the most seasoned administrators: the dreaded request for the campus to sponsor Eve Ensler's *The Vagina Monologues*.

This trepidation is due in large part to a campaign against the play spearheaded by the Cardinal Newman Society. Per its Web site, the Cardinal Newman Society is "dedicated to renewing and strengthening Catholic identity at America's 224 Catholic colleges and universities."[2] The CNS accomplishes this primarily through mail and e-mail campaigns directed at those institutions that, according to the leadership of the CNS (the founder and president, Patrick Reilly, is a graduate of Jesuit-run Fordham University), are not acting in accord with Catholic teaching. As a result of effective fund-raising over the last several years, the CNS has recently expanded from existing primarily as a letterhead to becoming a full-fledged organization with a staff of six and with a budget of $1 million. There are several specific targets of the CNS, including individual faculty members; in fact, CNS publicized a list of employees of Catholic schools who donated to the Kerry campaign during the 2004 election. The CNS regularly investigates commencement speakers, recipients of honorary degrees, and invited lecturers to assess their respect for Catholic teaching. According to the society's Web site, "Our bishops have declared that 'the Catholic community and Catholic institutions should not honor those who act in defiance of our fundamental moral principles. They should not be given awards, honors or platforms which would suggest support for their actions.' Nevertheless, in the spring of 2006 24 Catholic colleges and universities hosted scandalous commencement speakers and honorees including advocates of abortion rights, stem-cell research, physician-assisted suicide, homosexual marriage and women's ordination."[3] According to CNS, this number represents "more than 10 percent of the 224 Catholic colleges and universities in the U.S., consistent with past years," and is cause for considerable alarm.[4]

It is against *The Vagina Monologues*, in particular, that the CNS has waged its most ardent war. In 2006, preventing performances of the play became the specific campaign agenda of the CNS—and it considered its campaign victorious. Again, to quote from the society's Web site, "The Cardinal Newman Society's 2006 campaign to stop 'The

Vagina Monologues' performances and public readings on Catholic campuses across the United States was a success. A then-record-low 22 Catholic colleges and universities hosted the 'Monologues' in February and March, a significant decline from 27 performances or readings in 2005, 29 in 2004, and 32 in 2003. As you will see on this page, our campaign is working and we are reclaiming Catholic campuses for Catholic values one school at a time!"[5] The numbers differ slightly depending on the source consulted. Per the V-Day Web site maintained by the group promoting productions of *The Vagina Monologues* on college campuses, 1,100 colleges and universities across the country offered performances of the play in 2005.[6] Of that number, forty were Catholic. Partly as a result of the CNS campaign, however, the number of performances occurring annually on Catholic campuses has, indeed, shown a steady decline. The site states that nineteen performances were scheduled around Valentine's Day in 2008.[7]

This decline is not surprising, given the nature and organizational structure of the CNS campaign. Catholic campuses whose names appear on the V-Day Web site receive a letter from CNS alerting university leadership to the upcoming performance. Letters are also sent to the presiding bishop of the local diocese as well as to CNS members in the area. All are encouraged to use whatever means necessary to stop the production. In this letter, the play is referred to as "The V***** Monologues." The word "vagina" is thus relegated to the category of words that should not be spoken, much less typed. To offer some sense of the tenor of the CNS campaign, their press release taking credit for the decrease in performances states in part: "'Every year, more Catholic college and university leaders are coming to their senses about this vile play,' said CNS president Patrick J. Reilly. He continued, 'Still, it's astonishing that officials could not immediately recognize a conflict with the values that are fundamental to Catholic higher education. Which of the remaining 22 institutions will be last to embrace lesbian activity, masturbation, statutory rape and extramarital perversity?'"

Given this context, it should be easy to understand why student affairs administrators on Catholic campuses dread the annual request by students to perform *The Vagina Monologues*. The decision to allow or prohibit the play is loaded with significance that goes far beyond that typically associated with extracurricular programming. Such a decision requires interrogating definitions of academic freedom, artistic expression, and censorship. It demands engagement from university administration, staff, faculty, students, and even alumni about the nature of Catholic identity and of Catholic educational institutional values. It entails thoughtful and critical inquiry into Catholic theology and culture. And inevitably, someone in the dialogue will not be satisfied. But as Fr. O'Meara and Dr. Hathaway will show, examining these issues is precisely what should be expected of any university.

A Theological Inquiry
Gregory J. O'Meara, S.J.

The Cardinal Newman Society's attack on performances of Eve Ensler's *The Vagina Monologues* at Jesuit and other Catholic colleges and universities is at least paradoxical. The rationale that the CNS proffers to ban these performances relies on a premise of the following sort: "This play must be banned because it conflicts with the teaching of the church." Such a claim is, in part, a theological one. This section of the chapter attempts to consider the CNS's claimed theological justification in light of post–Vatican II theological method as explained by the late Bernard Lonergan, S.J. According to proper post–Vatican II theological method, if the play could be understood as an "external cultural factor" that reveals something about what it is to be a human being, then it is a proper subject for theological discussion, and the theological basis asserted by the CNS for prohibiting performances of the play at Catholic universities is undermined.

As a matter of context, few dispute that both faculty members and administrators at Jesuit and Catholic institutions navigate fairly competently a wide swath of material not easily understood. It is presumed that our faculties are relatively adept at theological reflection about matters ranging from patristic conceptions of the Trinity to current thought on the Incarnation and sacramental interpretations of the world in literature and film. Few, if any, objections are sounded to the handling of more current debates by our departments involving the death penalty, limits on proposed genetic research, crises in health insurance policy, and applications of the just war theory. Further, Catholic universities and colleges apparently address, in appropriately Catholic contexts, issues of world hunger, the lack of potable water, female genital mutilation, responses to torture, and approaches to the Holocaust. These discussions are perforce complicated and call for nuanced responses with varying degrees of certainty and frank assertions of the inability to speak before what we rightly call mysteries. Nonetheless, the ability to present, if not clear answers, then at least relatively adequate questions does not seem to be doubted on these matters. Thus, the idea that departments that habitually explore issues of this magnitude should somehow be stymied, tongue tied or lapse into heretical incoherence because Ensler's play involves references to lesbianism or has the word "vagina" in the title is simply odd.

One approach to the theological arguments for performing or prohibiting Ensler's play in Catholic and Jesuit universities is rooted in a robust understanding of the word "tradition." Speaking in Wuhan, China, in fall of 2006, Rowan Williams, the archbishop of Canterbury, noted:

> It is taken for granted that those who exercise power in a society need to be formed in a particular culture. They need to learn how to reflect on the social interactions around them; they need to learn how to evaluate the reasons that people give for actions and policies. Part of that training—how to evaluate reasons and arguments—and also ideals and aims—has always involved references to the basic texts of a culture—whether sacred or secular—which are regarded as setting out patterns of human society that continue to serve as an orientation.[8]

Those who work in higher education are ineluctably part of a tradition. We do close readings of texts, musical scores, artistic renderings, and artifacts within our shared history both to draw out what we see as possessing value within them and to assess the value of what we encounter in our world today. This fearless and searching encounter with classic texts helps develop sinewy intellects; in the interaction with the text, our students, and we better understand the world beyond the classroom.

David Tracy illustrates how the intellect is formed in a tradition through the medium of authentic conversation required to tease out the implications of reality.

Real conversation occurs only when the participants allow the question, the subject matter, to assume primacy. It occurs only when our usual fears about our own self-image die: whether that fear is expressed either in arrogance or scrupulosity matters little. That fear dies only because we are carried along, and sometimes away, by the subject matter itself into the rare event or happening named "thinking" and "understanding." For understanding happens; it occurs not as the pure result of personal achievement but in the back and forth movement of the conversation itself.[9]

By engaging in conversation, participants encounter not only the people in the room but also the classic texts that undergird our intellectual tradition. Tracy defines a classic text as one that bears an "excess of meaning" that "demands constant interpretation." He continues, "The classic text's real disclosure is its claim to attention on the ground that an event of understanding proper to finite human beings has here found expression. . . . Only its constant repetition by later finite, historical, temporal beings who will risk asking its questions and listening, critically and tactfully, to its responses can actualize the event of understanding beyond its present fixation in a text. Every classic lives as a classic only if it finds readers willing to be provoked by its claim to attention."[10]

We are likewise part of a theological tradition, which also has classic texts that can be used to measure and assess the values we see displayed in our world. Of course the category of theological classics must include scripture, but it also includes the works of theologians, such as those designated patristic writers Tertullian, Hippolytus, Chrysostom, and Augustine. St. Augustine describes in some detail not only his religious conversion but his embarrassment at having erections in public as well.[11] Because it matters to people, sexuality is well within the scope of theological reflection. The CNS admits as much when it cites sections of the catechism and papal encyclicals dealing with sexuality on its Web site.[12] The CNS wishes to see tradition as a bulwark, a fixed position that brooks no dissent. Therefore, CNS maintains that *The Vagina Monologues* "presents a view of women's dignity, love and sexuality that significantly contradicts Catholic teaching."[13] This reference begs the question, Why is contradiction inimical to academic endeavor?

To explore the significance of this question, it is helpful to consult the work of Robert Wuthnow, who sees society as beset by "unexamined assumptions which prevent us from exploring as many possibilities as we should."[14] While grasping the surface content of statements proffered to support a particular argument, academics can fail to interrogate the complicated and divergent bases upon which that argument stands, ignoring that positions advanced as unquestioned may well rest on premises unsupported by the vagaries of history.[15] Wuthnow's observations surely hold true for many assertions about what constitutes "the teaching of the church" and the relationship Catholic universities should have to that teaching. The work of Bernard Lonergan, S.J., explores this tension.

In a paper published in 1968, Lonergan set forth his understanding of what needed to be done to accomplish the *aggiornamento*, the renewal, the "bringing things up to date," called for in the Second Vatican Council.[16] Lonergan observed that when those at the Council asserted that theology needed to be brought up to date, they necessarily implied that theology had fallen behind the times. Lonergan identified this slippage as occurring in the year 1680. He chose this date because of a congruence of intellectual historians here. Herbert Butterfield notes the date as marking the origins of modern science, Paul Hazard names this as the beginning of the Enlightenment, and Yves Congar places here the beginnings of dogmatic theology. According to Lonergan, when the world began to shake off medieval categories that bounded its intellectual conceptions, the Church retreated intellectually to assure itself that it still possessed certainty, blissfully untroubled by evidence adduced in the state, the marketplace, the laboratory.[17]

Lonergan explores the methodological assumptions underlying theological styles. Originally, "dogmatic theology" referred simply to the body of theological knowledge distinct from moral or historical theology.[18] Lonergan notes that in 1680, the method of dogmatic theology shifted. Prior to that date, theology adopted the Thomistic method, wherein it was defined as "faith seeking understanding," a dynamic discipline that interrogated both external reality and its own internal presuppositions. Notably, the Thomistic method required constant bumping up against objections in the form of contradiction. By contrast, dogmatic theology after 1680 merely set forth a series of maxims or certitudes, more in the form of truths to be learned than questions to be asked, and the robust grappling with contradiction was discarded.[19] Lonergan maintains that this "conception of theology survived right into the twentieth century, and even today in some circles it is the only conception that is understood."[20]

Such an approach to theology is decidedly static and ahistorical. Not only is God seen as unchanging, but so too must be our way of expressing the inexpressible mystery. Lonergan finds this second claim to be the root of the difficulty. He observes, "Theology is a product not only of the religion it expounds but also of the cultural ideals and norms that set its problems and direct its solutions."[21] To prevent theology's "withering into insignificance," theologians need to address with "clarity and accuracy" external cultural factors that "undermine its past achievements and challenge it to new endeavors."[22] Simply put, theology needs to wrestle with the contradictions and counter-arguments of its age. Failure to do so shunts theology to the margins of the world in which we live.

Lonergan clarifies how the method of doing theology developed following Vatican II in three logical steps: First, before the Council, theological method was a deductive science; its conclusions were short, necessary, and timeless, based upon unalterable premises provided by scripture and tradition.[23] After the Council, theology uses scripture and tradition differently. These sources are treated as data that must be viewed in historical perspective.[24] The steps from data to interpretation are long, arduous, and context driven and generate conclusions that are at best probable.[25] Such an approach results in more modest sorts of conclusions, because "it does not preclude the uncovering of further relevant data, the emergence of new insights, the attainment of a more comprehensive view."[26] Second, the shift from a deductive to an empirical approach is required by our current view of history, which sees reality as evolving and developing.[27] We cannot return to a period wherein theologians could easily express themselves as certain, once for all time. Third, theology has discovered that much of its previous medieval apparatus is unwieldy or insufficient; therefore, rather than taking a view of human beings as transcendent individuals bounded by the mind-body problem, theology now focuses on human beings as historical beings possessed of "the richer and more concrete apprehension of [people] as incarnate subject[s]."[28]

Another way of understanding Lonergan's point on method might be to consider what sort of reasoning leads to truth claims in theology. Borrowing from Toulmin and Jonsen, pre–Vatican II dogmatic theology seems to employ "theoretical" reasoning and the style of theology described by Lonergan as using "practical" reasoning.[29] Theoretical reasoning employs the elegant and precise calculus displayed in geometric proofs.[30] It begins with unquestioned general principles from which all other conclusions can be derived. Theoretical reasoning is attractive because its conclusions must be accepted if one concedes the premises. The difficulty with theoretical reasoning is its limited applicability, because it addresses only the idealized, atemporal, and necessary.[31] Theoretical reasoning is informative when describing certain mathematical entities, but its usefulness diminishes outside that rarefied sphere. As Aristotle observed, "not all of our knowledge . . . is of this sort; nor do we have this theoretical kind of certainty in every field."[32]

Although some theological arguments may rest on theoretical reasons, Lonergan cautions against this method for most theological concerns. Rather than addressing ideal constructs that are based on truths always valid at all times and places, theological matters that deal with incarnate human life work in categories that are "concrete, temporal, and presumptive." In short, we do not begin with truths that we will presume and then pretend to derive. Theology is not about satisfying some infantile need for a sense of order or resolution. Rather, theology deals with mysteries, and mysteries are places for questions, not for answers. Theological method reflects that disposition and recognizes it is oriented more to questioning than answers.

With this understanding of method in place, the theologian must explore his or her connection to questions of history. Matters that are central in one epoch seem tangential in other periods. This observation is not meant to denigrate the importance of these disputes in the life of the Church or in the moral development of human beings; nevertheless, a sense of the historical basis for objections helps us to grapple with assertions that particular texts or issues conflict with the teaching of the Church. The teaching of the Church, if it is to be authentic, has to develop and change. Karl Rahner observes:

> The sum total of the norms of Christian living, together with a spe-
> cific way of life felt to be binding on Christians, may once have been
> developed and held confidently and unquestionably in a particular
> age. Nevertheless, they contained far more changeable elements than
> were ever conceived of as a matter of clear and conscious reflection
> by those belonging to that particular age itself. [The church is
> marked by an ineluctable] process of interaction between changeable
> and unchangeable factors which cannot be fully distinguished. . . .
> And this is something which must be sustained and endured in
> patience.[33]

Not everything the Church has once taught is properly seen as belonging to the unchangeable deposit of faith.

Although the object of faith itself, God, is unchanging, our beliefs,
the expression of our faith, are distinct from faith itself.[34] God is a
mystery and thus our attempts to speak of God are necessarily provi-
sional and inarticulate. We are, as a matter of faith, never able to
express who or what God is with clarity. The best we can do is attempt
to frame our beliefs. As Roger Haight, S.J., observes, "faith reaches out
and attaches itself to an object which is transcendent. The interpretation of that object employs the concepts and language of knowledge of
this world. But the world and human knowledge of it is constantly
moving and changing, and thus the interpretative position in relation
to the object of faith is always shifting. Beliefs change and should
change."[35] Because our expressions of the objects of faith change—that
is to say, because our beliefs change—we can no longer cling to one
formulation of belief as unambiguously true at all times. Rather,
because the world changes, we change, and how we see the world and
see God acting in it changes as well. Thus, our theological understanding is presumptive, concrete, and temporal. God, who is mystery, can
be revealed in places, situations, and texts not previously thought to
disclose the Divine.

An example of how historically bound theological reflection can be
is revealed by the work of John Cardinal Newman himself. In his mas-
terful biography of Newman, published in 2002, Frank Turner maps
out the major considerations that occupied the nineteenth-century
bishop's life. It is instructive to note where Newman's pen never strays.

In Victorian England, beset by changing mores and social upheaval, much of it frankly sexual and gender based in nature, Newman never once mentions sex or gender as a concern. He does not speak about promiscuity, adultery, prostitution, or homosexuality. These were simply not topics he ever thought important to address in terms of interest for the Church. Rather, like other divines of the time, he was concerned with whether Catholics could vote and remain Christians.[36]

Newman's neglect of sexual matters as central to Catholic teaching is neither idiosyncratic nor out of line with his tradition. Albert Jonsen and Stephen Toulmin point out that at the time of the founding of the Society of Jesus, the key question for moralists was whether financial institutions such as banks could morally charge interest on loans in violation of the Bible's prohibition against usury.[37] Questions of morality that dogged earlier eras focus on the state house and the public square, not on the expression of genital sexuality.

Of course, for the theologian who wrestles honestly with reality, our collision with the earthly leads to reflection on God's irruption into our previously settled lives and ways of looking at the world. Henri de Lubac notes: "Faith disturbs us and continually upsets the too-beautiful balance of our mental conceptions and our social structures. Bursting into a world that perpetually tends to close in on itself, God brings in the possibility of a harmony that is certainly superior but is to be attained only at the cost of a series of cleavages and struggles coextensive with time itself. . . . The earth, which without God could cease being a chaos only to become a prison, is in reality the magnificent and painful field where our eternal being is worked out."[38] The subject matter of theology is defined not only by the tradition, the classic texts with which we repeatedly wrestle, but also by our life experiences. Particularly for theologians writing in the postwar worlds, as Stephen Schloesser, S.J., observes, this encounter with the tragic, the temporal, and the terrestrial required a new approach to theology in Vatican II. Schloesser notes, "Seen against this horizon, the council's rupture with the past appears not only as a historical possibility. It seems to have been an ethical necessity."[39]

The implications of this theological method for Jesuit pedagogy make further uncomfortable demands on the educator. We must reconceive the authoritative structure built into academic ways of proceeding that many of us find congenial and easy. For if what is revealed by our constant clashing with reality is nothing less than the face of God, then our goal as educators must be to increase opportunities for addressing such cleavages and reflect on them in light of our tradition. Furthermore, we cease to be the experts, the "sages on the stage," who impart ready-formed truths to the women and men with whom we share the learning process. Rather, we must take seriously the contributions of our students and colleagues if we are to stumble along the path to enlightenment, because others may well be the face and voice that "continually [upset] the too-beautiful balance of our mental conceptions and our social structures."[40]

The theological method suggested by Lonergan, Rahner, and de Lubac need not differ substantially from the method for feminist theory proposed by Catharine MacKinnon in her groundbreaking work "Feminism, Marxism, Method and the State: An Agenda for Theory."[41] MacKinnon holds that the personal is the political and uses this understanding as a grounding for the method whereby women are able to cast off patriarchal structures. Upon this reclamation of the personal she builds the method of consciousness-raising, a method present in germ in Hegel's master-slave dialectic and later serving as the basis for theological reflection by Gustavo Gutierrez.[42] MacKinnon maintains that women enter into the political through their personal experiences. In consciousness-raising, women "[take] situated feelings and common detail . . . as the matter of political analysis" and "[explore] the terrain that is most damaged, most contaminated, yet therefore most women's own, most intimately known, most open to reclamation."[43] MacKinnon emphasizes that

> through consciousness-raising, women grasp the collective reality of women's condition from within the perspective of that experience, not from outside it. . . . Its claim to women's perspective *is* its claim to truth. . . . Feminism does not see its view as subjective, partial or undetermined but as a critique of the purported generality, disinterestedness, and universality of prior accounts. These have not been half right but have invoked the wrong whole. Feminism not only challenges masculine partiality but questions the universality imperative itself. Aperspectivity is revealed as a strategy of male hegemony.[44]

In the method detailed by MacKinnon, we see features of precisely what Lonergan sets forth in his description of theological method. Consider the dynamics of both practices. Initially, like theologians who reject dogmatic formulations, women who engage in consciousness-raising reflect on their lives as historical data. They then analyze and interpret these data by subjecting them to strategies of unmasking that reveal how matters treated as somehow "natural" or "necessary" are in fact social constructions chosen, consciously or not, by those in power. The world no longer is received as some sort of truth but becomes a place where important questions need to be asked. Second, like theologians encountering theological questions, women begin to see their own lives as evolving and developing rather than as static and prescribed. No one can claim to define his or her role once and for all. Simone de Beauvoir's insight that "one is not born a woman, one becomes one" is not a sad commentary describing women who are pampered into powerlessness but can become a paean to the grasping of rightful self-authority as women begin to claim their own identity, their own power. Finally, as this process continues, it becomes clear that the subject of feminist consciousness-raising is not women as mere victims of an oppressive structure. Rather, women are encountered more honestly as historical beings possessing what Lonergan terms the "richer and more concrete apprehension of [people] as incarnate subject[s]."[45]

Lonergan's use of the word "incarnate" to describe the subjects of theology is anything but accidental. The doctrine of the Incarnation means that Christ is made real in our human flesh. This was true of Jesus of Nazareth, born of a woman, who lived, preached, healed, and fed, who suffered, died, and was resurrected. The doctrine goes further. God also takes flesh again in the life of the imperfect world where we live. And if feminist theology means anything, it means that women are a locus, a place where the Incarnation is continued. We need to recognize and teach that it is in women's bodies and through women's voices that Christ is continually made present in this world.

This recognition of the role of women is precisely the sort of "external cultural factor" that challenges theology "to new endeavors."[46] In the post–Vatican II Thomistic tradition, the role and self-perception of women become a new *sed contra* that challenges the received wisdom of the past and urges the Church forward. One need not agree with all premises of every feminist philosopher or artist to enter into conversation with her. Nevertheless, their work as an expression of the Incarnation in the world constitutes matters rightly explored within our universities.

And so, having set forth the method and subject of theology after Vatican II, we can perhaps profitably reflect on the theological method employed by the CNS and ask if it passes muster. The CNS sees its mission as addressing ways in which Jesuit and Catholic universities deviate from the unchanging deposit of the faith. In newsletters posted on its Web site, the CNS mentions a fairly restricted category of concerns. We learn about CNS's opposition to performances of *The Vagina Monologues*, to gay and lesbian student groups and speakers, to abortion, and to birth control.[47] Notably absent are references to torture, the war in Iraq, or the plight of the poor, all of which have been mentioned prominently by the Holy See in recent years.

Naturally, we must grant the CNS its subject. Everything it mentions has at one time been roughly held or believed by some with authority in the Church. However, the paucity of its reasoning should trouble members of the academy asked to adopt uncritically the CNS's conclusions. The difficulty with the CNS's position is that it is shot through with the style of dogmatic theology specifically rejected by the Second Vatican Council. The CNS's argument is merely an appeal to authority that it assumes is unchanging. Its utter failure to engage the tradition in any interesting way renders the CNS's positions on *The Vagina Monologues* and other topics frankly unworthy of notice on our campuses. Surely, we are called to consider carefully the warrants of Church teaching as we wrestle with reality encountered daily, but to claim that intelligent discussion is foreclosed merely because some authority in the past said so is not a sufficient answer for us, for our students, for our profession as academics. Such claims to unquestioned authority are not permitted elsewhere in the academy, and as Lonergan demonstrates, they must not be permitted in theology.

That said, there are more troubling aspects to the reasoning employed by the CNS. Their materials reveal an intellectual gap by suggesting that merely asserting that a particular text "conflicts with the teaching of the church" is sufficient to justify a ban on reading a book, screening a film, or performing a play at a Jesuit and Catholic university. More specifically, it appears to maintain that artistic works that depict acts in conflict with Church teaching must be summarily rejected.[48] Surely this assertion is too broad to be countenanced. For example, the Church does not approve of incest, yet no one maintains that *Oedipus Rex* should not be performed by a Catholic university's theater department. The Church disapproves of sexual relationships outside the bond of matrimony, but that is not a reason for preventing student exposure to the works of Chaucer, Henry James, or Thomas Pynchon. In the non-literary arena, the Church has repeatedly stated its disapproval of the Bush doctrine championing "preemptive strikes" or torture as a legitimate strategy in warfare, but the Church's disapproval cannot credibly be given as a reason for eschewing robust discussion of these matters, both within and outside the classroom.

Thus, a stronger claim needs to be made to exclude *The Vagina Monologues* from consideration on Catholic college campuses. Lurking behind the objections seems to be not only a perceived conflict with Catholic teaching but also what might be described as a fundamental fear of contagion, of pollution, of the irredeemable coarsening of the spirit caused by merely witnessing this performance.[49] The language of the CNS describes *The Vagina Monologues* as just such a source of infection. "Banning the play is a means of demonstrating genuine commitment to reasoned dialogue on important issues without the vulgarity, obscenity, disrespect for human dignity and one-sided demagoguery that prevents true academic discourse."[50] In the same vein, the Web site continues that the very possibility that the University of Notre Dame may permit a performance of the play should give "Catholics around the world reason to believe that the University of Notre Dame, 'Our Lady's University,' will remain substandard as a Catholic institution for the foreseeable future."[51] Apparently, being open to the idea of permitting a performance so taints a Catholic university that its very identity as Catholic is called into question.

The reasoning behind such arguments rests on either or both of two premises: (1) The Catholic identity of the university in question is in dire straits, extraordinarily fragile, and precarious, subject to crumble when faced by the winds of opposition, or (2) *The Vagina Monologues* is such a powerful piece that it single-handedly can obliterate years of effort at articulating a Catholic voice in higher education.

The second objection can be dealt with more easily. It seems unlikely that within the context of a university where texts are, as a matter of course, subject to strenuous critique, a play that is so mainstream would pose the sorts of dangers feared. This conclusion arises from an examination of texts students regularly read and discuss as part of the ordinary liberal arts curriculum, which could be far more dangerous to Catholic and Christian values. Presumably, students are asked to read Western thinkers such as Freud, Marx, Feuerbach, Nietzsche, Jean-Paul Sartre, and Bertrand Russell. All of these attack both current instantiations of religious faith and the very possibility of religious belief in strong and concerted ways. Surely these thinkers carry more intellectual heft and pose a greater danger to Catholic belief than does the repeating of ordinary vulgarities or a discussion of stimulation leading to orgasm, but this context seems largely ignored by the play's detractors. It seems to me that if Catholic universities can handle the challenges proposed by the major atheist attacks on belief (and they can and should), then these same universities have nothing to fear from any frank discussion of female sexuality.

The initial objection has more nuances. Although the CNS itself may maintain the fundamental weakness of Catholic identity in most colleges and universities that describe themselves as Catholic, surely this would not be the position of colleges and universities that designate themselves as Catholic. Presumably, these schools see themselves as striving, in lesser and greater degree, toward a vision of upholding Catholic values in the modern world. Thus, it is unlikely that they would be persuaded by this view proffered by the CNS.

A weaker version of this position may have merit. Although colleges and universities may not see the fundamentally Catholic character of the institution as threatened by performance of the play, they may choose to ban it on the grounds that its performance is seen as somehow inconsistent with upholding and teaching Catholic values. This would be the message of Bishop John D'Arcy as set forth in his February 2004 letter, "Concerning a Presentation at Notre Dame."[52] In a measured and reasoned appeal to then-president Edward Malloy, CSC, Bishop D'Arcy does not seek to ban a performance but does quite rightly point to the dangers of a performance that may well be offensive to women and seems to be "antithetical to the church's teaching on human sexuality." This is precisely the sort of conversation we need to have about the play, and it should be welcomed in our colleges and universities. Different people can disagree about the merits of Archbishop D'Arcy's letter, but at least he refers back to the tradition and is willing to engage in dialogue with the university. Following a robust discussion, the university may decide that the play's merits are outweighed by its flaws, but only then can the play be discarded in line with the requirements of academic integrity. This approach is, as noted here, sorely lacking in the missives sent by the CNS.

In his 2003 Cardinal Hume Memorial Lecture, Eamon Duffy of Cambridge University observed: "All living traditions need and are nourished by some degree of self-scrutiny and debate, and they are not undermined by it; indeed, where they become fixed and immune from such self-scrutiny, they die. Tradition is not a weight holding us down, but a tool for fresh discovery. This is as true for religious traditions as for any other kind."[53] As members of the academy in the rich Roman Catholic tradition, we must take that tradition seriously and be willing to subject it to scrutiny and debate. This tradition calls us forward; we cannot permit it to wither to insignificance by failing to engage and discuss the world we live in. The CNS urges us to do just that. As Lonergan observes, their position fails to meet the demands of the tradition they claim as their own.

A Critical Analysis
Heather Hathaway

As Fr. O'Meara has stated, what is most necessary when considering any issue on an academic campus is critical and robust discussion. Eve Ensler's play *The Vagina Monologues* has not received that on most Catholic campuses for a variety of reasons. Dr. Quade has shown how negative attention from the Cardinal Newman Society has effectively stifled, if not altogether silenced, discussion of the play on many campuses. Fr. O'Meara has shown how simplistic applications of Catholic teachings to the play often justify its exclusion from the curriculum and co-curriculum. From my own disciplinary perspective as an English professor, I would argue that basic weaknesses in the play itself have made it an unpopular selection for literary, theater, or women's studies syllabi. But given the attention *The Vagina Monologues* commands annually from our students, and consequently from us as educators, it is in fact unreasonable *not* to discuss it. My goal here is to engage briefly in a critical evaluation of the play so as to suggest how an analysis of its strengths and weaknesses can actually be used, first to educate students about fundamental feminist ideals that stand at the heart of the Jesuit educational mission and second to fulfill our obligations as proponents of Ignatian pedagogy.

Quite frankly, the appeal of *The Vagina Monologues* to college students often surprises me. As a literature scholar, I find it limited artistically; as a longtime feminist, I find it limited philosophically and politically; as a faculty member and former administrator, I find that the controversy it generates, at least on Catholic campuses, distracts students from larger structural, political, and institutional forms of inequality that I believe they should also be engaging. At the same time, I must acknowledge that Ensler's play is culturally significant on a number of grounds. First, in focusing explicitly on women's bodies and women's sexuality, the play exists as an important artifact of a movement in the history of American feminism in which the reclamation of women's bodies by women was a significant step toward greater psychological and physical autonomy. Since this is an ongoing struggle for women worldwide—consider Afghanistan, for example, where women still face persecution if they do not obscure their bodies with burkas when in public—the play repeatedly issues a call for the right of women to own their bodies, themselves.[54]

Second, as poststructuralist feminists have shown, and as Ensler says herself in the "I Believe" piece she wrote for National Public Radio, there is a "power in naming things."[55] In saying the word "vagina" (a word that seems always to elicit snickers or giggles or blushing in ordinary settings) 128 times during each show, the play does go a long way toward demystifying and demarginalizing the linguistic taboo surrounding "vagina" and, in so doing, works toward, in Ensler's words, "rearrang[ing] our learned patterns of behavior, and redirect[ing] our thinking." In publicly uttering "a banished word, which represented a buried, neglected, dishonored part of the body"—and thereby empowering other women to do the same—Ensler has created a valuable cultural mechanism through which many women feel liberated from the shame they associate with their own sexuality.[56]

Finally, there is no question that The Vagina Monologues, as the impetus behind Ensler's larger V-Day Campaign, has mobilized thousands of women and men toward a realization of the depth of violence against women and girls and a desire to act against it. In 2008, over 3,700 V-Day benefits were held, all organized by community volunteers. Donations from performances of the play have generated such varied programs as a two-week festival of theater, spoken word, performance, and community events called "Until the Violence Stops: NY," which was intended to heighten awareness about gender violence in the city; community briefings on the missing and murdered women of Juárez, Mexico; women's summits in Afghanistan, South Asia, Israel, Palestine, and Jordan; the opening of the first shelters for women in Iraq; and the Karama program based out of Cairo, which works at the grassroots level to build networks ending violence against women and girls in Egypt, Sudan, Morocco, Tunisia, Algeria, Syria, and Lebanon. The V-Day Campaign has contributed more than $40 million to organizations working to eradicate violence against women in its many forms, and this can only be celebrated.[57]

So, The Vagina Monologues has done important cultural work on many different levels. But does this render it appropriate material for Catholic campuses? Does it meet the standards of most Catholic universities, outlined by Dr. Quade, so as to deem the play in keeping with the Catholic mission? Obviously, the CNS says no—but I say yes. Yes, because, by capitalizing on the energy The Vagina Monologues inevitably generates among students, we can challenge them to engage in a critical—not just a simplistically idolizing or admonishing—analysis of the issues the play raises. If we embrace our students' desire to engage the text, we can simultaneously defuse the political antagonisms that surround the question of whether it should or should not be performed on campus and concentrate instead on opening their minds to the more important concerns of feminists, Jesuits, and the Catholic Church more generally that The Vagina Monologues engages—namely, gender and global oppression.

Such a discussion might begin with a simple critique of the play and an analysis of its strengths and weaknesses from an aesthetic perspective. By most theatrical and literary standards, it is simply not a great work of art. Consider the form of presentation of the individual monologues. Because they are neither contextualized when the play is performed (though they are introduced in the published version) nor self-reflective, it is often difficult to determine Ensler's purpose in presenting them. Some monologues, such as "Because He Liked to Look at It," are intentionally light and often come off humorously. But when followed directly by the oddly titled "Not-So-Happy Fact," which declares that "genital mutilation has been inflicted on eighty to one hundred million girls and young women" (which would suggest that this is far more than a "not-so-happy" fact), or the very harrowing tale of a Bosnian war rape victim, "My Vagina Was My Village," this jarring juxtaposition leaves the viewer uncertain about what message is intended to be conveyed.[58] The play might also be considered limited aesthetically with regard to its level of theatrical production. No scenery, stage direction, or props shape the performance; rather, the audience is basically asked to sit for three hours and listen to a group of women deliver monologues about their vaginas. Obviously, this minimalism is advantageous and intentional on Ensler's part, because it enables groups of untrained performers (students, community members, etc.) to produce the work easily and well, with limited support. But few drama critics would argue that this makes for aesthetically superior theater. In fact, I would argue that the audience appeal of The Vagina Monologues lies more in the "who" than in the "what": who exactly is talking about her vagina? College students clearly find the articulation of sexuality on stage by their peers both daring and funny, and 1,800 people were drawn to the 2001 Madison Square Garden event to see the play performed by such luminaries as Glenn Close, Isabella Rossellini, Oprah Winfrey, Gloria Steinem, and Rosie Perez. But I doubt that any of these women, amateur or professional, identifies donning a pink pantsuit and screaming, "Cunt, cunt, cunt," as marking a high point in her theatrical career.

Forgiving its aesthetic limitations, one might argue that the work is valuable as a piece of feminist literature. Oddly, however, the very actresses who were so committed to the Madison Square Garden performance do not similarly commit themselves to feminism. Among the Hollywood icons in the 2001 Madison Square Garden performance, neither Isabella Rossellini nor Glenn Close (among others) would define herself as a feminist. When questioned about it by Sharon Lerner of the *Village Voice* at the post-performance fund-raiser, Rossellini stated that she did not think "violence against women" was a "feminist issue." Close went so far as to admit that she had "this clichéd image of what a feminist would be and I don't want to be that way." When asked how feminists are perceived, she stated: "They don't like men—you know, kind of, um, butch." So, as Lerner asked in her commentary on the evening, "*Feminism* is in the verbal gutter, while Close carries *cunt* to redemption?? 'That, to me, is about humanity,' the actress said of her word-purifying performance. 'It's about something that's bigger than what I kind of always thought feminism was.'"[59]

Not all art is or should be high art, however, so these limitations are fairly insignificant and can be easily overlooked, given the way in which the production has proved to empower women to embrace their bodies. At the same time, one must thoughtfully consider the play's dangerously essentialist equation of identity with biology. By focusing the performance itself so exclusively on the vagina and a woman's identification with it as a form of female empowerment, Ensler implies that the grounding of identity in anatomy makes sense. But, as critiques of the body's materiality and social constructions of gender by queer feminist theorists such as Judith Butler have shown (not to mention the history of women writ large), such essentialism risks affirming a reductive equation of personhood, identity, and gender with the physical embodiment and manifestation of one's sexual organs. This, in turn, actually leads to the very objectification of women that the V-Day Campaign seeks to challenge.

Similarly, one might discuss whether *The Vagina Monologues* reifies the vagina as normative in this culture, as Kim Q. Hall has shown in her article "Queerness, Disability, and *The Vagina Monologues*."[60] Basing her analysis on the Intersex Society of North America's critique of the play, Hall challenges Ensler's interpretation of the story of an intersex young woman from Oklahoma.[61] Ensler states:

One girl in Oklahoma told how she had been born without a vagina, and only realized it when she was fourteen. She was playing with her girlfriend. They compared their genitals and she realized hers was different, something was wrong. She went to the gynecologist with her father, the parent she was close to, and the doctor discovered that in fact she did not have a vagina or uterus. Her father was heartbroken, trying to repress his tears and sadness, so his daughter would not feel bad. On the way home from the doctor, in a noble attempt to comfort her, he said, "Darlin. We've got an interesting situation. You were born without a vagina. But the good news is we're gonna get you the best homemade pussy in America. And when you meet your husband he's gonna know we had it made especially for him."[62]

While there are a number of problems raised by this vignette, perhaps most obvious is the denial of the intersex young woman's basic human dignity in the suggestion that she is deficient and must be "fixed." In fact, Ensler lauds the patriarchal intervention by stating, "And they did get her a new pussy, . . . and when she brought her father back [to the play] two nights later, the love between them melted me."[63] As Hall explains, Ensler's tale reinforces the belief that "the relation between having a vagina and being a woman" is "fixed in nature, and [that] women who are born without vaginas are . . . fragmented women."[64] More important, as has been noted by the Intersex Society of North America in its 2002 "V-Day Challenge," this vignette reflects Ensler's dissonant portrayal of "the cutting of young women's genitals in Africa . . . versus the cutting of young intersex people's genitals in the United States."[65] Hall rightly observes that "to the extent that Ensler's reclamation and celebration of the vagina marginalizes intersexed bodies, it reinforces heteropatriarchal regulatory norms that have historically infused the vagina with the very meanings Ensler wishes to subject to critique."[66]

Equally problematic in this vignette is its presumption of the young woman's heterosexuality despite her discovery that she had no vagina at age fourteen when "playing with her girlfriend." Nothing at all is said about this: Ensler lets the assumption that the girl must be heterosexual go unchallenged, despite the ambiguity of the scene of sexual discovery. Rather oddly, in an allegedly feminist play about claiming a voice (certainly one of the hallmarks of second-wave feminism), the potentially lesbian voice of this young woman is notably silenced. Moreover, Ensler's retelling of this event with no sense of irony or admonition actually makes her complicit in both the girl's silencing by a traditional patriarchal order in which the father "corrects" the daughter so that she will be "appropriate" marriage material for a husband. This dangerously implies approval of compulsory heterosexuality as described by lesbian feminist Adrienne Rich, as well as of the historical practice of viewing women as commodities of exchange between men.[67]

Related to the play's problematic reduction of identity with biology is its naive assumption that unity among women can be created on the basis of their vaginas. Yes, having a vagina does link a certain subset of the human population based on a common sexual organ. But women are surely more than their vaginas, and to deny the differences among them created by nationality, class, race, ethnicity, religion, and the like, risks reinscribing, via the play, the second-wave feminist movement's marginalization of lesbians and women of color.[68] As third-wave and postcolonial feminists such as Trin T. Minh-ha, Chandra Mohanty, and Gayatri Spivak have shown, such universalizing notions of women and the violence committed against them are hallmarks of a "colonialist feminism" that fails to recognize cultural differences and contextualize forms of patriarchal violence within them.[69]

One might also offer a critique of *The Vagina Monologues* on the basis of its notably Western and bourgeois orientation. Although Ensler tries to avoid this by adding monologues about women from other nations and even shifting the focus of the V-Day Campaigns to international issues (the 2009 V-Day focus, for example, was on female oppression in the Democratic Republic of the Congo), the general tenor of the play implies that Western, and more specifically American, women celebrate their vaginas while third world women (in the play this is reflected in the monologues on Bosnian and African women in particular) are victimized by them. Clearly her intention, in including such monologues, is to highlight the violence inherent in rape as a war crime and in female genital mutilation. But, again to quote Hall, "because Ensler's discussion of genital mutilation presents a West that has moved beyond this practice while the non-Western world is construed as remaining trapped in a more patriarchal past," Ensler risks reifying the colonialist notion of the Western woman as progressive while third world women are powerless under the worst forms of patriarchy.[70] Western women become both the norm and the model to which to aspire, again reflecting a form of "Western privilege" (as well as white privilege) that risks hobbling global feminism.

The play is also problematic in its bourgeois assumption that most (if not all) women have the luxury actually to be "worried about vaginas." If one has to sell sex in order to live, the larger structural issues surrounding her perpetual poverty are probably more pressing. Educational inequity, economic oppression, political subjugation—all these issues are about far more than vaginas, and studying one's vagina is unlikely to combat them. As Germaine Greer, feminist anarchist and author of *The Female Eunuch* (1970), commented about her own participation in a V-Day reading, "In multiple performances that took place all over Britain on and around V-Day this year, sassier actresses than Ensler found themselves chanting, 'We were worried about vaginas. We were worried about vaginas,' though at the Mercury Theatre in Colchester, where I was one of their number, we all agreed that our vaginas were one thing we didn't have to worry about. Our kids, Afghanistan, the National Health, George W. Bush, breast cancer, MMR, the Middle East, aging parents, global warming, you name it—we were more worried about them than we were about vaginas."[71] Cultural critic Camille Paglia makes a similar point when she notes that "a day at a potato farm or crab-picking plant would do a hell of a lot more for" most women in terms of understanding oppression "than an evening at Madison Square Garden," chanting the c word with Glenn Close.[72] While this act may constitute some form of liberation for economically privileged women, a more powerful and comprehensive liberation will be signaled when structural and institutional sexism abates.[73]

Inquiry into all or any of these subjects, as provoked by an analysis of *The Vagina Monologues*, is a worthy enterprise in any college classroom. In particular, it is relevant in those on Catholic Jesuit campuses, where working toward social, economic, and political justice is one of these institutions' primary missions. Jo Reger and Lacey Story have documented how *The Vagina Monologues* valuably advances dialogue about such issues on two contrasting secular campuses. On a liberal campus on which women's rights were regularly addressed, student attention moved from issues directly related to feminism and sexuality toward larger concerns with human rights nationally and internationally. On a more conservative campus where issues pertaining to feminism and sexuality were not often discussed, the play opened the door for students to talk about and study such topics in arenas previously unknown to them.[74] Thus, the play itself, regardless of whether one chooses to concentrate on its strengths or limitations, can valuably serve as a catalyst to furthering discussions about myriad issues related to women's rights specifically and human rights, geopolitical history, and forms of oppression based on nationality, class, race, and ethnicity more broadly.

By engaging our students in these topics, in fact, we can go a long way toward fulfilling our obligation as educators to enact a pedagogy that fulfills the goals of Jesuit education: namely, nurturing critical thinking, demanding a rigorous interrogation of the norms that shape consciousness; attending to experience as a valuable way of knowing (experience being a key component of Ignatian spirituality); engaging in advocacy and the struggle for social change institutionally and systematically; and liberating students (and ourselves) to be women and men for others. I argue, in fact, that as educators on Jesuit campuses in particular, we have a *distinctive* obligation to engage *The Vagina Monologues* due to a perfect storm in which converge expectations of Ignatian pedagogy, patterns of young adult psychosexual development, and a vexed history of sexuality and religion.

First, as proponents of Jesuit education, we are called upon to practice an approach to learning and student development that is rooted in philosophical tradition of St. Ignatius. As described most recently in two documents, "The Characteristics of Jesuit Education" (1986) and "Ignatian Pedagogy: A Practical Approach" (1993), the expressed goal of Jesuit education is to transform students' views of themselves, of others, of social systems and societal structures, of the human community and the natural world.[75] To do so, educators are encouraged to be mindful of and apply the five tenets characteristic of Ignatian pedagogy: context, experience, reflection, action, and evaluation. Context involves meeting students where they are in terms of their familial, community, and cultural identities; the sociocultural, political, cultural, and institutional contexts in which their education occurs; and the experiences and knowledge students bring to their learning task. Experience refers to engaging students as whole people—head and heart, *pietas* and *veritas*, affective and cognitive. Reflection is required to help students understand the relationship between the content learned and its application to their own and others' aspects of life. Action refers to an internal and deed-based reordering of priorities and values. Finally, evaluation measures student growth, including academic mastery, but, more important, a determination of the students' growth in attitudes, priorities, and actions as aligned with the goals of Jesuit education.[76]

Of these, the most relevant to our obligation, as feminist Jesuit educators, to engage *The Vagina Monologues* are, perhaps, context, experience, and reflection. If we are to meet students where they are—if we are to honor their cultural identities and *contexts*, we have no choice but to engage their *experiences* as physical, as well as intellectual and affective, beings. Students are sexual entities, plain and simple. This is neither good nor bad, shameful nor honorable—it just *is*. The college years, in fact, as developmental psychologists from Jean Piaget to Erik Erikson to Carol Gilligan have shown, represent a peak moment in their psychosexual development. Particularly relevant to college professors because of our professional responsibilities are Arthur Chickering's "seven vectors" of college student development. Chickering has shown that, as part of developing mature interpersonal relationships (vector 4), students' capacity for healthy intimacy increases. Implicit in establishing identity (vector 5), they become more comfortable with their bodies and appearances and with their gender and sexual orientation. Identity formation, according to Chickering, "hinges on finding out what it means to be a man or a woman and coming to terms with one's sexuality."[77] In so doing, students grow in self-acceptance and self-esteem, and personal stability and integration. As our colleagues in student development know, attending to all vectors of the student development experience is the critical enterprise of the university. By using *The Vagina Monologues* to engage these issues on campus, whether in the classroom or outside it, we can make strides toward true *cura personalis,* care of the entire person.

As important, by responding to students holistically, by acknowledging their sexuality by offering information rather than judgment, we can go a long way toward healing the vexed relationship that traditionally exists between religion and sexuality. Numerous studies have shown that sexuality is often linked to shame, not only for those who have been abused (which is one of Ensler's main points, of course), but also for people with a high degree of religiosity.[78] Nancy Lesko, in her study "The Curriculum of the Body: Lessons from a Catholic High School," demonstrates that this is certainly true for Catholics.[79] Catholic writer Nancy Mairs's reflection on sexuality in *Ordinary Time: Cycles in Marriage, Faith, and Renewal* perhaps best captures the ambivalence that many Catholics experience about the body as a sexual entity:

> You would think, wouldn't you, that a faith founded on the premise of incarnation—of the Word-that-speaks-all-into-being made flesh to dwell among us—would hold in certain respect, perhaps outright reverence, the body, the very form in which the divine had elected to be housed. . . . The world may well end if you cut down its trees and pave it over, it may well end if you permit its people to go unfed and unclothed and uneducated while you prosper. But the world will not end if you touch your genitals. The world will not end even if you touch someone else's genitals. I can think of sound reasons for choosing not to do so, but fear and disgust should not be among them. Your body is not a pesthouse, it is simply a body: who you are: part of God's creation, a small part, true, but as real and lovely as the rest. If you love every part, evil will not enter the world through you.[80]

Granted, Mairs's perspective may be more representative of attitudes held by adult Catholics who grew up, prior to Vatican II reforms, believing that sexual thoughts, deeds, and words constituted venial sins significant enough to warrant denial of Holy Communion and to be forgiven only through the confines of the confessional. Similarly, the Church's teachings on sexuality were beneficially updated by the U.S. Bishops' 1991 document, *Human Sexuality: A Catholic Perspective for Education and Lifelong Learning*. Nonetheless, as educators in Catholic institutions, we must be attentive to the likelihood that pre–Vatican II ideas about sexuality still linger in the teachings and attitudes passed on to our students by their parents. The contested portrayal of sexuality in Ensler's *Monologues* can certainly help us initiate discussions with our students about how "wonderful [a] gift" and how "awesome [a] responsibility" human sexuality is, according to the bishop's treatise.[81]

Studies have also shown that the less information young women have about sex and sexuality, the higher degree of guilt and discomfort they feel about their bodies. This, in turn, puts them at higher risk in terms of both sexual danger and desire. According to Deborah Tolman:

> The "just say no" curriculum obscures the larger social inequities being played out on girls' bodies. . . . Even adults who are willing or able to acknowledge that girls experience sexual feelings worry that knowing about their own sexual desire will place girls in danger. But keeping girls in the dark about their power to choose based on their own feelings fails to keep them any safer from these dangers. Girls who trust their minds and bodies may experience a stronger sense of self, entitlement, and empowerment that could enhance their ability to make safe decisions. One approach to educating girls is for women to speak to them about the vicissitudes of sexual desire—which means that women must let themselves speak and know their own sexual feelings, as well as the pleasures and dangers associated with women's sexuality and the solutions we have wrought to the dilemma of desire: how to balance the realities of pleasure and danger in women's sexuality.[82]

While *The Vagina Monologues* may not be the ideal educational forum through which to raise these issues, denying its production on college campuses only reinforces the harmful beliefs that sexuality is shameful and that acknowledgment of oneself as a sexual being runs counter to Catholic teaching.

Rather than run from Ensler's *Vagina Monologues* in response to the intimidating tactics of the Cardinal Newman Society described by Dr. Quade or out of fear of contagion caused by merely witnessing the performance, to which Fr. O'Meara referred, I suggest that Catholic institutions should instead embrace the *Monologues* with the same spirit of open-mindedness and critical inquiry we would direct toward other imaginative artistic pieces. In reality, there is nothing in the play that Catholic institutions should be afraid of, theologically or otherwise. Rather, by examining both what the play does *and* what it does not do, we can find much to be mined that actually reinforces, when subject to critical and robust discussion, the fundamental ideals of Catholic, and particularly Jesuit, feminist education: respect for the dignity of each person; a commitment to community; service to those in need, particularly the poor, vulnerable, and suffering; and that age-old feminist tenet, solidarity. Most importantly, as Fr. O'Meara stated so eloquently, the play, regardless of what one might think about its merits or liabilities, can help us to "recognize and teach that it is in women's bodies and through women's voices that Christ is continually made present in this world."

13 Tilling the Soil

Preparing Women for the Vocation
of Ministry—A Challenge and Call

SUSAN M. MOUNTIN

"For hunchbacks, cripples, those with open sores and women in the church . . . we pray to the Lord." This powerful petition, reportedly offered by theologian Josephine Massingberd Ford, faculty member from the University of Notre Dame Theology Department, stunned Catholic theologians gathered for their annual meeting in the early 1970s. As one might expect, some worshippers tittered at this proclamation and some were simply mortified.

More than thirty-five years later, the cause of women and their place in the Catholic Church remains of paramount interest. A recent Web search indicated more than 1.7 million sites devoted to the question of Catholic women's ordination. The vast majority encourage the possibility. Organizations such as the Women's Ordination Conference, the Young Feminist Network, and FutureChurch have existed for years, creating a parallel theological framework for what is the "official" Church teaching on this volatile issue, which is not discussable, according to statements issued by the Vatican. The tension that exists around this topic evokes a range of responses from anger to apathy to frustration, whether one is for or against the idea. But this chapter is not about women's ordination, exactly. It is about the responsibility Jesuit institutions (and, by extension, all Catholic colleges and universities) have to attract, nurture, and support women for vocations in ministry, in light of current Church practice.

While scores of women choose to stay in the Catholic Church for a variety of reasons, other women leave.[1] Many enter seminaries of other Christian traditions, are ordained, and serve in Protestant congregations. They find that they can deny neither their gifts and abilities nor the powerful call of the Holy Spirit to serve the Christian community. One respects their right to respond to the call deep within to pastor and lead through ordained ministry. At the same time, the loss to the

Roman Catholic tradition of these talented, faith-filled women is painful and has a spiraling effect, as each woman who departs is likely to be friends with others who stay, and that action often results in a reexamination of their own commitment to the Catholic Church and leadership within it.

In spite of the policy on women's ordination and official Church teaching, women serve in official capacities in the Church in countless numbers. The Church even holds up their service and leadership. For instance, *Co-workers in the Vineyard of the Lord*, a U.S. Bishops' letter promulgated in November 2005, reports that of more than 30,000 lay ecclesial ministers in the Church, 64 percent (approximately 19,000) are laywomen and 16 percent (4,800) are religious women.[2] That startling statistic bears out what Catholics know firsthand from experience and observation: Eight out of ten lay ecclesial ministers in the Church are women.[3]

Yet the context is daunting. The demand for ecclesial ministers continues to grow. Ironically, at a time when numbers of priests and religious women are declining at an alarming rate, the U.S. Catholic population increased from 57.4 million in 1995 to 64.8 million in 2005 (about a 15% increase), according to the Center for Applied Research in the Apostolate.[4] In even greater numbers than ten years before, the Catholic faithful require pastoral services. Parents need to be prepared for the baptism of their children; children need to be catechized for First Communion and confirmation; couples need to be prepared for marriage; funerals, weddings, and other liturgies need to be planned; churches need to be decorated for the liturgical seasons; choirs need preparation; high school and college students have pastoral needs for catechesis, justice activities, Christian formation, and youth projects; the ill, the dying, and their families need care and the sacraments; the entire adult community of faith needs formation; and people need pastoral counseling.

The need of the faithful to be "hatched, matched and dispatched," as the saying goes, continues. Someone has to meet this need. The likelihood that it will be "Father" grows slimmer by the hour. A crying need for well-prepared, theologically trained religious education directors, youth ministers, catechists, parish administrators, religious educators, liturgists, and church musicians continues to expand. All are roles that can and are being held by the laity, according to the U.S. Bishops.[5] And many of the faithful who are on the receiving end don't often care anymore whether the pastoral functions are offered by laywomen, laymen, or ordained men.

But when young women, many of whom are reeling at the Church's refusal to address either the shortage of church ministers or the issue of women's ordination, find in themselves a call, a desire, a yearning that is deep within their core for priesthood, and that yearning is mirrored by the growing needs among the faithful, what response is appropriate? When on college campuses young women show up in far greater numbers than their male counterparts to attend retreats and be retreat leaders, serve in liturgical ministries, take service trips, explore Catholic social teaching, and meet in prayer and Bible study groups, what should happen?

If it is difficult in today's culture for a young man to express publicly an interest in priesthood, imagine how difficult it is for a young woman who feels equally and rightfully called to the same ministry to name her desires. Women in the Church have long been relegated to the behind-the-scenes work of cleaning the church, ironing and sewing vestments and altar cloths, teaching catechism, and singing in the choir. In the past thirty years, more women than men have stepped forward, without ordination, to do the priestly work (by virtue of their baptism) of pastoral leadership in parishes, on campuses, and in hospitals and schools and universities.

What, then, is the responsibility of Jesuit colleges and universities to the Church at large? Jesuit institutions of higher learning prepare leaders in a wide variety of fields, from health care and education to business to social work. They train theologians. Some schools have ministry preparation programs. The challenge, though, of nurturing women for ministry today must be seen within a context of this contemporary Church milieu.

The Society of Jesus peripherally though specifically addressed the issue in the documents of the Thirty-fourth General Congregation in the decree "Jesuits and the Situation of Women in Church and Civil Society." In the document, the Jesuits recognize the discrimination against and exclusion and abuse of women that has occurred throughout society. They apologize for any actions, behaviors, or words that have added to those experiences of exclusion. In short, pithy statements, they suggest remedies. The text invites "all Jesuits, as individuals and through their institutions, to align themselves in solidarity with women" and suggests specific examples for doing this, such as "explicit teaching of the essential equality of women and men in Jesuit ministries, especially in schools, colleges and universities"; "support for liberation movements which oppose the exploitation of women and encourage their entry into political and social life"; "appropriate presence of women in Jesuit ministries and institutions, not excluding the ministry of formation"; "genuine involvement of women in consultation and decision-making in our Jesuit ministries"; "promotion of the education of women and, in particular, the elimination of all forms of illegitimate discrimination between boys and girls in the educational process."[6] These suggestions may be the next-best-kept secret of the Catholic Church (behind Catholic social teaching).

This document then clearly identifies the difficulties that lie ahead:

> It would be idle to pretend that all the answers to the issues surrounding a new, more just relationship between women and men have been found, or are satisfactory to all. In particular, it may be anticipated that some other questions about the role of women in civil and ecclesial society will undoubtedly mature over time. Through committed and persevering research, through exposure to different cultures, and through reflection on experience, Jesuits hope to participate in clarifying these questions and in advancing the underlying issues of justice. The change of sensibilities which this involves will inevitably have implications for Church teaching and practice. In this context we ask Jesuits to live, as always, with the tension involved in being faithful to the teachings of the Church and at the same time trying to read accurately the signs of the times.[7]

Acknowledging the tension is certainly a great place to begin. But the call and challenge to those of us who work and minister in Jesuit colleges and universities is this: naming the real needs of our Catholic women who desire to minister by finding ways for them to test out their vocational call and creating a space for them to ask all the questions. In some respects this is an easy task. It is not brain surgery or nuclear science.

To "till the soil" of women's vocations to ministry, one must first recognize the rocky ground of the current context of Church polity. Providing a safe place for women to speak their desires may be the first step. It is rather scary to consider ministry as one's life work when not officially sanctioned by the Church hierarchy. Yet the *sensus fidelium* speaks loudly. While surely some people will only go to a priest for their pastoral needs, most of the faithful find a ready and willing ear and support in laywomen and men for all but the sacraments. While the hierarchy may be the rocky ground, the faithful are mostly good soil open to sprouting the seeds of ministry.

Women benefit from the same type of formation for ministry as do their male counterparts: field education, strong spiritual formation, a life of prayer, spiritual direction, strong mentoring, and good theological reflection. On the graduate level, these are plentiful in Master of Divinity and pastoral studies programs. But what can be done to bring women into the ministry pipeline earlier, while their strong motivational pull is at its peak in college?

On campuses, what can be done? Marquette University's Manresa Project has attempted in its nine-year history to address this situation in its Manresa Scholars and Intern Program and in a new venture called Partners in Ministry. The Manresa Project is the result of a $2 million grant from the Lilly Endowment for "programs for the theological exploration of vocation." Lilly encouraged schools receiving the grants to find meaningful ways to invite college students to think about both lay and ordained professional church ministry as a life goal. These programs provide real-life ministry opportunities for students, men and women alike, and a program of spiritual formation grounded in Ignatian spirituality and discernment. The basic foundation for the program includes ministry experience, theological reflection, formation in Ignatian spirituality, prayer, mentoring, and visioning.

Nurturing women for ministry is similar to what has nurtured men discerning ministry. What women need in addition is a safe place to ask the tough questions about ecclesial polity and exclusion. They need a place to at least consider what life might be like if they choose to leave the Catholic Church for another tradition that might value their gifts in a different way. They need to pray through that discernment with people who can allow them the room to entertain the possibility, even if it is contrary to the hope of our work. They need the support of mentors who trust the process of their exploration. They also need to face serious questions of what they would lose if they chose to leave the Catholic Church.

There are some risks. One Marquette alumna, Jessica Gazzola Rowley, who believes strongly that she is called to ministry completed her Master in Divinity at a Protestant seminary. She took courses in both Catholic and Protestant theology and came to the crossroads of having to choose. Seeking a place to support her own life goals, she became part of an ecumenical congregation and decided (after much prayerful and painful discernment) to minister in that church. She was ordained a priest in 2008 in a splinter community called the Ecumenical Catholic Church and is now an associate pastor in that large St. Louis parish community. Another woman who completed the program also left the Catholic Church, became Episcopalian, and is studying at an Episcopalian seminary for ordination. Her discernment has come with both desolation and consolation; she confesses to a great deal of spiritual pain in coming to her final conclusion. Yet she also has experienced a sense of freedom. The Catholic Church is losing a remarkably talented individual, which is a huge loss. Yet the wider church is gaining the prayerful leadership of this truly gifted individual, who in her spirituality will remain rooted in Catholicism even if her birth church does not welcome her fully. What is it about the rites and ritual, the tradition and history, the sacraments and prayer life that are left behind for women who feel they must leave? At the same time more than a dozen other alumnae of the program continued in Catholic graduate programs for ministry or theology and are now lay ministers in Catholic schools and parishes. Certainly there are those in the Roman Catholic Church who will proclaim their ordination invalid. Perhaps from their perspective they are. Yet if their vocations are from God, one might surmise that it is God who ordains these insightful, talented, and faith-filled women to do God's work.

On the other hand, how can those women who choose to stay explore the possibilities that exist if they continue in their commitment to the Roman Catholic tradition? Hearing the vocation journeys of women who have stuck with the Church through thick and thin and found life in the service of the Roman Catholic faith community may help. But as one young woman in our program pointed out, "it's a bit like describing why women in abusive relationships stay with their partners." Women often need to be affirmed in their fidelity and commitment to the Catholic Church in spite of its policy, and that may feel and look like staying in what some might term a bad relationship.

Looking around the Church, one finds evidence that millions of women stay. They continue to find in the ritual and practices, in the tradition and prayer, a source of life that surpasses their concerns. Frankly, some women do not mind the Church as it is. In a group setting for theological reflection, it is important for men and women alike to talk through current Church culture. And clearly some women, along with some men, do not believe women should ever be ordained.

Women and men on college campuses have multiple opportunities for ministry-related activities ranging from liturgical ministries, leading retreats, Bible studies, and prayer groups to faith and justice work. Indeed, if a survey were done of those involved on Jesuit campuses in campus ministry activities, women would likely outnumber men by a significant margin.

So what happens when some of these women, as college students, begin to have opportunities off campus as well? Female students in the Manresa Project have taken on the traditional roles of catechist and others roles as well, including those of confirmation director, music minister, liturgical ministry coordinator, and youth minister. Seeing their gifts and talents appreciated and valued by a local church community allows them to see themselves in a new way and to envision possibilities for their continued education in ministry. Many of them may not have known that they could get a master's degree in divinity, which would make them eminently employable in a parish or diocesan agency. Graduate programs in ministry are usually not represented at career fairs, so someone at every college needs to be a conduit to direct students to those programs.

At Marquette, in the past six years, twenty-six women have been involved in the ministry discernment program. One joined the ecumenical Catholic Church and is now ordained as a priest in that tradition. Another joined the Episcopal Church and is studying to be ordained as a priest. These decisions came with pain for each of them, but also with an inner assurance that they have been called to priesthood and must answer that call. Nineteen of them have gone on to graduate studies in theology or ministry or are currently working for Church-related agencies. While these are not huge numbers, and it is impossible to know how many would have gone into ministry anyway, the Manresa Project is hopeful that it is enabling women to take their role in the church as leaders who will shape future generations. Marquette is not the only Jesuit university to do this. Those who do this work are compelled to collaborate and share ideas for building this group of strong women who will likely shape the church of the future.

14 Women in Jesuit Higher Education

Ten Years Later

SUSAN A. ROSS

In 1999, I was asked to write an article for an issue of *Conversations*, the journal distributed to Jesuit colleges and universities, about the situation of women in these institutions.[1] Interestingly, that issue was titled "Dangerous Ideas." I focused on the statement issued by the Society of Jesus's General Congregation (GC) 34 on "Jesuits and the Situation of Women in Church and Civil Society," and I was fairly critical of the ways that my institution, Loyola University Chicago, had responded to GC 34's courageous statement, which called on the Jesuits to incorporate women more fully into their mission. I noted that the work of implementing the statement at Loyola had been given to some women religious on the staff; I also observed that my interactions with the Jesuits on campus, other than those related to academic issues, were minimal. I was critical of the president of Loyola University at the time for not insisting that the Jesuits themselves take up the task of implementation. After the article was printed, I received both praise and criticism for my comments. Some women faculty did not want to be associated with feminism, while others wrote to say that their experiences were very similar.

Ten years later, I am in my second year as chairperson of the Theology Department. The provost of Loyola is a woman. Five years ago, I accepted university ministry's invitation to participate in the Spiritual Exercises over the course of the year and developed a close friendship with the Jesuit priest who was assigned to be my spiritual director. I was asked to preach at the baccalaureate Mass a few years ago, and recently I was interviewed by the marketing department for a video about why high school students should consider coming to a Jesuit institution. I spoke enthusiastically about the Jesuit spirit on campus. So, one might conclude that everything has changed for the better for women in Jesuit institutions of higher education, or at least at Loyola.

But the answer is far more complicated than that. While some things have changed for the better, some things have stubbornly remained the same. In this chapter, I want to explore some of the issues that continue to be a challenge for women, particular women who identify as feminists, at Jesuit institutions. My starting point will be what has happened at Loyola Chicago over the last ten years, as a follow-up to my earlier article. I will focus on three areas: academics, administration, and atmosphere. While these three areas are not comprehensive and have a fair amount of overlap, they provide some measure of the situation for feminists in Jesuit higher education at the end of the first decade of the twenty-first century. To anticipate my conclusion, there is much, much more work that needs to be done before feminist women and men can be completely comfortable at Jesuit institutions.

Academics

Loyola University Chicago established its Women's Studies Program in 1979, the first of the twenty-eight Jesuit colleges and universities to do so. The program has thrived over the thirty years of its existence; in the fall of 2008, its name was formally changed to Women's Studies and Gender Studies (WSGS). In 2000, it became possible for students to declare a second major in women's studies and in 2000–2001, the program added a master's degree in women's studies, as well as a joint master's degree in social work. Now housed in the Ann Ida Gannon, BVM, Center for Women and Leadership, the program has more than forty faculty listed as associate faculty members and offers a wide range of courses at the undergraduate and graduate levels. At present, the program has just had a stand-alone major approved, and at least one joint faculty appointment is in process; another joint master's program is in development with the Theology Department.

The number of women faculty at Loyola has increased and, happily, so has the number of women full professors. Women students make up nearly two-thirds of the university's total enrollment, as is the case at many colleges and universities. WSGS courses enjoy strong enrollments, Women's History Month is supported by the Office of Student Life, and organizations developed by women students continue to grow: Along with the Gannon Scholars program, a leadership development program begun in the former Mundelein College (affiliated with Loyola in 1991), there are Women in Business and Women in Loyola Leadership.

In many ways, this is a very positive picture. But behind these glowing statistics, there remain some serious problems. In the summer of 2007, no full-time faculty member was willing to take on the directorship of the WSGS program, largely because of cutbacks in compensation and increased pressures on faculty members to publish. In the end, a new full-time but non-tenure-track faculty member took on the position and has provided strong and enthusiastic leadership. But her lack of tenure is a serious concern for the program. The program has also been encouraged to develop a stand-alone major, but problems with control over courses—still almost entirely in the hands of department chairs—as well as enrollment minimums and budgetary concerns continue to stymie this transition.

In the spring of 2009, the WSGS underwent its regular academic program review, and the two external reviews were largely very positive. But there remain some stubborn issues to be resolved. One is that WSGS has no faculty of its own. So, as the program plans to expand its offerings, ensuring that the required courses for a stand-alone major will be offered on a regular basis, the administration is still sorting through the complex issues that joint and dedicated faculty appointments will imply. (It is my sincere hope that by the time this volume is published, these appointments will be a reality!) Other Jesuit institutions, including Santa Clara University, have moved well ahead of Loyola in having joint and dedicated appointments to their programs. Thus, the program remains dependent on the good will of department chairs. Moreover, a process for the evaluation of faculty who have such appointments to the program has been proposed but remains, like the joint appointments, in administrative limbo. Unless and until the stranglehold of traditional departmental structures can be eased, and appropriate compensation structures can be developed, WSGS programs will be hampered in their ability to grow, and too many faculty will work for these programs essentially as volunteers. Professionalization of these programs is one of the major goals to be accomplished.

Women's studies has found a home in many Jesuit institutions, and it is no longer problematic for a new faculty member to focus on feminist or gender-related scholarship. But I wonder to what extent the real challenges that feminism has made to the academy have been met with an adequate response. Scholarship continues to be evaluated largely on traditional grounds, and departments are pressured to meet criteria for ranking, such as those established by the National Research Council, that are individualistic and traditional and tend not to rank collaborative work as highly. Interdisciplinary scholarship, while encouraged by the institutions, is also difficult to support concretely, as concerns about class sizes and FTEs continue to drive budgets.

Younger faculty, both women and men, who have an interest in WSGS are often leery of involvement in the program because of pressures to publish in their primary fields and because the service work on which these programs rely can be burdensome. This was one of the reasons that the program at Loyola was unable to find a tenured faculty member to take on the program's leadership. Even as a group of former women's studies program directors met to write a new constitution for the program, we ruefully acknowledged that it was we old-timers who came in early to work on this, not the younger faculty, who had the most stake in what we were writing. This is not to put the blame exclusively on them, however. Many younger faculty have families to care for, and the increasing demands of academia and of the tenure clock need to take priority. But their reluctance to give up time dedicated to department-related research means that the program will suffer without their contributions.

Are we better off today than ten years ago? In many ways, the answer is yes. The first generation of feminist scholars is reaching retirement age; they and their successors are department chairs, full professors, and established scholars, and they have educated many young women and men who are now continuing this process. Younger faculty, including men, expect to combine professional and personal—including parental—responsibilities in the course of their careers and see women's and gender-related issues as central and not marginal in their teaching and research.

Yet I still find that students resist the idea of inclusive language, course reading lists outside WSGS rarely include significant numbers of women writers, and the students in WSGS courses remain largely women. For too many faculty and students, feminist issues are of concern only to some women who consider themselves feminists. And while the addition of the term "gender studies" to the name of the program has already resulted in more faculty becoming a part of the program, women's studies and gender studies still remains at the bottom of the academic hierarchy.

Administration

In 2005, the president of Loyola University Chicago established a Commission on the Status of Women to explore the issues that concerned women faculty and staff. I served on the steering committee of that commission and spent many hours in meetings over the course of the following year. Modeled on a similar commission at Marquette University—the commission included both faculty and staff and sought to find out what the situation was for women on campus and to make appropriate recommendations.[2]

The impetus for the commission came from a meeting with the president and present and former women's studies program directors (a position I held in the early 1990s) who were concerned about the exodus of women faculty from administrative positions. Some women who had served in various academic administrative positions had found themselves "frozen out" of meetings, decision making, and even space. One told of discovering, when the offices in the area where she worked were moved from one location to another, that she no longer had an office! Another woman who chaired a committee and had prepared a report to present to the board of trustees was stunned when another (male) administrator withheld vital information from her and then gave a report from her area without consulting her ahead of time. Both of these women faculty members left their administrative posts.

The commission included both faculty and staff, which was both beneficial and problematic. Significantly, a number of senior women faculty members refused to have anything to do with the commission, saying that they had little confidence that this group would be able to have any meaningful impact on the university. The initial meeting with women faculty and staff provided plenty of stories from staff members, for example, on how opportunities for internal advancement were blocked, or about outside (male) candidates being chosen over more qualified internal female candidates. Faculty members expressed their frustration with a lack of strong female leadership in the administration. At one point, Loyola had three women deans, including those of the law, nursing, and education schools. At present, there is one (in nursing), and she is an interim dean. And although the university had gone through a major change in its governance structure in the early years of the current president's administration, a number of faculty members wondered how well this new structure was actually working.

The workings of the commission were sometimes hampered by the differences in the cultures of staff and faculty: For faculty who have tenure, there are few limits on what can be said, but for staff, job security is much more tenuous. Some staff members were reluctant to raise issues because of the effects that this might have on their own working situations. And, while the co-chairs of the commission had hoped to interview former women members of the administration, this idea was vetoed by the university's human resources department.

The commission's findings revealed a complex situation. While there was no evidence of outright salary discrimination, men and women alike reported that there was a culture at Loyola that discouraged women's participation at the highest levels. In fact, in 2006—the year of the commission's report—Loyola ranked at the bottom of the list of peer institutions in the number of women in senior leadership. A majority of faculty and staff agreed that there was "insufficient commitment to gender equity issues" on the part of the administration and that programs to develop women as leaders were lacking.

The commission made three sets of recommendations. The first had to do with recruiting and retention. The commission recommended that the university commit itself to "aggressively" recruiting women for senior leadership positions and to designing programs that would help to develop more women leaders among the faculty and staff already at Loyola. The second set of recommendations concerned implementation and assessment. The commission recommended that there be a Gender Equity Commission, that it be a part of the university's strategic plan, that it be charged with gathering data on a regular basis, and that there be educational programs mandated for search committees on the issue of gender equity. The third set of recommendations had to do with work-life balance. Unlike, for example, Boston College and John Carroll University, Loyola Chicago has no clear maternity or paternity leave policy. The commission recommended that such a policy be instituted at Loyola and that its preschool (established in the 1990s after efforts by the Women's Studies Program and Faculty Council) be expanded to offer infant care and that it operate on a sliding scale, making it more affordable for students and staff, as well as faculty.

Three years after the report of the commission was made, results are decidedly mixed. The recommended progress reports were delegated to the university's human relations office, which made one report, in the fall of 2006. Many of the formal recommendations, such as "funding and implementing targeted hiring initiatives" for administrative-level hires, were rejected on the basis that they were actually quota systems in disguise. (Commission members beg to differ.) Gender equity plays no role in the university's new strategic plan.

In my conversations with other women leaders at Jesuit institutions, similar concerns have been raised. The Association of Jesuit Colleges and Universities is in the process of gathering qualitative data on women at the nation's twenty-eight Jesuit colleges and universities to understand better the situation of women in leadership. What has emerged from many of these conversations is that the real issue has to do with the culture of Jesuit education and a sense that many schools are stuck in situations where little is done to challenge the present situation.

Yet there are also positive stories to be told, some at Loyola and even more in other places. A significant number of chairs of departments at Loyola, including some of the largest departments in the College of Arts and Sciences, are women. Marquette University—the first Catholic university to admit women to the university alongside men—is celebrating the centennial of its decision to begin coeducation in 1909 with a yearlong celebration featuring speakers from within and outside the university. Even more significantly, five of Marquette's twelve deans and seven out of seventeen key university leaders are women. A number of other Jesuit universities, including Santa Clara, Fordham, Loyola Marymount, and Seattle, offer majors in women's studies or WSGS programs and some, such as Santa Clara, have their own faculty.

Atmosphere and Culture

In my conversations with women faculty and administrators as I was planning this chapter, the topic of culture came up over and over. How does the culture of a Jesuit Catholic institution support women? The question of culture gets to what goes on beneath the official levels of administrative organization. How do the *real* decisions get made? Who holds the *real* power in these institutions? While there are women who hold senior administrative positions, some of them find themselves excluded from decision-making processes because of the culture in which decisions have long been made.

The Society of Jesus, unlike other large Catholic religious congregations like the Dominicans, Franciscans, or Benedictines, does not admit women to membership.[3] Moreover, the lengthy training that Jesuits undergo in their formation, while not strictly excluding women— women sometimes serve as spiritual directors, and often as teachers— involves an enculturation into a tradition that forges strong bonds among its members, as indeed it ought. The GC 34 statement, no doubt recognizing the all-male nature of the Jesuit culture, urged Jesuits to develop stronger personal bonds with women in their working and social relationships.

In my *Conversations* article, I commented on how few times I had been invited to lunch or dinner with my Jesuit colleagues. I am happy to report that this is no longer the case. Yet I suspect that I am one of only a few women faculty members who know many of the members of the Jesuit community, who know whom to call when there is a problem, and who can count on both personal and professional connections. As one colleague pointed out to me, the issue of Jesuits needing to have more associations with women is not simply a question of expanding the Jesuits' social life. Rather, when one knows someone fairly well, one is more comfortable in all kinds of communications. We are much more likely to listen to the people we know well, and we are also willing to overlook some of their failings. Possibly because of my comments in that article, I came to know better some of the Jesuits I had worked with for years, and some of them have become good friends. But I think that there is still much more that could be done by Jesuits and by the administrations of Jesuit colleges and universities to forge strong connections with the women in their institutions.

While many institutions of higher education need to confront a culture in which a group of "old boys" is effectively in charge despite the presence of women in administrative posts, the situation at Jesuit universities is that the members of the Society also live in communities and thus share both a formal and an informal network from which women are, by definition, excluded. Recently, a candidate for an endowed chair in women's leadership came to Loyola to interview. We talked about the issues that women face in academia and at Loyola, and the candidate nodded knowingly; she commented that this was very much the same situation at her secular institution. But when I noted that the male administrators at her institution did not live together as well as work together, she realized that there were indeed some important differences.

By this I do not mean to disparage the strong sense of community that is shared by members of a religious order whose mission is education; on the contrary, I wish to affirm the commitments of communities like the Jesuits. But, by definition, those who are not Jesuits are excluded from the more informal deliberations that often take place in community settings. One of the innovations that many men's and women's religious communities have developed since Vatican II is a group of "associates," people who have a strong affiliation with the community but who are laypeople and committed to their secular lives. I suggest that developing such a category for communities at the universities can assist Jesuits in knowing their lay colleagues better and including them in some of the kinds of informal gatherings that help to generate strong friendships.

Another issue that arose as I consulted my colleagues was the lack, in many institutions, including my own, of a consistent and fair family and maternal leave policy that does not penalize young faculty members who wish to have children before gaining tenure. Recall that this was one of the issues raised by Loyola's Commission on the Status of Women. At Loyola, most of the faculty I know who have children, or who have had children during their probationary period, were able to work out an arrangement with a department chair: If the baby was due at the end of a semester, then the faculty member would arrange for a substitute for the weeks when she would be unable to teach. If the timing was less auspicious, then the arrangement might involve more committee work and less teaching, or some kind of tradeoff with duties split between semesters. Or, again, perhaps a research leave or mid-probationary leave would be timed well enough to allow for time for childbirth and the crucial early months of a baby's life. But there is still no consistent policy that addresses the needs of faculty who do not want to make the choice between having a job and having children. When I wrote to the Loyola women's studies faculty members to ask for any anecdotal experiences that would be helpful for this chapter, one wrote me this message: "I remain appalled that LUC maintains the family leave policies that it has had for decades, especially in light of the emphasis on social justice and global service, and the fact that three different university constituents have recommended a different policy, i.e., the Women's Commission, Faculty Council, and Center for Faculty and Professional Development. The contradiction of the Jesuit mission with the difficulty young faculty have beginning their families in an environment that does not provide time for adjustment and development seems disingenuous." This faculty member's observation speaks for itself. There are, of course, wider issues to be taken into consideration: the nature of the academic tenure clock; the emphasis (as noted earlier) on solitary, monastic-type scholarship; the old boys' network. But the fact that the lives and struggles of lay faculty are not only often unknown to Jesuit administration but not even a serious consideration remains crucial. If justice on both the personal and social levels is to remain key in the mission of these institutions, then the issues that affect their own members—like the challenges that face the Catholic Church in its distribution of justice—need much greater attention than they receive at present. More transparency in institutional decision making, particularly when decisions are made within the Jesuit community, both informally and formally, that affect the college or university, is necessary so that the high ideals of Jesuit education are open to all and practiced among the institution's members.

Conclusions

Writing this chapter elicited many mixed feelings for me. On the one hand, I and many other feminists I know who teach at Jesuit colleges and universities are proud to be associated with the tradition and to participate in the mission of education that has been a hallmark of the Society of Jesus for over 450 years. I am moved by the dedication of so many members of the Society who care deeply for their work and by so many students who find in this mission a meaningful direction for their lives. WSGS has enjoyed the support of three presidents of Loyola, who have, on some occasions, defended the program against more narrow-minded alumni or community members who think that feminism and Catholicism are mutually exclusive. Each year Loyola's president has to respond to countless e-mails about the production of *The Vagina Monologues*, defending the need for the free exchange of ideas on a university campus. I think of students I have known and with whom I stay in touch whose Jesuit education was central in their choice of careers: legal work with victims of domestic violence, political activism, even academic work in theology!

Yet I also find myself discouraged at times when women's issues are seen as marginal to the institution's main goals, when meetings of university leaders are overwhelmingly male, when it seems that women's voices have not been a part of the conversations and deliberations that have led to important decisions. Women constitute over 60 percent of Loyola's student body, and similar statistics can be found in other Jesuit institutions. Yet leadership, at least in a number of these schools, continues to be a challenge for women.

What will it take? In 2007, the Chicago Foundation for Women used this phrase as their slogan for the year. At their annual luncheon, baskets were placed on each table and attendees were strongly encouraged—make that exhorted!—to contribute money right then and there to make violence against women a thing of the past. This phrase comes to mind as I write this conclusion. What will it take for women in Jesuit higher education to take on significant leadership, to make these institutions family and women friendly, to be places of justice and excellence for women and men alike? It will take at least these things: strong leadership that models an approach to encouraging women at the highest levels of the institution, campus mentoring and leadership programs for women with an interest in academic leadership, and an environment and culture that is women and family friendly. While much of the responsibility for this still falls on the Jesuits involved in higher education, women in these institutions need to keep pressing for change. Some Jesuit institutions are moving forward and serve as models for others; others have much more work to do. The fact that some Jesuit institutions are moving ahead needs to be known by all twenty-eight of the colleges and universities. But even more important, the promise of GC 34 is still unfilled. As we approach the fifteenth anniversary of that meeting in early 1995, we can do no better than return to some of the closing words of that document and remind our Jesuit brothers and colleagues of the work that they committed themselves to in 1995:

> Above all we want to commit the Society in a more formal and explicit way to regard this solidarity with women as integral to our mission. In this way we hope that the whole Society will regard this work for reconciliation between women and men in all its forms as integral to its interpretation of Decree 4 of GC 32 for our times. We know that a reflective and sustained commitment to bring about this respectful reconciliation can flow only from our God of love and justice who reconciles all and promises a world in which "there is neither Jew nor Greek, there is neither slave nor free, there is neither male nor female, for you are all one in Christ Jesus" (Gal 3:28).[4]

Afterword

CHARLES L. CURRIE, S.J.

To one involved in Jesuit higher education for over forty years, the impact of women on the enterprise is both clearly obvious and clearly impressive. In the early 1970s many of our schools were just becoming coeducational. Today, women now make up an average of 57 percent of the student population. More than 46 percent of faculty are women, and each year more women fill important administrative posts. Each survey shows signs of progress, but important gaps in the narrative remain. A detailed study of women faculty and administrators is currently underway to see what we are doing well and where we can do better.

The chapters in this volume recount how women are influencing Jesuit colleges and universities at the core of their mission, namely, where faculty teach and students learn. The contributors explore in many helpful ways the intersection of feminist pedagogy with Ignatian pedagogy, thus opening up opportunities for further dialogue and concerted action.

It is appropriate for Jesuit campuses to be places where the leadership of women in higher education is realized. Decree 14 from the Thirty-fourth General Congregation of Jesuits in 1995 was titled "Jesuits and the Situation of Women in Church and Civil Society." Jesuits and, by extension, Jesuit institutions were challenged "to listen carefully and courageously to the experience of women." Jesuits were also challenged, "as individuals and through their institutions, to align themselves in solidarity with women." The Congregation committed the Society "in a more formal and explicit way to regard this solidarity with women as integral to our mission" and linked that solidarity to our commitment to a faith that does justice.[1]

Interestingly, it was also a Decree 4 at the Thirty-second General Congregation in 1975 that challenged Jesuits and Jesuit institutions to practice a faith that does justice. Decree 4 states that "the mission of the Society of Jesus today is the service of faith, of which the promotion of justice is an absolute requirement."[2] Together, Decree 14 and Decree 4 link justice and solidarity with women.

The insights and strategies of feminist pedagogy, focusing on the student-teacher relationship of active and engaged learning leading to personal and social transformation, clearly resonate with Ignatian pedagogy, wherein teachers accompany learners in their growth and development to be "men and women for others."[3]

That resonance is apparent in the words of Fr. Peter-Hans Kolvenbach, who expanded the notion of educating the "whole person" to educating the "whole person of solidarity for the real world," with that solidarity being learned through "contact" rather than through "concepts." "Students . . . must let the gritty reality of this world into their lives, so they can learn to feel it, think about it critically, respond to its suffering, and engage it constructively."[4]

He also described a challenging and transforming role for faculty, whose mission is "tirelessly to pursue the truth and to form each student into a whole person of solidarity who will take responsibility for the real world." Their research "not only obeys the canons of each discipline, but ultimately embraces human reality in order to help make the world a more fitting place for six billion of us to inhabit. I want to affirm that university knowledge is valuable for its own sake and at the same time is knowledge that must ask itself, 'For whom? For what?'" He explained: "It is the nature of every university to be a social force, and it is the calling of every Jesuit university to take conscious responsibility for being a force for faith and justice. Every Jesuit academy of higher learning is called to live in a social reality . . . and to live for that social reality, to shed university intelligence upon it and to use university influence to transform it."[5]

Those trying to implement Fr. Kolvenbach's vision for education make common cause with the contributors to this volume writing about (and practicing) active and contextual learning, transformative education, critical pedagogy, and the triad of experience, reflection, and action found in both feminist and Ignatian pedagogies. The description of feminist educational strategies reminds one of the life-changing immersion experiences that are increasingly part of Jesuit education today.[6]

The origins and underpinnings of feminist pedagogy and of Ignatian pedagogy are different, in many ways very different, but the end result is often the same, as author after author describes—thus all the more reason for the two pedagogies to join forces to have a greater impact on our campuses. Not all faculty are comfortable engaging in transformational teaching and learning. Some will think it is not academically rigorous enough, when in actuality this kind of teaching and learning will be successful only if it is rigorous. Seeing feminist and Ignatian pedagogies working together and energizing one another can encourage others to explore these very contemporary educational strategies.

We can ardently hope that the dialogue between the two pedagogies described so well in this volume is just the beginning of a very fruitful relationship that will surely benefit not only Jesuit colleges and universities but, more important, the students they serve.

Appendix

Decree 14. Jesuits and the Situation of Women in Church and Civil Society

Thirty-fourth General Congregation of the Society of Jesus

Introduction

361 1. General Congregation 33 made a brief mention of the "unjust treatment and exploitation of women."[1] It was part of a list of injustices in a context of new needs and situations which Jesuits were called to address in the implementation of our mission. We wish to consider this question more specifically and substantially on this occasion. This is principally because, assisted by the general rise in consciousness concerning this issue, we are more aware than previously that it is indeed a central concern of any contemporary mission which seeks to integrate faith and justice. It has a universal dimension in that it involves men and women everywhere. To an increasing extent it cuts across barriers of class and culture. It is of personal concern to those who work with us in our mission, especially lay and religious women.

The Situation

362 2. The dominance of men in their relationship with women has found expression in many ways. It has included discrimination against women in educational opportunities, the disproportionate burden they are called upon to bear in family life, paying them a lesser wage for the same work, limiting their access to positions of influence when admitted to public life and, sadly but only too frequently, outright violence against women themselves. In some parts of the world, this violence still includes female circumcision, dowry deaths and the murder of unwanted infant girls. Women are commonly treated as objects in advertising and in the media. In extreme cases, for example in promoting international sex tourism, they are regarded as commodities to be trafficked.

363   3. This situation, however, has begun to change, chiefly because of the critical awakening and courageous protest of women themselves. But many men, too, have joined women in rejecting attitudes which offend against the dignity of men and women alike. Nonetheless, we still have with us the legacy of systematic discrimination against women. It is embedded within the economic, social, political, religious and even linguistic structures of our societies. It is often part of an even deeper cultural prejudice and stereotype. Many women, indeed, feel that men have been slow to recognize the full humanity of women. They often experience a defensive reaction from men when they draw attention to this blindness.

364   4. The prejudice against women, to be sure, assumes different forms in different cultures. Sensitivity is needed to avoid using any one, simple, measurement of what counts as discrimination. But it is nonetheless a universal reality. Further, in many parts of the world, women already cruelly disadvantaged because of war, poverty, migration or race, often suffer a double disadvantage precisely because they are women. There is a "feminization of poverty" and a distinctive "feminine face of oppression."

The Church Addresses the Situation

365   5. Church social teaching, especially within the last ten years, has reacted strongly against this continuing discrimination and prejudice. Pope John Paul II in particular, has called upon all men and women of good will, especially Catholics, to make the essential equality of women a lived reality. This is a genuine "sign of the times."[2] We need to join with inter-church and interreligious groups in order to advance this social transformation.

366   6. Church teaching certainly promotes the role of women within the family, but it also stresses the need for their contribution in the Church and in public life. It draws upon the text of Genesis, which speaks of men and women created in the image of God (Gn 1:27) and the prophetic praxis of Jesus in his relationship with women. These sources call us to change our attitudes and work for a change of structures. The original plan of God was for a loving relationship of respect, mutuality and equality between men and women, and we are called to fulfil this plan. The tone of this ecclesial reflection on Scripture makes it clear that there is an urgency in the challenge to translate theory into practice not only outside, but also within, the Church itself.

The Role and Responsibility of Jesuits

367   7. The Society of Jesus accepts this challenge and our responsibility for doing what we can as men and as a male religious order. We do not pretend or claim to speak for women. However, we do speak out of what we have learned from women about ourselves and our relationship with them.

368   8. In making this response we are being faithful, in the changed consciousness of our times, to our mission: the service of faith, of which the promotion of justice is an absolute requirement. We respond, too, out of the acknowledgement of our own limited but significant influence as Jesuits and as male religious within the Church. We are conscious of the damage to the People of God brought about in some cultures by the alienation of women who no longer feel at home in the Church, and who are not able with integrity to transmit Catholic values to their families, friends and colleagues.

Conversion

369   9. In response, we Jesuits first ask God for the grace of conversion. We have been part of a civil and ecclesial tradition that has offended against women. And, like many men, we have a tendency to convince ourselves that there is no problem. However unwittingly, we have often contributed to a form of clericalism which has reinforced male domination with an ostensibly divine sanction. By making this declaration we wish to react personally and collectively, and do what we can to change this regrettable situation.

Appreciation

370   10. We know that the nurturing of our own faith and much of our own ministry would be greatly diminished without the dedication, generosity, and joy that women bring to the schools, parishes, and other fields in which we labour together. This is particularly true of the work of lay and religious women among the urban and rural poor, often in extremely difficult and challenging situations. In addition, many religious congregations of women have adopted the *Spiritual Exercises* and our Jesuit *Constitutions* as the basis for their own spirituality and governance, becoming an extended Ignatian family. Religious and lay women have in recent years become expert in giving the Spiritual Exercises. As retreat directors, especially of the Exercises in daily life, they have enriched the Ignatian tradition, and our own understanding of ourselves and of our ministry. Many women have helped to reshape our theological tradition in a way that has liberated both men and women. We wish to express our appreciation for this generous contribution of women, and hope that this mutuality in ministry might continue and flourish.

Ways Forward

371 11. We wish to specify more concretely at least some ways in which Jesuits may better respond to this challenge to our lives and mission. We do not presume that there is any one model of male-female relationship to be recommended, much less imposed, throughout the world or even within a given culture. Rather we note the need for a real delicacy in our response. We must be careful not to interfere in a way that alienates the culture; rather we must endeavour to facilitate a more organic process of change. We should be particularly sensitive to adopt a pedagogy that does not drive a further wedge between men and women who in certain circumstances are already under great pressure from other divisive cultural or socio-economic forces.

372 12. In the first place, we invite all Jesuits to listen carefully and courageously to the experience of women. Many women feel that men simply do not listen to them. There is no substitute for such listening. More than anything else it will bring about change. Without listening, action in this area, no matter how well-intentioned, is likely to bypass the real concerns of women and to confirm male condescension and reinforce male dominance. Listening, in a spirit of partnership and equality, is the most practical response we can make, and is the foundation for our mutual partnership to reform unjust structures.

373   13. Secondly, we invite all Jesuits, as individuals and through their institutions, to align themselves in solidarity with women. The practical ways of doing this will vary from place to place and from culture to culture, but many examples come readily to mind:

374   13.1—explicit teaching of the essential equality of women and men in Jesuit ministries, especially in schools, colleges and universities;

375   13.2—support for liberation movements which oppose the exploitation of women and encourage their entry into political and social life;

376   13.3—specific attention to the phenomenon of violence against women;

377   13.4—appropriate presence of women in Jesuit ministries and institutions, not excluding the ministry of formation;

378   13.5—genuine involvement of women in consultation and decision-making in our Jesuit ministries;

379   13.6—respectful cooperation with our female colleagues in shared projects;

380   13.7—use of appropriately inclusive language in speech and official documents;

381   13.8—promotion of the education of women and, in particular, the elimination of all forms of illegitimate discrimination between boys and girls in the educational process.

Many of these, we are happy to say, are already being practised in different parts of the world. We confirm their value, and recommend a more universal implementation as appropriate.

382 14. It would be idle to pretend that all the answers to the issues surrounding a new, more just relationship between women and men have been found, or are satisfactory to all. In particular, it may be anticipated that some other questions about the role of women in civil and ecclesial society will undoubtedly mature over time. Through committed and persevering research, through exposure to different cultures and through reflection on experience, Jesuits hope to participate in clarifying these questions and in advancing the underlying issues of justice. The change of sensibilities which this involves will inevitably have implications for Church teaching and practice. In this context we ask Jesuits to live, as always, with the tension involved in being faithful to the teachings of the Church and at the same time trying to read accurately the signs of the times.

Conclusion

383 15. The Society gives thanks for all that has already been achieved through the often costly struggle for a more just relationship between women and men. We thank women for the lead they have given, and continue to give. In particular, we thank women religious, with whom we feel a special bond, and who have been pioneers in so many ways in their unique contribution to the mission of faith and justice. We are grateful, too, for what the Society and individual Jesuits have contributed to this new relationship, which is a source of great enrichment for both men and women.

384 16. Above all we want to commit the Society in a more formal and explicit way to regard this solidarity with women as integral to our mission. In this way we hope that the whole Society will regard this work for reconciliation between women and men in all its forms as integral to its interpretation of Decree 4 of GC 32 for our times. We know that a reflective and sustained commitment to bring about this respectful reconciliation can flow only from our God of love and justice who reconciles all and promises a world in which "there is neither Jew nor Greek, there is neither slave nor free, there is neither male nor female, for you are all one in Christ Jesus" (Gal 3:28).

Notes

Foreword

JEFFREY P. VON ARX, S.J.

1. John L. McCarthy and Jesuits, eds., *Documents of the Thirty-fourth General Congregation of the Society of Jesus: The Decrees of General Congregation Thirty-four, the Fifteenth of the Restored Society and the Accompanying Papal and Jesuit Documents* (St. Louis, Mo.: Institute of Jesuit Sources, 1995).

2. Ibid.

3. Ibid.

4. Ibid.

5. Quoted in John W. O'Malley, "How the First Jesuits Became Involved in Education," in *The Jesuit "Ratio Studiorum": 400th Anniversary Perspectives,* ed. Vincent J. Duminuco (New York: Fordham University Press, 2000), 66.

6. Ignacio Ellacuría, commencement address to Santa Clara University (Santa Clara, Calif., June 1982), http://www.scu.edu/Jesuits/ellacuria.html.

7. Society of Jesus, *The Decrees of General Congregation 35,* http://www.sjweb.info/35/documents/Decrees.pdf.

8. Ibid.

9. Ibid.

Introduction: Educating for Transformation—Jesuit and Feminist Approaches in the Classroom and Beyond

JOCELYN M. BORYCZKA AND ELIZABETH A. PETRINO

1. Kimberlé Crenshaw, "Mapping the Margins: Intersectionality, Identity Politics, and Violence against Women of Color," *Stanford Law Review* 43, no. 6 (1991): 1241–99.

2. Pedro Arrupe, "Men for Others," in *Foundations,* ed. C. E. Meirose (Washington, D.C.: Jesuit Secondary Education Association, 1973).

3. See Lisa Sowle Cahill's "Women and Men Working Together in Jesuit Institutions of Higher Learning," *Conversations* 4 (Fall 1993): 25, and Susan A.

Ross's "The Jesuits and Women: Reflections on the 34th General Congregation's Statement on Women in Church and Civil Society," *Conversations* 16 (Fall 1999): 20–28.

4. Rosemary A. DeJulio, "Women's Ways of Knowing and Learning: The Response of Mary Ward and Madeleine Sophie Barat to the *Ratio Studiorum*," in *The Jesuit "Ratio Studiorum": 400th Anniversary Perspectives*, ed. Vincent J. Duminuco (New York: Fordham University Press, 2000), 107–26.

5. Ibid.

6. International Commission on the Apostolate of Jesuit Education, "The Characteristics of Jesuit Education," in Duminuco, *The Jesuit "Ratio Studiorum*," 155.

7. Peter-Hans Kolvenbach, "Themes of Jesuit Higher Education" (address delivered at Georgetown University, Washington, D.C., June 7, 1989), http://onlineministries.creighton.edu/Heartland3/r-themes.html.

8. Peter-Hans Kolvenbach, "The Service of Faith and the Promotion of Justice in American Jesuit Higher Education," in *A Jesuit Education Reader*, ed. George W. Traub (Chicago: Loyola Press, 2008), 155.

9. For a brief overview of Jesuit education's early development, see the Boston College Jesuit Community's "Jesuits and Jesuit Education: A Primer," in Traub, *A Jesuit Education Reader*, 42, and John W. O'Malley's "How the First Jesuits Became Involved in Education," in Duminuco, *The Jesuit "Ratio Studiorum*," 56–79.

10. Peter-Hans Kolvenbach, "The Jesuit University in the Light of the Ignatian Charism" (address delivered to the International Meeting of Jesuit Higher Education, Rome, May 27, 2001), http://users.online.be/~sj.eur.news/doc/univ2001e.htm.

11. Ibid.

12. International Commission on the Apostolate of Jesuit Education, "Ignatian Pedagogy: A Practical Approach, 1993," in Duminuco, *The Jesuit "Ratio Studiorum*," 238.

13. Ibid., 253.

14. Ibid., 257.

15. The recent publications in *NWSA Journal* and a variety of texts demonstrate this growing field: Gail E. Cohee, Elisabeth Daumer, Theresa D. Kemp, Paula M. Krebs, Sue Lafky, and Sandra Runzo, eds., *The Feminist Teacher Anthology: Pedagogies and Classroom Strategies* (New York: Teachers College Press, 1998); Frances Maher and Mary Kay Thompson Tetreault, *The Feminist Classroom: Dynamics of Gender, Race, and Privilege* (New York: Rowman & Littlefield, 2001); Amie A. Macdonald and Susan Sánchez-Casal, *Twenty-first-Century Feminist Classrooms: Pedagogies of Identity and Difference* (New York: Palgrave Macmillan, 2002); Nancy A. Naples and Karen Bojar, eds., *Teaching*

Feminist Activism: Strategies from the Field (New York: Routledge, 2002); and Robbin D. Crabtree, David Alan Sapp, and Adela C. Licona, eds., *Feminist Pedagogy: Looking Back to Move Forward* (Baltimore, Md.: Johns Hopkins University Press, 2009).

16. Crabtree, Sapp, and Licona, *Feminist Pedagogy*, 1–3.

17. See Patricia Hill Collins's *Black Feminist Thought: Knowledge, Consciousness, and the Politics of Empowerment*, 2nd ed. (New York: Routledge, 2000).

18. Maher and Tetreault, *The Feminist Classroom*.

19. Lee Anne Bell, Sharon Washington, Gerald Weinstein, and Barbara Love, "Knowing Ourselves as Instructors," in *The Critical Pedagogy Reader*, ed. Antonia Darder, Marta Baltodano, and Rodolfo D. Torres (New York: Routledge, 2003), 464.

20. Teaching students how to engage in feminist activism, in activities ranging from community action projects to service-learning, represents a cornerstone of feminist pedagogy. See, for example, Naples and Bojar, *Teaching Feminist Activism*. Jennifer Baumgardner and Amy Richards translate this perspective into an approach directed at mobilizing the next generation of women to take action on feminist issues in *Grassroots: A Field Guide for Feminist Activism* (New York: Farrar, Straus and Giroux, 2005).

21. bell hooks, *Teaching Community: A Pedagogy of Hope* (New York: Routledge, 2003), 163.

1. "Do as I Do, Not as I Say": The Pedagogy of Action

ELIZABETH A. DREYER

I want to express my appreciation to Drs. Margaret Miles, Barbara Mujica, and Gillian Ahlgren, who read and made helpful comments on an earlier draft of this chapter.

1. Viewing women in their own right is part of a larger canvas of recent historical work on the Renaissance and early modern Europe that views the period under the rubric of the individual and society. A key early catalyst for this discussion was Swiss historian Jacob Burckhardt's *The Civilization of the Renaissance in Italy*, trans. S. G. C. Middlemore (1860; New York: Modern Library, 2002). While scholars have moved beyond Burckhardt's position, his name is still regularly referenced. See William J. Connell, ed., *Society and Individual in Renaissance Florence* (Berkeley: University of California Press, 2002). The emphasis on the individual that was emerging during this period should be understood in the context of deep social and community ties, not as a type of individualism common today that involves alienation from family and society.

2. For a psychological analysis of Ignatius's relationships with the women in and beyond his family, see W. W. Meissner, *Ignatius of Loyola: The Psychology of a Saint* (New Haven, Conn.: Yale University Press, 1992). In the chapter

"Women," Meissner notes the important role women played throughout Ignatius's life: "It is safe to say that, had it not been for the assistance of important women at critical points in the early history of the Society of Jesus, that organization may have met a far different fate" (238).

3. See John W. Coakley, *Women, Men, and Spiritual Power: Female Saints and Their Male Collaborators* (New York: Columbia University Press, 2006); Jodi Bilinkoff, *Related Lives: Confessors and Their Female Penitents, 1450–1750* (Ithaca, N.Y.: Cornell University Press, 2005); Kimberley M. Benedict, *Empowering Collaborations: Writing Partnerships between Religious Women and Scribes in the Middle Ages* (New York: Routledge, 2004); Catherine Mooney, ed., *Gendered Voices: Medieval Saints and Their Interpreters* (Philadelphia: University of Pennsylvania Press, 1999); Janette Dillon, "Holy Women and Their Confessors or Confessors and Their Holy Women? Margery Kempe and Continental Tradition," in *Prophets Abroad: The Reception of Continental Holy Women in Late-Medieval England*, ed. Rosalynn Voaden (Cambridge: D. S. Brewer, 1996), 115–40; Grace Jantzen, *Power, Gender, and Christian Mysticism* (Cambridge: Cambridge University Press, 1995); Clare A. Lees, ed., *Medieval Masculinities: Regarding Men in the Middle Ages* (Minneapolis: University of Minnesota Press, 1994); Brian Patrick McGuire, "Holy Women and Monks in the Thirteenth Century: Friendship or Exploitation?" *Vox Benedictina* 6 (1989): 343–74; Jo Ann McNamara, "The Rhetoric of Orthodoxy: Clerical Authority and Female Innovation in the Struggle with Heresy," in *Maps of Flesh and Light: The Religious Experience of Medieval Women Mystics*, ed. Ulrike Wiethaus (Syracuse, N.Y.: Syracuse University Press, 1993), 9–27; Ute Stargardt, "Male Clerical Authority in the Spiritual (Auto)biographies of Medieval Holy Women," in *Women as Protagonists and Poets in the German Middle Ages: An Anthology of Feminist Approaches to Middle High German Literature*, ed. Albrecht Classen (Göppingen, Germany: Kümmerle Verlag, 1991), 209–38; Alison Weber, *Teresa of Avila and the Rhetoric of Femininity* (Princeton, N.J.: Princeton University Press, 1990).

4. Mary Elizabeth Perry, *Gender and Disorder in Early Modern Seville* (Princeton, N.J.: Princeton University Press, 1990), 8.

5. All numeric references in parentheses in the text are to Hugo Rahner, ed., *Saint Ignatius Loyola: Letters to Women*, trans. Kathleen Pond and S. A. H. Weetman (New York: Herder & Herder, 1960). Rahner organizes the letters according to the social positions of the women and their relationships with Ignatius and the Society of Jesus: royalty, nobility, benefactresses, spiritual daughters, mothers of Jesuits, and friends. Rahner's goals include uncovering the story of Ignatius the saint and learning about the spiritual care of women in the post-Reformation era of the sixteenth century.

6. Because of my interest in philanthropy, I have not considered the letters in the sections in Rahner's volume titled "Letters to Spiritual Daughters" and "Letters to the Mothers of Fellow-Jesuits."

7. While my focus is Catholic women, there is an impressive literature on Protestant women within the Reformation context. A sampling includes Roland H. Bainton, *Women of the Reformation in Germany and Italy* (Minneapolis, Minn.: Augsburg Press, 1971); Renate Bridenthal, Susan Mosher Stuard, and Merry E. Wiesner-Hanks, eds., *Becoming Visible: Women in European History*, 3rd ed. (Boston: Houghton Mifflin, 1998), 175–201; Merry E. Wiesner, *Women and Gender in Early Modern Europe*, 2nd ed. (Cambridge: Cambridge University Press, 2000); Sherrin Marshall, ed., *Women in Reformation and Counter-Reformation Europe: Public and Private Worlds* (Bloomington: Indiana University Press, 1989); Jean R. Brink, Allison P. Coudert, and Maryanne C. Horowitz, eds., *The Politics of Gender in Early Modern Europe* (Kirksville, Mo.: Sixteenth Century Journal Publishers, 1989); Lyndal Roper, *The Holy Household: Women and Morals in Reformation Augsburg* (Oxford: Clarendon Press, 1989); Jane Dempsey Douglass, "Women and the Continental Reformation," in *Religion and Sexism: Images of Woman in the Jewish and Christian Traditions*, ed. Rosemary Radford Ruether (New York: Simon and Schuster, 1974), 292–318.

8. Strikingly different portrayals of Mary Magdalene provide evidence of this ambivalence, from Donatello's emaciated wooden statue in the Uffizi to Titian's voluptuous seductress. I thank Gillian Ahlgren for calling my attention to these artistic representations.

9. Fear of women's power found frequent expression in paintings of the biblical images of Judith cutting off the head of Holofernes from the book of Judith and Salome with the head of John the Baptist (Mk. 6.21–29). Examples include Caravaggio's 1599 painting *Judith Beheading Holofernes* and Titian's *Salome with the Head of John the Baptist* (c. 1515).

10. Dale Kent suggests that Florence had the highest literacy rate of any European society in the fifteenth century—over 30 percent of the population. Kent, "Michele del Giogante's House of Memory," in Connell, *Society and Individual*, 111.

11. Constance Furey claims that while educated males tended to downplay female intellectual prowess in the Middle Ages, they praised it during the early modern period. She cites comments such as that made by Bishop Gian Matteo Giberti about Vittoria Colonna (1492–1547): "Her intellect was able to draw her through its own strength and show her the way to God." Constance Furey, "'Intellects Inflamed in Christ': Women and Spiritualized Scholarship in Renaissance Christianity," *Journal of Religion* 84, no. 1 (2004): 3 n. 7. Some elite women participated in the humanist movement, led by Erasmus, among

others, which promoted intellectual sophistication as well as virtuous moral character. Furey mentions the work of Marguerite of Navarre (1492–1549), sister of the French king, and Cassandra Fedele (1465–1558), who, skilled in Latin, dialectic, and rhetoric, gave public lectures at the University of Padua.

12. Confraternities and guilds were important sources of medieval social cohesion and charitable works. We know that Venice had 120 confraternities in 1500; by 1700, the number had grown to 400. In the fifteenth century, as a result of growing attempts to limit women's power and freedom, female membership was curtailed or limited to all-female subgroups within the larger body. Women were more likely to be beneficiaries of confraternity charity than benefactresses. Peter Matheson, ed., *A People's History of Christianity*, vol. 5, *Reformation Christianity* (Minneapolis, Minn.: Fortress Press, 2007), 158–60. See also Giovanna Cassagrande, "Confraternities and Lay Female Religiosity in Late Medieval and Renaissance Umbria," in *The Politics of Ritual Kinship: Confraternities and Social Order in Early Modern Italy*, ed. Nicholas Terpstra, Cambridge Studies in Italian History and Culture (Cambridge: Cambridge University Press, 2007), 48–66; Nicholas Terpstra, *Lay Confraternities and Civic Religion in Renaissance Bologna*, Cambridge Studies in Italian History and Culture (Cambridge: Cambridge University Press, 2002), 116–32.

13. Peter Burke, "How to Be a Counter-Reformation Saint," in *Religion and Society in Early Modern Europe, 1500–1800*, ed. Kaspar von Greyerz (London: Allen and Unwin, 1984), 45–55.

14. See Gabriella Zarri, "Living Saints: A Typology of Female Sanctity in the Early Sixteenth Century," in *Women and Religion in Medieval and Renaissance Italy*, ed. Daniel Bornstein and Roberto Rusconi, trans. Margery J. Schneider (Chicago: University of Chicago Press, 1996), 221–22. Laws against female preaching were passed in Zwickau and Memmingen. See Merry E. Wiesner, "Nuns, Wives, and Mothers: Women and the Reformation in Germany," in Marshall, *Women in Reformation and Counter-Reformation Europe*, 15–17.

15. The appellation "mother" was frequently applied to women who supported the poor. Mary Elizabeth Perry devotes a chapter to "Mothers of the Poor" in early modern Seville. Perry, *Gender and Disorder*, 153–76. A contemporary account of the life of Leonor Mascarenhas described her as "Mother of the Society of Jesus." Rahner, *Saint Ignatius Loyola*, 417.

16. See, for example, Milagros Ortega Costa, "Spanish Women in the Reformation," in Marshall, *Women in Reformation and Counter-Reformation Europe*, 89–119.

17. Examples of comportment literature include Luis de Léon's 1583 *La Perfecta Casada*, [*The Perfect Wife*] (Salamanca: Iuan Fernandez, 1583); Hermann Knust, *Dos obras didácticas y dos leyendas* (Madrid: Sociedad de Bibliófilos, 1978); Martín de Córdoba, *Jardin de las nobles doncellas: A Critical Edition*

and Study, ed. Harriet Goldberg (Chapel Hill: University of North Carolina Press, 1974); Juan Luis Vives's *Education of a Christian Woman* (1524) and Thomas Elyot's *The Defense of Good Women* (1545), both in William St. Clair and Irmgard Maassen, eds., *Conduct Literature for Women, 1500–1640* (London: Pickering & Chatto, 2000), 1:17–318, 2:201–64. For a summary of the controversies surrounding Desiderius Erasmus's treatises on marriage, see the introduction by Michael J. Heath to Erasmus's *The Institution of Christian Matrimony*, in *Collected Works of Erasmus*, ed. John W. O'Malley and Louis A. Perraud (Toronto: University of Toronto Press, 1999), 69:203–13.

18. Influential clerical leaders such as Jean Gerson (1363–1429), chancellor of the University of Paris, had voiced skepticism about the origins of female religious experience. See *On the Testing of Spirits (De probatione spirituum)*, written at the Council of Constance in 1415 to contest the visionary experience of Bridget of Sweden, who was a candidate for sainthood. An earlier text with a similar theme, *On Distinguishing True from False Revelations (De distinctione verarum revelationum a falsis)*, can be found in *Gerson: Early Works*, trans. Brian Patrick McGuire, Classics of Western Spirituality (Mahwah, N.J.: Paulist Press, 1998), 334–64. See also Dyan Elliott, "Seeing Double: John Gerson, the Discernment of Spirits, and Joan of Arc," *American Historical Review* 107, no. 1 (2002): 26–54.

19. See Gillian T. W. Ahlgren, "Negotiating Sanctity: Holy Women in Sixteenth-Century Spain," *Church History*, 65 no. 3 (1995): 373–88.

20. See J. Waterworthed, ed. and trans., *The Canons and Decrees of the Sacred and Oecumenical Council of Trent* (London: Dolman, 1848), 240.

21. Elizabeth A. Lehfeldt examines the significant complexities involved in the implementation of enclosure and the tensions between enclosure and the Church's emphasis on active ministry. She offers Ignatius of Loyola and Teresa of Avila as representative of the contrasting values of active and contemplative ministry. Lehfeldt, *Religious Women in Golden Age Spain: The Permeable Cloister* (Hampshire, UK: Ashgate, 2005), 175–94; Lehfeldt, "Sacred and Secular Spheres: Religious Women in Golden Age Spain," *History Compass* 3 (2005): 1–5. See also Ulrike Strasser, "Embodying the Middle Ages, Advancing Modernity: Religious Women in Sixteenth- and Seventeenth-Century Europe and Beyond," in *Between the Middle Ages and Modernity: Individual and Community in the Early Modern World*, ed. Charles H. Parker and Jerry H. Bentley (New York: Rowman & Littlefield, 2007), 238.

22. John Coakley, *Women, Men, and Spiritual Power*, 211–13.

23. See William Monter, "Women and the Italian Inquisitions," in *Women in the Middle Ages and the Renaissance: Literary and Historical Perspectives*, ed. Mary Beth Rose (Syracuse, N.Y.: Syracuse University Press, 1986), 73–87; Robin Briggs, *Witches and Neighbors: The Social Context of European Witchcraft*

(Oxford: Blackwell, 2002); Anne Llewellyn Barstow, *Witchcraze* (New York: Harper Collins, 1994); Alan Charles Kors and Edward Peters, *Witchcraft in Europe, 400–1700* (Philadelphia: University of Pennsylvania Press, 2001); Joseph Klaits, *Servants of Satan* (Indianapolis: University of Indiana Press, 1985); Brian Levack, *The Witch-Hunt in Early Modern Europe* (Harlow, UK: Pearson Longman, 2006).

24. See John M. Najemy, "Giannozzo and His Elders: Alberti's Critique of Renaissance Patriarchy," in Connell, *Society and Individual*, 57.

25. Albrecht Classen, "Female Epistolary Literature from Antiquity to the Present: An Introduction," *Studia Neophilologica* 60 (1988): 7. Classen notes that letters written by women such as Julia Gonzaga, Vittoria Colonna, Isabella de'Este, and Emilia Pia "convey an amazing liveliness and humour, combined with equal vivacity and witticism"—qualities that contrast significantly with the style of women's letters to Ignatius. See also Karen Cherewatuk and Ulrike Wiethaus, eds., *Dear Sister: Medieval Women and the Epistolary Genre* (Philadelphia: University of Pennsylvania Press, 1993); Elizabeth C. Goldsmith, ed., *Writing the Female Voice: Essays on Epistolary Literature* (Boston: Northeastern University Press, 1989); Adriano Prosperi's "Spiritual Letters," in *Women and Faith: Catholic Religious Life in Italy from Late Antiquity to the Present*, ed. Lucetta Scaraffia and Gabriella Zarri (Cambridge, Mass.: Harvard University Press, 1999), 113–28; Jane Couchman and Ann Crabb, eds., *Women's Letters across Europe, 1400–1700* (Hampshire, UK: Ashgate, 2005); and Barbara Mujica, *Teresa de Avila: Lettered Woman* (Nashville, Tenn.: Vanderbilt University Press, 2009).

26. See Giles Constable, *Letters and Letter-Collections* (Turnhout, Belgium: Editions Brepols, 1976).

27. Albrecht Classen, "Footnotes to the German Canon: Maria von Wolkenstein and Argula von Grumbach," in Brink, Coudert, and Horowitz, *The Politics of Gender*, 132.

28. Constable, *Letters and Letter-Collections*, 15.

29. The guarded language of these letters also reflects broader social conventions. Humanist clerical authors and reformers such as Erasmus and Giovanni della Casa wrote about proper dress and behavior for the aristocracy—self-control, discipline, and restraint were important virtues. See John K. Brackett, "The Florentine Criminal Underworld: The Underside of the Renaissance," in Connell, *Society and Individual*, 303. See also N. Elias, *The Civilizing Process: The History of Manners and State Formation and Civilization*, trans. E. Jephcott (Oxford: Oxford University Press, 1978), 42–44.

30. On this aspect of the Exercises, see Elena Carrera, "The Emotions in Sixteenth-Century Spanish Spirituality," *Journal of Religious History* 31, no. 3 (2007): 235–52.

31. A description of the ways in which letters foster spiritual community can be found in Lisa M. C. Weston, "Reading the Textual Shadows of Anglo-Saxon Monastic Women's Friendships," *Magistra* 14, no. 1 (2008): 68–78.

32. For a detailed account of women's contributions to the Collegio Romano and the first permanent Jesuit novitiate for the Roman Province, see Carolyn Valone, "Piety and Patronage: Women and the Early Jesuits," in *Creative Women in Medieval and Early Modern Italy: A Religious and Artistic Renaissance*, ed. E. Ann Matter and John Coakley (Philadelphia: University of Pennsylvania Press, 1994), 157–84.

33. On women's active ministries, see Natalie Davis, "City Women and Religious Change," in *Society and Culture in Early Modern France* (Stanford, Calif.: Stanford University Press, 1975), 65–95; Ruth Liebowitz, "Virgins in the Service of Christ: The Dispute over an Active Apostolate for Women during the Counter-Reformation," in *Women of Spirit: Female Leadership in the Jewish and Christian Traditions*, ed., Rosemary Radford Ruether and Eleanor McLaughlin (New York: Simon and Schuster, 1979), 131–52.

34. In the face of the Lutheran challenge in France, Teresa of Avila wrote: "It seemed to me that I would have given a thousand lives to save one soul out of the many that were being lost there." She described what she and her sisters could do: "We would all be occupied in prayer for those who are the defenders of the Church and for preachers and for learned men who protect her from attack." *The Collected Works of St. Teresa of Avila*, vol. 2, *Way of Perfection*, trans. Otilio Rodriguez and Kieran Kavanaugh (Washington, D.C.: Institute of Carmelite Studies, 1980), 41–42. Maria de San José Salazar testified in Teresa's canonization process that Teresa's efforts at reform had a deeply apostolic character in spite of claustration. Cited in Gillian T. W. Ahlgren, *Teresa of Avila and the Politics of Sanctity* (Ithaca, N.Y.: Cornell University Press, 1995), 36.

35. Schools for girls were housed within the walls of the convent, obviating the need for the nuns to leave the premises for their educational work.

36. See Friedrich von Hügel, *The Mystical Element of Religion: A Study of Catherine of Genoa* (1908; New York: Herder & Herder, 1999).

37. See Gabriella Zarri, "From Prophecy to Discipline, 1450–1650," in Scaraffia and Zarri, *Women and Faith*, 83–91.

38. See Margaret Mary Littlehales, *Mary Ward: Pilgrim and Mystic* (London: Burns & Oates, 1998).

39. A similar theme emerges in the theology and spirituality of Ignatius's contemporary Teresa of Avila. In the *Interior Castle* she distinguishes between gifts related to human effort (*contentos*) and those experienced as the gratuitous gift of God (*gustos*)—what Ignatius called "consolation without cause." See Elizabeth A. Dreyer, "The *Interior Castle*: An Exposition on the Giftedness of Mystical Prayer," *Spiritual Life* 31 (1985): 170–77.

40. This courtly attitude toward Mary is visible in the famous story about the Moor who, Ignatius judged, had insulted the honor of the Virgin. Ignatius's first impulse was to kill the Moor, but instead he allowed his donkey to make the decision. If the donkey followed the path of the Moor, he would kill him. If the donkey took the other road, he would not. Happily, the donkey made the right decision.

41. The role of women in ministry from earliest Christianity is documented in the New Testament. These women included Mary Magdalen; Lydia of Thyatira, who offered her home for worship in Philippi (Acts 16.14–15); Euodia, Syntyche, and Phoebe (Rom. 16); and the couple Priscilla and Acquilla (Rom. 16.3; 1 Cor. 16.19). For an interesting study of early Christian women's role in collecting the bones of the martyrs and giving them a proper burial on their own private property, see Nicola Denzey, *The Bone Gatherers: The Lost Worlds of Early Christian Women* (Boston: Beacon Press, 2007).

42. See Katherine Gill, "Women and the Production of Religious Literature in the Vernacular, 1300–1500," and Ann M. Roberts, "Chiara Gambacorta of Pisa as Patroness of the Arts," in Matter and Coakley, *Creative Women*, 64–104 and 120–54.

43. Olwen Hufton examines, within the context of the financial history of early modern Europe, the processes by which Jesuits located, acquired, and managed funds for the early Jesuit colleges, which were marked by a shortage of cash and available funds and a preponderance of debt. He claims that establishing these colleges gave birth to "the modern educational fundraiser, one instantly recognizable to the development office of a prestigious university in our time." Hufton shows how widows could be important financial resources inasmuch as they were free to donate their dowries to charitable causes. Hufton, "Every Tub on Its Own Bottom: Funding a Jesuit College in Early Modern Europe," in *The Jesuits II: Cultures, Sciences, and the Arts, 1540–1773*, ed. John W. O'Malley, Gauvin Alexander Bailey, Steven J. Harris, and T. Frank Kennedy (Toronto: University of Toronto Press, 2007), 7, 15ff. See also Hufton's "Altruism and Reciprocity: The Early Jesuits and Their Female Patrons," *Renaissance Studies* 15, no. 2 (2001): 328–53.

44. For political reasons, Ignatius chose the husband of Donna Maria Frassoni, Duke Hercules of Ferrara, as the official founder of the college at Ferrara. This meant that Donna Maria, who, it is estimated, spent 70,000 gold scudi on the Jesuit church and college in Ferrara, had to be satisfied with the title of "Anonymous Foundress"—an example of the gender discrimination that was part of the cultural fabric of the period. Rahner, *Saint Ignatius Loyola*, 199, 200.

45. An example of intimate personal involvement in the care of the poor can be found in the instructions of Miguel de Mañara to members of a brotherhood he founded in seventeenth-century Spain. When they brought in a poor

sick man from the city, the brothers were instructed to "meet him with love and lower him in your arms from the conveyance and carry him to the infirmary. And before putting him to bed, wash his feet and kiss them." Perry, *Gender and Disorder*, 163. A survey of the poor in Seville in 1667 suggests that poverty had become almost exclusively a problem for women and children, even though two-thirds of the licenses to beg in 1675 were issued to males. Perry, *Gender and Disorder*, 172, 176.

46. The canonization depositions for St. Francesca Bussa dei Ponziani, a fifteenth-century Roman laywoman, emphasize her simplicity in contrast to the mores of Roman noblewoman, who favored jewels and expensive clothing, cosmetics, wigs, and high-heeled shoes. Anna Esposito, "St. Francesca and the Female Religious Communities of Fifteenth-Century Rome," in Bornstein and Rusconi, *Women and Religion*, 198–99. For a case study of the ascetic practices of women in Florence, see Julius Kirshner, "*Li Emergenti Bisogni Matrimoniali in Renaissance Florence*," in Connell, *Society and Individual*, 79–109.

47. References to Ignatius's patience are frequent in Rahner's commentary. See Rahner, *Saint Ignatius Loyola*, 113, 202, 222, 242, 433, 447, 460, 463, 467, 470.

48. See Constance Jordan, "Renaissance Women and the Question of Class," in *Sexuality and Gender in Early Modern Europe: Institutions, Texts, Images*, ed. James Grantham Turner (Cambridge: Cambridge University Press, 1993), 90–106.

49. Teresa of Avila, Prologue 3, in *Way of Perfection*, 40.

50. See Weber, *Teresa of Avila*; Elizabeth Rapley, *The Dévotes: Women and Church in Seventeenth-Century France* (Montreal: McGill–Queen's University Press, 1990); Diane Willen, "Women and Religion in Early Modern England," in Marshall, *Women in Reformation and Counter-Reformation Europe*, 140–65.

51. Self-deprecating language is also largely absent in Teresa's letters. Its appearance in formal treatises is probably due to the scrutiny of such documents by ecclesial authorities, a scrutiny that would not apply to letters. I thank Barbara Mujica for calling attention to this aspect of Teresa's letters.

52. In another situation, Ignatius made a significant effort to fulfill the requests of Doña Leonor Osorio for rosaries that carried special indulgences and other favors by contacting various cardinals at St. Peter's. Polanco wrote to the Fathers in Sicily, complaining. One cardinal thought Ignatius took her requests too seriously but also noted that Ignatius's heart was in it. "For does not everyone know that it is characteristic of him to perform energetically all things that he undertakes?" Rahner, *Saint Ignatius Loyola*, 447.

53. For an examination of images that portray the linkage between action and contemplation, see Dominique Rigaux, "Women, Faith, and Image in the Late Middle Ages," in Scaraffia and Zarri, *Women and Faith*, 72–82.

54. John W. O'Malley, "Introduction: The Pastoral, Social, Ecclesiastical, Civic, and Cultural Mission of the Society of Jesus," in O'Malley et al., *The Jesuits II*, xxxiii.

55. Elizabeth Rhodes, "Join the Jesuits, See the World: Early Modern Women in Spain and the Society of Jesus," in O'Malley et al., *The Jesuits II*, 38.

56. Steven Haliczer, *Sexuality in the Confessional* (Oxford: Oxford University Press, 1995), 112; Rhodes, "Join the Jesuits," 43–45.

57. Jesuits were often seen as more desirable spiritual directors than others. This may be due to the fact that Jesuits were more carefully screened and received extensive education beyond that of diocesan clergy and other religious orders. This training may also partially explain data that show Jesuits were less likely to abuse the spiritual direction relationship than other priests.

58. Perry, *Gender and Disorder*, 98.

59. Margery A. Ganz writes: "Proper behavior was required on both sides of the patron-client relationship. . . . Honor required that the client properly express his gratitude and demonstrate his loyalty to the patron; the patron, in turn, was expected to do favors and aid his clients in achieving their goals. A man with a wide network of friends and relatives was perceived as accruing honor and profit, while shame was attributed to those who failed to either demonstrate proper gratitude or produce the requested favors." Ganz, "Perceived Insults and Their Consequences: Acciaiuoli, Neroni, and Medici Relationships in the 1460s," in Connell, *Society and Individual*, 155–56.

2. Mary, the Hidden Catalyst: Reflections from an Ignatian Pilgrimage to Spain and Rome

MARGO J. HEYDT AND SARAH J. MELCHER

1. John W. O'Malley, *The First Jesuits* (Cambridge, Mass.: Harvard University Press, 1993); Joseph A. Munitiz and Philip Endean, trans., *Saint Ignatius of Loyola: Personal Writings* (London: Penguin, 1996).

2. Louis A. Bonacci, "The Marian Presence in the Life and Works of Saint Ignatius Loyola: From Private Revelation to Spiritual Exercises—The Cloth of Loyola's Allegiance" (doctoral thesis, International Marian Research Institute, University of Dayton, 2002), 16–17.

3. W. W. Meissner, *Ignatius of Loyola: The Psychology of a Saint* (New Haven, Conn.: Yale University Press, 1992), 8–9.

4. Ibid., 11.

5. Ibid., 10.

6. James W. Reites, "Ignatius and Ministry with Women," *The Way*, Supplement 74 (Summer 1992): 7–19.

7. This painting's influence on Ignatius is discussed in Hugo Rahner, ed., *Saint Ignatius Loyola: Letters to Women*, trans. Kathleen Pond and S. A. H. Weetman (New York: Herder & Herder, 1960), 116.

8. See also Munitiz and Endean, *Saint Ignatius of Loyola*, 14–16 and O'Malley, *The First Jesuits*, 24.

9. O'Malley, *The First Jesuits*, 24.

10. Munitiz and Endean, *Saint Ignatius of Loyola*, 16.

11. Ibid., 18.

12. William J. Young, trans., *Letters of St. Ignatius of Loyola* (Chicago: Loyola Press, 1959), 349–50.

13. Munitiz and Endean, *Saint Ignatius of Loyola*, 19.

14. The requirement to treat women with chivalry is part of the "four commandments." See Keith Busby, ed., *Raoul de Hodenc: Le roman des Eles /The Anonymous Ordene de chevalerie* (Amsterdam: John Benjamins, 1983, 112–13 (lines 263–303). See also Maurice Keen, *Chivalry* (New Haven, Conn.: Yale University Press, 1984), 6–8.

15. Brian R. Price, ed., *Ramon Lull's Book of Knighthood and Chivalry*, trans. William Caxton (Union City, Calif.: Chivalry Bookshelf, 2004), 25.

16. Ibid., 35.

17. Geoffroi de Charny, *A Knight's Own Book of Chivalry*, trans. Elspeth Kennedy (Philadelphia: University of Pennsylvania Press, 2005), 53.

18. Though Ignatius read romances rather than treatises on chivalry, the latter genre gives a better overview of the requirements and the culture of chivalry. In addition, the treatises on chivalry were influenced both by the romances and by ecclesiastical opinion. See Keen, *Chivalry*, 6.

19. Munitiz and Endean, *Saint Ignatius of Loyola*, 20. See also O'Malley, *The First Jesuits*, 24–25.

20. Munitiz and Endean, *Saint Ignatius of Loyola*, 297–98.

21. Ibid., 311–12.

22. Ibid., 305–6.

23. Ibid., 74, 77, 78, 81.

24. Ibid., 78.

25. For example, see Young, *Letters*, 11.

26. Munitiz and Endean, *Saint Ignatius of Loyola*, 64.

27. For more information about this ordination and the circumstances surrounding it, see John W. Padberg, "Secret, Perilous Project," *Company* 17 (1999): 28–29, and Joan Roccasalvo, "Ignatian Women Past and Future," *Review for Religious* 62 (2003): 38–62.

28. Rahner, *Saint Ignatius Loyola*, 290.

29. Research uncovering the influence of women on the early Jesuits continues. For example, see Lisa Fullam, "Juana, S.J.: The Past (and Future) Status

of Women in the Society of Jesus," *Studies in the Spirituality of Jesuits* 31, no. 5 (1999): 1–41; Elizabeth Rhodes, "Join the Jesuits, See the World: Early Modern Women in Spain and the Society of Jesus," in John W. O'Malley, Gauvin Alexander Bailey, Steven J. Harris, and T. Frank Kennedy, eds., *The Jesuits II: Cultures, Sciences, and the Arts, 1540–1773* (Toronto: University of Toronto Press, 2007), 33–49; and Amalee Meehan, "Partners in Ministry: The Role of Women in Jesuit Education," *America*, May 12, 2008, 22–24.

30. O'Malley, *The First Jesuits*, 75.

31. Joseph N. Tylenda, *Jesuit Saints and Martyrs: Short Biographies of the Saints, Blessed, Venerables, and Servants of God of the Society of Jesus* (Chicago: Loyola Press, 1998), 110.

32. M. C. Durkin, *"Ours": Jesuit Portraits* (Strasbourg: Editions du Signe, 2006).

33. Meehan, "Partners in Ministry," 24.

34. Mary Garvin, "Dusting off a Document," *Conversations* 29 (Spring 2006): 38.

35. Susan A. Ross, "The Jesuits and Women: Reflections on the 34th General Congregation's Statement on Women in Church and Civil Society," *Conversations* 16 (Fall 1999): 21–22.

36. Ibid., 24.

37. Roger Haight, "Lessons from an Extraordinary Era: Catholic Theology since Vatican II," *America*, March 17, 2008, 11–16.

38. Ibid.

3. Early Jesuit Pedagogy and the Subordination of Women: Resources from the *Ratio Studiorum*

COLLEEN McCLUSKEY

1. It should be noted, however, that this practice was controversial among early Jesuits, although it was vigorously supported by Ignatius Loyola himself. John W. O'Malley, *The First Jesuits* (Cambridge, Mass.: Harvard University Press, 1993), 188–92.

2. John W. O'Malley, "How the First Jesuits Became Involved in Education," and John W. Padberg, "Development of the *Ratio Studiorum*," both in *The Jesuit "Ratio Studiorum": 400th Anniversary Perspectives*, ed. Vincent Duminuco (New York: Fordham University Press, 2000), 56–74 and 80–100.

3. For a nice summary of its development, see Padberg, "Development of the *Ratio Studiorum*."

4. For further information about the *modus Parisiensis*, see Gabriel Codina, "The 'Modus Parisiensis,'" in Duminuco, *The Jesuit "Ratio Studiorum*," 28–49;

John W. O'Malley, "The Jesuit Educational Enterprise in Historical Perspective," in *Jesuit Higher Education: Essays on an American Tradition of Excellence*, ed. Rolando E. Bonachea (Pittsburgh: Duquesne University Press, 1989), 10–25.

5. Padberg, "Development of the *Ratio Studiorum*," 82.

6. Ibid.

7. O'Malley, *The First Jesuits*, 75. Rosemary A. DeJulio has an extensive discussion of Loyola's female acquaintances in "Patrons, Pupils, and Partners: The Participation of Women in Ignatian Spirituality and Pedagogy" (PhD diss., Fordham University, 2000).

8. A number of wealthy women were inspired to become patrons of Jesuit projects, including Marchesa Vittoria della Tolfa, who contributed land and monetary resources to establish the Collegio Romano, and Giovanna d'Aragona Colonna and Isabella Feltria della Rovere Sanseverino, who provided the resources to build the first permanent Jesuit novitiate in Rome. See Carolyn Valone, "Piety and Patronage: Women and the Early Jesuits," in *Creative Women in Medieval and Early Modern Italy: A Religious and Artistic Renaissance*, ed. E. Ann Matter and John Coakley (Philadelphia: University of Pennsylvania Press, 1994), 157–84. See also DeJulio, "Patrons, Pupils, and Partners," 75–87.

9. See John W. Padberg, "Juana: Princess and Jesuit Scholastic," *National Jesuit News* 4, no. 2 (1974): 1, 4–6. See also DeJulio, "Patrons, Pupils, and Partners," 56–57.

10. O'Malley, *The First Jesuits*, 76; DeJulio, "Patrons, Pupils, and Partners," 57.

11. O'Malley, *The First Jesuits*, 75; DeJulio, "Patrons, Pupils, and Partners," 40–45; Jennifer Cameron, *A Dangerous Innovator: Mary Ward (1585–1645)* (Strathfield, NSW: St. Pauls Publications, 2000), 89–92.

12. O'Malley, *The First Jesuits*, 178–88.

13. In the 1880s, two women were allowed to take some classes at Georgetown University in the Medical College, but there is no mention that they matriculated as medical students.

14. Claude Pavur, trans., *The Ratio Studiorum: The Official Plan for Jesuit Education* (St. Louis, Mo.: Institute of Jesuit Sources, 2005), 117 [259]. Although I have depended upon Pavur's excellent translation to locate relevant passages, I have consulted the Latin text that he provides in the facing columns. For text citations, I have provided first the page numbers of Pavur's translation and in brackets the numbers found both in his translation and in the critical edition.

15. For example, see Bat-Ami Bar On, ed., *Engendering Origins: Critical Feminist Readings in Plato and Aristotle* (Albany: State University of New York Press,

1994); Lisa Sowle Cahill, *Sex, Gender, and Christian Ethics* (Cambridge: Cambridge University Press, 1996); Sabina Lovibond, "Feminism in Ancient Philosophy: The Feminist Stake in Greek Rationality," in *The Cambridge Companion to Feminism in Philosophy*, ed. Miranda Fricker and Jennifer Hornsby (Cambridge: Cambridge University Press, 2000), 10–28; Jean Porter, *Natural and Divine Law: Reclaiming the Tradition for Christian Ethics* (Grand Rapids, Mich.: William B. Eerdmans, 1999); and Cristina L. H. Traina, *Feminist Ethics and Natural Law: The End of the Anathemas* (Washington, D.C.: Georgetown University Press, 1999).

16. Eve Browning Cole, "Women, Slaves, and 'Love of Toil' in Aristotle's Moral Philosophy," in Bar On, *Engendering Origins*, 127–44; Elizabeth Clark and Herbert Richardson, "Thomas Aquinas: The Man Who Should Have Known Better," in *Women and Religion: A Feminist Sourcebook of Christian Thought* (New York: Harper and Row, 1977), 78–101.

17. See *Gen. an.* 767b5–768a7.

18. *NE* 1158b12–22.

19. *NE* 1158b23–26; *NE* 1161a20–25. Aristotle leaves open the nature of the goods involved; they might include material goods, political and social status, and educational and economic opportunities—in short, all the benefits ordinarily reserved for males in a patriarchal culture.

20. See for example, Cole, "Women, Slaves, and 'Love of Toil.'"

21. There are many editions and translations of Aquinas's works. For my references to *Summa theologiae*, I used the Marietti edition: Thomas Aquinas, *Summa theologiae*, ed. Petri Caramello (Rome: Marietti, 1952). The most prominent translation is that of the English Dominican Fathers, originally published in 1911 and reissued in 1981 by Christian Classics.

22. The topics of *Summa theologiae* are divided into what are called questions, and each question generally has three or more articles. Aquinas did not complete part 3 in his lifetime; the final part was compiled after his death from material found in his *Sentences* commentary, which is an early work. This includes the questions on marriage. However, since the *Ratio Studiorum* refers to part 3, this suggests that the early Jesuits used this edited version rather than the original material found in the *Sentences* commentary.

23. *ST* 3 Suppl. 60.

24. *ST* 3 Suppl. 59.3.

25. See *ST* 3 Suppl. 65, 66, and 67. A rare exception is his discussion of whether a divorced woman may remarry. See *ST* 3 Suppl. 67.4. Aquinas's discussion of these issues in *Summa theologiae* is put in the context of whether they violate the natural law. Interestingly, Aquinas argues against divorce and polygamy in *Summa contra gentiles* on the grounds that these practices harm the wife insofar as they violate equality and leave her in a state of servility.

This discussion in *Summa contra gentiles* is very complex and, as I shall mention later, involves a very thin notion of equality, but it does at least consider the issues from the wife's point of view. Nevertheless, the *Ratio Studiorum* does not include texts from *Summa contra gentiles* in the curriculum.

26. See *ST* 3. Suppl. 44.2.ad 1, 53.1.ad 1, 54.3.

27. See *ST* 1.92.1.

28. Aquinas draws upon Aristotle's discussion of friendship in book 8 of *Nicomachean Ethics* for this idea and develops it to a greater extent than did Aristotle in his (Aquinas's) commentary on the *Ethics*, especially in his discussion of book 8, chapter 7.

29. *ST* 1.92.2; *In NE* 8.12; *In IV sent.* 32.1.3; *ST* 3. Suppl. 44–47; *SCG* 3.124.

30. *ST* 3. Suppl. 64. For more information on marriage practices in the Middle Ages, see James A. Brundage, *Law, Sex, and Christian Society in Medieval Europe* (Chicago: University of Chicago Press, 1987); and David d'Avray, *Medieval Marriage: Symbolism and Society* (New York: Oxford University Press, 2005).

31. See *ST* 1.92.2; *In NE* 8.12.

32. Colleen McCluskey, "An Unequal Relationship between Equals: Thomas Aquinas on Marriage," *History of Philosophy Quarterly* 24 (2007): 1–18.

33. Many of my colleagues are actually quite shocked to learn that Aquinas held such views, which tells me that these passages are not read even today.

34. Francesco C. Cesareo, "Quest for Identity: The Ideals of Jesuit Education in the Sixteenth Century," in *The Jesuit Tradition in Education and Missions: A 450-Year Perspective*, ed. Christopher Chapple (Scranton, Pa.: University of Scranton Press, 1993), 26. Merry E. Wiesner also raises this view in *Women and Gender in Early Modern Europe*, 2nd ed. (Cambridge: Cambridge University Press, 2000), 152–53.

35. Wiesner, *Women and Gender*, 143–44.

36. Ruth Kelso, *Doctrine for the Lady of the Renaissance* (Urbana: University of Illinois Press, 1956); Wiesner, *Women and Gender*, especially chaps. 1 and 4; Meg Lota Brown and Kari Boyd McBride, *Women's Roles in the Renaissance* (Westport, Conn.: Greenwood Press, 2005), 27–52.

37. Wiesner, *Women and Gender*, 146–49.

38. Ibid., 148–49.

39. See Rosemary A. DeJulio, "Women's Ways of Knowing and Learning: The Response of Mary Ward and Madeleine Sophie Barat to the *Ratio Studiorum*," in Duminuco, *The Jesuit "Ratio Studiorum,"* 107–26.

40. Thomas Worcester, "'Neither Married nor Cloistered': Blessed Isabelle in Catholic Reformation France," *Sixteenth Century Journal* 30 (1999): 457–72. Of course, women did not always live up to the ideal, and throughout Europe's history, a certain percentage of the female population never married or

entered a convent. See Judith M. Bennett and Amy M. Froide, eds., *Single-women in the European Past, 1250–1800* (Philadelphia: University of Pennsylvania Press, 1999).

41. Loyola's correspondence with women has been translated and published. See Hugo Rahner, ed., *Saint Ignatius Loyola: Letters to Women*, trans. Kathleen Pond and S. A. H. Weetman (New York: Herder & Herder, 1960).

42. Valone, "Piety and Patronage," 162, 178–80.

43. Worcester, "Neither Married nor Cloistered," 460.

44. Ibid., 469–70.

45. Ibid., 469.

46. Many of the papers in Bennett and Froide, *Singlewomen in the European Past*, address these issues. See also Wiesner, *Women and Gender*, 102–40, and Brown and McBride, *Women's Roles*, 89–124, for discussions of women's economic roles in the early modern period.

47. For more information about Mary Ward, see Marion Norman, "A Woman for All Seasons: Mary Ward (1585–1645), Renaissance Pioneer of Women's Education," *Pedagogica Historica* 23 (1983): 125–43; Cameron, *A Dangerous Innovator*; DeJulio, "Patrons, Pupils, and Partners," 98–115; and DeJulio, "Women's Ways of Knowing and Learning," 109–18. For information about Madeleine Barat, see DeJulio, "Patrons, Pupils, and Partners," 116–27; DeJulio, "Women's Ways of Knowing and Learning," 118–26. This group of women might also include Angela Merici, founder of the Ursulines. Although originally founded as a non-cloistered order in 1540, they faced papal orders to adopt the cloister. Many houses accepted the cloister while others resisted. All continued their teaching mission, albeit under severe conditions. Merici herself was an older contemporary of Loyola's and therefore was not directly influenced by the *Ratio Studiorum*, but later Ursuline schools show evidence of its influence on their curriculum and teaching methods. See Margaret Gorman, "The Influence of Ignatian Spirituality on Women's Teaching Orders in the United States," in Chapple, *The Jesuit Tradition*, 182–202, especially 190–92; William Monter, "Protestant Wives, Catholic Saints, and the Devil's Handmaid: Women in the Age of Reformations," in *Becoming Visible: Women in European History*, 2nd ed., ed. Renate Bridenthal, Claudia Koonz, and Susan Stuard (Boston: Houghton Mifflin, 1987), 209–10.

48. Wiesner, *Women and Gender*, 233–34; DeJulio, "Patrons, Pupils, and Partners," 114. The Institute was officially revived in the late nineteenth century. See Gorman, "The Influence of Ignatian Spirituality," 192–93.

49. DeJulio, "Women's Ways of Knowing and Learning," 111–14 and 120–21.

50. Cameron, *A Dangerous Innovator*, 92–93.

51. Wiesner, *Women and Gender*, 144–49. Although educational opportunities increased for girls in the early modern period, they lagged behind the increase in educational opportunities for boys, especially in urban areas. Thus, at least in some areas, the literacy gap between boys and girls increased. See Wiesner, *Women and Gender*, 143–71, for a detailed discussion of this topic.

52. Gorman, "The Influence of Ignatian Spirituality," 132–35. Ward had a further motive for emphasizing religious studies insofar as her schools were founded originally for ex-patriot English Catholic girls who would return home to a land hostile to the practice of their religion.

53. Wiesner, *Women and Gender*, 154–58.

54. Ibid., 154, also 160.

55. French women seem to be the exception. See Wiesner, *Women and Gender*, 158.

56. How individuals come to recognize injustices in their social/cultural systems and whether one can be held accountable for failing to do so are interesting and difficult questions. For discussion of these issues, see Ann Ferguson, "Can I Choose Who I Am? And How Would That Empower Me? Gender, Race, Identities, and the Self," and Lynn Hankinson Nelson, "Who Knows? What Can They Know? And When?" both in *Women, Knowledge, and Reality: Explorations in Feminist Philosophy*, 2nd ed., ed. Ann Garry and Marilyn Pearsall (New York: Routledge, 1996), 108–26 and 286–97.

57. John L. McCarthy and Jesuits, eds., *Documents of the Thirty-fourth General Congregation of the Society of Jesus: The Decrees of General Congregation Thirty-four, the Fifteenth of the Restored Society and the Accompanying Papal and Jesuit Documents* (St. Louis, Mo.: Institute of Jesuit Sources, 1995).

58. Ibid., 175–76, no. 372.

59. Ibid., 176, nos. 374, 381.

60. What approach to social change one should adopt is a matter of some controversy among feminists. The dominant approach has been, at least historically, the route of equal rights and opportunities, but at least one feminist has argued that such an approach prioritizes and privileges lesser evils at the expense of greater evils. See Claudia Card, *The Atrocity Paradigm* (Oxford: Oxford University Press, 2002), especially chap. 5. I will not address Card's worry here, but in my view, the general approaches I raise here could be adopted with Card's concerns in mind.

61. See Decree 17 in McCarthy and Jesuits, *Documents of the Thirty-fourth General Congregation*, 189–94, nos. 404–15.

62. Ibid., 177, no. 382.

63. Ibid.

64. Ibid., 184, no. 396.

65. Gorman, "The Influence of Ignatian Spirituality," 182–202.

4. "The Personal Is Political": At the Intersections
of Feminist and Jesuit Education

JOCELYN M. BORYCZKA AND ELIZABETH A. PETRINO

1. For a description of Ignatian pedagogy, see Vincent J. Duminuco, "A New *Ratio* for a New Millennium?" in *The Jesuit "Ratio Studiorum": 400th Anniversary Perspectives*, ed. Duminuco (New York: Fordham University Press, 2000), 158 and Appendix B.

2. Here pedagogy is broadly conceived to describe best teaching practices and the Ignatian perspective of including a worldview and vision of the ideal person to be educated.

3. See American Association of University Women Educational Foundation, *How Schools Shortchange Girls: A Study of Major Findings on Girls and Education* (Washington, D.C.: AAUW Educational Foundation, 1992), and the follow-up study, American Association of University Women, *Gender Gaps: Where Schools Still Fail Our Children* (New York: Marlowe, 1998), which includes valuable data on the impact of technology on learning among male and female students.

4. See American Association of University Women Educational Foundation, *How Schools Shortchange Girls*, 72.

5. John L. McCarthy and Jesuits, eds., *Documents of the Thirty-fourth General Congregation of the Society of Jesus: The Decrees of General Congregation Thirty-four, the Fifteenth of the Restored Society and the Accompanying Papal and Jesuit Documents* (St. Louis, Mo.: Institute of Jesuit Sources, 1995), 172.

6. Ibid., 176.

7. Quoted in Sara Evans's *Personal Politics: The Roots of Women's Liberation in the Civil Rights Movement and the New Left* (New York: Vintage Books, 1980), 213.

8. For an account of how consciousness-raising generated women's liberation in the late 1960s, see ibid., chap. 9.

9. See Pamela Allen, "The Small Group Process," in *Radical Feminism: A Documentary Reader*, ed. Barbara A. Crow (New York: New York University Press, 2000), 277–81.

10. Ibid., 277.

11. Lee Anne Bell, Sharon Washington, Gerald Weinstein, and Barbara Love, "Knowing Ourselves as Instructors," in *The Critical Pedagogy Reader*, ed. Antonia Darder, Marta Baltodano, and Rodolfo D. Torres (New York: Routledge, 2003), 464.

12. McCarthy and Jesuits, *Documents of the Thirty-fourth General Congregation*, 63.

13. Ibid., 61.

14. Ibid., 60.

15. Ibid., 61.

5. *Paideia* and the Political Process: The Unexplored Coincidence of Jesuit and Feminist Pedagogical Visions

PAUL LAKELAND

1. bell hooks, *Teaching to Transgress: Education and the Practice of Freedom* (New York: Routledge, 1994).

2. In Deborah Rosenfelt, ed., *Female Studies VII: Going Strong, New Courses / New Programs* (Old Westbury, N.Y.: Feminist Press, 1973), 187.

3. A Letter to the Community at Alcala, 1543, *Letters of St. Ignatius of Loyola*, selected and translated by William J. Young, S.J. (Chicago: Loyola, 1959), p. 440.

4. Walter Ong, review of *Classical Rhetoric in English Poetry*, by Brian Vickers, *College English* 33, no. 5 (1972): 612–16.

5. See Henry A. Giroux, *Disturbing Pleasures: Learning Popular Culture* (New York: Routledge, 1994).

6. Jennifer M. Gore, *The Struggle for Pedagogies: Critical and Feminist Discourses as Regimes of Truth* (New York: Routledge, 1993), 27–31.

7. These remarks and the quotation from Paul VI, offered without further reference, can be found in Peter-Hans Kolvenbach, "Ignatian Pedagogy Today," in *The Jesuit "Ratio Studiorum": 400th Anniversary Perspectives*, ed. Vincent J. Duminuco (New York: Fordham University Press, 2000), 285.

8. Ignacio Ellacuría, commencement address to Santa Clara University (Santa Clara, Calif., June 1982), http://www.scu.edu/Jesuits/ellacuria.html.

9. International Commission on the Apostolate of Jesuit Education, "The Characteristics of Jesuit Education," in Duminuco, *The Jesuit "Ratio Studiorum,"* 182.

10. Ibid., 185.

11. International Commission on the Apostolate of Jesuit Education, "Ignatian Pedagogy: A Practical Approach, 1993," in Duminuco, *The Jesuit "Ratio Studiorum,"* 240.

12. Vincent J. Duminuco, "A New *Ratio* for a New Millennium?" in Duminuco, *The Jesuit "Ratio Studiorum,"* 157.

13. Ibid., 156.

14. James Fowler, *Weaving the New Creation: Stages of Faith and the Public Church* (San Francisco: HarperSanFrancisco, 1996), 137.

15. Ellacuría, commencement address.

16. International Commission on the Apostolate of Jesuit Education, "The Characteristics of Jesuit Education," 191, 190.

17. Ibid., 192.

18. Jürgen Habermas, *The Theory of Communicative Action*, vol. 2, *Lifeworld and System: A Critique of Functionalist Reason*, trans. Thomas McCarthy (Boston: Beacon Press, 1987), 196.

19. Ellacuría, commencement address.

6. Feminist Pedagogy, the Ignatian Paradigm, and Service-Learning: Distinctive Roots, Common Objectives, and Intriguing Challenges

ROBBIN D. CRABTREE, JOSEPH A. DeFEO, AND MELISSA M. QUAN

1. Sharan B. Merriam, *An Update on Adult Learning Theory* (San Francisco: Jossey-Bass, 1993), 8.

2. Allan Luke and Carmen Luke, "Pedagogy," in *The Encyclopedia of Language and Linguistics*, ed. R. E. Asher and J. M. Simpson (Tarrytown, N.Y.: Elsevier Science/Pergamon, 1994), 566–68.

3. See, for example, Paulo Freire, *Pedagogy of the Oppressed* (New York: Continuum, 1970); Henry A. Giroux, *Pedagogy and the Politics of Hope: Theory, Culture, and Schooling* (Boulder, Colo.: Westview Press, 1997); Ira Shor, *When Students Have Power: Negotiating Authority in a Critical Pedagogy* (Chicago: University of Chicago Press, 1996).

4. Gail E. Cohee, Elisabeth Daumer, Theresa D. Kemp, Paula M. Krebs, Sue Lafky, and Sandra Runzo, eds., *The Feminist Teacher Anthology: Pedagogies and Classroom Strategies* (New York: Teachers College Press, 1998).

5. See Carmen Luke, ed., *Feminisms and Pedagogies of Everyday Life* (Albany: State University of New York Press, 1996).

6. For example, Estelle B. Freedman, "Small Group Pedagogy: Consciousness Raising in Conservative Times," *NWSA Journal* 2, no. 4 (1990): 603–23; Suzanna Rose, "The Protest as a Teaching Technique for Promoting Feminist Action," *NWSA Journal* 1, no. 3 (1989): 486–90.

7. See, most notably, Mary Field Belenky, Blythe McVicker Clinchy, Nancy Rule Goldberger, and Jill Mattuck Tarule, *Women's Ways of Knowing: The Development of Self, Voice, and Mind* (New York: Basic Books, 1986). Also see Patti Lather, *Getting Smart: Feminist Research and Pedagogy with/in the Postmodern* (New York: Routledge, 1991).

8. Also see Dale M. Bauer, "Feminist Bywords: Authority," *NWSA Journal* 3, no. 1 (1990): 95–97.

9. Becky Ropers-Huilman, "Scholarship on the Other Side: Power and Caring in Feminist Education," *NWSA Journal* 11, no. 1 (1999): 132.

10. Carolyn M. Shrewsbury takes up these issues as her primary focus in "What Is Feminist Pedagogy?" *Women's Studies Quarterly* 15, no. 3–4 (1987): 6–14. Also see Robbin D. Crabtree and David Alan Sapp, "Theoretical, Political, and Pedagogical Challenges in the Feminist Classroom: Our Struggles to Walk the Walk," *College Teaching* 51, no. 4 (2003): 131–40.

11. Pamela L. Caughie and Richard Pearce, "Resisting 'the Dominance of the Professor': Gendered Teaching, Gendered Subjects," *NWSA Journal* 4, no. 2 (1992): 198.

12. M. G. Lewis, foreword to *Feminist Teaching in Theory and Practice: Situating Power and Knowledge in Poststructural Classrooms*, by Becky Ropers-Huilman (New York: Teachers College Press, 1998), xv.

13. Also see Frances Maher and Mary Kay Thompson Tetreault, *The Feminist Classroom: Dynamics of Gender, Race, and Privilege* (New York: Rowman & Littlefield, 2001), for an analysis of gender and race privilege in the classroom context.

14. Carol Gilligan, *In a Different Voice: Psychological Theory and Women's Development* (Cambridge, Mass.: Harvard University Press, 1982).

15. See, for example, bell hooks, "Feminist Theory: A Radical Agenda," in *Multicultural Experiences, Multicultural Theories*, ed. Mary F. Rogers (New York: McGraw-Hill, 1996), 56–61; bell hooks, *Killing Rage: Ending Racism* (New York: Henry Holt, 1995); and bell hooks, *Teaching to Transgress: Education and the Practice of Freedom* (New York: Routledge, 1994), on the erotic nature of teaching. See Miriam Wallace, "Beyond Love and Battle: Practicing Feminist Pedagogy," *Feminist Teacher* 12, no. 3 (1999): 184–97, on psychoanalytic views of feminist pedagogy.

16. For example, E. M. Novek, "Service-Learning Is a Feminist Issue: Transforming Communication Pedagogy," *Women's Studies in Communication* 22, no. 2 (1999): 230–40.

17. See especially Margaret L. Anderson and Patricia Hill Collins, eds., *Race, Class, and Gender: An Anthology* (New York: Wadsworth, 1998).

18. Shrewsbury, "What Is Feminist Pedagogy?"

19. For example, Sara Munson Deats and Lagretta Tallent Lenker, eds., *Gender and Academe: Feminist Pedagogy and Politics* (New York: Rowman & Littlefield, 1994).

20. See Amie A. Macdonald and Susan Sánchez-Casal, eds., *Twenty-first-Century Feminist Classrooms: Pedagogies of Identity and Difference* (New York: Palgrave Macmillan, 2002).

21. For example, Susan Johnston, "Not for Queers Only: Pedagogy and Postmodernism," *NWSA Journal* 7, no. 1 (1995): 109–22; Ropers-Huilman, *Feminist Teaching in Theory and Practice*.

22. Crabtree and Sapp, "Theoretical, Political, and Pedagogical Challenges."

23. Jo Ann Pagano, "Moral Fictions: The Dilemma of Theory and Practice," in *Stories Lives Tell: Narrative and Dialogue in Education*, ed. Carol Witherell and Nel Noddings (New York: Teachers College Press, 1991), 194.

24. Ropers-Huilman, "Scholarship on the Other Side," 132.

25. George Ganss, ed., *Ignatius of Loyola: Spiritual Exercises and Selected Works* (Mahwah, N.J.: Paulist Press, 1991), 44, 231.

26. International Commission on the Apostolate of Jesuit Education, "Ignatian Pedagogy: A Practical Approach, 1993," in *The Jesuit "Ratio Studiorum": 400th Anniversary Perspectives*, ed. Vincent J. Duminuco (New York: Fordham University Press, 2000), 249.

27. James L. Connor and Fellows of the Woodstock Theological Center, *The Dynamism of Desire: Bernard J. F. Lonergan, S.J., on the Spiritual Exercises of Saint Ignatius of Loyola* (St. Louis, Mo.: Institute of Jesuit Sources, 2006), 25; John W. O'Malley, *The First Jesuits* (Cambridge, Mass.: Harvard University Press, 1993), 18.

28. O'Malley, *The First Jesuits*, 18.

29. International Commission on the Apostolate of Jesuit Education, "Ignatian Pedagogy," 240.

30. John L. McCarthy and Jesuits, eds., *Documents of the Thirty-fourth General Congregation of the Society of Jesus: The Decrees of General Congregation Thirty-four, the Fifteenth of the Restored Society and the Accompanying Papal and Jesuit Documents* (St. Louis, Mo.: Institute of Jesuit Sources, 1995), 11, no. 414.

31. James M. Bowler, "The Transformative Power of Jesuit Education: A Reflection on Ignatian Pedagogy," in *Ignatian Pedagogy for the Challenges of Humanism Today*, ed. Wita Pasierbka (Krakow, Poland: Wyższa Szkoła Filozoficzno-Pedagogiczna Ignatianum, 2008), 4; Dean Brackley, *The Call to Discernment in Troubled Times: New Perspectives on the Transformative Wisdom of Ignatius of Loyola* (New York: Crossroads, 2004), 11, 12; Connor and Fellows of the Woodstock Theological Center, *The Dynamism of Desire*, 25.

32. Vincent J. Duminuco, "A New *Ratio* for a New Millennium?" in Duminuco, *The Jesuit "Ratio Studiorum*," 155.

33. John W. Padberg, ed., *Documents of the Thirty-first and Thirty-second General Congregations of the Society of Jesus: An English Translation of the Official Latin Texts of the General Congregations and of the Accompanying Papal Documents* (St. Louis, Mo.: Institute of Jesuit Sources, 1977).

34. International Commission on the Apostolate of Jesuit Education, "Ignatian Pedagogy," 243.

35. See ibid. for more detail about the vision and methodology of Ignatian pedagogy.

36. Ibid., 254.

37. Robert J. Starratt, *Building an Ethical School: A Practical Response to the Moral Crisis in Schools* (London: Falmer, 1994), 22.

38. Ibid.

39. Howard Gray, "The Experience of Ignatius Loyola: Background to Jesuit Education," in Duminuco, *The Jesuit "Ratio Studiorum*," 15.

40. International Commission on the Apostolate of Jesuit Education, "Ignatian Pedagogy," 260.

41. Ibid., 261.

42. Duminuco, "A New *Ratio*," 155.

43. International Commission on the Apostolate of Jesuit Education, "Ignatian Pedagogy," 262.

44. Janet Eyler and Dwight E. Giles Jr., *Where's the Learning in Service-Learning?* (San Francisco: Jossey-Bass, 1999), 66.

45. John Dewey, *Experience and Education* (New York: Touchstone, 1944); David A. Kolb, *Experiential Learning* (Englewood Cliffs, N.J.: Prentice Hall, 1984); Freire, *Pedagogy of the Oppressed*.

46. Dewey, *Experience and Education*; Kolb, *Experiential Learning*; Freire, *Pedagogy of the Oppressed*.

47. Timothy Stanton, Dwight E. Giles Jr., and Nadinne Cruz, *Service-Learning: A Movement's Pioneers Reflect on Its Origins, Practice, and Future* (San Francisco: Jossey-Bass, 1999); John Thelin, *A History of American Higher Education* (Baltimore, Md.: Johns Hopkins University Press, 2004).

48. Stanton, Giles, and Cruz, *Service-Learning*.

49. Robert Bringle and Julie Hatcher, "Implementing Service Learning in Higher Education," *Journal of Higher Education* 67 (1996): 221-22.

50. Jeffrey P. F. Howard, "Academic Service Learning: A Counternormative Pedagogy," in *Academic Service Learning: A Pedagogy of Action and Reflection*, ed. Robert A. Rhoads and Jeffrey P. F. Howard (San Francisco: Jossey-Bass, 1998), 21-30.

51. Alexander Astin and Linda Sax, "How Undergraduates Are Affected by Service Participation," *Journal of College Student Development* 39 (1998): 251-63; Alexander Astin, Linda Sax, and Juan Avalos, "Long-Term Effects of Volunteerism during the Undergraduate Years," *Review of Higher Education* 22 (1999): 187-202; Judith Boss, "The Effect of Community Service Work on the Moral Development of College Ethics Students," *Journal of Moral Education* 23, no. 2 (1994): 183-98.

52. Dewey, *Experience and Education*.

53. Julie Hatcher and Robert Bringle, "Reflection: Bridging the Gap between Service and Learning," *College Teaching* 45, no. 4 (1997): 153-58.

54. Jeffrey P. F. Howard, ed., *Service-Learning Course Design Workbook* (Ann Arbor: Edward Ginsberg Center for Community Service, University of Michigan, 2001).

55. Ibid.

56. Benjamin Barber and Richard Battistoni, "A Season of Service: Introducing Service Learning into the Liberal Arts Curriculum," *Political Science and Politics* 26 (1993): 235–62; Howard, *Service-Learning Course Design Workbook.*

57. Howard, *Service-Learning Course Design Workbook.*

58. John Dewey, *Democracy and Education* (Toronto: Collier-Macmillan, 1916).

59. Howard, *Service-Learning Course Design Workbook,* 23.

60. Ibid.; Joseph Kahne and Joel Westheimer, "In the Service of What? The Politics of Service-Learning," *Phi Delta Kappa* 77, no. 9 (1996): 593–99.

61. Jeremy Cohen and Dennis Kinsey, "'Doing Good' and Scholarship: A Service-Learning Study," *Journalism Educator* 48, no. 4 (1994): 4–14; Kahne and Westheimer, "In the Service of What?"

62. Kahne and Westheimer, "In the Service of What?" 596.

63. Barber and Battistoni, "A Season of Service"; Howard, *Service-Learning Course Design Workbook*; Barbara Jacoby, "Service-Learning in Today's Higher Education," in *Service-Learning in Higher Education: Concepts and Practices,* ed. Barbara Jacoby (San Francisco: Jossey-Bass, 1996), 3–25.

64. Barber and Battistoni, "A Season of Service"; Howard, *Service-Learning Course Design Workbook*; Kahne and Westheimer, "In the Service of What?"

65. Barber and Battistoni, "A Season of Service"; Kahne and Westheimer, "In the Service of What?"

66. Howard, *Service-Learning Course Design Workbook,* 38.

67. Kahne and Westheimer, "In the Service of What?"

68. Ibid., 597.

69. Freire, *Pedagogy of the Oppressed,* 100–101.

70. Hatcher and Bringle, "Reflection: Bridging the Gap," 153

71. Barber and Battistoni, "A Season of Service."

72. Tamara Williams and Erin McKenna, "Negotiating Subject Positions in a Service-Learning Context: Toward a Feminist Critique of Experiential Learning," in Macdonald and Sánchez-Casal, *Twenty-first-Century Feminist Classrooms,* 135–54.

73. Louis J. Puhl, *The Spiritual Exercises of St. Ignatius: Based on Studies in the Language of the Autograph* (Chicago: Loyola Press, 1951), 7 n. 18.

74. Nadinne Cruz, presentation to the Campus Compact Professional Development Institute (Providence, R.I., July 2006).

75. Lewis, foreword to *Feminist Teaching,* xv.

76. See, in particular, Janet Eyler, Dwight E. Giles Jr., Christine M. Stenson, and Charlene J. Gray, *At a Glance: What We Know about the Effects of Service-Learning on College Students, Faculty, Institutions and Communities, 1993–2000,* 3rd ed. (Nashville, Tenn.: Vanderbilt University, 2001).

77. For a rare exception, see Julie Brown, "Theory or Practice: What Exactly Is Feminist Pedagogy?" *Journal of General Education* 41 (1992): 51–63.

7. The Intersection of Race, Class, and Gender in Jesuit and Feminist Education: Finding Transcendent Meaning in the Concrete

M. SHAWN COPELAND

1. Michael J. Buckley, *The Catholic University as Promise and Project: Reflections in a Jesuit Idiom* (Washington, D.C.: Georgetown University Press, 1998), 57.

2. Ibid., 57–58.

3. Society of Jesus in the United States, "Communal Reflection on the Jesuit Mission in Higher Education: A Way of Proceeding," in *A Jesuit Education Reader*, ed. George W. Traub (Chicago: Loyola Press, 2002), 183.

4. John W. O'Malley, "How Humanistic Is the Jesuit Tradition? From the 1599 *Ratio Studiorum* to Now," http://www.bc.edu/offices/mission/exploring/jesuniv/omalley_humanistic.html.

5. Ibid.

6. Society of Jesus in the United States, "Communal Reflection," 6–7.

7. Boston College, *What Are We? An Introduction to Boston College and Its Jesuit and Catholic Tradition* (Chestnut Hill, Mass.: Center for Ignatian Spirituality, Boston College, 2002), 17.

8. Timothy Hanchin, "Messianic or Bourgeois?" *America*, May 8, 2006, 12.

9. Society of Jesus in the United States, "Communal Reflection," 7–8.

10. See Anne M. Clifford, *Introducing Feminist Theology* (Maryknoll, N.Y.: Orbis, 2001), 16–17; Eve Browning Cole, *Philosophy and Feminist Criticism: An Introduction* (New York: Paragon House, 1991), 1–2. See also Jean Baker Miller, *Toward a New Psychology of Women* (Boston: Beacon Press, 1976); Carol Gilligan, *In a Different Voice: Psychological Theory and Women's Development* (Cambridge, Mass.: Harvard University Press, 1982); Mary Field Belenky, Blythe McVicker Clinchy, Nancy Rule Goldberger, and Jill Mattuck Tarule, *Women's Ways of Knowing: The Development of Self, Voice, and Mind* (New York: Basic Books, 1986).

11. Clifford, *Introducing Feminist Theology*, 23.

12. Sandra M. Schneiders, *With Oil in Their Lamps: Faith, Feminism, and the Future* (Mahwah, N.J.: Paulist Press, 2000), 8.

13. Third-wave feminism assumes women's equality and inclusion at every level of society but also insists on grounding its analysis in multiracial, multiethnic, multi-issue concerns, including respect for gay, lesbian, bisexual, and transgender persons, and on collaborating in working for social change with people from all socioeconomic backgrounds. See Sangamithra Iyer, "Riding the Third Wave: The *Satya* Interview with Rebecca Walker," *Satya*, Jan. 2005, http://www.rebeccawalker.com/article_2005_riding-the-third-wave.htm.

14. Alice Walker problematizes the word "womanist" by making "black feminist or feminist of color" the first definition of the term. "Womanist" also denotes "responsible, in charge, *serious*. Also, committed to survival and wholeness of entire people, male *and* female. Not a separatist, except periodically for health. Traditionally universalist, as in: " 'Mama, why are we brown, pink, and yellow, and our cousins are white, beige, and black?' " Ans.: " 'Well, you know the colored race is just like a flower garden, with every color flower represented.' " Alice Walker, *In Search of Our Mothers' Gardens: Womanist Prose* (San Diego, Calif.: Harcourt Brace Jovanovich, 1983), xi–xii.

15. Bernard Lonergan asks: "How, indeed, is a mind to become conscious of its own bias when that bias springs from a communal flight from understanding and is supported by the whole texture of a civilization? How can new strength and vigour be imparted to the detached and disinterested desire to understand without the reinforcement acting as an added bias? How can human intelligence hope to deal with the unintelligible yet objective situations which the flight from understanding creates and expands and sustains?" Lonergan, *Collected Works of Bernard Lonergan,* vol. 3, *Insight: A Study of Human Understanding* (Toronto: University of Toronto Press, 1992), xiv.

16. Iris Marion Young, *Justice and the Politics of Difference* (Princeton, N.J.: Princeton University Press, 1990), 41.

17. See Lonergan, *Insight,* chaps. 6 and 7.

18. Lorraine Code, "Experience, Knowledge, and Responsibility," in *Feminist Perspectives in Philosophy,* ed. Morwenna Griffiths and Margaret Whitford (Bloomington: Indiana University Press, 1988), 191.

19. Jean Ziegler, "The Right to Food: Report of the Special Rapporteur on the Right to Food," Economic and Social Council, United Nations, Jan. 24, 2005, 4. Ziegler served in this post from 2000 through 2008. See also Arundhati Roy, *The Cost of Living* (New York: Modern Library, 1999).

20. United Nations, *Human Development Report, 2005* (New York: United Nations Development Programme, 2005), 4, http://hdr.undp.org/en/media/HDR05_complete.pdf.

21. Ibid.

22. Zygmunt Bauman, *Globalization: The Human Condition* (New York: Columbia University Press, 1998), 70; Howard Winant, "The New Imperialism, Globalization, and Racism," in *The New Politics of Race: Globalism, Difference, Justice* (Minneapolis: University of Minnesota Press, 2004), 135.

23. See David K. Shipler, *The Working Poor: Invisible in America* (New York: Vintage Books, 2005); Barbara Ehrenreich, *Nickel and Dimed in America: On (Not) Getting by in America* (New York: Henry Holt, 2001); Jonathan Kozol, *Rachel and Her Children: Homeless Families in America* (New York: Fawcett Columbine, 1988); Jeffrey Reiman, *The Rich Get Richer and the Poor Get Prison: Ideology, Class, and Criminal Justice* (Boston: Pearson, 2004).

24. Eduardo Bonilla-Silva, *Racism without Racists: Color-Blind Racism and the Persistence of Racial Inequality in the United States* (Lanham, Md.: Rowman & Littlefield, 2003). The four main "frames" of color-blind racism are abstract liberalism, which involves a set of ideas linked to political and economic liberalism—equal opportunity, individualism, choice, and persuasion— rather than compulsion in achieving social policy; naturalization, which "allows whites to explain away racial phenomena by suggesting that they are natural occurrences"; cultural racism, which replaces the essentialism once held by biology to explain deviations from a putative white norm as the result of inferior culture and cultural norms; and minimization of racism, which downplays the role of racial discrimination as a "central factor affecting the life chances" of people of color. Taken together, Bonilla-Silva argues, "these frames form an impregnable yet elastic wall that barricades whites from the United States' racial reality" (28–29, 30–52, 47, 119). He interprets data gathered from a structured survey conducted regionally (the Midwest, the South, and the West Coast) among black and white university students as well as a "probalistic survey" of black and white Detroit residents (12–15). See also Patricia J. Williams, *Seeing a Color-Blind Future: The Paradox of Race* (New York: Farrar, Straus and Giroux, 1997); Richard Rodriguez, *Brown: The Last Discovery of America* (New York: Viking, 2002); Frank H. Wu, *Yellow: Race in America beyond Black and White* (New York: Basic Books, 2002).

25. Michael Omi and Howard Winant, *Racial Formation in the United States: From the 1960s to the 1990s*, 2nd ed. (New York: Routledge, 1994), 55.

26. On the macro-level, racial formation process interprets contemporary social relations and the shifting meanings and relevance of race in a global context over historical time. Thus, race as a social construct demonstrates considerable flexibility. Omi and Winant argue that given the increasingly complex and globalized concept of race, racial formation process manages the "competing racial projects [or] efforts to institutionalize racial meanings and identities in particular social structures, notably those of individual, family, community, and state." Michael Omi and Howard Winant, "On the Theoretical Status of the Concept of Race," in *Race, Identity, and Representation in Education*, ed. Cameron McCarthy and Warren Crichlow (New York: Routledge, 1993), 7. The desire of women and men of mixed racial parentage to name themselves, the struggles of egalitarian movements against racial backlash, the postcolonial interrogations of empire, the decentering of powerful binary logics (for example, white/black, colonizer/colonized, as well as the sly concealment of discourses and exercises of racial domination)—these sometimes contradictory enterprises reinforce the protean character of race. Moreover, these enterprises may generate new forms of social oppression and responses that deploy race not only to expose its toxic limitations but also

to reimagine and reconfigure social matrices to evoke the achievement and flourishing of authentic humanity.

27. Omi and Winant, *Racial Formation,* 60.

28. James Boggs, *Racism and the Class Struggle* (New York: Monthly Review Press, 1970), 147–48. See also David Theo Goldberg, *Racist Culture: Philosophy and the Politics of Meaning* (Oxford: Blackwell, 1993).

29. There is opposition between an educated imagination and a biased one. Where the biased imagination is inattentive, incurious, and self-absorbed, the educated imagination is attentive, perceptive, and expansive. Where the biased imagination is obtuse, exclusionary, and narrow, the educated imagination is supple, inclusive, and open. Where the biased imagination is furtive and self-centered, corrupt and spiteful, the educated imagination is free and generous, moral and unstinting. Where the biased imagination is accusatory and irresponsible, the educated imagination is committed and responsible. Where the biased imagination thrives on fear and despair, the educated imagination flourishes with trust and hope.

30. Stuart Hall, "New Ethnicities," in *Stuart Hall: Critical Dialogues in Cultural Studies,* ed. David Morley and Kuan-Hsing Chen (London: Routledge, 1996), 446–47.

31. Anthony Paul Farley, "The Black Body as Fetish Object," *Oregon Law Review* 76, no. 3 (1997): 475.

32. Stephanie Wildman, "The Persistence of White Privilege," *Washington University Journal of Law & Policy* 18 (2005): 253.

33. Martha C. Nussbaum, *Cultivating Humanity: A Classical Defense of Reform in Liberal Education* (Cambridge, Mass.: Harvard University Press, 1997), 84.

8. Teaching for Social Justice in the Engaged Classroom: The Intersection of Jesuit and Feminist Moral Philosophies

KAREN L. SLATTERY, ANA C. GARNER,
JOYCE M. WOLBURG, AND LYNN H. TURNER

1. While we recognize the multiple perspectives that could be called feminist, we use the term in its most basic form as a philosophy that is devoted to the improvement of the status of women and a commitment to taking seriously the issues affecting women.

2. Rita C. Manning, *Speaking from the Heart: A Feminist Perspective on Ethics* (Lanham, Md.: Rowman & Littlefield, 1992); L. Robertson, "Feminist Teacher Education: Applying Feminist Pedagogies to the Preparation of New Teachers," *Feminist Teacher* 8, no. 1 (1994): 11–15; Peter-Hans Kolvenbach, "Themes

of Jesuit Higher Education" (address delivered at Georgetown University, Washington, D.C., June 7, 1989), http://onlineministries.creighton.edu/ Heartland3/r-themes.html.

3. We acknowledge that not all feminists subscribe to an ethic of care—see, for example, Claudia Card, review of *Feminist Morality: Transforming Culture, Society, and Politics*, by Virginia Held, *Feminist Ethics* 4 (1995): 938–40; Virginia Held, "Liberalism and the Ethics of Care," in *On Feminist Ethics and Politics*, ed. Claudia Card (Lawrence: University Press of Kansas, 1999), 288–309; Sara Ruddick, "Injustice in Families: Assault and Domination," in *Justice and Care: Essential Readings in Feminist Ethics*, ed. Virginia Held (Boulder, Colo.: Westview Press, 1995), 203–24—but for the purposes of our discussion, we have chosen the ethic of care as representative of many feminists' approach to ethics and morality.

4. Virginia Held, "Feminist Transformations of Moral Theory," Philosophy and Phenomenological Research 50 (1990): 344.

5. Joan Tronto, *Moral Boundaries: A Political Argument for an Ethic of Care* (New York: Routledge, 1993).

6. Dorothy Van Soest, "Strange Bedfellows: A Call for Reordering National Priorities from Three Social Justice Perspectives," *Social Work* 39, no. 6 (1994): 710–17.

7. John Rawls, *Theory of Justice* (Cambridge, Mass.: Belknap Press of Harvard University Press, 1971), 379.

8. P. M. Morris, "The Capabilities Perspective: A Framework for Social Justice," *Families in Society* 83, no. 4 (2002): 365–73.

9. Lawrence R. Frey, W. Barnett Pearce, Mark A. Pollock, Lee Artz, and Bren A. O. Murphy, "Looking for Justice in All the Wrong Places: On a Communication Approach to Social Justice," *Communication Studies* 47, no. 1–2 (1996): 110–27.

10. Ibid., 110.

11. Ibid., 111.

12. Lisa Sowle Cahill, "Women and Men Working Together in Jesuit Institutions of Higher Learning," *Conversations* 4 (Fall 1993): 25.

13. Georgia Harkness, *Christian Ethics* (Nashville, Tenn.: Abingdon Press, 1957).

14. Pope Benedict XVI, "Encyclical Letter *Deus Caritas Est* of the Supreme Pontiff Benedict XVI to the Bishops, Priests and Deacons, Men and Women Religious and All the Lay Faithful on Christian Love, " (2005), 11. Retrieved, 9/18/06. http://www.vatican.va/holyfather/benedict_xvi/encyclicals/ documents/hf_ben-xvi_enc_20051225_deus-caritas-est_en.html

15. Matt. 22.34–40.

16. Pontifical Council for Justice and Peace, "The social agenda: A collection of magisterial texts" (2000). Retrieved, 12/17/07. http://www.thesocialagenda.org

17. Martin R. Tripole, "Justice and Jesuit Higher Education: Another Perspective," *Conversations* 23 (Spring 2003): 46.

18. Ibid.

19. Carol Gilligan, *In a Different Voice: Psychological Theory and Women's Development* (Cambridge, Mass.: Harvard University Press, 1982).

20. Rosemarie Tong (2000), "Feminist Ethics." *Stanford Encyclopedia of Philosophy.* Retrieved 4/1/04. http://setis.library.usyd.edu.au/standord/archives/fall2000.

21. Nel Noddings, *Caring: A Feminine Approach to Ethics and Moral Education* (Berkeley: University of California Press, 1984); Ruddick, "Injustice in Families"; Virginia Held, *Feminist Morality: Transforming Culture, Society, and Politics* (Chicago: University of Chicago Press, 1993).

22. Virginia Held, *The Ethics of Care: Personal, Political, and Global* (New York: Oxford University Press, 2006).

23. Tronto, *Moral Boundaries*; Tong, "Feminist Ethics."

24. Tong, "Feminist Ethics."

25. Held, *The Ethics of Care*; Eva Kittay, *Love's Labor: Essays on Women, Equality, and Dependency* (New York: Routledge, 1999).

26. Tronto, *Moral Boundaries*, 110.

27. Douglas Jacobson and Rodney Sawatsky, *Gracious Christianity: Living the Love We Profess* (Grand Rapids, Mich.: Baker Academic, 2006), 43.

28. Second Vatican Council, "Gaudium et Spes, Pastoral Constitution on the Church in the Modern World" (1965), Part One, No. 27. Retrieved 1/18/2007. http://222.osjspm.org/majordoc_gaudium_et_spes_part_one.aspx.

29. Held, *The Ethics of Care*, 86.

30. Ibid., 71.

31. Jacobson and Sawatsky, *Gracious Christianity*.

32. Pope Benedict XVI, "Encyclical Letter *Deus Caritas Est* of the Supreme Pontiff Benedict XVI to the Bishops, Priests and Deacons, Men and Women Religious and All the Lay Faithful on Christian Love."

33. Noddings, *Caring: A Feminine Approach*, 3.

34. Ibid.

35. Jacobson and Sawatsky, *Gracious Christianity*, 45.

36. Joseph Daoust, "Of Kingfishers and Dragonflies: Faith and Justice at the Core of Jesuit Education," *Conversations* 19 (Spring 2001): 13–20.

37. Pope Benedict XVI, "Encyclical Letter *Deus Caritas Est* of the Supreme Pontiff Benedict XVI to the Bishops, Priests and Deacons, Men and Women Religious and All the Lay Faithful on Christian Love."

38. Ibid., 16.

39. Susan Moller Okin, *Justice, Gender and the Family* (New York: Basic Books, 1989).

40. Virginia Held, "The Meshing of Care and Justice," in *Feminist Ethics*, ed. Moira Gatens (Brookfield, Vt.: Ashgate, 1998), 540.

41. See, for example, Tronto, *Moral Boundaries*; Selma Sevenhuijsen, "Caring in the Third Way: The Relation between Obligation, Responsibility and Care in Third Way Discourse," *Critical Social Policy* 20, no. 5 (2000): 5–37; Linda Steiner and Chad M. Okrusch, "Care as a Virtue for Journalists," *Journal of Mass Media Ethics* 21 (2006): 102–22; Garry Pech and Rhona Leibel, "Writing in Solidarity: Steps toward an Ethic of Care for Journalism," *Journal of Mass Media Ethics* 21 (2006): 141–55.

42. Kolvenbach, "Themes of Jesuit Higher Education" Address delivered at Georgetown University, Washington, D.C., June 7, 1989. http://onlineministries.creighton.edu/Heartland3/r-themes.html

43. Laura K. Guerrero, Peter A. Andersen, and Melanie R. Trost, "Communication and Emotion: Basic Concepts and Approaches," in *Handbook of Communication and Emotion: Research, Theory, Applications, and Contexts,* ed. Peter A. Andersen and Laura K. Guerrero (San Diego, Calif.: Academic Press, 1998), 3–4.

44. Kerry Ann Rockquemore and Regan Harwell Schaffer, "Toward a Theory of Engagement: A Cognitive Mapping of Service-Learning Experiences," *Michigan Journal of Community Service Learning* 7 (2000): 14–25.

45. John MacMurray, *Reason and Emotion* (Amherst, N.Y.: Humanity Books, 1992), 29.

46. Robert Jensen, *The Heart of Whiteness: Confronting Race, Racism, and White Privilege* (San Francisco: City Lights, 2005).

47. Dean Brackley, "Higher Standards for Higher Education: The Christian University and Solidarity" (address delivered at Creighton University, Omaha, Neb., Nov. 4, 1999), http://www.creighton.edu/CollaborativeMinistry/brackley.html.

48. Ibid., 7.

49. Jocelyn M. Boryczka, "A Brief Overview of Feminism and Feminist Pedagogy" (paper delivered at the "Jesuit and Feminist Education: Transformative Discourses for Teaching and Learning" conference, Fairfield University, Fairfield, Conn., Oct. 2006); Brackley, "Higher Standards for Higher Education."

50. Brackley, "Higher Standards for Higher Education."

51. Tronto, *Moral Boundaries*; Traci M. Levy, "At the Intersection of Intimacy and Care: Redefining 'Family' through the Lens of a Public Ethic of Care," *Politics & Gender* 1 (2005): 65–95.

52. Jocelyn M. Boryczka and Elizabeth A. Petrino, "The Personal Is Political: At the Intersections of Feminist and Jesuit Education" (paper delivered at the "Jesuit and Feminist Education: Transformative Discourses for Teaching and Learning" conference, Fairfield University, Fairfield, Conn., Oct. 2006), 9.

53. Carolyn M. Shrewsbury, "What Is Feminist Pedagogy?" *Women's Studies Quarterly* 15, no. 3–4 (1987): 9.

54. Kolvenbach, "Themes of Jesuit Higher Education."

55. Carolyn M. Shrewsbury, "What Is Feminist Pedagogy?"

56. MacMurray, *Reason and Emotion,* 79.

57. Ibid.

58. Ibid., 61.

59. Rawls, *Theory of Justice.*

9. Transformative Education in a Broken World: Feminist and Jesuit Pedagogy on the Importance of Context

THERESA WEYNAND TOBIN

1. Frances Maher and Mary Kay Thompson Tetreault, *The Feminist Classroom: Dynamics of Gender, Race, and Privilege* (Lanham, Md.: Rowman & Littlefield, 2001), chap. 7.

2. International Commission on the Apostolate of Jesuit Education, "Ignatian Pedagogy: A Practical Approach, 1993," in *The Jesuit "Ratio Studiorum": 400th Anniversary Perspectives,* ed. Vincent J. Duminuco (New York: Fordham University Press, 2000), 243.

3. Ibid., 247.

4. Ibid., 248.

5. Ibid.

6. In their article on sexism, Ann Cudd and Leslie E. Jones discuss the nature and levels of sexism, and I believe much of their discussion can be applied to the phenomenon of heterosexism too, in particular, their distinction between levels and kinds. See Cudd and Jones, "Sexism," in *Feminist Theory: A Philosophical Anthology,* ed. Ann Cudd and Robin Andreasen (Oxford: Blackwell, 2005), 73–83.

7. See *Catechism of the Catholic Church* (Vatican City: Libreria Editrice Vaticana, 1993), http://www.vatican.va/archive/catechism/ccc_toc.htm. See pt. 3, sec. 2, chap. 2, especially articles 2332, 2357, 2358, and 2359.

8. "Vatican to 'Ban New Gay Priests,'" *BBC World News,* Sept. 2005, http://news.bbc.co.uk/1/hi/world/europe/4276912.stm.

9. bell hooks, "Toward a Revolutionary Feminist Pedagogy," in *Falling into Theory: Conflicting Views of Reading Literature* (New York: Bedford/St. Martin's Press, 2000), 83.

10. Carol Gilligan, *In a Different Voice: Psychological Theory and Women's Development* (Cambridge, Mass.: Harvard University Press, 1982).

11. Nel Noddings and other feminist thinkers developed Gilligan's initial insights into full-blown ethics of care. See Nel Noddings, *Caring: A Feminine Approach to Ethics and Moral Education* (Berkeley: University of California Press, 1984); Virginia Held, *The Ethics of Care: Personal, Political, and Global* (New York: Oxford University Press, 2006).

12. See Joan Tronto, *Moral Boundaries: A Political Argument for an Ethic of Care* (New York: Routledge, 1993).

13. Iris Marion Young, *Justice and the Politics of Difference* (Princeton, N.J.: Princeton University Press, 1990), 45, quoting Epstein, "Gay Politics, Ethnic Identity: The Limits of Social Constructionism," *Socialist Review* 17 (May–Aug. 1987): 9–54.

14. Young, *Justice,* 43.

15. Ibid., 93.

16. Laurie Finke quoted by Maher and Tetreault, *The Feminist Classroom,* 64.

17. Teresa McKenna, "Borderness and Pedagogy: Exposing Culture in the Classroom," in *The Critical Pedagogy Reader,* ed. Antonia Darder, Marta Baltodano, and Rodolfo D. Torres (New York: Routledge, 2003), 430–39.

18. Ibid., 435.

19. Ibid.

20. Maher and Tetreault, *The Feminist Classroom,* 213.

21. hooks, "Toward a Revolutionary Feminist Pedagogy," 83.

10. Consciousness-Raising as Discernment: Using Jesuit and Feminist Pedagogies in a Protestant Classroom

MARY J. HENOLD

1. See Mary J. Henold, *Catholic and Feminist: The Surprising History of the American Catholic Feminist Movement* (Chapel Hill: University of North Carolina Press, 2008).

2. Anita Shreve, *Women Together, Women Alone: The Legacy of the Consciousness-Raising Movement* (New York: Viking Penguin, 1989), 53–55; Rachel Blau DuPlessis and Ann Snitow, eds., *The Feminist Memoir Project: Voices from Women's Liberation* (New York: Three Rivers Press, 1998), 7–8.

3. DuPlessis and Snitow, *The Feminist Memoir Project,* 7–8.

4. I should stress here that I am no expert in Jesuit spirituality; I am merely a product of it. I was raised in a Jesuit parish, attended a Jesuit university, served in the Jesuit Volunteer Corps, and did the Spiritual Exercises (Nineteenth Annotation) in graduate school.

5. Pierre Wolff, *Discernment: The Art of Choosing Well* (Liguori, Mo.: Liguori Publications, 2003), 25–26.

11. De Certeau and "Making Do": The Case of Gay Men and Lesbians on a Jesuit Campus

DAVID GUDELUNAS

1. Ian Buchanan, *Michel de Certeau: Cultural Theorist* (Thousand Oaks, Calif.: Sage, 2001); Ben Highmore, *Michel de Certeau: Analyzing Culture* (New York: Continuum, 2006).

2. Buchanan, *Michel de Certeau.*

3. Henry Jenkins, *Textual Poachers: Television Fans and Participatory Culture* (New York: Routledge, 1992).

4. John Fiske, *Understanding Popular Culture* (New York: Routledge, 1989).

5. Michel de Certeau, *The Practice of Everyday Life* (Berkeley: University of California Press, 1984), xiii.

6. Ibid., xvii.

7. Ibid., 35.

8. Ibid., 37.

9. Ibid., 92.

10. Ibid., xii.

11. Ibid., 35.

12. Ibid., xxi.

12. Textual Deviance: Eve Ensler's *The Vagina Monologues* and Catholic Campuses

HEATHER HATHAWAY, GREGORY J. O'MEARA, S.J., AND STEPHANIE QUADE

1. American Association of University Professors, "Informal Glossary of AAUP Terms and Abbreviations," http://www.aaup.org/AAUP/about/mission/glossary.htm.

2. Cardinal Newman Society, "About Us," http://www.cardinalnewman society.org/AboutUs/tabid/53/Default.aspx.

3. Cardinal Newman Society, "Campus Speaker Monitoring Project," http://www.cardinalnewmansociety.org/CampusSpeakerMonitoring/tabid/64/Default.aspx.

4. Ibid.

5. Cardinal Newman Society, "About the CNS Campaign to End the V-Monologues on Catholic Campuses," http://www.cardinalnewmansociety.org/LoveResponsibility/CampaigntoStoptheVMonologues/tabid/63/Default.aspx.

6. V-Day, "Today, Valentine's Day is V-Day 2005 in over 1100 Colleges and Communities," Feb. 14, 2005, http://www.vday.org/node/1420.

7. Cardinal Newman Society, "19 Planned Performances in 2008; Play Returns to Notre Dame," http://www.cardinalnewmansociety.org/LoveResponsibility/CampaigntoStoptheVMonologues/tabid/63/ctl/Details/mid/445/ItemID/85/Default.aspx.

8. Rowan Williams, "What Is a University?" (address delivered in Wuhan, China, Oct. 13, 2006), http://www.archbishopofcanterbury.org/sermons_speeches/061013.htm.

9. David Tracy, *The Analogical Imagination: Christian Theology and the Culture of Pluralism* (New York: Crossroads, 1981), 101.

10. Ibid.

11. See, for example, Augustine, *The Confessions*, 2.3.6: "Sed ubi sexto illo et decimo anno, interposito otio ex necessitate domestica, feriatus ab omni schola cum parentibus esse coepi, excesserunt caput meum vepres libidinum, et nulla erat eradicans manus. quin immo ubi me ille pater in balneis vidit pubescentem et inquieta indutum adolescentia, quasi iam ex hoc in nepotes gestiret, gaudens matri indicavit." Garry Wills offers the following translation: "So in my sixteenth year, in an idleness caused by my father's impecunious state, with no school to attend, I began again to stay with my parents, and the thorns of my own drives, with no one to weed them out from around me, shot up above my head. So much was this true that when my father saw in the baths that my childhood was gone and I was clothed with unstable young manhood, he mentioned this to my mother, overjoyed with anticipation of having grandchildren by me." Garry Wills, *Saint Augustine's Sin* (New York: Viking, 2003), 39.

12. See, for example, Cardinal Newman Society, "Catholic Teachings on Sexuality," http://www.cardinalnewmansociety.org/LoveResponsibility/CampaigntoStoptheVMonologues/CatholicTeachingsonSexuality/tabid/88/Default.aspx.

13. Ibid.

14. Robert Wuthnow, *American Mythos: Why Our Best Efforts to Be a Better Nation Fall Short* (Princeton, N.J.: Princeton University Press, 2006), 11.

15. Ibid., 232–33.

16. Bernard Lonergan, "Theology in Its New Context," in *Bernard Lonergan: A Second Collection*, ed. William Ryan and Bernard Tyrrell (Toronto: University of Toronto Press, 1974), 55; originally published in *Theology of Renewal*,

vol. 1, *Renewal of Religious Thought,* ed. L. K. Shook (New York: Herder & Herder, 1968), 36–46.

17. Ibid., 55.

18. Ibid., 57.

19. Ibid.

20. Ibid.

21. Ibid., 58.

22. Ibid.

23. Ibid.

24. Ibid.

25. Ibid., 59.

26. Ibid.

27. Ibid.

28. Ibid., 61.

29. These two approaches are distinguished and discussed at great length in Albert Jonsen and Stephen Toulmin, *The Abuse of Casuistry: A History of Moral Reasoning* (Berkeley: University of California Press, 1988), 22–46. Of course, there are more refined explanatory methods that can be relied upon at this stage. Wittgenstein, among others, warned against the idea that only one set of methods yielded certainty. Instead, he noted that there are many different sorts of uncertainty, and we have different ways of approaching them. See, for example, Ludwig Wittgenstein, *On Certainty* (Oxford: Blackwell, 1969). Ricoeur agrees with Wittgenstein's observation: "There is no one privileged mode of explanation in history. This is a feature that history shares with the theory of action to the degree that the penultimate referent of historical discourse is those interactions capable of engendering the social bond. It is not surprising therefore that history unfolds the full range of modes of explanation likely to make human interaction intelligible. On the one side, the series of repeatable facts of quantitative history lend themselves to a causal analysis and to the establishing of regularities that draw the idea of a cause, in the sense of efficacy, toward that of lawfulness, toward the model of 'if . . . then' relation." Paul Ricoeur, *Memory, History, Forgetting,* trans. Kathleen Blamey and David Pellauer (Chicago: University of Chicago Press, 2004), 184–85.

Still, as Jonsen and Toulmin observe, from all these possible methods, there are really two broad approaches to reasoning in practical fields such as law or ethics. "We inherit two distinct ways of discussing ethical issues: One of these frames these issues in terms of principles, rules, and other general ideas; the other focuses on the specific features of particular kinds of moral cases. In the first way general ethical rules relate to specific moral cases in a *theoretical* manner, with universal rules serving as 'axioms' from which particular moral judgments are deduced as theorems. In the second, this relation is frankly *practical,* with general moral rules serving as 'maxims,' which can be fully understood only in terms of paradigmatic cases that define their meaning and force." Jonsen and Toulmin, *The Abuse of Casuistry,* 22.

30. "The rigor of geometry was so appealing, indeed, that for many Greek philosophers formal deduction became the ideal of *all* rational argument. . . . In due course, too (the hope was) other sciences would find their own unquestioned general principles to serve as their starting points, in explaining, for example, the natures of animals, plants, and the other permanent features of the world." Jonsen and Toulmin, *The Abuse of Casuistry,* 25.

31. In theoretical fields such as geometry, statements or arguments were idealized, atemporal, and necessary:

   a. They were "idealized" in the following sense. Concrete physical objects, cut out of metal in the shapes of triangles or circles, can never be made with perfect precision. . . . The idealized "straight lines" and "circles" of geometry, by contrast, exemplify such truths with perfect exactness.
   b. They were "atemporal" in the following sense. Any geometrical theorem that is true at one time or on one occasion will be true at any time and at any occasion. . . .
   c. Finally, theoretical arguments were "necessary" in a twofold sense. The arguments of Euclidean geometry depended for their validity both on the correctness of the initial axioms and definitions and on the inner consistency of the subsequent deductions. Granted Euclid's axioms, all of his later theorems were "necessary consequences" of those initial truths. If any of the theorems were questioned, conversely, this implied either that their starting point was incorrect or else that the steps taken in passing to the theorems were formally fallacious. (Ibid., 26–27)

32. Ibid., 25, citing Aristotle, *Nicomachean Ethics,* 6.iii–vii.

33. Karl Rahner, "Basic Observations on the Subject of Changeable and Unchangeable Factors in the Church," in *Theological Investigations,* vol. IX, trans. Graham Harrison (London: Herder & Herder, 1972), 14.

34. Roger Haight, *Dynamics of Theology* (Maryknoll, N.Y.: Orbis, 1990), 26.

35. Ibid., 28.

36. Frank Miller Turner, *John Henry Newman: The Challenge to Evangelical Religion* (New Haven, Conn.: Yale University Press, 2002).

37. Jonsen and Toulmin, *The Abuse of Casuistry,* 181–94.

38. Stephen Schloesser, "Against Forgetting: Memory, History, Vatican II," *Theological Studies* 67 (2006): 310, citing Henri de Lubac, *At the Service of the Church: Henri de Lubac Reflects on the Circumstances that Occasioned His Writings,* trans. Anne Elizabeth Englund (San Francisco: Ignatius, 1993), 55.

39. Schloesser, "Against Forgetting," 279.

40. De Lubac, *At the Service of the Church,* cited in ibid., 39.

41. Catharine A. MacKinnon, "Feminism, Marxism, Method and the State: An Agenda for Theory," *Signs* 7, no. 3 (1982): 515–44.

42. Gustavo Gutierrez, *A Theology of Liberation: History, Politics, and Salvation,* rev. ed. (New York: Orbis, 1988).

43. MacKinnon, "Feminism, Marxism, Method and the State," 536.

44. Ibid., 536–37 (internal citation omitted).

45. Lonergan, "Theology in Its New Context," 61.

46. Ibid., 58.

47. Cardinal Newman Society, "CNS News and Announcements Archive," http://www.cardinalnewmansociety.org/News/tabid/54/Default.aspx.

48. See, for example, Cardinal Newman Society, "Catholic Teachings on Sexuality."

49. See, for example, Mary Douglas, *Purity and Danger* (New York: Routledge, 1966).

50. Cardinal Newman Society, "Response to University of Notre Dame Statement on Academic Freedom," April 5, 2006, http://www.cardinal newmansociety.org/Publications/News/Notre_Dame.

51. Ibid.

52. John D'Arcy, "Concerning a Presentation at Notre Dame," Feb. 2004, http://www.cardinalnewmansociety.org/LoveResponsibility/CampaigntoStoptheVMonologues/BishopDArcyStatementontheMonologues/tabid/89/Default.aspx.

53. The lecture was later published as a chapter titled "Tradition and Authority," in Eamon Duffy, *Faith of Our Fathers: Reflections on Catholic Tradition* (New York: Continuum, 2004), 171.

54. The Boston Women's Health Collective first published *Our Bodies, Ourselves* in 1973, in an effort to "disseminate women's experience and knowledge as valid information" and "challenge the paternalistic medical system." At the time, the book was revolutionary. Its legacy is ongoing through the Our Bodies Ourselves, an organization that is still run by the Boston Women's Health Book Collective. Like Ensler's play, *Our Bodies, Ourselves* generated a worldwide movement to improve women's health, especially with regard to reproduction and sexuality. See Our Bodies Ourselves, "A Letter from the Founders," http://www.ourbodiesourselves.org/book/inside/letter.asp.

55. Eve Ensler, "The Power and Mystery of Naming Things," *NPR,* March 20, 2006. http://www.npr.org/templates/story/story.php?storyId=5285531.

56. Ibid.

57. V-Day, "About V-Day," http://www.vday.org/contents/vday/aboutvday.

58. Eve Ensler, *The Vagina Monologues* (New York: Dramatists Play Service, 2000), 18–22.

59. Sharon Lerner, "Clit Club," *Village Voice*, Feb. 13, 2001, http://www
.villagevoice.com/2001-02-13/news/clit-club.

60. Kim Q. Hall in "Queerness, Disability, and *The Vagina Monologues*,"
Hypatia 20, no. 1 (2005): 99–119. Hall's article, as I will show, raises a number
of important issues that can valuably inform a classroom discussion of *The
Vagina Monologues*, even if students lack the theoretical sophistication required
to appreciate Hall's analysis in full.

61. "Intersex" is a term used to describe individuals with reproductive or
sexual anatomy that is atypical. Individuals may possess, for example, external
female genitalia with internal male anatomy. A person who is intersex may
also possess chromosomal variations. As in this vignette, intersex anatomy may
go unrecognized until puberty. I refer to the intersex individual in question
here as a "young woman" because, according to Ensler, that is how she identifies herself. The Intersex Society of North America states that "many intersex
people are perfectly comfortable adopting either a male or female gender identity and are not seeking a genderless society or to label themselves as a member
of a third gender class. . . . In fact, many of the people with intersex we
know—both those subjected to early surgeries and those who escaped surgery—very happily accepted a gender assignment of male or female (either the
one given them at birth or one they chose later for themselves later in life)."
Intersex Society of North America, "Why Doesn't ISNA Want to Eradicate
Gender?" http://www.isna.org/faq/not_eradicating_gender.

62. Ensler, *The Vagina Monologues*, 30.

63. Ibid.

64. Hall, "Queerness, Disability, and *The Vagina Monologues*," 109.

65. Intersex Society of North America, quoted by Hall, "Queerness, Disability, and *The Vagina Monologues*," 100–101.

66. Hall, "Queerness, Disability, and *The Vagina Monologues*," 101.

67. Hall makes a similar point on pages 103 and 108 of her essay. See also
Adrienne Rich, "Compulsory Heterosexuality and Lesbian Existence," *Journal
of Women's History* 15, no. 3 (2003): 11–48.

68. Indeed, this fissure seems to be a perennial issue at the National Wom-
en's Studies Association annual conference. It was again addressed in the keynote address of the 2008 convention, delivered by Patricia Hill Collins, a social
theorist whose research, scholarship, and activism have examined intersecting
power relations of race, gender, social class, sexuality, and nation.

69. Hall, "Queerness, Disability, and *The Vagina Monologues*," 106, citing
Chandra Talpade Mohanty, "Under Western Eyes: Feminist Scholarship and
Colonial Discourse," in *Third World Women and the Politics of Feminism*, ed.
Chandra Talpade Mohanty, Ann Russo, and Lourdes Torres (Bloomington:
Indiana University Press, 1991), 58.

70. Hall, "Queerness, Disability, and *The Vagina Monologues*," 103, citing Mohanty, "Under Western Eyes," 73–74.

71. Germaine Greer, "The V-Word Is No Victory for Women," *Daily Telegraph*, March 1, 2002. Greer makes a number of other important points in this scathing critique, including her observation of the irony of Ensler's celebration of a word ("vagina") that, in Greer's mind, "is the nastiest kind of name for the female genitalia because it is the Latin for 'sword-sheath.' There is more to the female sex than the accommodation of a male weapon, and much more to female sexual apparatus than a hole. Having decided to focus on the hole rather than the doughnut, as it were, Ensler happily disappears up it. These days, she is apt to talk of herself as living in her vagina, as if she had transformed herself into the sword, turning herself inside out in an orgy of inverted penis-envy."

72. Camille Paglia, "The Bush Look," *Salon*, Feb. 28, 2005, http://archive.salon.com/people/col/pagl/2001/02/28/bush/print.html. At the same time, in contrast to Paglia, I do not believe Ensler is "obsess[ed] with male evil." She does, in fact, draw important attention to very real issues of violence against women, most of which has a sexual component to it, whether it be war rape or incest. Nor do I agree with her assertion "That the psychological poison of Ensler's archaic creed of victimization is being spread to impressionable women students is positively criminal."

73. A similar class bias can be found in the monologue "I Was There in the Room," which recounts Ensler's witnessing of her granddaughter's birth. Here Ensler recounts a Western, privileged vision of birth in which mothers-in-law (as well as mothers and husbands) can be present, not to aid in the process because no one else is around, but rather because they have the luxury of witnessing, in a hospital room complete with all the latest lifesaving devices, the miracle of birth. For women who do not have access to decent health care, birth is not always a miracle—indeed, it can often lead to their own deaths. In this respect, Paglia is spot on in her critique of Ensler's bourgeois bias: "Today's upper-middle-class Western women, with their efficient, schematized lives, are so removed from elemental mysteries that they are naively susceptible to feverish charlatans and cultists like Ensler, who encourages the delusion that they are in full control of their reproductive system and that everything negative or ambivalent about it has been imposed by the prejudice of misogynous males."

74. Jo Reger and Lacey Story, "Talking about My Vagina: Two College Campuses and *The Vagina Monologues*," in *Different Wavelengths: Studies of the Contemporary Women's Movement*, ed. Jo Reger (New York: Routledge, 2005), 139–60.

75. Both of these were issued and can be obtained from the International Center for Jesuit Education, Rome.

76. For a valuable discussion of the relationship between Ignatian and critical pedagogical methods, see Sharon M. Chubbuck, "Socially Just Teaching and the Complementarity of Ignatian Pedagogy and Critical Pedagogy," *Christian Higher Education* 6, no. 3 (2007): 239–65.

77. Arthur W. Chickering and Linda Reisser, "The Seven Vectors," in *College Student Development and Academic Life: Psychological, Intellectual, Social, and Moral Issues*, ed. Karen Arnold and Ilda Carreiro King (New York: Garland, 1997), 2–20.

78. See, for example, Mark Paul Gunderson and James Leslie McCary, "Sexual Guilt and Religion," *Family Coordinator* 28, no. 2 (1979): 353–57.

79. Nancy Lesko, "The Curriculum of the Body: Lessons from a Catholic High School," in *Becoming Feminine: The Politics of Popular Culture*, ed. Leslie Roman (Philadelphia: Falmer, 1988), 123–42.

80. Nancy Mairs, *Ordinary Time: Cycles in Marriage, Faith, and Renewal* (Boston: Beacon Press, 1993).

81. United States Catholic Conference, *Human Sexuality: A Catholic Perspective for Education and Lifelong Learning* (Washington, D.C.: United States Catholic Conference, 1991).

82. Deborah L. Tolman, "Doing Desire: Adolescent Girls' Struggles for/ with Sexuality," *Gender and Society* 8, no. 3 (1994): 340 (internal citation omitted), citing Lynn Segal, introduction to *Sex Exposed: Sexuality and the Pornography Debate*, ed. Lynn Segal and M. McIntosh (New Brunswick, N.J.: Rutgers University Press, 1993).

13. Tilling the Soil: Preparing Women for the Vocation of Ministry—A Challenge and Call

SUSAN M. MOUNTIN

1. Alice McDermott, "The Church in the 21st Century: Why Women Choose to Stay" (paper delivered at Boston College, Chestnut Hill, Mass., Sept. 2005).

2. United States Conference of Catholic Bishops, *Co-workers in the Vineyard of the Lord: A Resource for Guiding the Development of Lay Ecclesial Ministry* (Washington, D.C.: United States Conference of Catholic Bishops, 2005).

3. In a more recent report, the Center for Applied Research in the Apostolate reported that 61 percent of those studying for lay ministry programs (certificate and degree) are women. That includes 12,462 studying for certificates in lay ministry and 5,473 studying for graduate degrees in ministry. Women studying to do ministry number nearly 10,940. There were only 3,483 men in priestly formation in 2009–10. Mary L. Gautier, *Catholic Ministry Formation*

Enrollments: Statistical Overview for 2009–2010 (Washington, D.C.: Center for Applied Research in the Apostolate, 2010).

4. Center for Applied Research in the Apostolate, "Frequently Requested Church Statistics," http://cara.georgetown.edu/bulletin/index.htm.

5. United States Conference of Catholic Bishops, *Co-workers in the Vineyard of the Lord.*

6. John L. McCarthy and Jesuits, eds., *Documents of the Thirty-fourth General Congregation of the Society of Jesus: The Decrees of General Congregation Thirty-four, the Fifteenth of the Restored Society and the Accompanying Papal and Jesuit Documents* (St. Louis, Mo.: Institute of Jesuit Sources, 1995).

7. Ibid.

14. Women in Jesuit Higher Education: Ten Years Later

SUSAN A. ROSS

I would like to acknowledge the generous assistance of Dr. Bren Ortega Murphy, who reviewed this manuscript and offered many helpful suggestions for revision.

1. Susan A. Ross, "The Jesuits and Women: Reflections on the 34th General Congregation's Statement on Women in Church and Civil Society," *Conversations* 16 (Fall 1999): 20–28.

2. Commission of the Status of Women at Loyola University Chicago, "Report of the Commission of the Status of Women at Loyola University Chicago," May 2006, http://luc.edu/diversity/pdfs/womens_commission_report.pdf.

3. John W. O'Malley, *The First Jesuits* (Cambridge, Mass.: Harvard University Press, 1993).

4. John L. McCarthy and Jesuits, eds., *Documents of the Thirty-fourth General Congregation of the Society of Jesus: The Decrees of General Congregation Thirty-four, the Fifteenth of the Restored Society and the Accompanying Papal and Jesuit Documents* (St. Louis, Mo.: Institute of Jesuit Sources, 1995).

Afterword

CHARLES L. CURRIE, S.J.

1. John L. McCarthy and Jesuits, eds., *Documents of the Thirty-fourth General Congregation of the Society of Jesus: The Decrees of General Congregation Thirty-four, the Fifteenth of the Restored Society and the Accompanying Papal and Jesuit Documents* (St. Louis, Mo.: Institute of Jesuit Sources, 1995).

2. John W. Padberg, ed., *Documents of the Thirty-first and Thirty-second General Congregations of the Society of Jesus: An English Translation of the Official Latin Texts of the General Congregations and of the Accompanying Papal Documents* (St. Louis, Mo.: Institute of Jesuit Sources, 1977), 411.

3. Pedro Arrupe, "Men for Others," in *Foundations*, ed. C. E. Meirose (Washington, D.C.: Jesuit Secondary Education Association, 1973), 32.

4. Peter-Hans Kolvenbach, "The Service of Faith and the Promotion of Justice in American Jesuit Higher Education," in *A Jesuit Education Reader*, ed. George W. Traub (Chicago: Loyola Press, 2008), 156, 159.

5. Ibid., 159.

6. See, for example, the Casa de Solidaridad program at the University of Central America in El Salvador.

Appendix: 14. Jesuits and the Situation of Women in Church and Civil Society

1. GC 33, D 1, n. 48.

2. John Paul II, Apostolic letter *Mulieris Dignitatem* and Apostolic Exhortation *Christifideles Laici*; Message for the World Day of Peace, 1 January 1995.

Bibliography

Ahlgren, Gillian T. W. "Negotiating Sanctity: Holy Women in Six-teenth-Century Spain." *Church History* 65, no. 3 (1995): 373–88.

———. *Teresa of Avila and the Politics of Sanctity.* Ithaca, N.Y.: Cornell University Press, 1995.

Allen, Pamela. "The Small Group Process." In *Radical Feminism: A Documentary Reader*, edited by Barbara A. Crow, 277–81. New York: New York University Press, 2000.

American Association of University Women. *Gender Gaps: Where Schools Still Fail Our Children.* New York: Marlowe, 1998.

American Association of University Women Educational Foundation. *How Schools Shortchange Girls: A Study of Major Findings on Girls and Education.* Washington, D.C.: AAUW Educational Foundation, 1992.

Anderson, Margaret L., and Patricia Hill Collins, eds. *Race, Class, and Gender: An Anthology.* New York: Wadsworth, 1998.

Ansley, Fran, and John Gaventa. "Researching for Democracy and Democratizing Research." *Change* 29, no. 1 (1997): 46–53.

Aquinas, Thomas. *Summa theologiae.* Edited by Petri Caramello. Rome: Marietti, 1952.

Arrupe, Pedro. "Men for Others." In *Foundations*, edited by C. E. Meirose, 31–40. Washington, D.C.: Jesuit Secondary Education Association, 1973.

Astin, Alexander, and Linda Sax. "How Undergraduates Are Affected by Service Participation." *Journal of College Student Development* 39 (1998): 251–63.

Astin, Alexander, Linda Sax, and Juan Avalos. "Long-Term Effects of Volunteerism during the Undergraduate Years." *Review of Higher Education* 22 (1999): 187–202.

Bainton, Roland H. *Women of the Reformation in Germany and Italy.* Minneapolis, Minn.: Augsburg Press, 1971.

Barber, Benjamin, and Richard Battistoni. "A Season of Service: Introducing Service Learning into the Liberal Arts Curriculum." *Political Science and Politics* 26 (1993): 235–62.

Bar On, Bat-Ami, ed. *Engendering Origins: Critical Feminist Readings in Plato and Aristotle.* Albany: State University of New York Press, 1994.

Barstow, Anne Llewellyn. *Witchcraze.* New York: Harper Collins, 1994.

Bauer, Dale M. "Feminist Bywords: Authority." *NWSA Journal* 3, no. 1 (1990): 95–97.

Bauman, Zygmunt. *Globalization: The Human Condition.* New York: Columbia University Press, 1998.

Baumgardner, Jennifer, and Amy Richards. *Grassroots: A Field Guide for Feminist Activism.* New York: Farrar, Straus and Giroux, 2005.

Belenky, Mary Field, Blythe McVicker Clinchy, Nancy Rule Goldberger, and Jill Mattuck Tarule. *Women's Ways of Knowing: The Development of Self, Voice, and Mind.* New York: Basic Books, 1986.

Bell, Lee Anne, Sharon Washington, Gerald Weinstein, and Barbara Love. "Knowing Ourselves as Instructors." In *The Critical Pedagogy Reader,* edited by Antonia Darder, Marta Baltodano, and Rodolfo D. Torres, 464–78. New York: Routledge, 2003.

Benedict, Kimberley M. *Empowering Collaborations: Writing Partnerships between Religious Women and Scribes in the Middle Ages.* New York: Routledge, 2004.

Bennett, Judith M., and Amy M. Froide, eds. *Singlewomen in the European Past, 1250–1800.* Philadelphia: University of Pennsylvania Press, 1999.

Bilinkoff, Jodi. *Related Lives: Confessors and Their Female Penitents, 1450–1750.* Ithaca, N.Y.: Cornell University Press, 2005.

Boggs, James. *Racism and the Class Struggle.* New York: Monthly Review Press, 1970.

Bonacci, Louis A. "The Marian Presence in the Life and Works of Saint Ignatius Loyola: From Private Revelation to Spiritual Exercises—The Cloth of Loyola's Allegiance." Doctoral thesis, International Marian Research Institute, University of Dayton, 2002.

Bonilla-Silva, Eduardo. *Racism without Racists: Color-Blind Racism and the Persistence of Racial Inequality in the United States.* Lanham, Md.: Rowman & Littlefield, 2003.

Boryczka, Jocelyn M. "A Brief Overview of Feminism and Feminist Pedagogy." Paper delivered at the "Jesuit and Feminist Education: Transformative Discourses for Teaching and Learning" conference, Fairfield University, Fairfield, Conn., Oct. 2006.

Boryczka, Jocelyn M., and Elizabeth A. Petrino. "The Personal Is Political: At the Intersections of Feminist and Jesuit Education." Paper delivered at the "Jesuit and Feminist Education: Transformative Discourses for Teaching and Learning" conference, Fairfield University, Fairfield, Conn., Oct. 2006.

Boss, Judith. "The Effect of Community Service Work on the Moral Development of College Ethics Students." *Journal of Moral Education* 23, no. 2 (1994): 183–98.

Boston College. *What Are We? An Introduction to Boston College and Its Jesuit and Catholic Tradition.* Chestnut Hill, Mass.: Center for Ignatian Spirituality, Boston College, 2002.

Boston College Jesuit Community. "Jesuits and Jesuit Education: A Primer." In *A Jesuit Education Reader,* edited by George W. Traub, 38–42. Chicago: Loyola Press, 2008.

Bowler, James M. "The Transformative Power of Jesuit Education: A Reflection on Ignatian Pedagogy." In *Ignatian Pedagogy for the Challenges of Humanism Today,* edited by Wita Pasierbka. Krakow, Poland: Wyższa Szkoła Filozoficzno-Pedagogiczna Ignatianum, 2008.

Boyer, Ernest L., and Fred M. Hechinger. *Higher Learning in the Nation's Service.* Washington, D.C.: Carnegie Foundation for the Advancement of Teaching, 1981.

Brackett, John K. "The Florentine Criminal Underworld: The Underside of the Renaissance." In Connell, *Society and Individual,* 293–314.

Brackley, Dean. *The Call to Discernment in Troubled Times: New Perspectives on the Transformative Wisdom of Ignatius of Loyola.* New York: Crossroads, 2004.

———. "Higher Standards for Higher Education: The Christian University and Solidarity." Address delivered at Creighton University, Omaha, Neb., Nov. 4, 1999. http://www.creighton.edu/CollaborativeMinistry/brackley.html.

Bridenthal, Renate, Susan Mosher Stuard, and Merry E. Wiesner-Hanks, eds. *Becoming Visible: Women in European History.* 3rd ed. Boston: Houghton Mifflin, 1998.

Briggs, Robin. *Witches and Neighbors: The Social Context of European Witchcraft.* Oxford: Blackwell, 2002.

Bringle, Robert, and Julie Hatcher. "Implementing Service Learning in Higher Education." *Journal of Higher Education* 67 (1996): 221–39.

Brink, Jean R., Allison P. Coudert, and Maryanne C. Horowitz, eds. *The Politics of Gender in Early Modern Europe.* Kirksville, Mo.: Sixteenth Century Journal Publishers, 1989.

Brown, Julie. "Theory or Practice: What Exactly Is Feminist Pedagogy?" *Journal of General Education* 41 (1992): 51–63.

Brown, Meg Lota, and Kari Boyd McBride. *Women's Roles in the Renaissance.* Westport, Conn.: Greenwood Press, 2005.

Brundage, James A. *Law, Sex, and Christian Society in Medieval Europe.* Chicago: University of Chicago Press, 1987.

Buchanan, Ian. *Michel de Certeau: Cultural Theorist.* Thousand Oaks, Calif.: Sage, 2001.

Buckley, Michael J. *The Catholic University as Promise and Project: Reflections in a Jesuit Idiom.* Washington, D.C.: Georgetown University Press, 1998.

Burckhardt, Jacob. *The Civilization of the Renaissance in Italy.* Translated by S. G. C. Middlemore. New York: Modern Library, 2002. First published 1860.

Burke, Peter. "How to Be a Counter-Reformation Saint." In *Religion and Society in Early Modern Europe, 1500–1800,* edited by Kaspar von Greyerz, 45–55. London: Allen and Unwin, 1984.

Busby, Keith, ed. *Raoul de Hodenc: Le roman des Eles /The Anonymous Ordene de chevalerie.* Amsterdam: John Benjamins, 1983.

Cahill, Lisa Sowle. *Sex, Gender, and Christian Ethics.* Cambridge: Cambridge University Press, 1996.

———. "Women and Men Working Together in Jesuit Institutions of Higher Learning." *Conversations* 4 (Fall 1993): 25.

Cameron, Jennifer. *A Dangerous Innovator: Mary Ward (1585–1645).* Strathfield, NSW: St. Pauls Publications, 2000.

Caputo, Richard. "Social Justice, the Ethics of Care, and Market Economies." *Families in Society* 83, no. 4 (2002): 355–65.

Card, Claudia. *The Atrocity Paradigm.* Oxford: Oxford University Press, 2002.

———. Review of *Feminist Morality: Transforming Culture, Society, and Politics*, by Virginia Held. *Feminist Ethics* 4 (1995): 938–40.

Carrera, Elena. "The Emotions in Sixteenth-Century Spanish Spirituality." *Journal of Religious History* 31, no. 3 (2007): 235–52.

Cassagrande, Giovanna. "Confraternities and Lay Female Religiosity in Late Medieval and Renaissance Umbria." In *The Politics of Ritual Kinship: Confraternities and Social Order in Early Modern Italy*, edited by Nicholas Terpstra, 48–66. Cambridge Studies in Italian History and Culture. Cambridge: Cambridge University Press, 2007.

Catechism of the Catholic Church. Vatican City: Libreria Editrice Vaticana, 1993. http://www.vatican.va/archive/catechism/ccc_toc.htm

Caughie, Pamela L., and Richard Pearce. "Resisting 'the Dominance of the Professor': Gendered Teaching, Gendered Subjects." *NWSA Journal* 4, no. 2 (1992): 187–99.

Cesareo, Francesco C. "Quest for Identity: The Ideals of Jesuit Education in the Sixteenth Century." In *The Jesuit Tradition in Education and Missions: A 450-Year Perspective*, edited by Christopher Chapple, 17–33. Scranton, Pa.: University of Scranton Press, 1993.

Charny, Geoffroi de. *A Knight's Own Book of Chivalry*. Translated by Elspeth Kennedy. Philadelphia: University of Pennsylvania Press, 2005.

Cherewatuk, Karen, and Ulrike Wiethaus, eds. *Dear Sister: Medieval Women and the Epistolary Genre*. Philadelphia: University of Pennsylvania Press, 1993.

Chickering, Arthur W., and Linda Reisser. "The Seven Vectors." In *College Student Development and Academic Life: Psychological, Intellectual, Social, and Moral Issues*, edited by Karen Arnold and Ilda Carreiro King, 2–20. New York: Garland, 1997.

Chubbuck, Sharon M. "Socially Just Teaching and the Complementarity of Ignatian Pedagogy and Critical Pedagogy." *Christian Higher Education* 6, no. 3 (2007): 239–65.

Clark, Elizabeth, and Herbert Richardson. "Thomas Aquinas: The Man Who Should Have Known Better." In *Women and Religion: A Feminist Sourcebook of Christian Thought*, 78–101. New York: Harper and Row, 1977.

Classen, Albrecht. "Female Epistolary Literature from Antiquity to the Present: An Introduction." *Studia Neophilologica* 60 (1988): 3–13.

————. "Footnotes to the German Canon: Maria von Wolkenstein and Argula von Grumbach." In *The Politics of Gender in Early Modern Europe*, edited by Jean R. Brink, Allison P. Coudert, and Maryanne C. Horowitz, 131–48. Kirksville, Mo.: Sixteenth Century Journal Publishers, 1989.

Clifford, Anne M. *Introducing Feminist Theology.* Maryknoll, N.Y.: Orbis, 2001.

Coakley, John W. *Women, Men, and Spiritual Power: Female Saints and Their Male Collaborators.* New York: Columbia University Press, 2006.

Code, Lorraine. "Experience, Knowledge, and Responsibility." In *Feminist Perspectives in Philosophy*, edited by Morwenna Griffiths and Margaret Whitford, 187–204. Bloomington: Indiana University Press, 1988.

Codina, Gabriel. "The 'Modus Parisiensis.'" In Duminuco, *The Jesuit "Ratio Studiorum,"* 28–49.

Cohee, Gail E., Elisabeth Daumer, Theresa D. Kemp, Paula M. Krebs, Sue Lafky, and Sandra Runzo, eds. *The Feminist Teacher Anthology: Pedagogies and Classroom Strategies.* New York: Teachers College Press, 1998.

Cohen, Jeremy, and Dennis Kinsey. "'Doing Good' and Scholarship: A Service-Learning Study." *Journalism Educator* 48, no. 4 (1994): 4–14.

Cole, Eve Browning. *Philosophy and Feminist Criticism: An Introduction.* New York: Paragon House, 1991.

————. "Women, Slaves, and 'Love of Toil' in Aristotle's Moral Philosophy." In *Engendering Origins: Critical Feminist Readings in Plato and Aristotle*, edited by Bat-Ami Bar On, 127–44. Albany: State University of New York Press, 1994.

Collins, Patricia Hill. *Black Feminist Thought: Knowledge, Consciousness, and the Politics of Empowerment.* 2nd ed. New York: Routledge, 2000.

Commission of the Status of Women at Loyola University Chicago. "Report of the Commission of the Status of Women at Loyola University Chicago." May 2006. http://luc.edu/diversity/pdfs/womens_commission_report.pdf.

Connell, William J., ed. *Society and Individual in Renaissance Florence.* Berkeley: University of California Press, 2002.

Connor, James, L., and Fellows of the Woodstock Theological Center. *The Dynamism of Desire: Bernard J. F. Lonergan, S.J., on the Spiritual Exercises of Saint Ignatius of Loyola.* St. Louis, Mo.: Institute of Jesuit Sources, 2006.

Constable, Giles. *Letters and Letter-Collections.* Turnhout, Belgium: Editions Brepols, 1976.

Córdoba, Martín de. *Jardin de las nobles doncellas: A Critical Edition and Study.* Edited by Harriet Goldberg. Chapel Hill: University of North Carolina Press, 1974.

Costa, Milagros Ortega. "Spanish Women in the Reformation." In Marshall, *Women in Reformation and Counter-Reformation Europe,* 89–119.

Couchman, Jane, and Ann Crabb, eds. *Women's Letters across Europe, 1400–1700.* Hampshire, UK: Ashgate, 2005.

Crabtree, Robbin D., and David Alan Sapp. "Theoretical, Political, and Pedagogical Challenges in the Feminist Classroom: Our Struggles to Walk the Walk." *College Teaching* 51, no. 4 (2003): 131–40.

Crabtree, Robbin D., David Alan Sapp, and Adela C. Licona, eds. *Feminist Pedagogy: Looking Back to Move Forward.* Baltimore, Md.: Johns Hopkins University Press, 2009.

Crenshaw, Kimberlé. "Mapping the Margins: Intersectionality, Identity Politics, and Violence against Women of Color." *Stanford Law Review* 43, no. 6 (1991): 1241–99.

Cruz, Nadinne. Presentation to the Campus Compact Professional Development Institute, Providence, R.I., July 2006.

Cudd, Ann, and Leslie E. Jones. "Sexism." In *Feminist Theory: A Philosophical Anthology,* edited by Ann Cudd and Robin Andreasen, 73–83. Oxford: Blackwell, 2005.

Daoust, Joseph. "Of Kingfishers and Dragonflies: Faith and Justice at the Core of Jesuit Education." *Conversations* 19 (Spring 2001): 13–20.

Davis, Natalie. "City Women and Religious Change." In *Society and Culture in Early Modern France,* 65–95. Stanford, Calif.: Stanford University Press, 1975.

D'Avray, David. *Medieval Marriage: Symbolism and Society.* New York: Oxford University Press, 2005.

De Certeau, Michel. *The Practice of Everyday Life.* Berkeley: University of California Press, 1984.

Deats, Sara Munson, and Lagretta Tallent Lenker, eds. *Gender and Academe: Feminist Pedagogy and Politics.* New York: Rowman & Littlefield, 1994.

DeFeo, Joseph Anthony. "Old Wine in New Skin: Ignatian Pedagogy, Compatible with and Contributing to Jesuit Higher Education." PhD diss., Fordham University, 2009.

DeJulio, Rosemary A. "Patrons, Pupils, and Partners: The Participation of Women in Ignatian Spirituality and Pedagogy." PhD diss., Fordham University, 2000.

————. "Women's Ways of Knowing and Learning: The Response of Mary Ward and Madeleine Sophie Barat to the *Ratio Studiorum*." In Duminuco, *The Jesuit "Ratio Studiorum,"* 107–26.

Denzey, Nicola. *The Bone Gatherers: The Lost Worlds of Early Christian Women.* Boston: Beacon Press, 2007.

Dewey, John. *Democracy and Education.* Toronto: Collier-Macmillan, 1916.

————. *Experience and Education.* New York: Touchstone, 1944.

Dillon, Janette. "Holy Women and Their Confessors or Confessors and Their Holy Women? Margery Kempe and Continental Tradition." In *Prophets Abroad: The Reception of Continental Holy Women in Late-Medieval England*, edited by Rosalynn Voaden, 115–40. Cambridge: D. S. Brewer, 1996.

Douglas, Mary. *Purity and Danger.* New York: Routledge, 1966.

Douglass, Jane Dempsey. "Women and the Continental Reformation." In *Religion and Sexism: Images of Woman in the Jewish and Christian Traditions,* edited by Rosemary Radford Ruether, 292–318. New York: Simon and Schuster, 1974.

Dreyer, Elizabeth A. "The *Interior Castle*: An Exposition on the Giftedness of Mystical Prayer." *Spiritual Life* 31 (1985): 170–77.

Duffy, Eamon. *Faith of Our Fathers: Reflections on Catholic Tradition.* New York: Continuum, 2004.

Duminuco, Vincent J., ed. *The Jesuit "Ratio Studiorum": 400th Anniversary Perspectives.* New York: Fordham University Press, 2000.

————. "A New *Ratio* for a New Millennium?" In Duminuco, *The Jesuit "Ratio Studiorum,"* 145–61.

DuPlessis, Rachel Blau, and Ann Snitow, eds. *The Feminist Memoir Project: Voices from Women's Liberation.* New York: Three Rivers Press, 1998.

Durkin, M. C. *"Ours": Jesuit Portraits*. Strasbourg: Editions du Signe, 2006.

Ehrenreich, Barbara. *Nickel and Dimed in America: On (Not) Getting by in America*. New York: Henry Holt, 2001.

Elias, N. *The Civilizing Process: The History of Manners and State Formation and Civilization*. Translated by E. Jephcott. Oxford: Oxford University Press, 1978.

Ellacuría, Ignacio. Commencement address to Santa Clara University, Santa Clara, Calif., June 1982. http://www.scu.edu/Jesuits/ellacuria.html.

Elliott, Dyan. "Seeing Double: John Gerson, the Discernment of Spirits, and Joan of Arc." *American Historical Review* 107, no. 1 (2002): 26–54.

Ensler, Eve. *The Vagina Monologues*. New York: Dramatists Play Service, 2000.

Esposito, Anna. "St. Francesca and the Female Religious Communities of Fifteenth-Century Rome." In *Women and Religion in Medieval and Renaissance Italy*, edited by Daniel Bornstein and Roberto Rusconi, translated by Margery J. Schneider, 197–218. Chicago: University of Chicago Press, 1996.

Evans, Sara. *Personal Politics: The Roots of Women's Liberation in the Civil Rights Movement and the New Left*. New York: Vintage Books, 1980.

Eyler, Janet, and Dwight E. Giles Jr. *Where's the Learning in Service-Learning?* San Francisco: Jossey-Bass, 1999.

Eyler, Janet, Dwight E. Giles Jr., and Angela Schmiede. *A Practitioner's Guide to Reflection in Service Learning: Student Voices and Reflections*. Nashville, Tenn.: Vanderbilt University, 1996.

Eyler, Janet, Dwight E. Giles Jr., Christine M. Stenson, and Charlene J. Gray. *At a Glance: What We Know about the Effects of Service-Learning on College Students, Faculty, Institutions and Communities, 1993–2000*. 3rd ed. Nashville, Tenn.: Vanderbilt University, 2001.

Farley, Anthony Paul. "The Black Body as Fetish Object." *Oregon Law Review* 76, no. 3 (1997): 475–535.

Ferguson, Ann. "Can I Choose Who I Am? And How Would That Empower Me? Gender, Race, Identities, and the Self." In *Women, Knowledge, and Reality: Explorations in Feminist Philosophy*, 2nd ed., edited by Ann Garry and Marilyn Pearsall, 108–26. New York: Routledge, 1996.

Fiske, John. *Understanding Popular Culture.* New York: Routledge, 1989.

Fowler, James. *Weaving the New Creation: Stages of Faith and the Public Church.* San Francisco: HarperSanFrancisco, 1996.

Freedman, Estelle B. "Small Group Pedagogy: Consciousness Raising in Conservative Times." *NWSA Journal* 2, no. 4 (1990): 603–23.

Freire, Paulo. *Pedagogy of the Oppressed.* New York: Continuum, 1970.

Frey, Lawrence R., W. Barnett Pearce, Mark A. Pollock, Lee Artz, and Bren A. O. Murphy. "Looking for Justice in All the Wrong Places: On a Communication Approach to Social Justice." *Communication Studies* 47, no. 1–2 (1996): 110–27.

Fullam, Lisa. "Juana, S.J.: The Past (and Future) Status of Women in the Society of Jesus." *Studies in the Spirituality of Jesuits* 31, no. 5 (1999): 1–41.

Furey, Constance. "'Intellects Inflamed in Christ': Women and Spiritualized Scholarship in Renaissance Christianity." *Journal of Religion* 84, no. 1 (2004): 1–22.

Gabelnick, F. "Educating a Committed Citizenry." *Change* 29, no. 1 (1997): 30–35.

Ganss, George, ed. *Ignatius of Loyola: Spiritual Exercises and Selected Works.* Mahwah, N.J.: Paulist Press, 1991.

Ganz, Margery A. "Perceived Insults and Their Consequences: Acciaiuoli, Neroni, and Medici Relationships in the 1460s." In Connell, *Society and Individual,* 155–72.

Garvin, Mary. "Dusting off a Document." *Conversations* 29 (Spring 2006): 38.

Gautier, Mary L. *Catholic Ministry Formation Enrollments: Statistical Overview for 2009–2010.* Washington, D.C.: Center for Applied Research in the Apostolate, 2010.

Gerson, Jean. *Gerson: Early Works.* Translated by Brian Patrick McGuire. Classics of Western Spirituality. Mahwah, N.J.: Paulist Press, 1998.

Gill, Katherine. "Women and the Production of Religious Literature in the Vernacular, 1300–1500." In Matter and Coakley, *Creative Women,* 64–104.

Gilligan, Carol. *In a Different Voice: Psychological Theory and Women's Development*. Cambridge, Mass.: Harvard University Press, 1982.

Giroux, Henry A. *Disturbing Pleasures: Learning Popular Culture*. New York: Routledge, 1994.

———. *Pedagogy and the Politics of Hope: Theory, Culture, and Schooling*. Boulder, Colo.: Westview Press, 1997.

Goldberg, David Theo. *Racist Culture: Philosophy and the Politics of Meaning*. Oxford: Blackwell, 1993.

Goldsmith, Elizabeth C., ed. *Writing the Female Voice: Essays on Epistolary Literature*. Boston: Northeastern University Press, 1989.

Gore, Jennifer M. *The Struggle for Pedagogies: Critical and Feminist Discourses as Regimes of Truth*. New York: Routledge, 1993.

Gorman, Margaret. "The Influence of Ignatian Spirituality on Women's Teaching Orders in the United States." In *The Jesuit Tradition in Education and Missions: A 450-Year Perspective*, edited by Christopher Chapple, 182–202. Scranton, Pa.: University of Scranton Press, 1993.

Gray, Howard. "The Experience of Ignatius Loyola: Background to Jesuit Education." In Duminuco, *The Jesuit "Ratio Studiorum,"* 1–22.

Guerrero, Laura K., Peter A. Andersen, and Melanie R. Trost. "Communication and Emotion: Basic Concepts and Approaches." In *Handbook of Communication and Emotion: Research, Theory, Applications, and Contexts*, edited by Peter A. Andersen and Laura K. Guerrero, 5–24. San Diego, Calif.: Academic Press, 1998.

Gunderson, Mark Paul, and James Leslie McCary. "Sexual Guilt and Religion." *Family Coordinator* 28, no. 2 (1979): 353–57.

Gutierrez, Gustavo. *A Theology of Liberation: History, Politics, and Salvation*. Rev. ed. New York: Orbis, 1988.

Habermas, Jürgen. *The Theory of Communicative Action*. Vol. 2, *Lifeworld and System: A Critique of Fundamentalist Reason*. Trans. Thomas McCarthy . Boston: Beacon Press, 1987.

Haight, Roger. *Dynamics of Theology*. Maryknoll, N.Y.: Orbis, 1990.

———. "Lessons from an Extraordinary Era: Catholic Theology since Vatican II." *America*, March 17, 2008, 11–16.

Haliczer, Steven. *Sexuality in the Confessional*. Oxford: Oxford University Press, 1995.

Hall, Kim Q. "Queerness, Disability, and *The Vagina Monologues*." *Hypatia* 20, no. 1 (2005): 99–119.

Hall, Stuart. "New Ethnicities." In *Stuart Hall: Critical Dialogues in Cultural Studies*, edited by David Morley and Kuan-Hsing Chen, 441–49. London: Routledge, 1996.

Hanchin, Timothy. "Messianic or Bourgeois?" *America*, May 8, 2006, 12.

Harkness, Georgia. *Christian Ethics*. Nashville, Tenn.: Abingdon Press, 1957.

Hatcher, Julie, and Robert Bringle. "Reflection: Bridging the Gap between Service and Learning." *College Teaching* 45, no. 4 (1997): 153–58.

Heath, Michael J. Introduction to *The Institution of Christian Matrimony*. In *Collected Works of Erasmus*, edited by John W. O'Malley and Louis A. Perraud, 69:203–13. Toronto: University of Toronto Press, 1999.

Held, Virginia. *The Ethics of Care: Personal, Political, and Global*. New York: Oxford University Press, 2006.

———. *Feminist Morality: Transforming Culture, Society, and Politics*. Chicago: University of Chicago Press, 1993.

———. "Feminist Transformations of Moral Theory." *Philosophy and Phenomenological Research* 50 (1990): 321–44.

———. "Liberalism and the Ethics of Care." In *On Feminist Ethics and Politics*, edited by Claudia Card, 288–309. Lawrence: University Press of Kansas, 1999.

———. "The Meshing of Care and Justice." In *Feminist Ethics*, edited by Moira Gatens, 530–37. Brookfield, Vt.: Ashgate, 1998.

Henold, Mary J. *Catholic and Feminist: The Surprising History of the American Catholic Feminist Movement*. Chapel Hill: University of North Carolina Press, 2008.

Highmore, Ben. *Michel de Certeau: Analyzing Culture*. New York: Continuum, 2006.

hooks, bell. "Feminist Theory: A Radical Agenda." In *Multicultural Experiences, Multicultural Theories*, edited by Mary F. Rogers, 56–61. New York: McGraw-Hill, 1996.

———. *Killing Rage: Ending Racism*. New York: Henry Holt, 1995.

———. *Teaching Community: A Pedagogy of Hope*. New York: Routledge, 2003.

———. *Teaching to Transgress: Education and the Practice of Freedom*. New York: Routledge, 1994.

———. "Toward a Revolutionary Feminist Pedagogy." In *Falling into Theory: Conflicting Views of Reading Literature*, 80–81. New York: Bedford/St. Martin's Press, 2000.

Howard, Jeffrey P. F. "Academic Service Learning: A Counternormative Pedagogy." In *Academic Service Learning: A Pedagogy of Action and Reflection*, edited by Robert A. Rhoads and Jeffrey P. F. Howard, 21–30. San Francisco: Jossey-Bass, 1998.

———, ed. *Service-Learning Course Design Workbook.* Ann Arbor: Edward Ginsberg Center for Community Service, University of Michigan, 2001.

Hufton, Olwen. "Altruism and Reciprocity: The Early Jesuits and Their Female Patrons." *Renaissance Studies* 15, no. 2 (2001): 328–53.

———. "Every Tub on Its Own Bottom: Funding a Jesuit College in Early Modern Europe." In O'Malley et al., *The Jesuits II*, 5–23.

Hügel, Friedrich von. *The Mystical Element of Religion: A Study of Catherine of Genoa.* New York: Herder & Herder, 1999. First published 1908.

International Commission on the Apostolate of Jesuit Education. "The Characteristics of Jesuit Education." In Duminuco, *The Jesuit "Ratio Studiorum,"* 163–216.

———. "Ignatian Pedagogy: A Practical Approach, 1993." In Duminuco, *The Jesuit "Ratio Studiorum,"* 234–93.

Jacobson, Douglas, and Rodney Sawatsky. *Gracious Christianity: Living the Love We Profess.* Grand Rapids, Mich.: Baker Academic, 2006.

Jacoby, Barbara. "Service-Learning in Today's Higher Education." In *Service-Learning in Higher Education: Concepts and Practices*, edited by Barbara Jacoby. San Francisco: Jossey-Bass, 1996.

Jaeger, Werner. *Early Christianity and Greek Paideia.* London: Oxford University Press, 1969.

———. *Paideia: The Ideals of Greek Culture.* Vol. 2, *In Search of the Divine Center.* Translated by Gilbert Highet. New York: Oxford University Press, 1976.

Jantzen, Grace. *Power, Gender, and Christian Mysticism.* Cambridge: Cambridge University Press, 1995.

Jenkins, Henry. *Textual Poachers: Television Fans and Participatory Culture.* New York: Routledge, 1992.

Jensen, Robert. *The Heart of Whiteness: Confronting Race, Racism, and White Privilege*. San Francisco: City Lights, 2005.

Johnston, Susan. "Not for Queers Only: Pedagogy and Postmodernism." *NWSA Journal* 7, no. 1 (1995): 109–22.

Jonsen, Albert, and Stephen Toulmin. *The Abuse of Casuistry: A History of Moral Reasoning*. Berkeley: University of California Press, 1988.

Jordan, Constance. "Renaissance Women and the Question of Class." In *Sexuality and Gender in Early Modern Europe: Institutions, Texts, Images*, edited by James Grantham Turner, 90–106. Cambridge: Cambridge University Press, 1993.

Kahne, Joseph, and Joel Westheimer. "In the Service of What? The Politics of Service-Learning." *Phi Delta Kappa* 77, no. 9 (1996): 593–99.

Keen, Maurice. *Chivalry*. New Haven, Conn.: Yale University Press, 1984.

Kelso, Ruth. *Doctrine for the Lady of the Renaissance*. Urbana: University of Illinois Press, 1956.

Kent, Dale. "Michele del Giogante's House of Memory." In Connell, *Society and Individual*, 110–36.

Kirshner, Julius. "*Li Emergenti Bisogni Matrimoniali* in Renaissance Florence." In Connell, *Society and Individual*, 79–109.

Kittay, Eva. *Love's Labor: Essays on Women, Equality, and Dependency*. New York: Routledge, 1999.

Klaits, Joseph. *Servants of Satan*. Indianapolis: Indiana University Press, 1985.

Knust, Hermann, ed. *Dos obras didácticas y dos leyendas*. Madrid: Sociedad de Bibliófilos, 1978.

Kolb, David A. *Experiential Learning*. Englewood Cliffs, N.J.: Prentice Hall, 1984.

Kolvenbach, Peter-Hans. "Ignatian Pedagogy Today." In Duminuco, *The Jesuit "Ratio Studiorum,"* 276–91 .

———. "The Jesuit University in the Light of the Ignatian Charism." Address delivered to the International Meeting of Jesuit Higher Education, Rome, May 27, 2001. http://users.online.be/~sj.eur.news/doc/univ2001e.htm.

———. "The Service of Faith and the Promotion of Justice in American Jesuit Higher Education." In *A Jesuit Education Reader*, edited by George W. Traub, 144–62. Chicago: Loyola Press, 2008.

———. "Themes of Jesuit Higher Education." Address delivered at Georgetown University, Washington, D.C., June 7, 1989. http://onlineministries.creighton.edu/Heartland3/r-themes.html.

Kors, Alan Charles, and Edward Peters. *Witchcraft in Europe, 400–1700*. Philadelphia: University of Pennsylvania Press, 2001.

Kozol, Jonathan. *Rachel and Her Children: Homeless Families in America*. New York: Fawcett Columbine, 1988.

Kraft, Richard. "Service Learning: An Introduction to Its Theory, Practice, and Effects." *Education and Urban Society* 28, no. 2 (1996): 131–59.

Lather, Patti. *Getting Smart: Feminist Research and Pedagogy with/in the Postmodern*. New York: Routledge, 1991.

Lees, Clare A., ed. *Medieval Masculinities: Regarding Men in the Middle Ages*. Minneapolis: University of Minnesota Press, 1994.

Lehfeldt, Elizabeth A. *Religious Women in Golden Age Spain: The Permeable Cloister*. Hampshire, UK: Ashgate, 2005.

———. "Sacred and Secular Spheres: Religious Women in Golden Age Spain." *History Compass* 3 (2005): 1–5.

Léon, Luis de. *La perfecta casada* [*The Perfect Wife*]. Madrid, 1804–16.

Lesko, Nancy. "The Curriculum of the Body: Lessons from a Catholic High School." In *Becoming Feminine: The Politics of Popular Culture*, edited by Leslie Roman, 123–42. Philadelphia: Falmer, 1988.

Levack, Brian. *The Witch-Hunt in Early Modern Europe*. Harlow, UK: Pearson Longman, 2006.

Levy, Traci M. "At the Intersection of Intimacy and Care: Redefining 'Family' through the Lens of a Public Ethic of Care." *Politics & Gender* 1 (2005): 65–95.

Lewis, M. G. Foreword to *Feminist Teaching in Theory and Practice: Situating Power and Knowledge in Poststructural Classrooms*, by Becky Ropers-Huilman, xiii–xvi. New York: Teachers College Press, 1998.

Liebowitz, Ruth. "Virgins in the Service of Christ: The Dispute over an Active Apostolate for Women during the Counter-Reformation." In *Women of Spirit: Female Leadership in the Jewish and Christian Traditions*, edited by Rosemary Radford Ruether and Eleanor McLaughlin, 131–52. New York: Simon and Schuster, 1979.

Littlehales, Margaret Mary. *Mary Ward: Pilgrim and Mystic*. London: Burns & Oates, 1998.

Lonergan, Bernard. *Collected Works of Bernard Lonergan*. Vol. 3, *Insight: A Study of Human Understanding*. Toronto: University of Toronto Press, 1992.

———. "Theology in Its New Context." In *Bernard Lonergan: A Second Collection*, edited by William Ryan and Bernard Tyrrell, 55–67. Toronto: University of Toronto Press, 1974.

Lovibond, Sabina. "Feminism in Ancient Philosophy: The Feminist Stake in Greek Rationality." In *The Cambridge Companion to Feminism in Philosophy*, edited by Miranda Fricker and Jennifer Hornsby, 10–28. Cambridge: Cambridge University Press, 2000.

Luke, Allan, and Carmen Luke. "Pedagogy." In *The Encyclopedia of Language and Linguistics*, edited by R. E. Asher and J. M. Simpson, 566–68. Tarrytown, N.Y.: Elsevier Science/Pergamon, 1994.

Luke, Carmen, ed. *Feminisms and Pedagogies of Everyday Life*. Albany: State University of New York Press, 1996.

Macdonald, Amie A., and Susan Sánchez-Casal, eds. *Twenty-first-Century Feminist Classrooms: Pedagogies of Identity and Difference*. New York: Palgrave Macmillan, 2002.

MacKinnon, Catharine A. "Feminism, Marxism, Method and the State: An Agenda for Theory." *Signs* 7, no. 3 (1982): 515–44.

MacMurray, John. *Reason and Emotion*. Amherst, N.Y.: Humanity Books, 1992.

Maher, Frances, and Mary Kay Thompson Tetreault. *The Feminist Classroom: Dynamics of Gender, Race, and Privilege*. New York: Rowman & Littlefield, 2001.

Mairs, Nancy. *Ordinary Time: Cycles in Marriage, Faith, and Renewal*. Boston: Beacon Press, 1993.

Manning, Rita C. *Speaking from the Heart: A Feminist Perspective on Ethics*. Lanham, Md.: Rowman & Littlefield, 1992.

Marshall, Sherrin, ed. *Women in Reformation and Counter-Reformation Europe: Public and Private Worlds*. Bloomington: Indiana University Press, 1989.

Matheson, Peter, ed. *A People's History of Christianity*. Vol. 5, *Reformation Christianity*. Minneapolis, Minn.: Fortress Press, 2007.

Matter, E. Ann, and John Coakley, eds. *Creative Women in Medieval and Early Modern Italy: A Religious and Artistic Renaissance*. Philadelphia: University of Pennsylvania Press, 1994.

McCarthy, John L., and Jesuits, eds. *Documents of the Thirty-fourth General Congregation of the Society of Jesus: The Decrees of General Congregation Thirty-four, the Fifteenth of the Restored Society and the Accompanying Papal and Jesuit Documents*. St. Louis, Mo.: Institute of Jesuit Sources, 1995.

McCluskey, Colleen. "An Unequal Relationship between Equals: Thomas Aquinas on Marriage." *History of Philosophy Quarterly* 24 (2007): 1–18.

McDermott, Alice. "The Church in the 21st Century: Why Women Choose to Stay." Paper delivered at Boston College, Chestnut Hill, Mass., Sept. 2005.

McGuire, Brian Patrick. "Holy Women and Monks in the Thirteenth Century: Friendship or Exploitation?" *Vox Benedictina* 6 (1989): 343–74.

McKenna, Teresa. "Borderness and Pedagogy: Exposing Culture in the Classroom." In *The Critical Pedagogy Reader*, edited by Antonia Darder, Marta Baltodano, and Rodolfo D. Torres, 430–39. New York: Routledge, 2003.

McNamara, Jo Ann. "The Rhetoric of Orthodoxy: Clerical Authority and Female Innovation in the Struggle with Heresy." In *Maps of Flesh and Light: The Religious Experience of Medieval Women Mystics*, edited by Ulrike Wiethaus, 9–27. Syracuse, N.Y.: Syracuse University Press, 1993.

Meehan, Amalee. "Partners in Ministry: The Role of Women in Jesuit Education." *America*, May 12, 2008, 22–24.

Meissner, W. W. *Ignatius of Loyola: The Psychology of a Saint*. New Haven, Conn.: Yale University Press, 1992.

Merriam, Sharan B. *An Update on Adult Learning Theory*. San Francisco: Jossey-Bass, 1993.

Michelson, Elana. "'Auctoritee' and 'Experience': Feminist Epistemology and the Assessment of Experiential Learning." *Feminist Studies* 22, no. 3 (1996): 627–55.

Miller, Jean Baker. *Toward a New Psychology of Women*. Boston: Beacon Press, 1976.

Monter, William. "Protestant Wives, Catholic Saints, and the Devil's Handmaid: Women in the Age of Reformations." In *Becoming Visible: Women in European History*, 2nd ed., edited by Renate Bridenthal,

Claudia Koonz, and Susan Stuard, 203–20. Boston: Houghton Mifflin, 1987.

———. "Women and the Italian Inquisitions." In *Women in the Middle Ages and the Renaissance: Literary and Historical Perspectives,* edited by Mary Beth Rose, 73–87. Syracuse, N.Y.: Syracuse University Press, 1986.

Mooney, Catherine, ed. *Gendered Voices: Medieval Saints and Their Interpreters.* Philadelphia: University of Pennsylvania Press, 1999.

Morris, P. M. "The Capabilities Perspective: A Framework for Social Justice." *Families in Society* 83, no. 4 (2002): 365–73.

Mujica, Barbara. *Teresa de Avila: Lettered Woman.* Nashville, Tenn.: Vanderbilt University Press, 2009.

Munitiz, Joseph A., and Philip Endean, trans. *Saint Ignatius of Loyola: Personal Writings.* London: Penguin, 1996.

Najemy, John M. "Giannozzo and His Elders: Alberti's Critique of Renaissance Patriarchy." In Connell, *Society and Individual,* 51–78.

Naples, Nancy A., and Karen Bojar, eds. *Teaching Feminist Activism: Strategies from the Field.* New York: Routledge, 2002.

Nelson, Lynn Hankinson. "Who Knows? What Can They Know? And When?" In *Women, Knowledge, and Reality: Explorations in Feminist Philosophy,* 2nd ed., edited by Ann Garry and Marilyn Pearsall, 286–97. New York: Routledge, 1996.

Noddings, Nel. *Caring: A Feminine Approach to Ethics and Moral Education.* Berkeley: University of California Press, 1984.

Norman, Marion. "A Woman for All Seasons: Mary Ward (1585–1645), Renaissance Pioneer of Women's Education." *Pedagogica Historica* 23 (1983): 125–43.

Novek, E. M. "Service-Learning Is a Feminist Issue: Transforming Communication Pedagogy." *Women's Studies in Communication* 22, no. 2 (1999): 230–40.

Nussbaum, Martha C. *Cultivating Humanity: A Classical Defense of Reform in Liberal Education.* Cambridge, Mass.: Harvard University Press, 1997.

Okin, Susan Moller. *Justice, Gender and the Family.* New York: Basic Books, 1989.

O'Malley, John W. *The First Jesuits.* Cambridge, Mass.: Harvard University Press, 1993.

———. "How Humanistic Is the Jesuit Tradition? From the 1599 *Ratio Studiorum* to Now." http://www.bc.edu/offices/mission/exploring/jesuniv/omalley_humanistic.html.

———. "How the First Jesuits Became Involved in Education." In Duminuco, *The Jesuit "Ratio Studiorum,"* 56–79.

———. "Introduction: The Pastoral, Social, Ecclesiastical, Civic, and Cultural Mission of the Society of Jesus." In O'Malley et al., *The Jesuits II*, xxiii–xxxvi.

———. "The Jesuit Educational Enterprise in Historical Perspective." In *Jesuit Higher Education: Essays on an American Tradition of Excellence*, edited by Rolando E. Bonachea, 10–25. Pittsburgh: Duquesne University Press, 1989.

O'Malley, John W., Gauvin Alexander Bailey, Steven J. Harris, and T. Frank Kennedy, eds. *The Jesuits II: Cultures, Sciences, and the Arts, 1540–1773*. Toronto: University of Toronto Press, 2007.

Omi, Michael, and Howard Winant. "On the Theoretical Status of the Concept of Race." In *Race, Identity, and Representation in Education*, edited by Cameron McCarthy and Warren Crichlow, 2–10. New York: Routledge, 1993.

———. *Racial Formation in the United States: From the 1960s to the 1990s*. 2nd ed. New York: Routledge, 1994.

Ong, Walter. Review of *Classical Rhetoric in English Poetry*, by Brian Vickers. *College English* 33, no. 5 (1972):612–16.

Padberg, John W. "Development of the *Ratio Studiorum*." In Duminuco, *The Jesuit "Ratio Studiorum,"* 80–100.

———, ed. *Documents of the Thirty-first and Thirty-second General Congregations of the Society of Jesus: An English Translation of the Official Latin Texts of the General Congregations and of the Accompanying Papal Documents*. St. Louis, Mo.: Institute of Jesuit Sources, 1977.

———. "Juana: Princess and Jesuit Scholastic." *National Jesuit News* 4, no. 2 (1974): 1, 4–6.

———. "Secret, Perilous Project." *Company* 17 (1999): 28–29.

Pagano, Jo Ann. "Moral Fictions: The Dilemma of Theory and Practice." In *Stories Lives Tell: Narrative and Dialogue in Education*, edited by Carol Witherell and Nel Noddings, 193–206. New York: Teachers College Press, 1991.

Pavur, Claude, trans. *The Ratio Studiorum: The Official Plan for Jesuit Education*. St. Louis, Mo.: Institute of Jesuit Sources, 2005.

Pech, Garry, and Rhona Leibel. "Writing in Solidarity: Steps toward an Ethic of Care for Journalism." *Journal of Mass Media Ethics* 21 (2006): 141–55.

Perry, Mary Elizabeth. *Gender and Disorder in Early Modern Seville*. Princeton, N.J.: Princeton University Press, 1990.

Pope Benedict XVI, "Encyclical Letter *Deus Caritas Est* of the Supreme Pontiff Benedict XVI to the Bishops, Priests and Deacons, Men and Women Religious and All the Lay Faithful on Christian Love," (2005), 11. Retrieved 9/18/06. http://www.vatican.va/holyfather/benedict_xvi/encyclicals/documents/hf_ben-xvi_enc_20051225_deus-caritas-est_en.html.

Pontifical Council for Justice and Peace, "The social agenda: A collection of magisterial texts" (2000). Retrieved 12/17/07. http://www.thesocialagenda.org.

Porter, Jean. *Natural and Divine Law: Reclaiming the Tradition for Christian Ethics*. Grand Rapids, Mich.: William B. Eerdmans, 1999.

Price, Brian R., ed. *Ramon Lull's Book of Knighthood and Chivalry*. Translated by William Caxton. Union City, Calif.: Chivalry Bookshelf, 2004.

Prosperi, Adriano. "Spiritual Letters." In Scaraffia and Zarri, *Women and Faith*, 113–28.

Puhl, Louis J. *The Spiritual Exercises of St. Ignatius: Based on Studies in the Language of the Autograph*. Chicago: Loyola Press, 1951.

Rahner, Hugo, ed. *Saint Ignatius Loyola: Letters to Women*. Translated by Kathleen Pond and S. A. H. Weetman. New York: Herder & Herder, 1960.

Rahner, Karl. "Basic Observations on the Subject of Changeable and Unchangeable Factors in the Church." *Theological Investigations*. Vol. 9. Trans. Karl H. Kruger and Boniface Kruger. London: Darton, Longman, and Todd, 1974, 3–23.

Rapley, Elizabeth. *The Dévotes: Women and Church in Seventeenth-Century France*. Montreal: McGill–Queen's University Press, 1990.

Rawls, John. *Theory of Justice*. Cambridge, Mass.: Belknap Press of Harvard University Press, 1971.

Reger, Jo, and Lacey Story. "Talking about My Vagina: Two College Campuses and *The Vagina Monologues*." In *Different Wavelengths: Studies of the Contemporary Women's Movement*, edited by Jo Reger, 139–60. New York: Routledge, 2005.

Reiman, Jeffrey. *The Rich Get Richer and the Poor Get Prison: Ideology, Class, and Criminal Justice*. Boston: Pearson, 2004.

Reites, James W. "Ignatius and Ministry with Women." *The Way*, Supplement 74 (Summer 1992): 7–19.

Rhodes, Elizabeth. "Join the Jesuits, See the World: Early Modern Women in Spain and the Society of Jesus." In O'Malley et al., *The Jesuits II*, 33–49.

Rich, Adrienne. "Compulsory Heterosexuality and Lesbian Existence." *Journal of Women's History* 15, no. 3 (2003): 11–48.

Ricoeur, Paul. *Memory, History, Forgetting*. Translated by Kathleen Blamey and David Pellauer. Chicago: University of Chicago Press, 2004.

Rigaux, Dominique. "Women, Faith, and Image in the Late Middle Ages." In Scaraffia and Zarri, *Women and Faith*, 72–82.

Roberts, Ann M. "Chiara Gambacorta of Pisa as Patroness of the Arts." In Matter and Coakley, *Creative Women*, 120–54.

Robertson, L. "Feminist Teacher Education: Applying Feminist Pedagogies to the Preparation of New Teachers." *Feminist Teacher* 8, no. 1 (1994): 11–15.

Roccasalvo, Joan. "Ignatian Women Past and Future." *Review for Religious* 62 (2003): 38–62.

Rockquemore, Kerry Ann, and Regan Harwell Schaffer. "Toward a Theory of Engagement: A Cognitive Mapping of Service-Learning Experiences." *Michigan Journal of Community Service Learning* 7 (2000): 14–25.

Rodriguez, Richard. *Brown: The Last Discovery of America*. New York: Viking, 2002.

Roper, Lyndal. *The Holy Household: Women and Morals in Reformation Augsburg*. Oxford: Clarendon Press, 1989.

Ropers-Huilman, Becky. *Feminist Teaching in Theory and Practice: Situating Power and Knowledge in Poststructural Classrooms*. New York: Teachers College Press, 1998.

———. "Scholarship on the Other Side: Power and Caring in Feminist Education." *NWSA Journal* 11, no. 1 (1999): 118–35.

Rose, Suzanna. "The Protest as a Teaching Technique for Promoting Feminist Action." *NWSA Journal* 1, no. 3 (1989): 486–90.

Rosenfelt, Deborah, ed. *Female Studies VII: Going Strong, New Courses/ New Programs.* Old Westbury, N.Y.: Feminist Press, 1973.

Ross, Susan A. "The Jesuits and Women: Reflections on the 34th General Congregation's Statement on Women in Church and Civil Society." *Conversations* 16 (Fall 1999): 20–28.

Roy, Arundhati. *The Cost of Living.* New York: Modern Library, 1999.

Ruddick, Sara. "Injustice in Families: Assault and Domination." In *Justice and Care: Essential Readings in Feminist Ethics,* edited by Virginia Held, 203–24. Boulder, Colo.: Westview Press, 1995.

Scaraffia, Lucetta, and Gabriella Zarri. *Women and Faith: Catholic Religious Life in Italy from Late Antiquity to the Present.* Cambridge, Mass.: Harvard University Press, 1999.

Schloesser, Stephen. "Against Forgetting: Memory, History, Vatican II." *Theological Studies* 67 (2006): 275–319.

Schneiders, Sandra M. *With Oil in Their Lamps: Faith, Feminism, and the Future.* Mahwah, N.J.: Paulist Press, 2000.

Sevenhuijsen, Selma. "Caring in the Third Way: The Relation between Obligation, Responsibility and Care in Third Way Discourse." *Critical Social Policy* 20, no. 5 (2000): 5–37.

Shipler, David K. *The Working Poor: Invisible in America.* New York: Vintage Books, 2005.

Shor, Ira. *When Students Have Power: Negotiating Authority in a Critical Pedagogy.* Chicago: University of Chicago Press, 1996.

Shreve, Anita. *Women Together, Women Alone: The Legacy of the Consciousness-Raising Movement.* New York: Viking Penguin, 1989.

Shrewsbury, Carolyn M. "What Is Feminist Pedagogy?" *Women's Studies Quarterly* 15, no. 3–4 (1987): 6–14.

Sirianni, Carmen, and Lewis Friedland. "Civic Innovation and American Democracy." *Change* 29, no. 1 (1997): 14–23.

Society of Jesus. *The Decrees of General Congregation 35.* http://www .sjweb.info/35.

Society of Jesus in the United States. "Communal Reflection on the Jesuit Mission in Higher Education: A Way of Proceeding." In *A Jesuit Education Reader,* edited by George W. Traub, 177–94. Chicago: Loyola Press, 2002.

Stanton, Timothy, Dwight E. Giles Jr., and Nadinne Cruz. *Service-Learning: A Movement's Pioneers Reflect on Its Origins, Practice, and Future*. San Francisco: Jossey-Bass, 1999.

Stargardt, Ute. "Male Clerical Authority in the Spiritual (Auto)biographies of Medieval Holy Women." In *Women as Protagonists and Poets in the German Middle Ages: An Anthology of Feminist Approaches to Middle High German Literature*, edited by Albrecht Classen, 209–38. Göppingen, Germany: Kümmerle Verlag, 1991.

Starratt, Robert J. *Building an Ethical School: A Practical Response to the Moral Crisis in Schools*. London: Falmer, 1994.

St. Clair, William, and Irmgard Maassen, eds. *Conduct Literature for Women, 1500–1640*. Vols. 1–2. London: Pickering & Chatto, 2000.

Steiner, Linda, and Chad M. Okrusch. "Care as a Virtue for Journalists." *Journal of Mass Media Ethics* 21 (2006): 102–22.

Strasser, Ulrike. "Embodying the Middle Ages, Advancing Modernity: Religious Women in Sixteenth- and Seventeenth-Century Europe and Beyond." In *Between the Middle Ages and Modernity: Individual and Community in the Early Modern World*, edited by Charles H. Parker and Jerry H. Bentley, 231–50. New York: Rowman & Littlefield, 2007.

Teresa of Avila. *The Collected Works of St. Teresa of Avila*. Vol. 2, *Way of Perfection*. Translated by Otilio Rodriguez and Kieran Kavanaugh. Washington, D.C.: Institute of Carmelite Studies, 1980.

Terpstra, Nicholas. *Lay Confraternities and Civic Religion in Renaissance Bologna*. Cambridge Studies in Italian History and Culture. Cambridge: Cambridge University Press, 2002.

Thelin, John. *A History of American Higher Education*. Baltimore, Md.: Johns Hopkins University Press, 2004.

Tolman, Deborah L. "Doing Desire: Adolescent Girls' Struggles for/with Sexuality." *Gender and Society* 8, no. 3 (1994): 324–42.

Tong, Rosemarie. *Feminine and Feminist Ethics*. Belmont, Calif.: Wadsworth, 1993.

———. "Feminist Ethics." In *Stanford Encyclopedia of Philosophy*, edited by Edward N. Zalta. Stanford, Calif.: Stanford University Press, 2000. http://plato.stanford.edu.

Tracy, David. *The Analogical Imagination: Christian Theology and the Culture of Pluralism*. New York: Crossroads, 1981.

Traina, Cristina L. H. *Feminist Ethics and Natural Law: The End of the Anathemas*. Washington, D.C.: Georgetown University Press, 1999.

Tripole, Martin R. "Justice and Jesuit Higher Education: Another Perspective." *Conversations* 23 (Spring 2003): 46–48.

Tronto, Joan. *Moral Boundaries: A Political Argument for an Ethic of Care*. New York: Routledge, 1993.

Turner, Frank Miller. *John Henry Newman: The Challenge to Evangelical Religion*. New Haven, Conn.: Yale University Press, 2002.

Tylenda, Joseph N. *Jesuit Saints and Martyrs: Short Biographies of the Saints, Blessed, Venerables, and Servants of God of the Society of Jesus*. Chicago: Loyola Press, 1998.

United Nations. *Human Development Report, 2005*. New York: United Nations Development Programme, 2005. http://hdr.undp.org/en/media/HDR05_complete.pdf.

United States Catholic Conference. *Human Sexuality: A Catholic Perspective for Education and Lifelong Learning*. Washington, D.C.: United States Catholic Conference, 1991.

United States Conference of Catholic Bishops. *Co-workers in the Vineyard of the Lord: A Resource for Guiding the Development of Lay Ecclesial Ministry*. Washington, D.C.: United States Conference of Catholic Bishops, 2005.

Valone, Carolyn. "Piety and Patronage: Women and the Early Jesuits." In Matter and Coakley, *Creative Women*, 157–84.

Van Soest, Dorothy. "Strange Bedfellows: A Call for Reordering National Priorities from Three Social Justice Perspectives." *Social Work* 39, no. 6 (1994): 710–17.

Walker, Alice. *In Search of Our Mothers' Gardens: Womanist Prose*. San Diego, Calif.: Harcourt Brace Jovanovich, 1983.

Wallace, Miriam. "Beyond Love and Battle: Practicing Feminist Pedagogy." *Feminist Teacher* 12, no. 3 (1999): 184–97.

Waterworthed, J., ed. and trans. *The Canons and Decrees of the Sacred and Oecumenical Council of Trent*. London: Dolman, 1848.

Weber, Alison. *Teresa of Avila and the Rhetoric of Femininity*. Princeton, N.J.: Princeton University Press, 1990.

Weston, Lisa M. C. "Reading the Textual Shadows of Anglo-Saxon Monastic Women's Friendships." *Magistra* 14, no. 1 (2008): 68–78.

Wiesner, Merry E. "Nuns, Wives, and Mothers: Women and the Reformation in Germany." In Marshall, *Women in Reformation and Counter-Reformation Europe*, 8–28.

———. *Women and Gender in Early Modern Europe*. 2nd ed. Cambridge: Cambridge University Press, 2000.

Wildman, Stephanie. "The Persistence of White Privilege." *Washington University Journal of Law & Policy* 18 (2005): 253–65.

Willen, Diane. "Women and Religion in Early Modern England." In Marshall, *Women in Reformation and Counter-Reformation Europe*, 140–65.

Williams, Patricia J. *Seeing a Color-Blind Future: The Paradox of Race*. New York: Farrar, Straus and Giroux, 1997.

Williams, Rowan. "What Is a University?" Address delivered in Wuhan, China, Oct. 13, 2006. http://www.archbishopofcanterbury.org/sermons_speeches/061013.htm.

Williams, Tamara, and Erin McKenna. "Negotiating Subject Positions in a Service-Learning Context: Toward a Feminist Critique of Experiential Learning." In *Twenty-first-Century Feminist Classrooms: Pedagogies of Identity and Difference*, edited by Amie A. Macdonald and Susan Sánchez-Casal, 135–54. New York: Palgrave Macmillan, 2002.

Wills, Garry. *Saint Augustine's Sin*. New York: Viking, 2003.

Winant, Howard. "The New Imperialism, Globalization, and Racism." In *The New Politics of Race: Globalism, Difference, Justice*, 129–49. Minneapolis: University of Minnesota Press, 2004.

Wittgenstein, Ludwig. *On Certainty*. Oxford: Blackwell, 1969.

Wolff, Pierre. *Discernment: The Art of Choosing Well*. Liguori, Mo.: Liguori Publications, 2003.

Worcester, Thomas. "'Neither Married nor Cloistered': Blessed Isabelle in Catholic Reformation France." *Sixteenth Century Journal* 30 (1999): 457–72.

Wu, Frank H. *Yellow: Race in American beyond Black and White*. New York: Basic Books, 2002.

Wuthnow, Robert. *American Mythos: Why Our Best Efforts to Be a Better Nation Fall Short*. Princeton, N.J.: Princeton University Press, 2006.

Young, Iris Marion. *Justice and the Politics of Difference*. Princeton, N.J.: Princeton University Press, 1990.

Young, William J., trans. *Letters of St. Ignatius of Loyola*. Chicago: Loyola Press, 1959.

Zarri, Gabriella. "From Prophecy to Discipline, 1450–1650." In Scaraffia and Zarri, *Women and Faith*, 83–91.

———. "Living Saints: A Typology of Female Sanctity in the Early Sixteenth Century." In *Women and Religion in Medieval and Renaissance Italy*, edited by Daniel Bornstein and Roberto Rusconi, translated by Margery J. Schneider, 219–304. Chicago: University of Chicago Press, 1996.

Ziegler, Jean. "The Right to Food: Report of the Special Rapporteur on the Right to Food." Economic and Social Council, United Nations, Jan. 24, 2005.

Contributors

JOCELYN M. BORYCZKA is associate professor of politics and co-director of the Peace and Justice Studies Program at Fairfield University, where she co-organized with Elizabeth Petrino the "Jesuit and Feminist Education: Transformative Discourses for Teaching and Learning" conference in 2006. She teaches feminist, contemporary, and modern political theory and was honored to win Alpha Sigma Nu Teacher of the Year at Fairfield in 2006. Her research interests are in feminist ethics, conceptual histories, virtue and vice, and women's social movements. Her recent publications have appeared in *Politics & Gender, Feminist Theory: An International Interdisciplinary Journal, Feminist Interpretations of Alexis de Tocqueville*, and *The Oxford Encyclopedia of Women in World History*. She earned her PhD from the Graduate Center, City University of New York, and is currently working on an article on direct action and feminist pedagogy, and a book on how the politics of virtue and vice shape American women's struggle for full democratic citizenship.

M. SHAWN COPELAND is an associate professor of theology at Boston College. She has taught at Marquette University; Yale University Divinity School; and the Institute for Black Catholic Studies, Xavier University of Louisiana, New Orleans. Copeland is recognized as one of the most important influences in North America in drawing attention to issues surrounding ministry to African American Catholics. A prolific author, she has written more than eighty-five articles and book chapters, is editor of *Uncommon Faithfulness: The Black Catholic Experience* (2009), and is author of *Enfleshing Freedom: Body, Race and Being* (2010).

ROBBIN D. CRABTREE is dean of the College of Arts and Sciences at Fairfield University, where she is professor and past chair of the Communication Department; she also served as director of the Office of

Service Learning from 2006 to 2008. Crabtree's teaching interests include international and intercultural communication, media analysis, public argument, and women's studies. Her research emphasizes understanding media in relation to revolution, development, and globalization. She has also published extensively on service-learning theory and practice with particular emphasis on international contexts. Most recently, her co-edited book on feminist pedagogy was published by Johns Hopkins University Press. Before coming to Fairfield University, Crabtree was on the faculty at DePauw University (1990–93) and New Mexico State University (1993–2001); she also was a visiting professor at Universidade do Sul in Santa Catarina, Brazil, and Saint Louis University in Madrid, Spain. She earned her PhD from the University of Minnesota. In addition to academic administration, teaching, and research, Crabtree has professional experience in public radio and with nonprofit organizations. Crabtree is a member of the inaugural cohort of the Ignatian Colleagues Program.

CHARLES L. CURRIE, S.J., was named president of the Association of Jesuit Colleges and Universities in 1997. A native of Philadelphia, Fr. Currie studied at Fordham University, Boston College, and Woodstock College and holds a PhD from the Catholic University of America. After teaching at Georgetown in the 1960s, Fr. Currie served as president of both Wheeling Jesuit University and Xavier University. Immediately prior to being named president of the Association of Jesuit Colleges and Universities, he served as rector of the Jesuit Community at Saint Joseph's University. Fr. Currie is the recipient of many awards, including eleven honorary degrees.

JOSEPH A. DeFEO is the Associate Dean of Students and Director of Student Development at Fairfield University. His current work includes the creation and coordination of residential colleges for sophomore students, including the facilitation of the monthly mentoring and biannual retreat program for each community. He is also involved in the formation of a discernment program for seniors. His research centers on the Ignatian pedagogical paradigm (Ignatian pedagogy) and how faculty, staff, and students can find points of engagement with Ignatian pedagogy both in and outside the classroom. Before coming to Fairfield

University, DeFeo taught in the Theology Department (1997–2001) at Jesuit High School in Portland, Oregon. He also served as a Jesuit volunteer (1989–90) and staff member (1990–95) for the Northwest chapter of Jesuit Volunteer Corps. He received his undergraduate degree (1987) and master's degree in theology (1989) from Boston College. In addition to his administrative roles, DeFeo is a spiritual director in training, accompanying students and staff through the Spiritual Exercises of St. Ignatius of Loyola through Fairfield's Ignatian spirituality programs. He earned his PhD from Fordham University and currently lives in Bethel, Connecticut, with his wife and two children.

ELIZABETH A. DREYER is professor of religious studies at Fairfield University. In addition to writing articles and essays for scholarly and popular journals, Dreyer teaches and lectures throughout the United States and abroad. Publications include *Holy Power, Holy Presence: Rediscovering Medieval Metaphors for the Holy Spirit* (2007); *Passionate Spirituality: Hildegard of Bingen and Hadewijch of Brabant* (2005); *Minding the Spirit: The Study of Christian Spirituality*, edited with Mark S. Burrows (2005); *The Cross in Christian Tradition: Paul to Bonaventure*, which she edited (2000); and *Earth Crammed with Heaven: A Spirituality of Everyday Life* (1994). Dreyer is also the creator and general editor of the nine-volume series "Called to Holiness: Spirituality for Catholic Women" (see www.calledtoholiness.org). Within this series, she authored the volume *Making Sense of God: A Woman's Perspective* (2008). Primary academic interests include a critical retrieval of the medieval Christian tradition, the history of Christian mysticism, the use of feminist methodologies in historical theology, contextual analysis and contemporary applications of the spiritual legacy of Ignatius Loyola, art as a historical resource, and contemporary lay spirituality. In 2004, she received the Elizabeth Ann Seton Medal from Mt. St. Joseph College in Cincinnati, Ohio, awarded each year to a woman for outstanding contributions to Catholic theology in the United States. She lives in Hamden, Connecticut, with her husband, John B. Bennett, provost emeritus, Quinnipiac University.

ANA C. GARNER is associate professor in the Department of Journalism in the J. William and Mary Diederich College of Communication at

Marquette University. She holds a PhD in mass communication and an MA in journalism, both from the University of Iowa, and a BA in sociology from Douglass College, Rutgers University. She teaches courses in magazine design and production, media criticism, race and gender issues in the mass media, and qualitative research methods. Recent publications that she has co-authored include "The Patriotic Good Mother of World War II: A Study of a Cultural Ideal," in *Journalism Studies;* "Mothers of Soldiers in Wartime: A National News Narrative," in *Critical Studies in Media Communication;* and "Narrative Analysis of Sexual Etiquette in Teenage Magazines," in the *Journal of Communication.*

DAVID GUDELUNAS is an associate professor of communication and director of the Communication Internship Program at Fairfield University in Connecticut. He received his MA and PhD from the Annenberg School for Communication at the University of Pennsylvania and his BA is from the University of San Francisco. Gudelunas researches and teaches in the areas of critical and cultural studies; gender, sexuality, and communication; media history; and communication industries. He is the author of *Confidential to America: Newspaper Advice Columns and Sexual Education* (2008) and is widely published in the areas of popular communication as well as the intersections of sexuality and communication. Gudelunas is a member of the International Communication Association, the Popular Culture Association, and the National Communication Association, for which he serves as vice-chair of the LGBT Caucus. He is on the editorial boards of *Sexuality and Culture* and *Critical Studies in Media Communication.* He also serves on the academic advisory board of the Online Policy Group. At Fairfield, he serves on the research committee and as the first male faculty member of the Women's Studies Steering Committee. Gudelunas is currently working on a new book project about the history of shopping from home. Originally from Palm Springs, California, Gudelunas lives in Manhattan, where he likes to read, write, run around Chelsea with his dog Davey, and generally cause trouble.

HEATHER HATHAWAY is an associate professor of English at Marquette University. She received her BA in English and American studies from

Wesleyan University and her PhD in the history of American civilization from Harvard University. Her research focuses on questions surrounding American identity at the individual, cultural, and national levels, with a particular focus on race and ethnicity. She also has a long-standing interest in women's and gender studies. She is the author of *Caribbean Waves: Relocating Claude McKay and Paule Marshall* (1999) and co-editor of *Race and the Modern Artist* (2003) and *Conversations with Paule Marshall* (2006). Her current research focuses on Japanese American internment.

MARY J. HENOLD is an associate professor of American history at Roanoke College, a liberal arts college in southwest Virginia. She is the author of *Catholic and Feminist: The Surprising History of the American Catholic Feminist Movement*, named an Outstanding Academic Title of 2009 by *Choice*. Henold received her PhD from the University of Rochester in 2003, assisted by a dissertation fellowship from the Louisville Institute. She then went on to teach for two years at Valparaiso University as a postdoctoral fellow in the Lilly Fellows Program. At Roanoke College, Henold teaches American social and cultural history and women's/gender history. Her research interests center on Catholic women and the American Catholic Church in the 1960s and 1970s.

MARGO J. HEYDT is associate professor in the Department of Social Work of Xavier University in Cincinnati, Ohio. She received her MSW from West Virginia University, and her women's studies certificate and EdD in counseling from the University of Cincinnati. Heydt has been co-chair of the Gender and Diversity Studies Minor Steering Committee for several years. Issues such as violence against women, sexual child abuse, addiction, and diversity have been longtime specialties for Heydt in her practice as well as teaching and research. Her current projects include consulting with a religious order regarding its efforts to address issues of sexual abuse.

PAUL LAKELAND is the Aloysius P. Kelley S.J. Professor of Catholic Studies and the director of the Center for Catholic Studies at Fairfield University, where he has taught for twenty-nine years, mostly in Catholic ecclesiology, liberation theology, and religion and literature. He was educated at Heythrop Pontifical Athenaeum, Oxford University, the University of London, and Vanderbilt University, where he received his PhD in 1981. His most recent books are *Postmodernity: Christian Identity in a Fragmented Age* (1997); *The Liberation of the Laity: In Search of an Accountable Church* (2003), which received the 2004 U.S. Catholic Press Association Award for the best book in theology; *Catholicism at the Crossroads: How the Laity Can Save the Church* (2007), which also received an award in the social concerns category in 2008 from the Catholic Press Association; and *Church: Living Communion* (2009). His latest publication is *Yves Congar, O.P.: Essential Writings* (2010), which he edited and for which he wrote an extended critical introduction.

COLLEEN McCLUSKEY is associate professor of philosophy at Saint Louis University, Missouri. She received a BA in philosophy from the University of Washington and her PhD from the University of Iowa. Her research interests include feminism, the history of medieval philosophy, and ethics. She is a co-author (with Rebecca Konyndyk DeYoung and Christina Van Dyke) of a monograph titled *Aquinas's Ethics: Theoretical Foundations, Moral Theory, and Theological Context* (2009). Other recent publications include "Thomas Aquinas and the Epistemology of Moral Wrongdoing," in *Action and Science: The Epistemology of the Practical Sciences in the 13th and 14th Centuries* (edited by Matthias Lutz-Bachmann and Alexander Fidora, 2008), and "An Unequal Relationship of Equals: Thomas Aquinas on Marriage," in *History of Philosophy Quarterly*. She is currently working on a paper on the implications of Thomas Aquinas's view of emotions in motherhood and a book manuscript on his account of moral wrongdoing.

SARAH J. MELCHER is associate professor of Hebrew scriptures and chair of the Theology Department of Xavier University, Cincinnati, Ohio. She holds a PhD in Hebrew Bible from Emory University and a MDiv from Louisville Presbyterian Theological Seminary. Melcher was co-editor of and contributor to *This Abled Body: Rethinking Disabilities in Biblical Studies* (2007) and editor of and contributor to *Discerning the Body: Metaphors of the Body in the Bible* (2010). Melcher has published numerous articles on disability in the Bible, sexual practice in the Pentateuch, and African American biblical interpretation. Currently she is working in collaboration with Amos Yong to establish a book series on religion and disability.

SUSAN M. MOUNTIN has been director of the Manresa Project, a grant-funded program for the theological exploration of vocation at Marquette University, since 2002. Before that she served as a campus minister and adjunct faculty member, teaching in the College of Journalism, the College of Communication, the School of Education, and the Honors Program. She has a master's in theological studies from St. Francis Seminary and a PhD in philosophy and the history of education from Marquette University. She was formerly associate editor at the *Milwaukee Catholic Herald* and *U.S. Catholic*. She teaches courses on Dorothy Day and the Catholic worker movement, Ignatian spirituality and social justice/social activism, and Christian discipleship. She has been published in *America, St. Anthony Messenger, Jesuit Journeys, Momentum,* and *U.S. Catholic* and has a chapter in *Dorothy Day and the Catholic Worker Movement,* which she co-edited with William Thorn and Phil Runkel (2001).

GREGORY J. O'MEARA, S.J., is an associate professor at Marquette University Law School. Fr. O'Meara teaches criminal law, legal ethics, evidence, and contemporary legal theory. Research areas include applying narrative theory to appellate decision-making and trial strategy, and issues of ineffective assistance of counsel for criminal defendants. He received his BA from the University of Notre Dame; his JD from the University of Wisconsin; his LLM from New York University; and his MDiv from Weston Jesuit School of Theology.

ELIZABETH A. PETRINO is associate professor of English and co-director of the American Studies Program at Fairfield University, where she teaches American literature, poetry, and gender studies. She co-organized with Jocelyn Boryczka the "Jesuit and Feminist Education: Transformative Discourses for Teaching and Learning" conference at Fairfield in 2006. She is the author of *Emily Dickinson and Her Contemporaries: American Women's Verse, 1820–1885* (1998). Named a Reese Fellow in American Bibliography and the History of the Book at the American Antiquarian Society (2007–8) and elected a member of the board of directors of the Emily Dickinson International Society (2009–11), she has published articles on Emily Dickinson and her American female literary peers in *The Emily Dickinson Journal, ATQ: 19th-Century American Literature and Culture, Tulsa Studies in Women's Literature,* and *Legacy: A Journal of American Women Writers* and has written book chapters for *Cambridge Companion to Nineteenth-Century American Women's Writing* (2005), *Options for Teaching Nineteenth-Century American Poetry* (2007), and *Emily Dickinson: Critical Insights* (2010). She is currently at work on creating an anthology of nineteenth-century American women's social protest literature and, with the aid of a Corrigan Scholarship, a volume of selected works by Lydia Sigourney, a popular poet, essayist, and reformer. She earned her MA and PhD from Cornell University.

STEPHANIE QUADE is the dean of students at Marquette University, where she has been involved in the creation and implementation of policies governing student organizations. She is also a lecturer in the Department of English at Marquette. Professional affiliations include the Association of Student Conduct Administrators, the National Association of Student Personnel Administrators, and the Jesuit Association of Student Personnel Administrators. She earned her MA from the University of Maryland, and her BA and PhD from Marquette University.

MELISSA M. QUAN is associate director of the Center for Faith and Public Life and director of service-learning at Fairfield University. She served as interim executive director of Connecticut Campus Compact during its transition to Fairfield as host university from 2008 to 2009. Prior to joining Fairfield University, Quan served as assistant director of Evergreen Network Inc., a community-based organization in Bridgeport, Connecticut serving women, men, and children affected by HIV/AIDS. Quan is an alumna of the Jesuit Volunteer Corps (1998–99), through which she initially served with Evergreen Network Inc. Quan works to integrate her commitment to service throughout her life, serving as a mentor through the Charter Oak Scholarship Program and as a board member of Hispanos Unidos Inc. in New Haven, Connecticut. Quan received her MA in education at Fairfield University with a concentration on service-learning and civic education.

SUSAN A. ROSS is a professor of theology and a faculty scholar at Loyola University Chicago, where she is the chairperson of the Theology Department. She received her PhD from the University of Chicago and has also taught at St. Norbert College and Duquesne University. She is the author of *For the Beauty of the Earth: Women, Sacramentality and Justice* (2006), *Extravagant Affections: A Feminist Sacramental Theology* (1998), and numerous journal articles and book chapters and is the co-editor of five books and journal issues. She has been the recipient of a Louisville Institute Sabbatical Grant, the Book of the Year Award from the College Theology Society in 1999, and the Ann O'Hara Graff Award of the Women's Seminar of the Catholic Theological Society of America. She serves as vice president and a member of the editorial board of *Concilium: International Theological Journal*. She is currently at work on a book titled *Seeking Light and Beauty: A Theological Anthropology*.

KAREN L. SLATTERY is an associate professor in the Department of Broadcast and Electronic Communication at Marquette University. Her research focuses on media ethics, journalism history, and gender issues. Recently, she is the co-author of "The Patriotic Good Mother of World War II: A Study of a Cultural Ideal," in *Journalism Studies*, and "Mothers of Soldiers in Wartime: A National News Narrative," in *Critical Studies in Media Communication*. She writes a bimonthly ethics column for digitaljournalist.org.

THERESA WEYNAND TOBIN is assistant professor of philosophy at Marquette University, where she teaches and writes on ethical theory, feminist philosophy, medical ethics, and global ethics. Her published articles concern moral reasoning in contexts of religious diversity and social inequality, and feminist approaches to doing philosophical ethics. Recent publications include "Using Rights to Counter 'Gender-Specific' Wrongs," in *Human Rights Review*, and "On Their Own Ground: Strategies of Resistance for Sunni Muslim Women," in *Hypatia*. She also has interests in the relationship between faith and feminism and is an active member of the Marquette University Center for Peacemaking.

LYNN H. TURNER joined the faculty of Marquette University's College of Communication in 1985. She earned her PhD at Northwestern University and has a master's degree from the University of Iowa and a

baccalaureate degree from the University of Illinois. She is now professor in communication studies at Marquette, where she teaches at both
the undergraduate and graduate levels and serves as the director of the
interdisciplinary minor in family studies. Her research areas include
interpersonal, gendered, and family communication. She has co-
authored and co-edited over ten books as well as many articles and
book chapters. Her articles have appeared in various journals, including
Management Communication Quarterly, the *Journal of Applied Communication Research*, *Women and Language*, the *Journal of Family Communication*, and *Western Journal of Communication*. Her books include *From the
Margins to the Center: Contemporary Women and Political Communication*
(co-authored with Patricia Sullivan, 1996), which won the 1997 Best
Book Award from the Organization for the Study of Communication,
Language and Gender; *Gender in Applied Communication Contexts* (co-
edited with Patrice Buzzanell and Helen Sterk, 2004); *Introducing Communication Theory*, 4th ed. (2010), and *Perspectives on Family Communication*, 3rd ed. (2006), both of which were co-authored with Richard
West; and *The Family Communication Sourcebook* (co-edited with Richard West, 2006). She serves on the editorial board of several journals,
including the *Journal of Family Communication*, *Communication Teacher*,
and *Communication Studies*. She was the recipient of the Marquette
University College of Communication Outstanding Research Award in
1999 and 2007.

JEFFREY P. VON ARX, S.J., became the eighth president of Fairfield University in 2004. A historian by discipline, Fr. von Arx began his academic career at Georgetown University, where he taught in the history
department from 1982 until 1998, serving as the chair of the department from 1991 to 1997, and where he was the founder and director of
Georgetown's Center for Australian and New Zealand Studies in the
School of Foreign Service. He then became the dean of Fordham College at Rose Hill in 1998, where he remained until his appointment to
Fairfield. Fr. von Arx graduated from Princeton University in 1969 and
entered the Society of Jesus that summer. He went on to receive an
MA and MPhil in history from Yale University and completed his PhD
there in 1980. In 1981, Fr. von Arx received an MDiv from Weston
School of Theology and was ordained a priest. A noted scholar and

historian, Fr. von Arx is the author of numerous articles as well as the books *Progress and Pessimism: Religion, Politics and History in Late Nineteenth-Century Britain* (1985) and *Varieties of Ultramontanism* (1998).

JOYCE M. WOLBURG is professor and associate dean in the Diederich College of Communication at Marquette University. Her research interests include social and ethical issues in advertising, international advertising, effective message strategies for smoking cessation campaigns and anti–binge drinking campaigns, regulation of advertising, and the ritual meaning of behavior. Her work has appeared in various journals, including the *Journal of Advertising, Journal of Consumer Affairs*, the *Journal of Advertising Research*, the *Journal of Current Research and Issues in Advertising*, and the *Journal of Consumer Marketing*. She co-authored *Advertising, Society, and Consumer Culture* with Roxanne Hovland (2010) and received her PhD in communication at the University of Tennessee, Knoxville.

Index